SHONEN JUMP MANGA

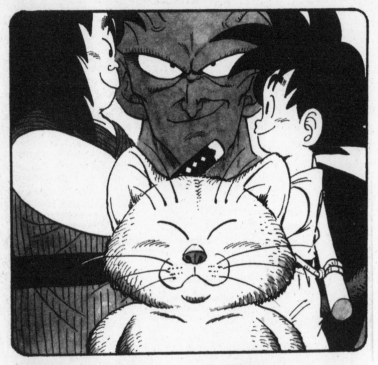

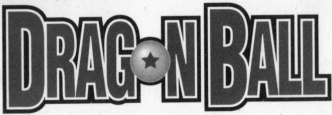

Vol. 13

DB: 13 of 42

STORY AND ART BY
AKIRA TORIYAMA

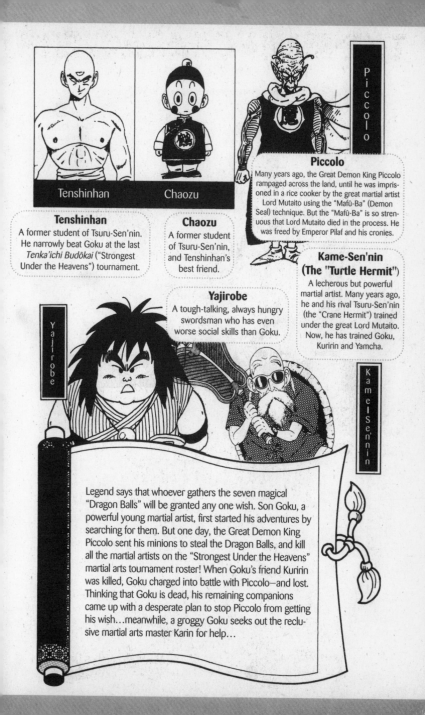

Tenshinhan

Chaozu

Piccolo

Piccolo
Many years ago, the Great Demon King Piccolo rampaged across the land, until he was imprisoned in a rice cooker by the great martial artist Lord Mutaito using the "Mafū-Ba" (Demon Seal) technique. But the "Mafū-Ba" is so strenuous that Lord Mutaito died in the process. He was freed by Emperor Pilaf and his cronies.

Tenshinhan
A former student of Tsuru-Sen'nin. He narrowly beat Goku at the last *Tenka'ichi Budōkai* ("Strongest Under the Heavens") tournament.

Chaozu
A former student of Tsuru-Sen'nin, and Tenshinhan's best friend.

Kame-Sen'nin (The "Turtle Hermit")
A lecherous but powerful martial artist. Many years ago, he and his rival Tsuru-Sen'nin (the "Crane Hermit") trained under the great Lord Mutaito. Now, he has trained Goku, Kuririn and Yamcha.

Yajirobe
A tough-talking, always hungry swordsman who has even worse social skills than Goku.

Yajirobe

Kame Sen'nin

Legend says that whoever gathers the seven magical "Dragon Balls" will be granted any one wish. Son Goku, a powerful young martial artist, first started his adventures by searching for them. But one day, the Great Demon King Piccolo sent his minions to steal the Dragon Balls, and kill all the martial artists on the "Strongest Under the Heavens" martial arts tournament roster! When Goku's friend Kuririn was killed, Goku charged into battle with Piccolo—and lost. Thinking that Goku is dead, his remaining companions came up with a desperate plan to stop Piccolo from getting his wish…meanwhile, a groggy Goku seeks out the reclusive martial arts master Karin for help…

THE MAIN CHARACTERS

Son Goku

Monkey-tailed young Goku has always been stronger than normal. His grandfather Gohan gave him the *nyoibô*, a magic staff, and Kame-Sen'nin gave him the *kinto'un*, a magic flying cloud. Unfortunately, the *kinto'un* was destroyed by one of Piccolo's minions, so now Goku has to walk everywhere.

Bulma

A genius inventor, Bulma met Goku on her quest for the seven magical Dragon Balls.

Yamcha

A student of Kame-Sen'nin, and Bulma's on-and-off boyfriend. He was seriously injured by Tenshinhan and taken to the hospital.

Lunch

A strange woman whose personality changes whenever she sneezes.

Kuririn

Goku's former martial arts schoolmate under Kame-Sen'nin.

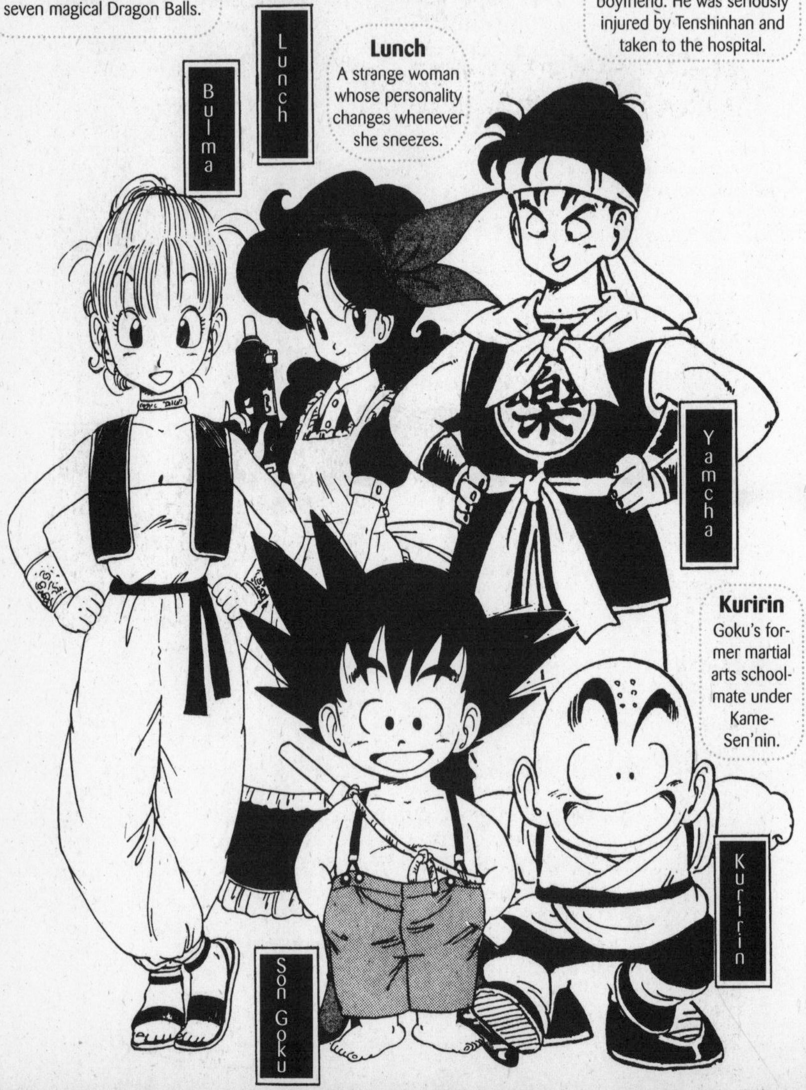

Bulma
Lunch
Yamcha
Son Goku
Kuririn

DRAGON BALL 13

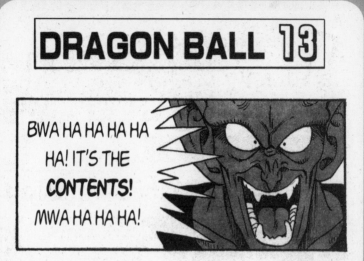

BWA HA HA HA HA HA! IT'S THE **CONTENTS!** MWA HA HA HA!

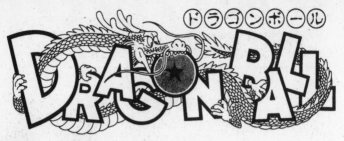

Tale 145
The Muten-Rôshi's Decision

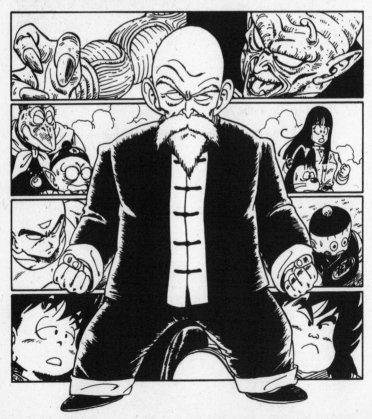

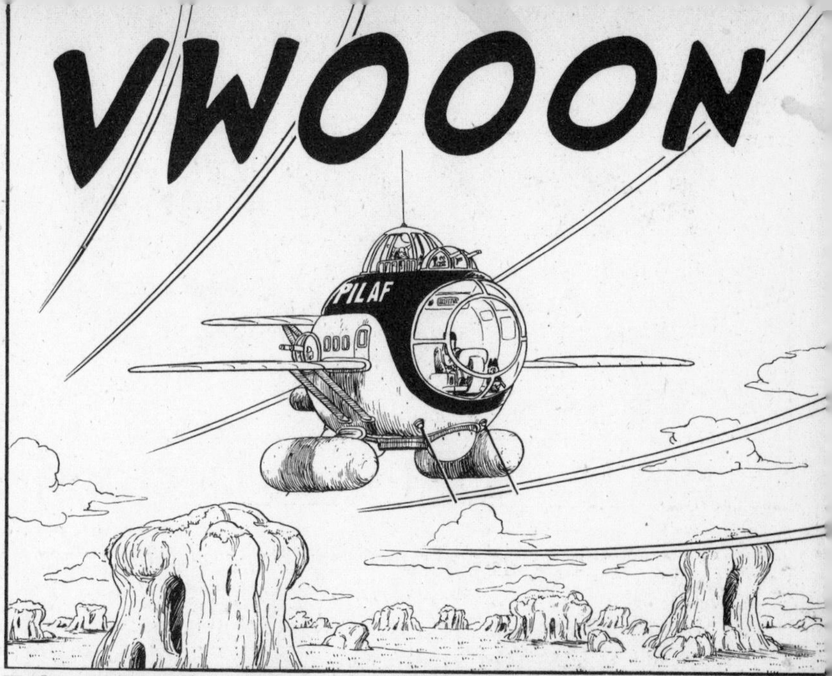
VWOOON
PILAF

Tale 145 • The Mûten-Roshi's Decision

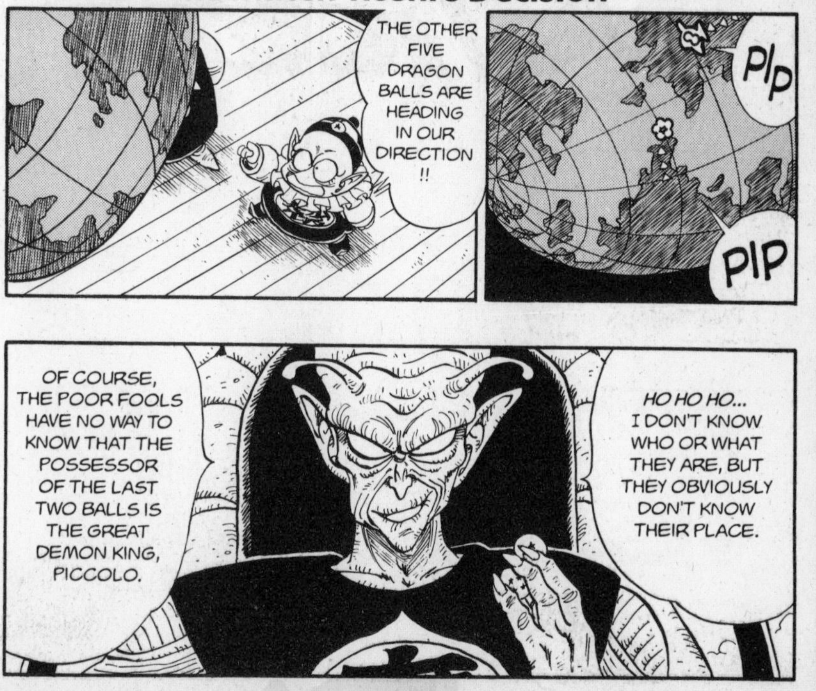
PIP
PIP
THE OTHER FIVE DRAGON BALLS ARE HEADING IN OUR DIRECTION !!
HO HO HO... I DON'T KNOW WHO OR WHAT THEY ARE, BUT THEY OBVIOUSLY DON'T KNOW THEIR PLACE.
OF COURSE, THE POOR FOOLS HAVE NO WAY TO KNOW THAT THE POSSESSOR OF THE LAST TWO BALLS IS THE GREAT DEMON KING, PICCOLO.

READ THIS WAY

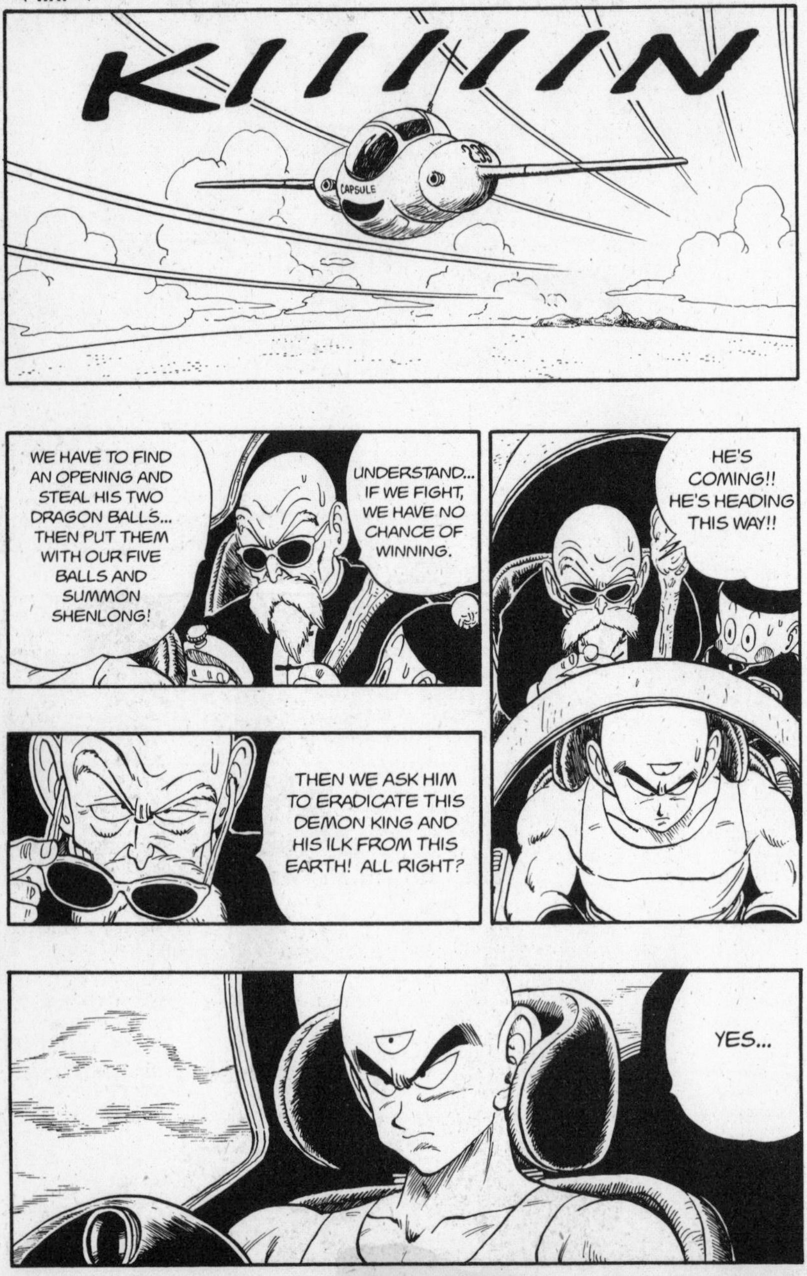
KIIIIIN
CAPSULE
HE'S COMING!! HE'S HEADING THIS WAY!!
UNDERSTAND... IF WE FIGHT, WE HAVE NO CHANCE OF WINNING.
WE HAVE TO FIND AN OPENING AND STEAL HIS TWO DRAGON BALLS... THEN PUT THEM WITH OUR FIVE BALLS AND SUMMON SHENLONG!
THEN WE ASK HIM TO ERADICATE THIS DEMON KING AND HIS ILK FROM THIS EARTH! ALL RIGHT?
YES...

READ THIS WAY

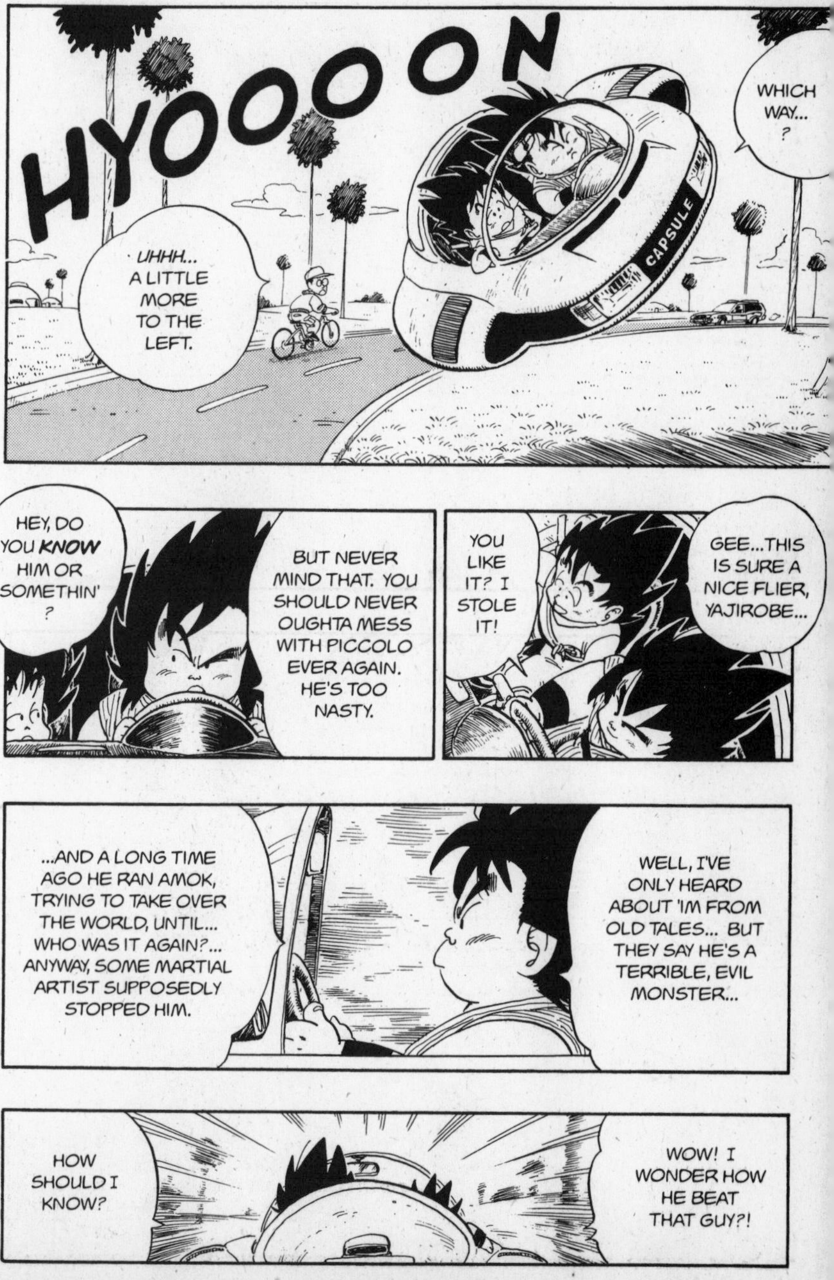
WHICH WAY...?
HYOOOON
CAPSULE
UHHH... A LITTLE MORE TO THE LEFT.
GEE...THIS IS SURE A NICE FLIER, YAJIROBE...
YOU LIKE IT? I STOLE IT!
BUT NEVER MIND THAT. YOU SHOULD NEVER OUGHTA MESS WITH PICCOLO EVER AGAIN. HE'S TOO NASTY.
HEY, DO YOU **KNOW** HIM OR SOMETHIN'?
WELL, I'VE ONLY HEARD ABOUT 'IM FROM OLD TALES... BUT THEY SAY HE'S A TERRIBLE, EVIL MONSTER...
...AND A LONG TIME AGO HE RAN AMOK, TRYING TO TAKE OVER THE WORLD, UNTIL... WHO WAS IT AGAIN?... ANYWAY, SOME MARTIAL ARTIST SUPPOSEDLY STOPPED HIM.
WOW! I WONDER HOW HE BEAT THAT GUY?!
HOW SHOULD I KNOW?

READ THIS WAY

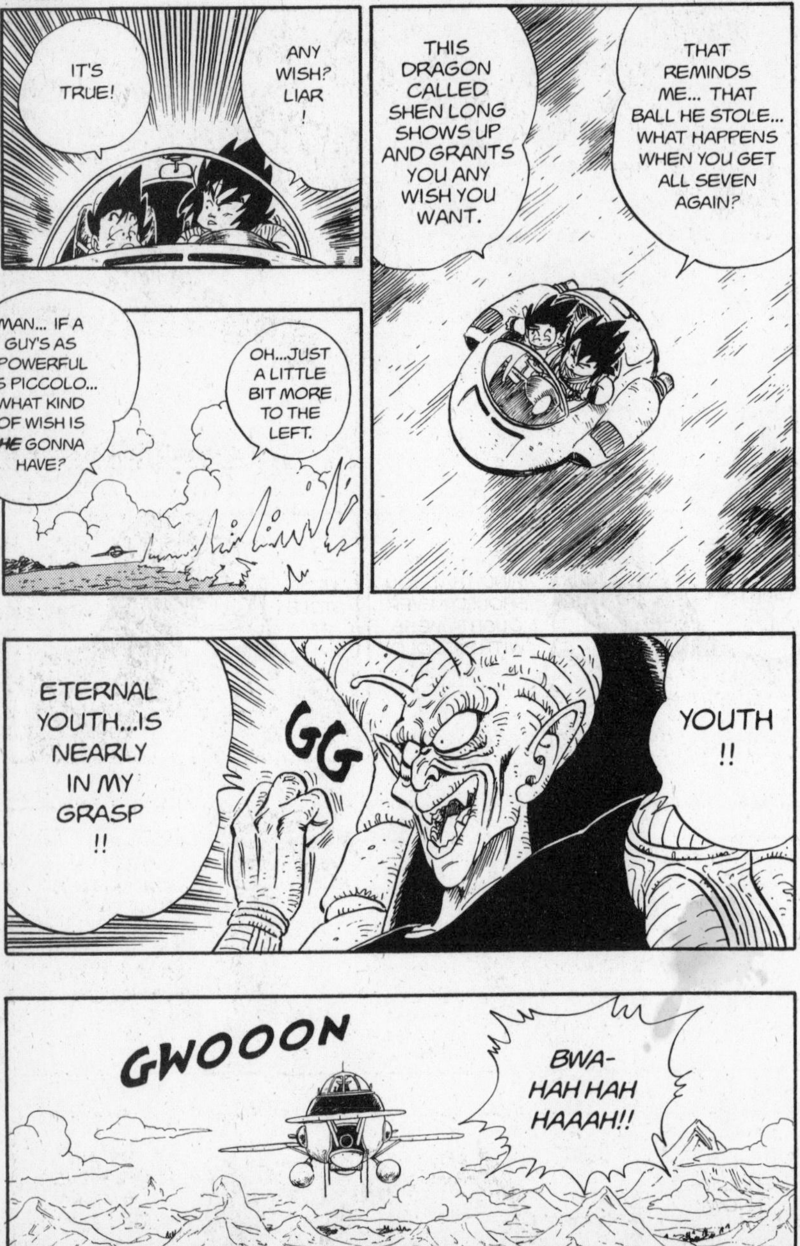

THAT REMINDS ME... THAT BALL HE STOLE... WHAT HAPPENS WHEN YOU GET ALL SEVEN AGAIN?
THIS DRAGON CALLED SHEN LONG SHOWS UP AND GRANTS YOU ANY WISH YOU WANT.
ANY WISH? LIAR!
IT'S TRUE!
OH...JUST A LITTLE BIT MORE TO THE LEFT.
MAN... IF A GUY'S AS POWERFUL AS PICCOLO... WHAT KIND OF WISH IS ***HE*** GONNA HAVE?
YOUTH!!
GG
ETERNAL YOUTH...IS NEARLY IN MY GRASP!!
BWA-HAH HAH HAAAH!!
GWOOON

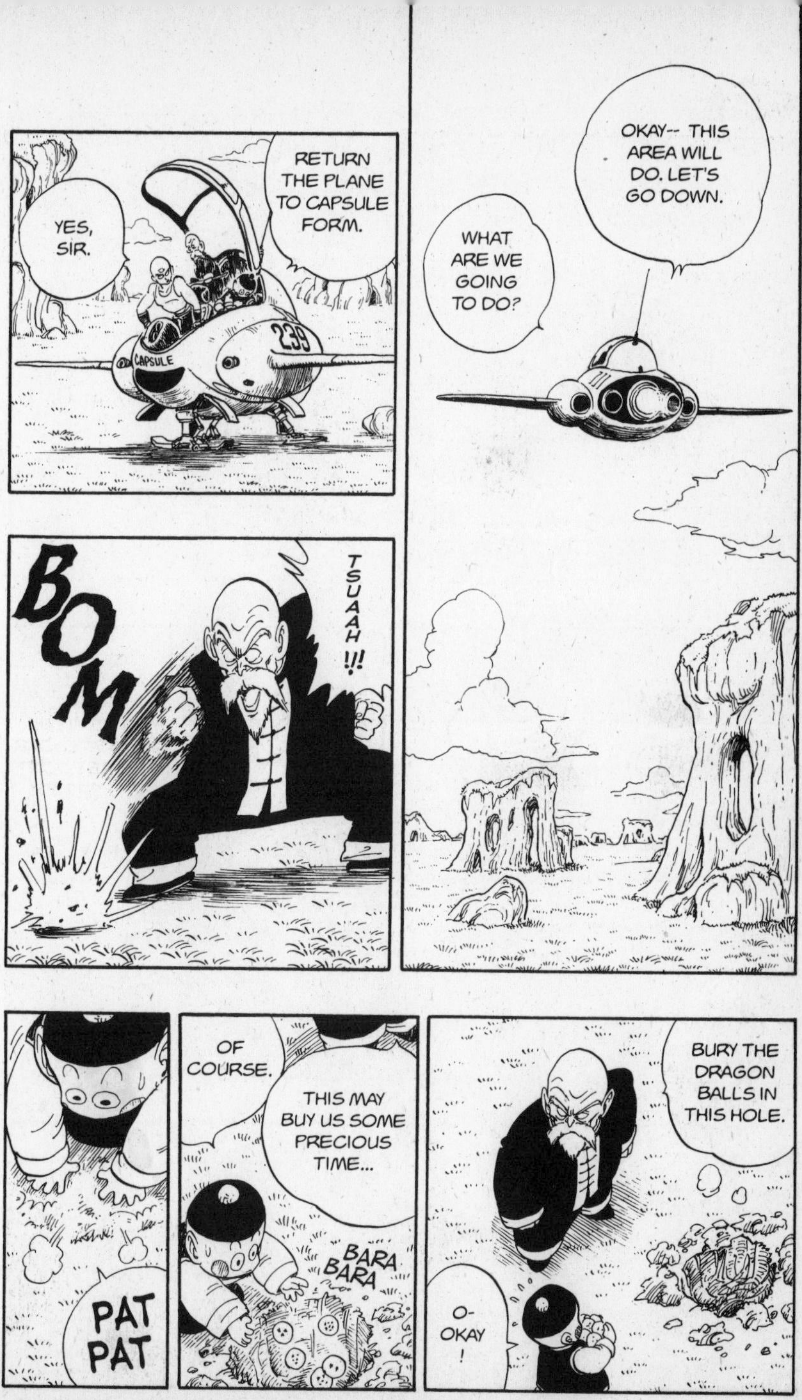
OKAY-- THIS AREA WILL DO. LET'S GO DOWN.
WHAT ARE WE GOING TO DO?
RETURN THE PLANE TO CAPSULE FORM.
YES, SIR.
239
CAPSULE
TSUAAH !!!
BOM
BURY THE DRAGON BALLS IN THIS HOLE.
O-OKAY !
OF COURSE.
THIS MAY BUY US SOME PRECIOUS TIME...
BARA BARA
PAT PAT

READ THIS WAY

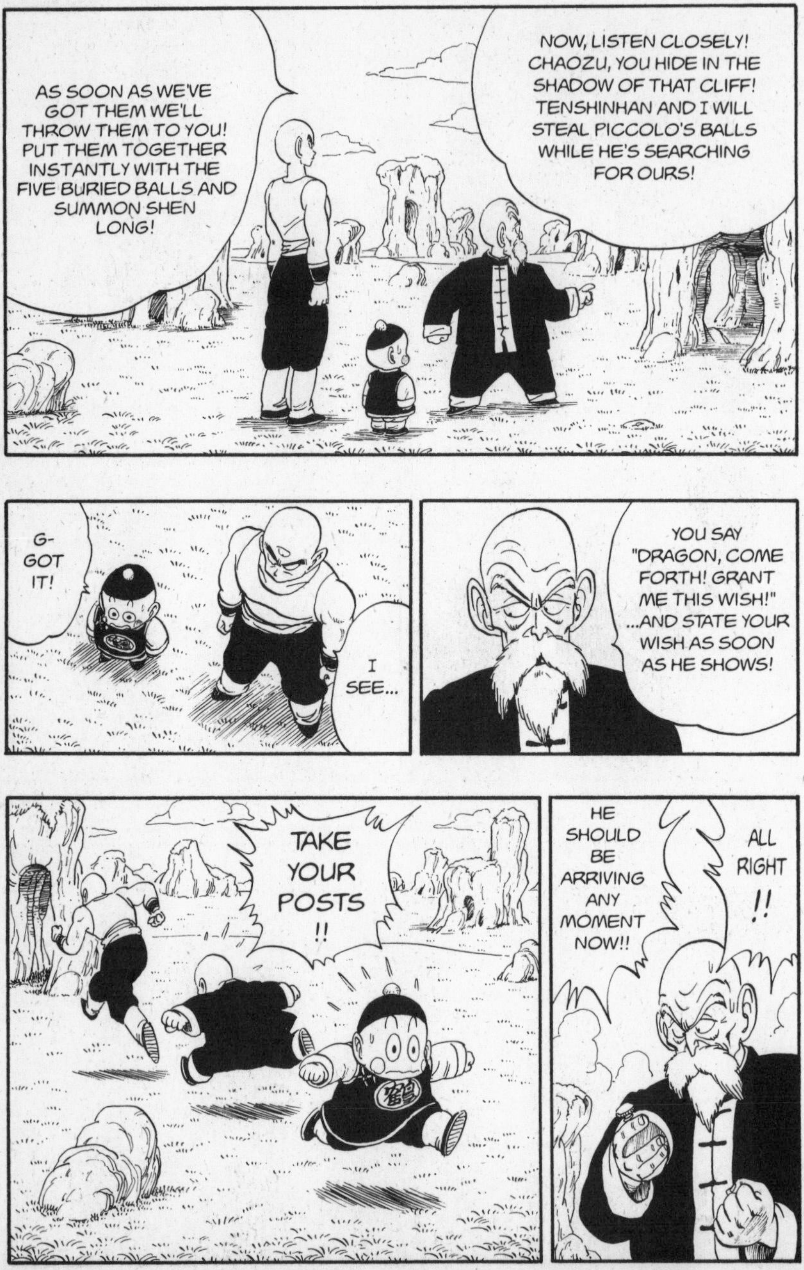

NOW, LISTEN CLOSELY! CHAOZU, YOU HIDE IN THE SHADOW OF THAT CLIFF! TENSHINHAN AND I WILL STEAL PICCOLO'S BALLS WHILE HE'S SEARCHING FOR OURS!
AS SOON AS WE'VE GOT THEM WE'LL THROW THEM TO YOU! PUT THEM TOGETHER INSTANTLY WITH THE FIVE BURIED BALLS AND SUMMON SHEN LONG!
YOU SAY "DRAGON, COME FORTH! GRANT ME THIS WISH!" ...AND STATE YOUR WISH AS SOON AS HE SHOWS!
I SEE...
G-GOT IT!
ALL RIGHT !!
HE SHOULD BE ARRIVING ANY MOMENT NOW!!
TAKE YOUR POSTS !!

READ THIS WAY

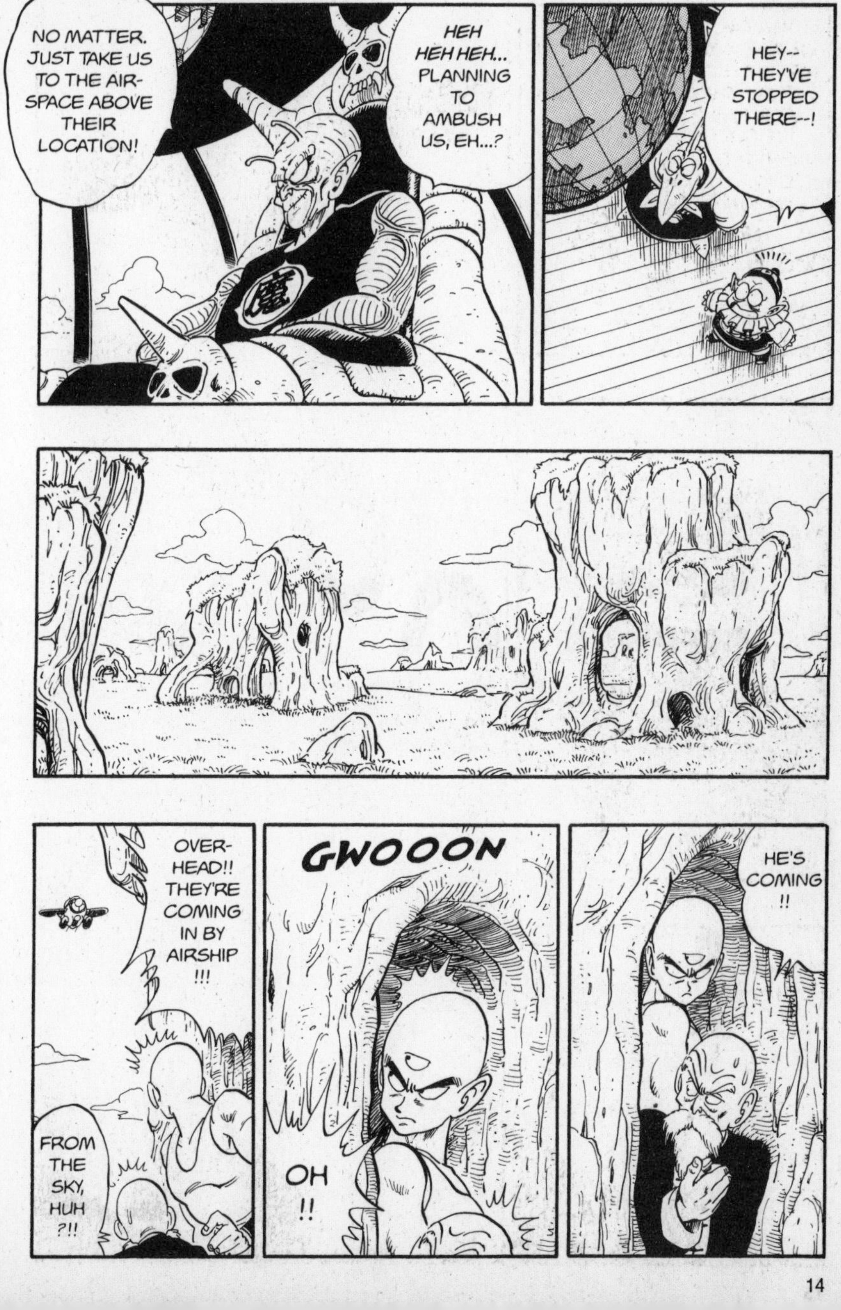

HEY-- THEY'VE STOPPED THERE--!
HEH HEH HEH... PLANNING TO AMBUSH US, EH...?
NO MATTER. JUST TAKE US TO THE AIR-SPACE ABOVE THEIR LOCATION!
HE'S COMING !!
GWOOON
OH !!
OVER-HEAD!! THEY'RE COMING IN BY AIRSHIP !!!
FROM THE SKY, HUH ?!!

READ THIS WAY

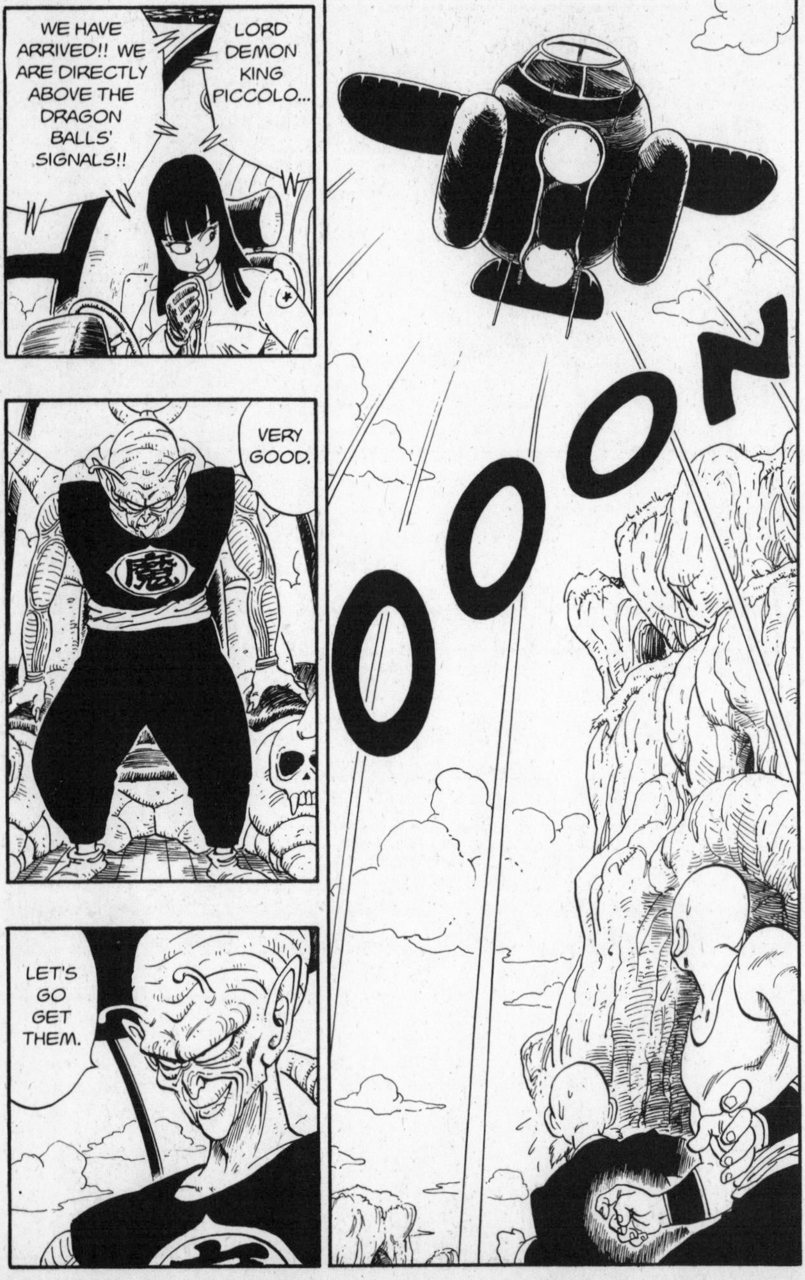
OOON
LORD DEMON KING PICCOLO...
WE HAVE ARRIVED!! WE ARE DIRECTLY ABOVE THE DRAGON BALLS' SIGNALS!!
VERY GOOD.
LET'S GO GET THEM.

READ THIS WAY

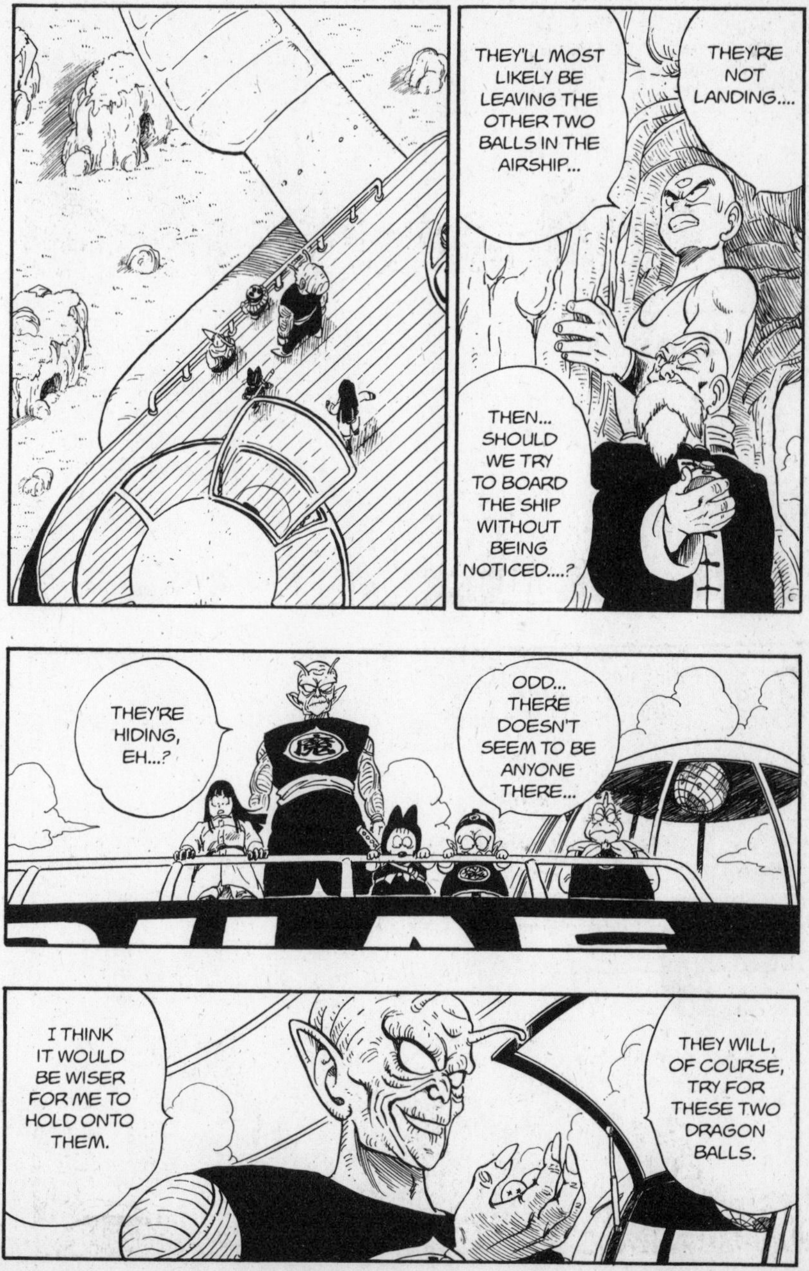

THEY'RE NOT LANDING....
THEY'LL MOST LIKELY BE LEAVING THE OTHER TWO BALLS IN THE AIRSHIP...
THEN... SHOULD WE TRY TO BOARD THE SHIP WITHOUT BEING NOTICED....?
ODD... THERE DOESN'T SEEM TO BE ANYONE THERE...
THEY'RE HIDING, EH...?
THEY WILL, OF COURSE, TRY FOR THESE TWO DRAGON BALLS.
I THINK IT WOULD BE WISER FOR ME TO HOLD ONTO THEM.

READ THIS WAY

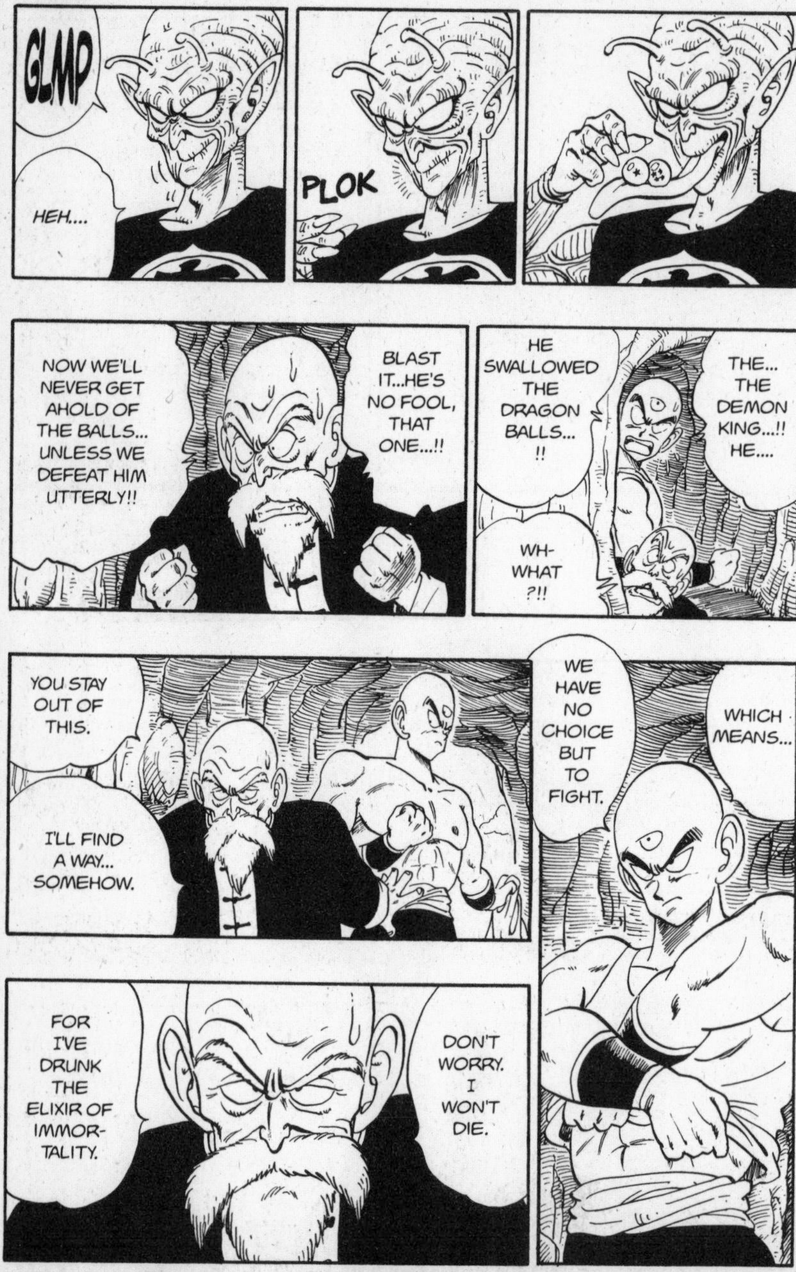
PLOK
GLMP
HEH....
THE... THE DEMON KING...!! HE....
HE SWALLOWED THE DRAGON BALLS... !!
WH-WHAT ?!!
BLAST IT...HE'S NO FOOL, THAT ONE...!!
NOW WE'LL NEVER GET AHOLD OF THE BALLS... UNLESS WE DEFEAT HIM UTTERLY!!
WHICH MEANS...
WE HAVE NO CHOICE BUT TO FIGHT.
YOU STAY OUT OF THIS.
I'LL FIND A WAY... SOMEHOW.
DON'T WORRY. I WON'T DIE.
FOR I'VE DRUNK THE ELIXIR OF IMMOR-TALITY.

READ THIS WAY

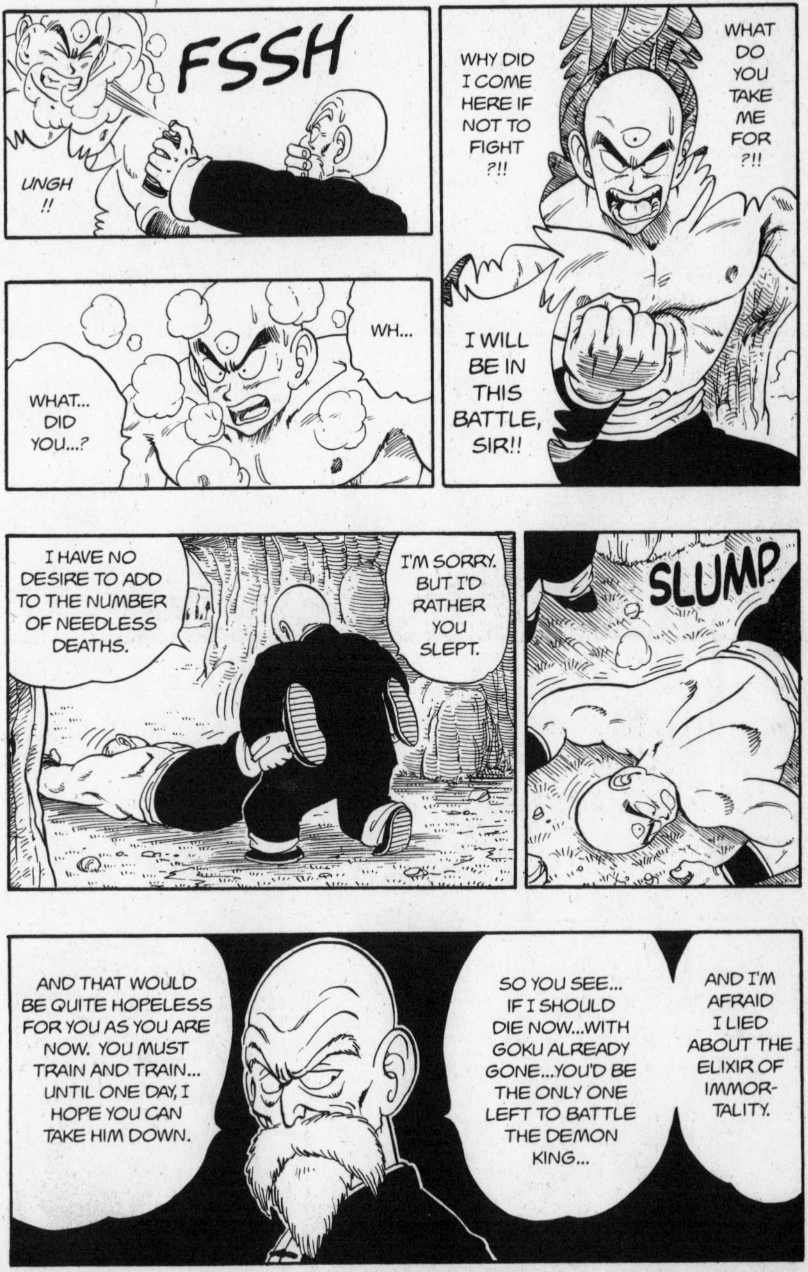
WHAT DO YOU TAKE ME FOR ?!!
WHY DID I COME HERE IF NOT TO FIGHT ?!!
I WILL BE IN THIS BATTLE, SIR!!
FSSH
UNGH !!
WH...
WHAT... DID YOU...?
SLUMP
I'M SORRY. BUT I'D RATHER YOU SLEPT.
I HAVE NO DESIRE TO ADD TO THE NUMBER OF NEEDLESS DEATHS.
AND I'M AFRAID I LIED ABOUT THE ELIXIR OF IMMORTALITY.
SO YOU SEE... IF I SHOULD DIE NOW...WITH GOKU ALREADY GONE...YOU'D BE THE ONLY ONE LEFT TO BATTLE THE DEMON KING...
AND THAT WOULD BE QUITE HOPELESS FOR YOU AS YOU ARE NOW. YOU MUST TRAIN AND TRAIN... UNTIL ONE DAY, I HOPE YOU CAN TAKE HIM DOWN.

READ THIS WAY

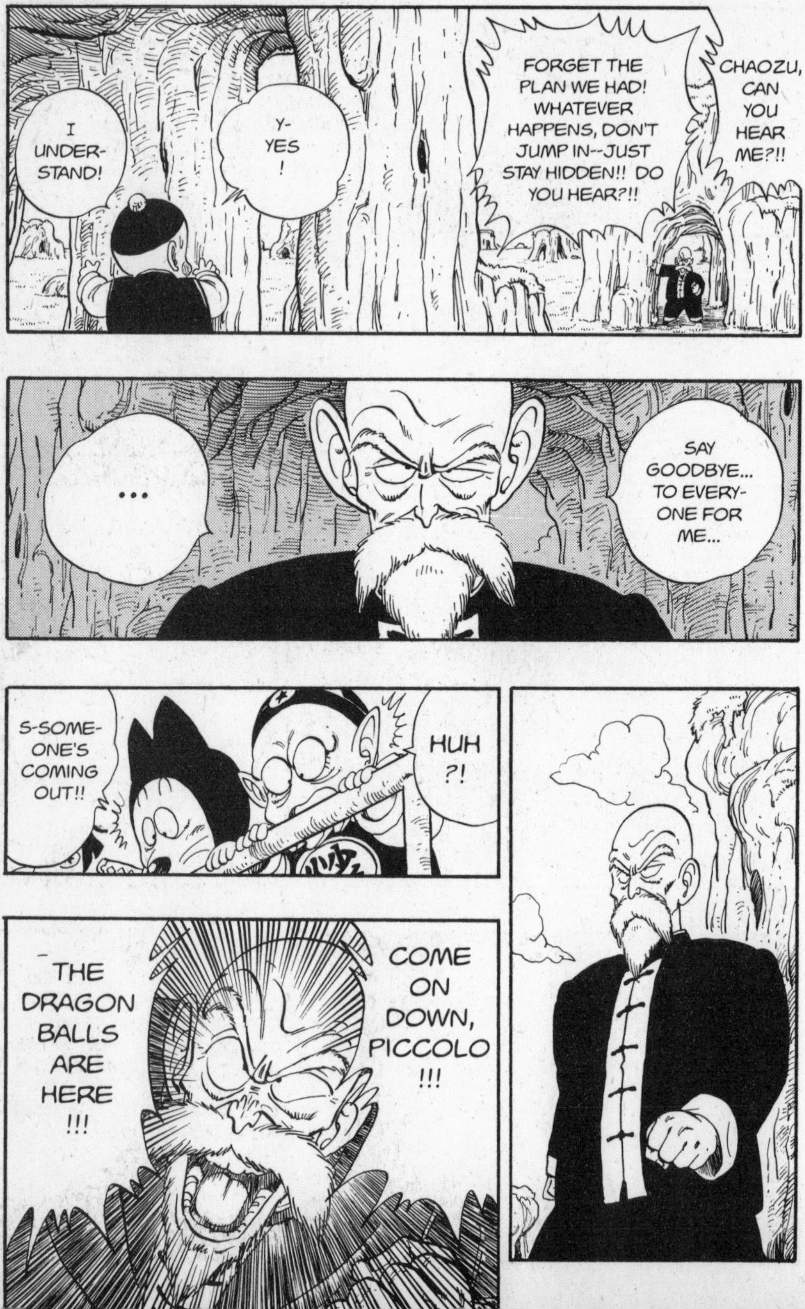
CHAOZU, CAN YOU HEAR ME?!!
FORGET THE PLAN WE HAD! WHATEVER HAPPENS, DON'T JUMP IN--JUST STAY HIDDEN!! DO YOU HEAR?!!
Y-YES!
I UNDERSTAND!
SAY GOODBYE... TO EVERYONE FOR ME...
...
HUH?!
S-SOMEONE'S COMING OUT!!
COME ON DOWN, PICCOLO!!!
THE DRAGON BALLS ARE HERE!!!

READ THIS WAY

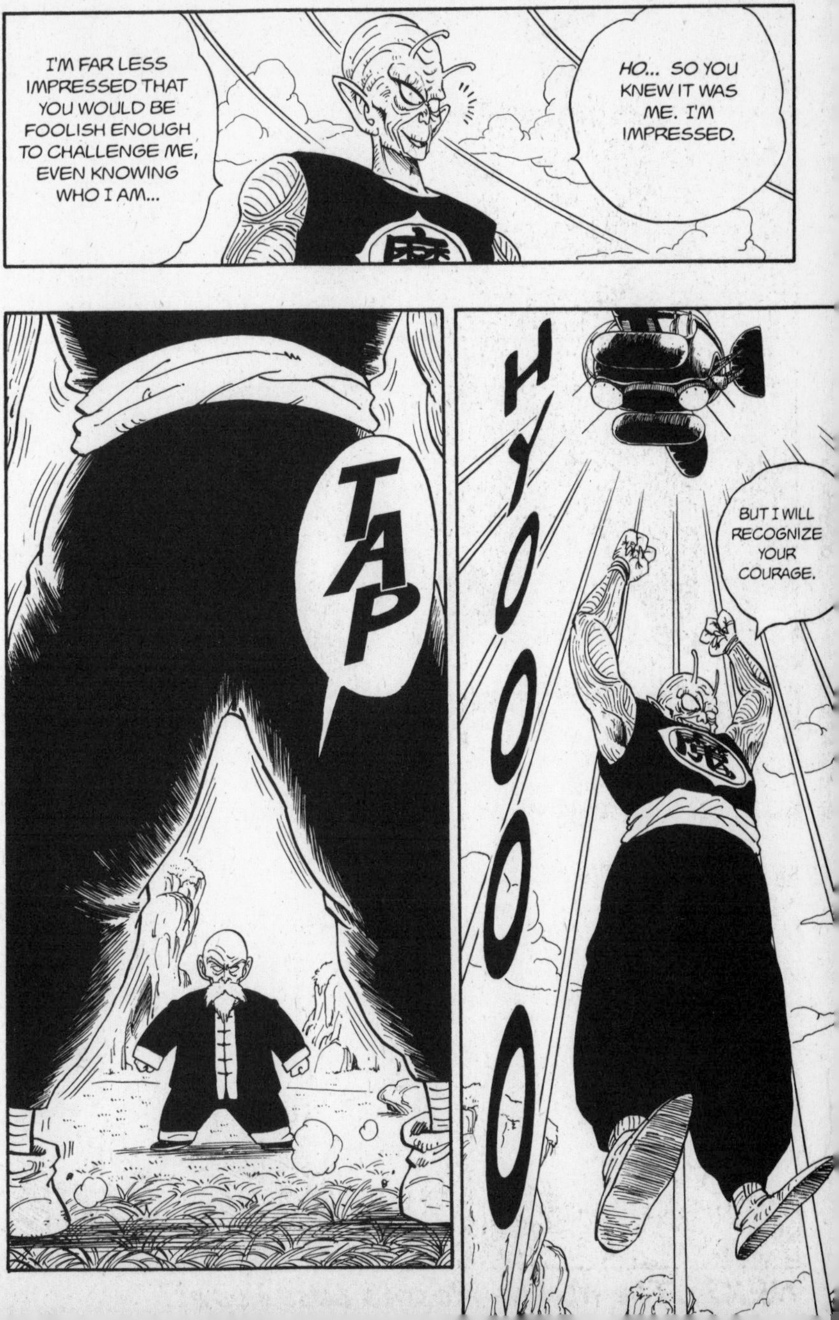
HO... SO YOU KNEW IT WAS ME. I'M IMPRESSED.
I'M FAR LESS IMPRESSED THAT YOU WOULD BE FOOLISH ENOUGH TO CHALLENGE ME, EVEN KNOWING WHO I AM...
BUT I WILL RECOGNIZE YOUR COURAGE.
HYOOOOO
TAP

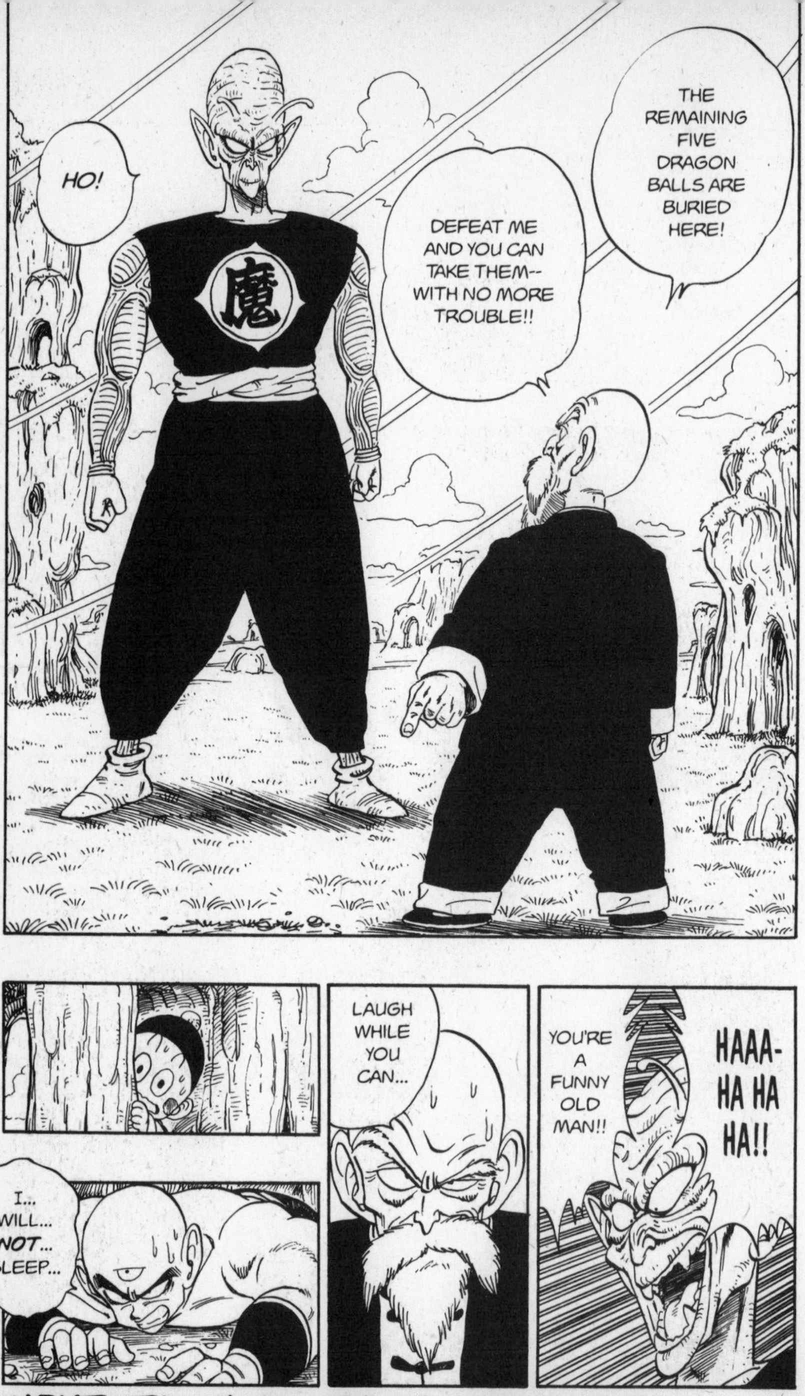
THE REMAINING FIVE DRAGON BALLS ARE BURIED HERE!
DEFEAT ME AND YOU CAN TAKE THEM-- WITH NO MORE TROUBLE!!
HO!
HAAA-HA HA HA!!
YOU'RE A FUNNY OLD MAN!!
LAUGH WHILE YOU CAN...
I... WILL... NOT... SLEEP...

NEXT: The Muten-Rôshi's Last Hope!!

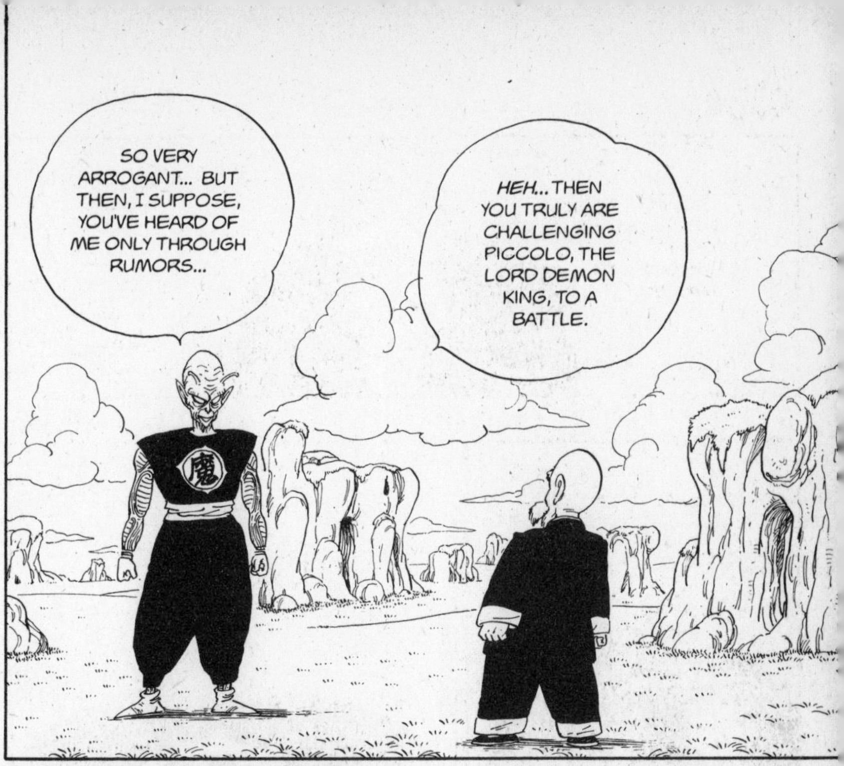
HEH... THEN YOU TRULY ARE CHALLENGING PICCOLO, THE LORD DEMON KING, TO A BATTLE.
SO VERY ARROGANT... BUT THEN, I SUPPOSE, YOU'VE HEARD OF ME ONLY THROUGH RUMORS...

Tale 146 • The Mafû-Ba

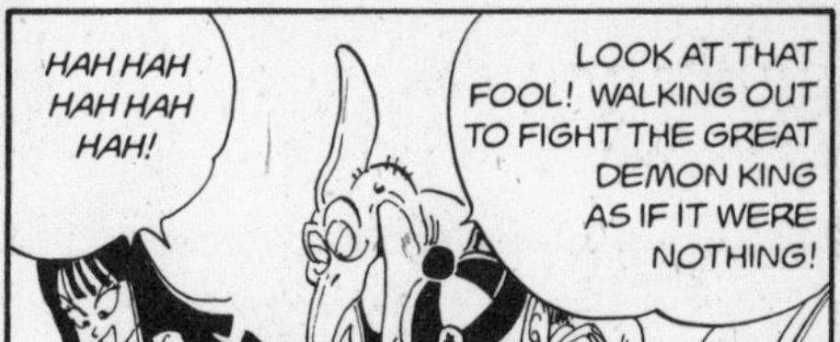
LOOK AT THAT FOOL! WALKING OUT TO FIGHT THE GREAT DEMON KING AS IF IT WERE NOTHING!
HAH HAH HAH HAH HAH!

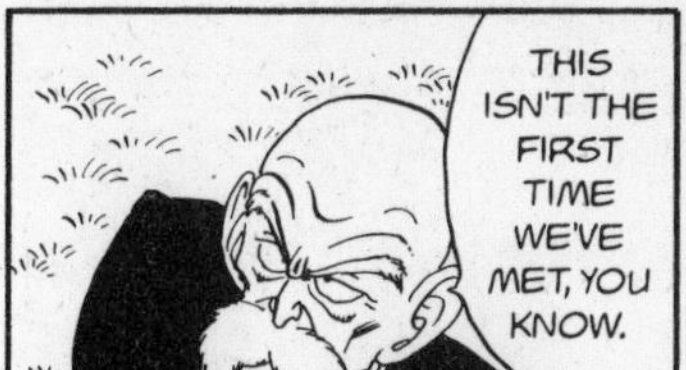
THIS ISN'T THE FIRST TIME WE'VE MET, YOU KNOW.

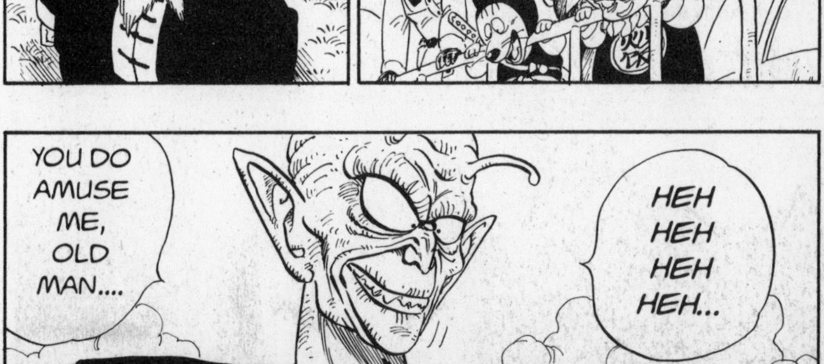
HEH HEH HEH HEH...
YOU DO AMUSE ME, OLD MAN....

READ THIS WAY

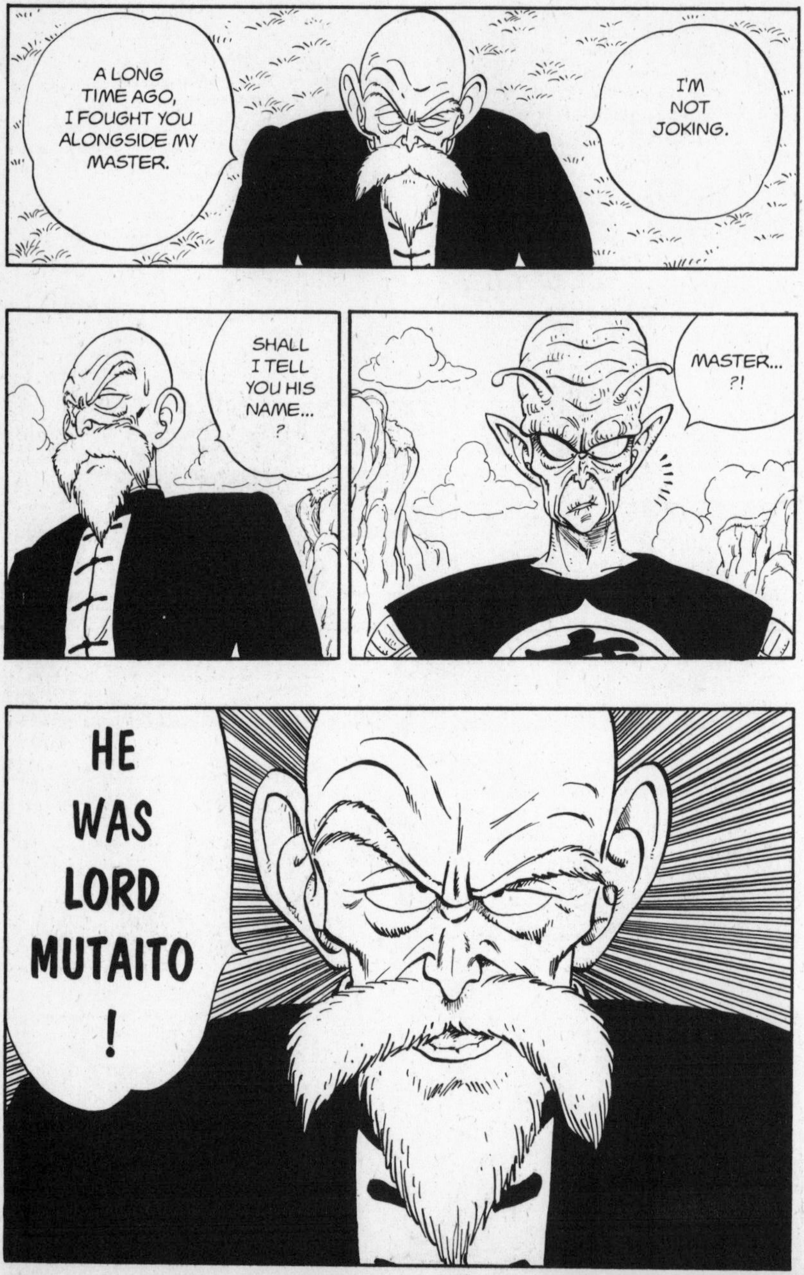
I'M NOT JOKING.
A LONG TIME AGO, I FOUGHT YOU ALONGSIDE MY MASTER.
MASTER...?!
SHALL I TELL YOU HIS NAME...?
HE WAS LORD MUTAITO!

READ THIS WAY

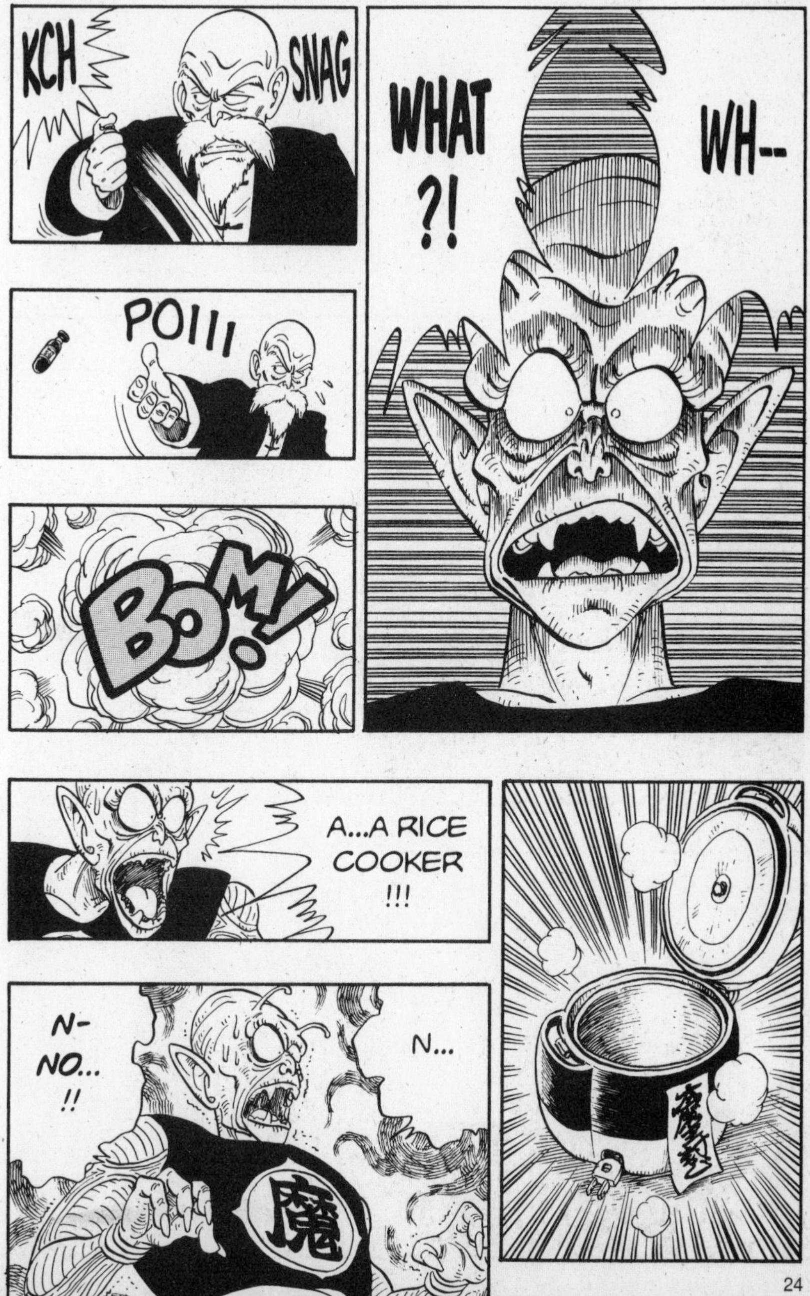

WH--
WHAT ?!
SNAG
KCH
POIII
BOOM!
A...A RICE COOKER !!!
N...
N-NO... !!
魔

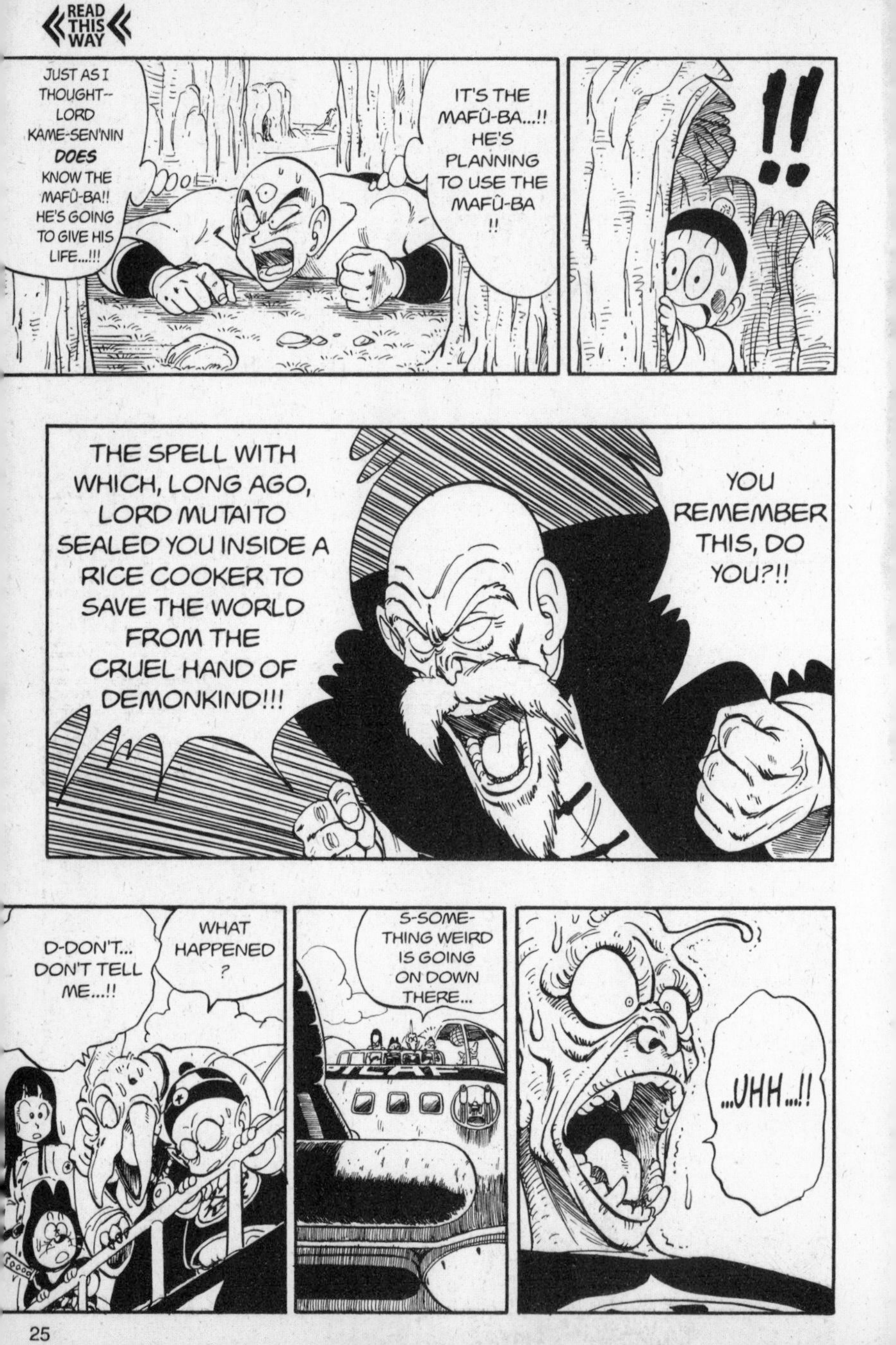
READ THIS WAY
!!
IT'S THE MAFÛ-BA...!! HE'S PLANNING TO USE THE MAFÛ-BA !!
JUST AS I THOUGHT-- LORD KAME-SEN'NIN DOES KNOW THE MAFÛ-BA!! HE'S GOING TO GIVE HIS LIFE...!!!
YOU REMEMBER THIS, DO YOU?!!
THE SPELL WITH WHICH, LONG AGO, LORD MUTAITO SEALED YOU INSIDE A RICE COOKER TO SAVE THE WORLD FROM THE CRUEL HAND OF DEMONKIND!!!
...UHH...!!
S-SOME-THING WEIRD IS GOING ON DOWN THERE...
WHAT HAPPENED ?
D-DON'T... DON'T TELL ME...!!

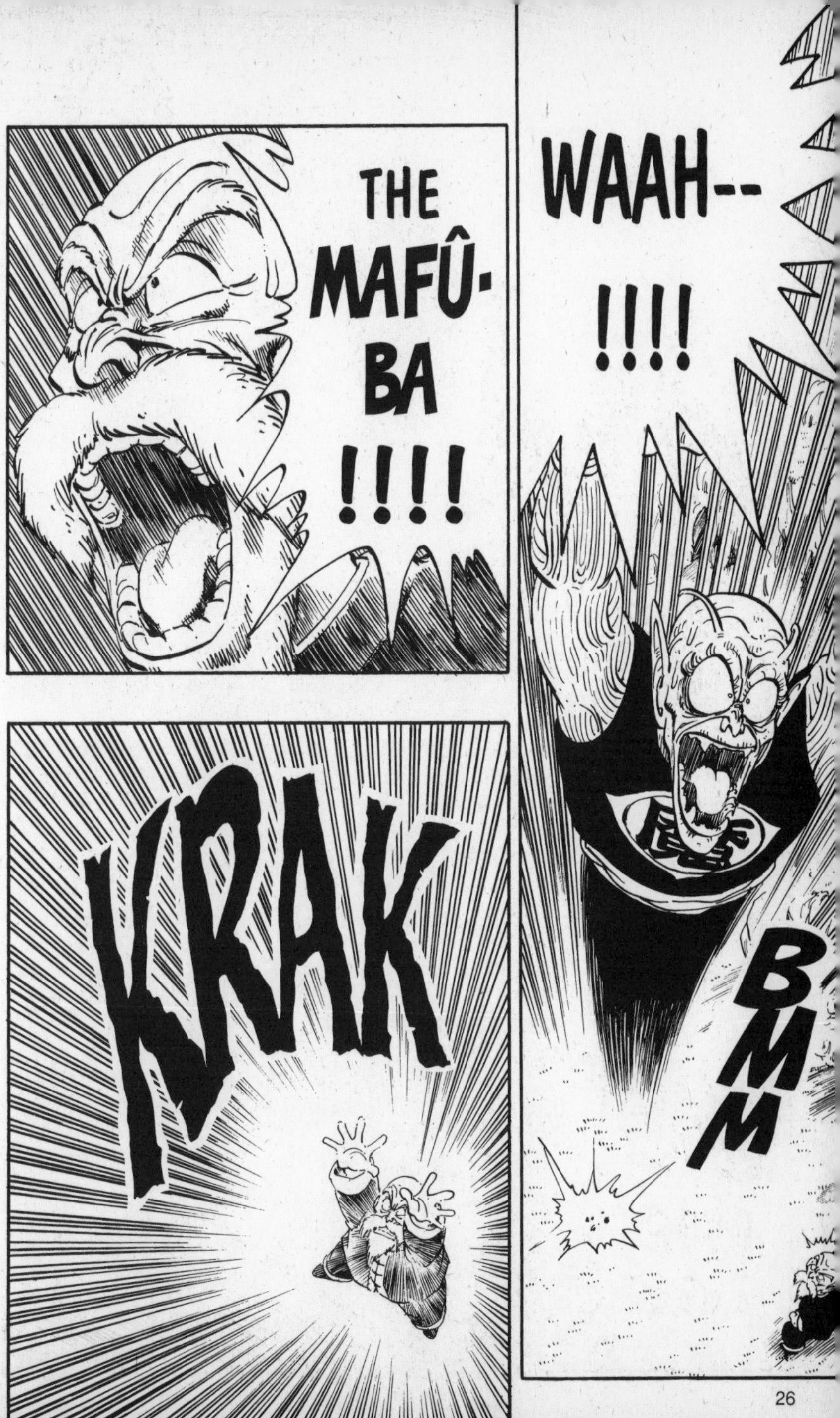
WAAH-- !!!!
BMM
THE MAFÛ-BA !!!!
KRAK

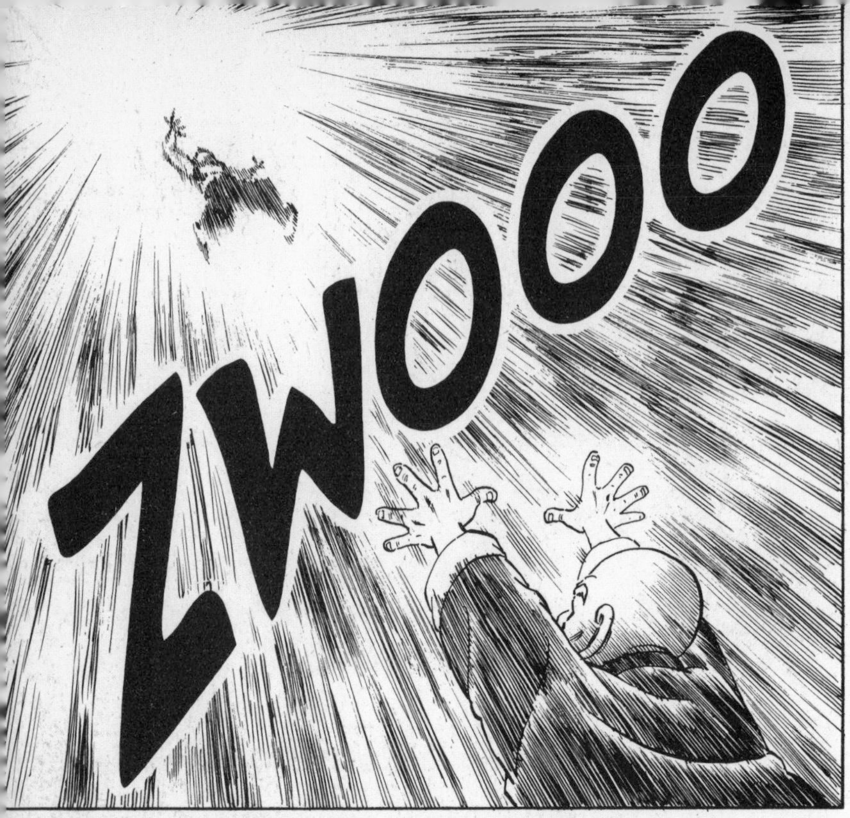
ZWOOOO

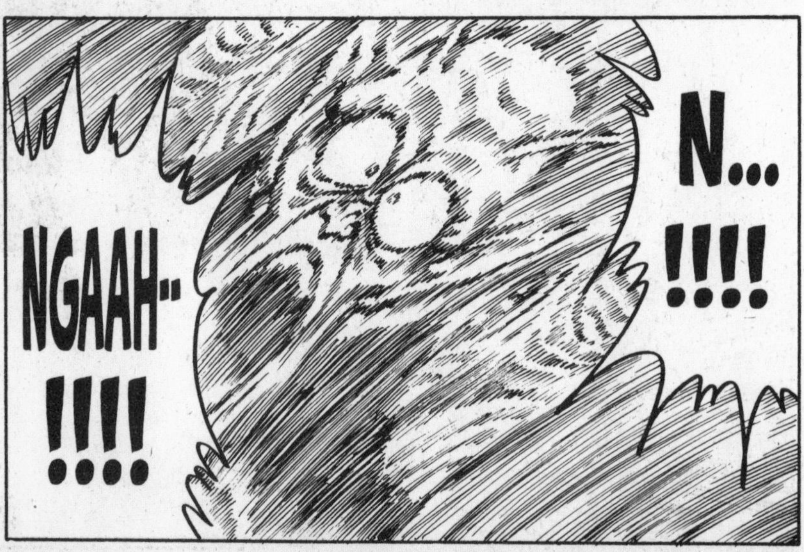
N...
!!!!
NGAAH--
!!!!

READ THIS WAY

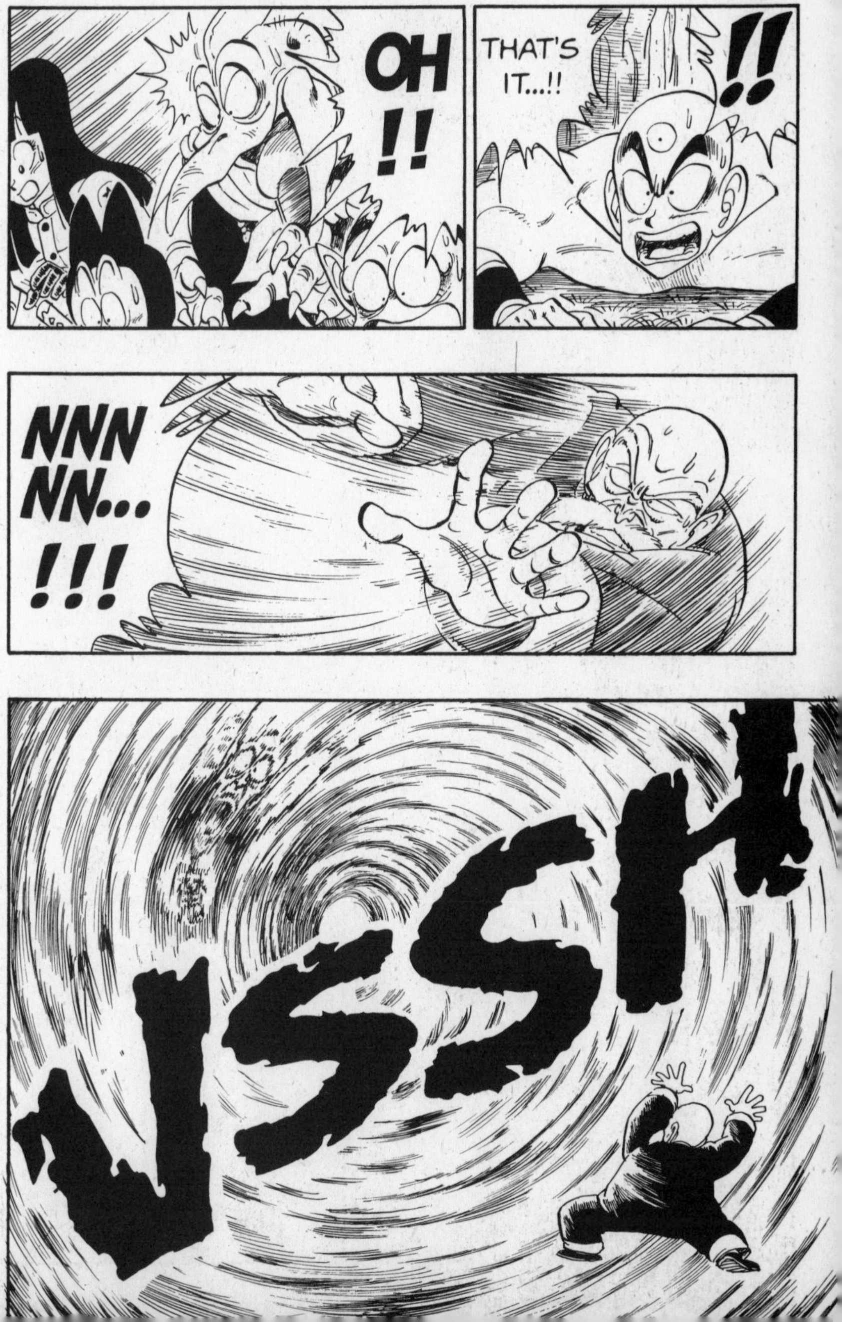
THAT'S IT...!!
!!
OH !!
NNNNN... !!!
VSSH!

READ THIS WAY

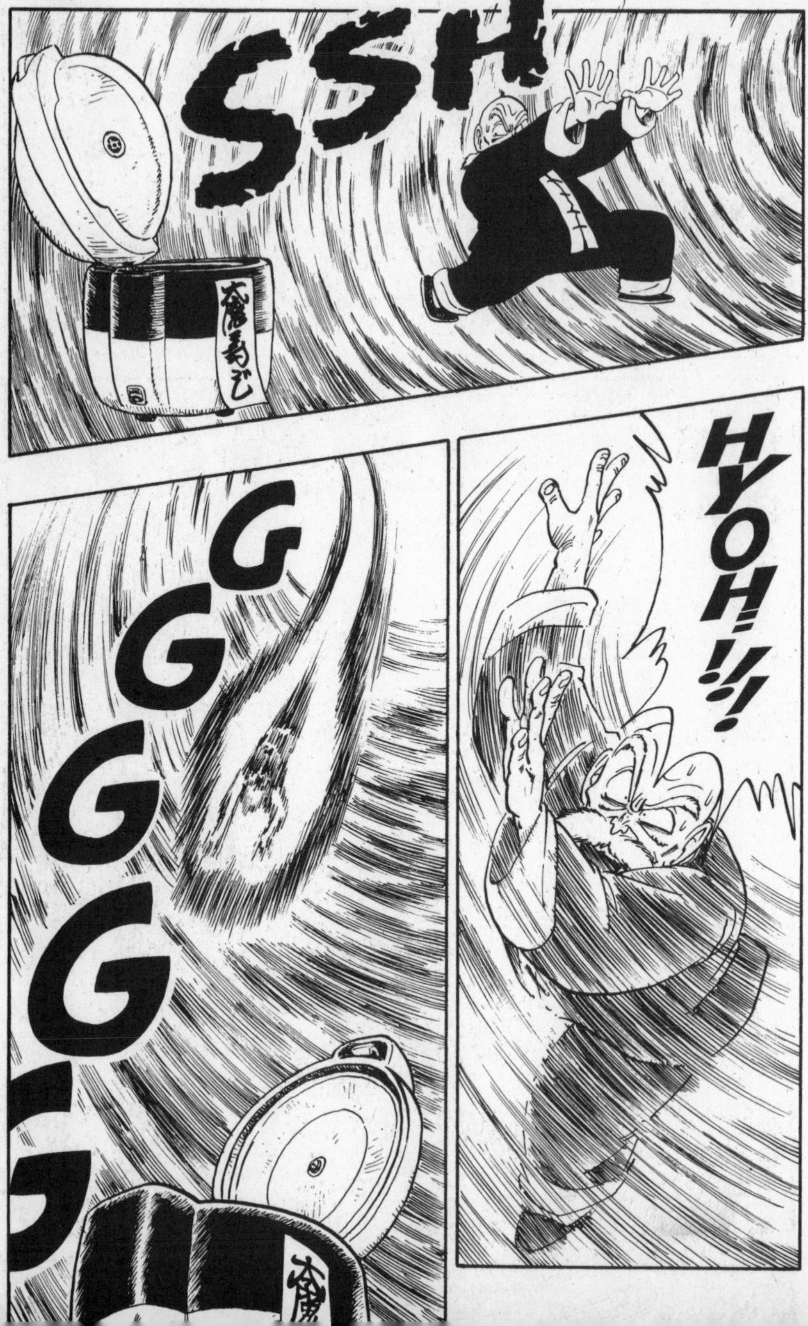
SSH
大魔封じ
HYOH!!!
GGGGG

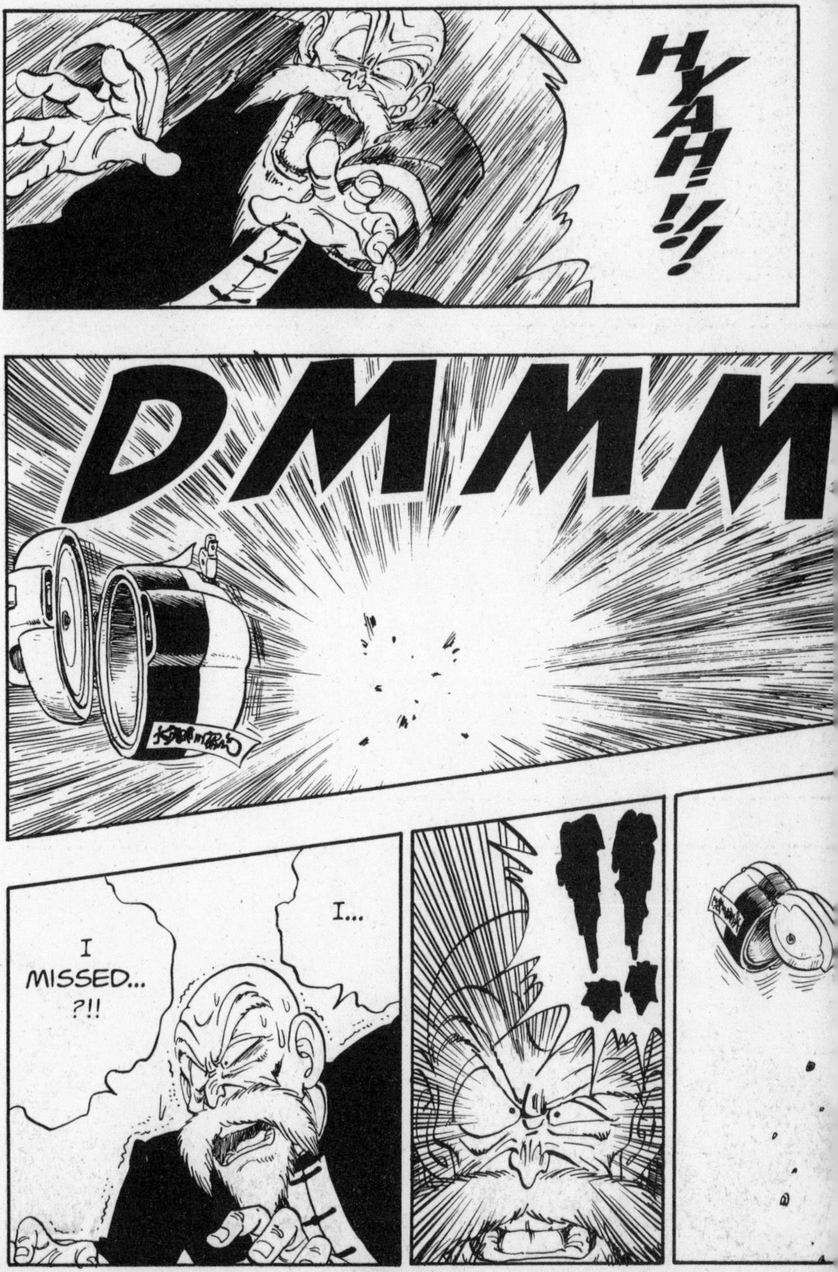
HYAH!!!
DMMM
!!
I...
I MISSED... ?!!

READ THIS WAY

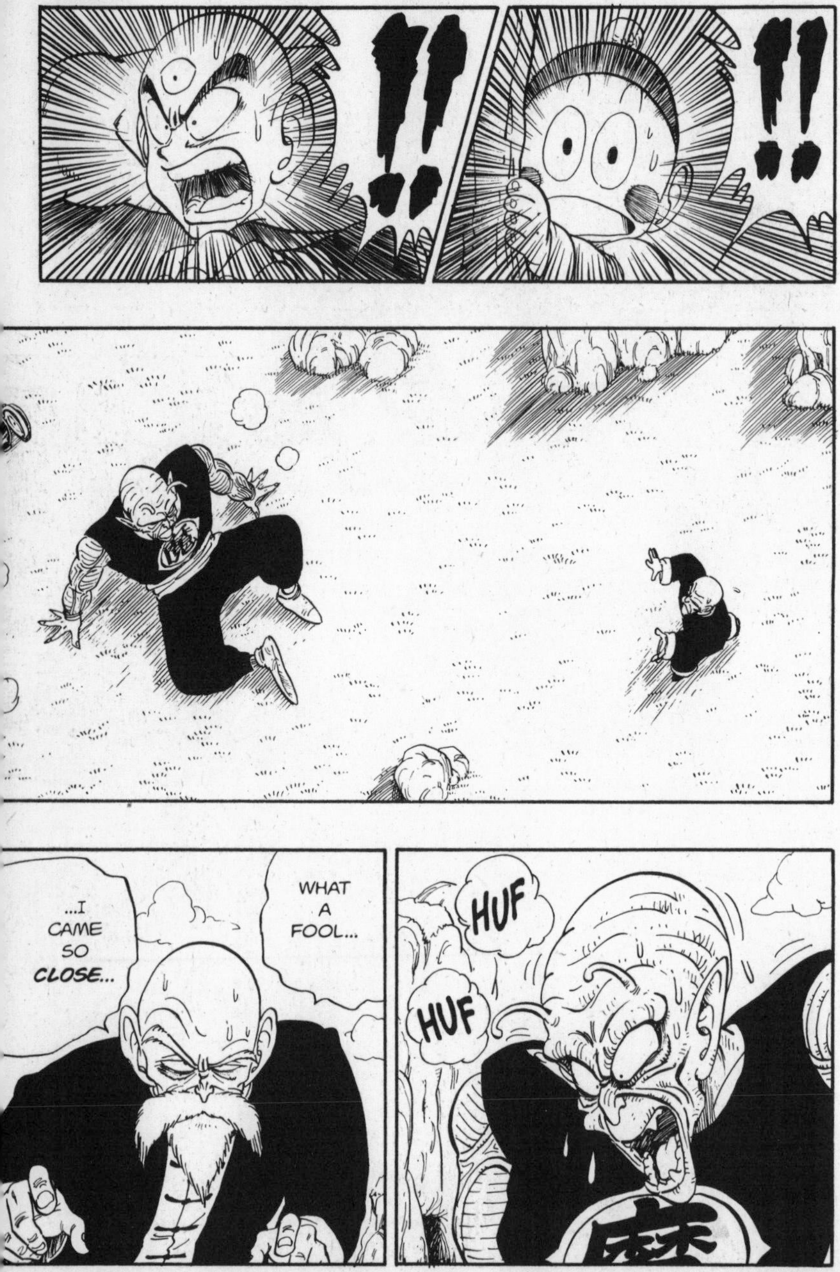
!!
!!
HUF
HUF
WHAT A FOOL...
...I CAME SO *CLOSE...*

READ THIS WAY

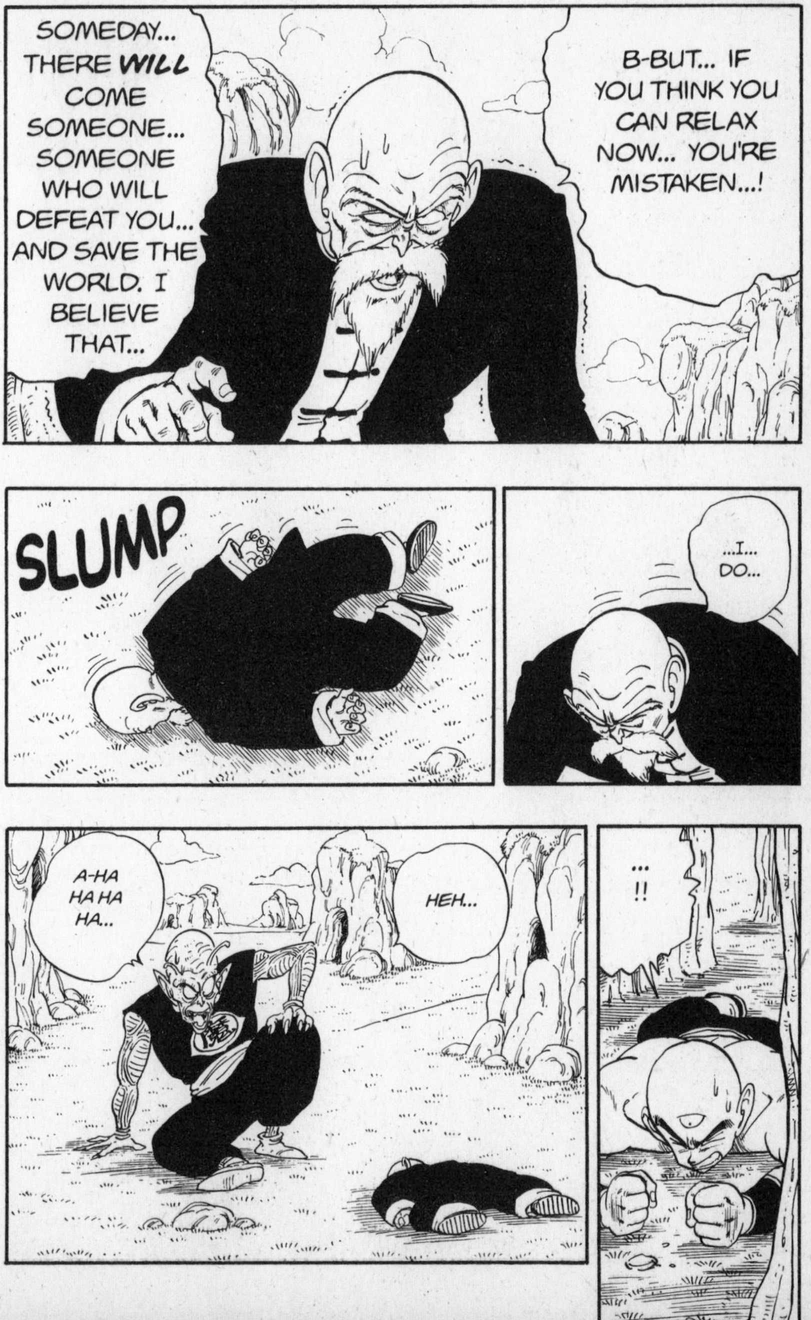

B-BUT... IF YOU THINK YOU CAN RELAX NOW... YOU'RE MISTAKEN...!
SOMEDAY... THERE WILL COME SOMEONE... SOMEONE WHO WILL DEFEAT YOU... AND SAVE THE WORLD. I BELIEVE THAT...
...I... DO...
SLUMP
... !!
HEH...
A-HA HA HA HA...

READ THIS WAY

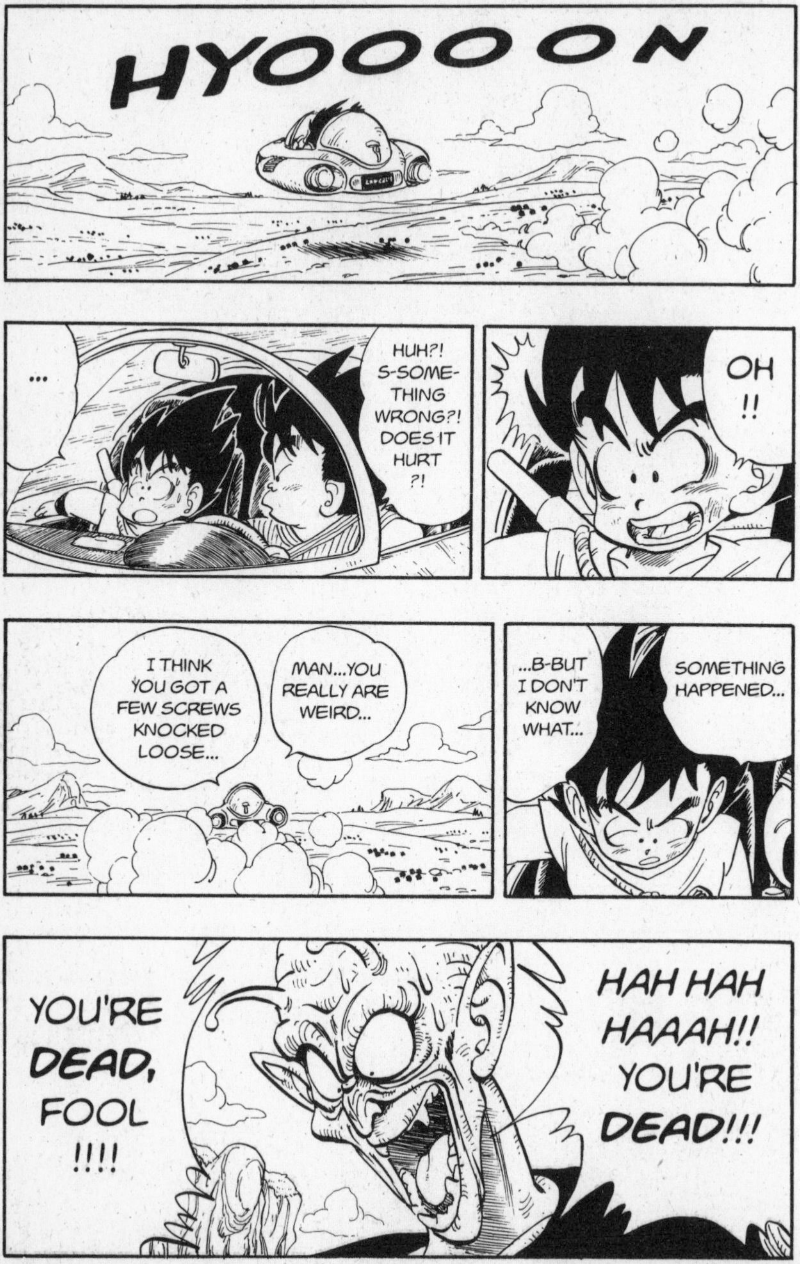
HYOOOON
OH !!
HUH?! S-SOMETHING WRONG?! DOES IT HURT ?!
...
SOMETHING HAPPENED...
...B-BUT I DON'T KNOW WHAT...
MAN...YOU REALLY ARE WEIRD...
I THINK YOU GOT A FEW SCREWS KNOCKED LOOSE...
HAH HAH HAAAH!! YOU'RE DEAD!!!
YOU'RE DEAD, FOOL !!!!

READ THIS WAY

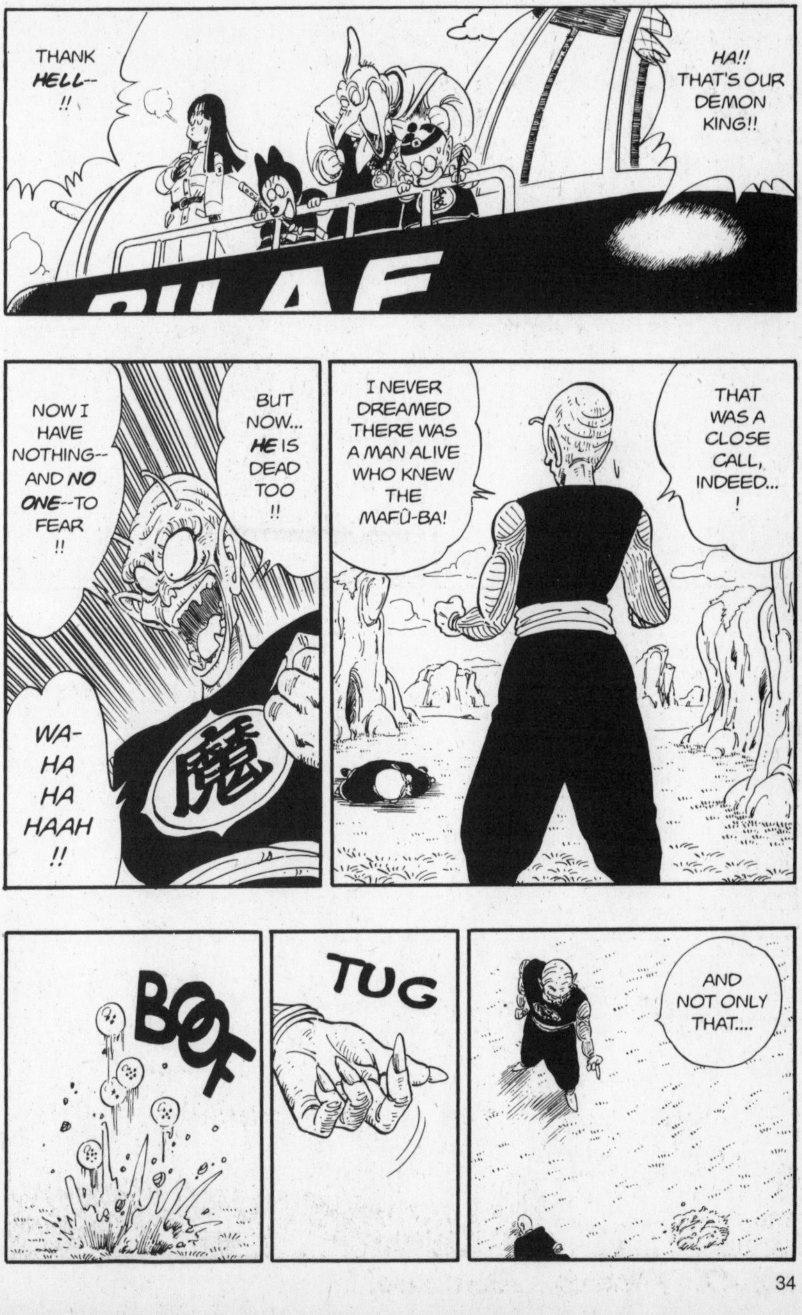

HA!! THAT'S OUR DEMON KING!!
THANK HELL-- !!
THAT WAS A CLOSE CALL, INDEED...!
I NEVER DREAMED THERE WAS A MAN ALIVE WHO KNEW THE MAFÛ-BA!
BUT NOW... HE IS DEAD TOO !!
NOW I HAVE NOTHING-- AND NO ONE--TO FEAR !!
WA-HA HA HAAH !!
AND NOT ONLY THAT....
TUG
BOOF

READ THIS WAY

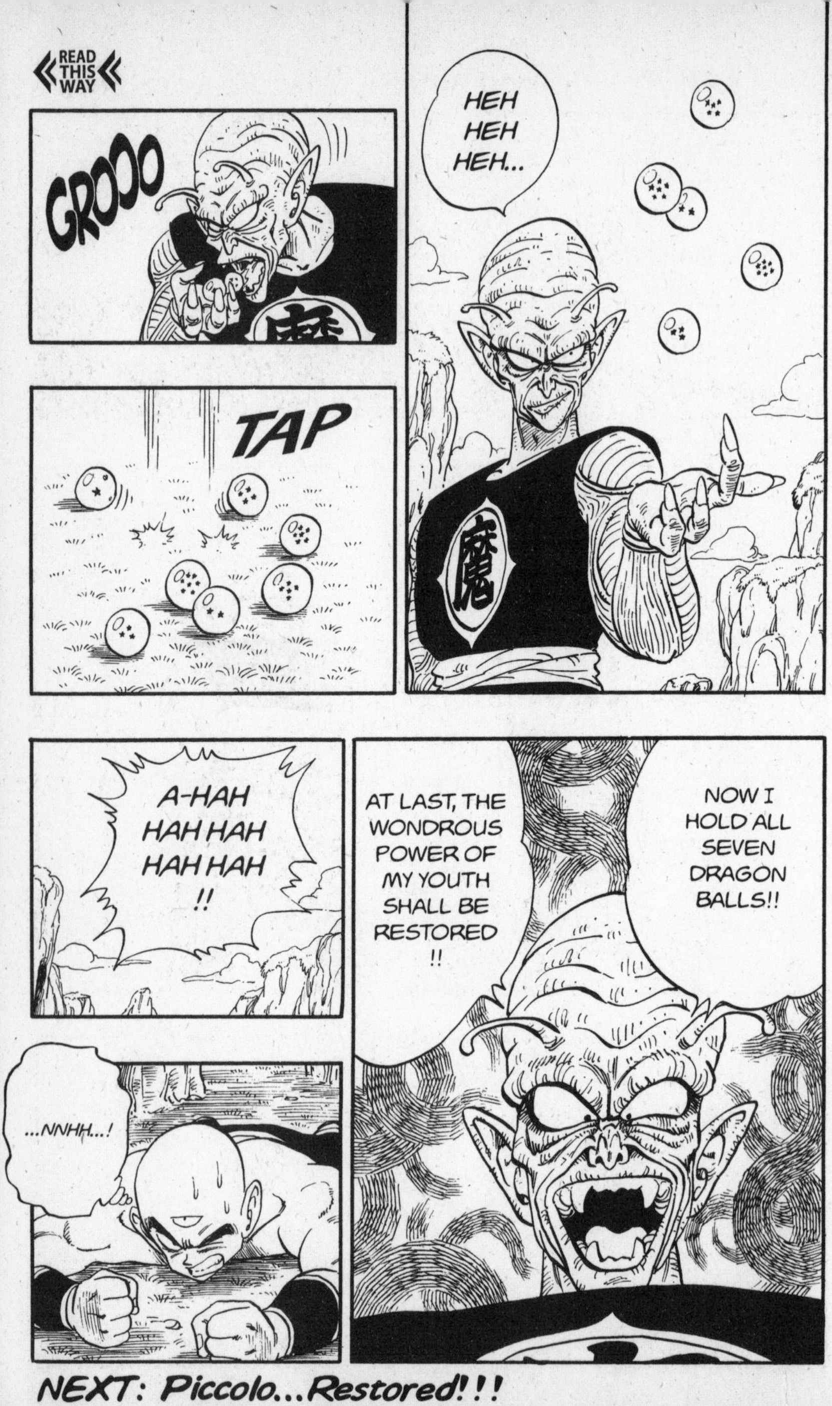
HEH HEH HEH...
GROOO
TAP
NOW I HOLD ALL SEVEN DRAGON BALLS!!
AT LAST, THE WONDROUS POWER OF MY YOUTH SHALL BE RESTORED !!
A-HAH HAH HAH HAH HAH !!
...NNHH...!

NEXT: Piccolo...Restored!!!

Tale 147 • The Demon King of Old... Restored!

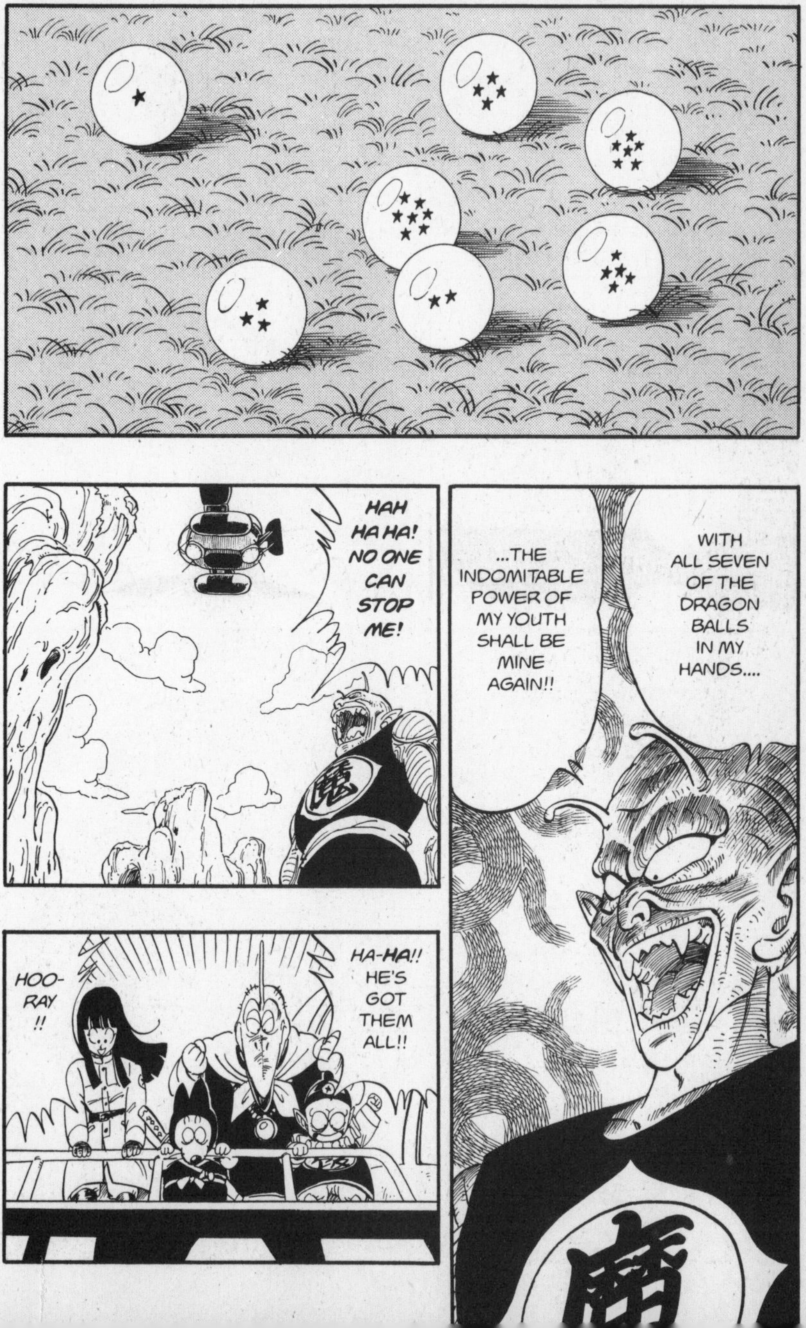
WITH ALL SEVEN OF THE DRAGON BALLS IN MY HANDS....
...THE INDOMITABLE POWER OF MY YOUTH SHALL BE MINE AGAIN!!
HAH HA HA! NO ONE CAN STOP ME!
HA-HA!! HE'S GOT THEM ALL!!
HOO-RAY !!

READ THIS WAY

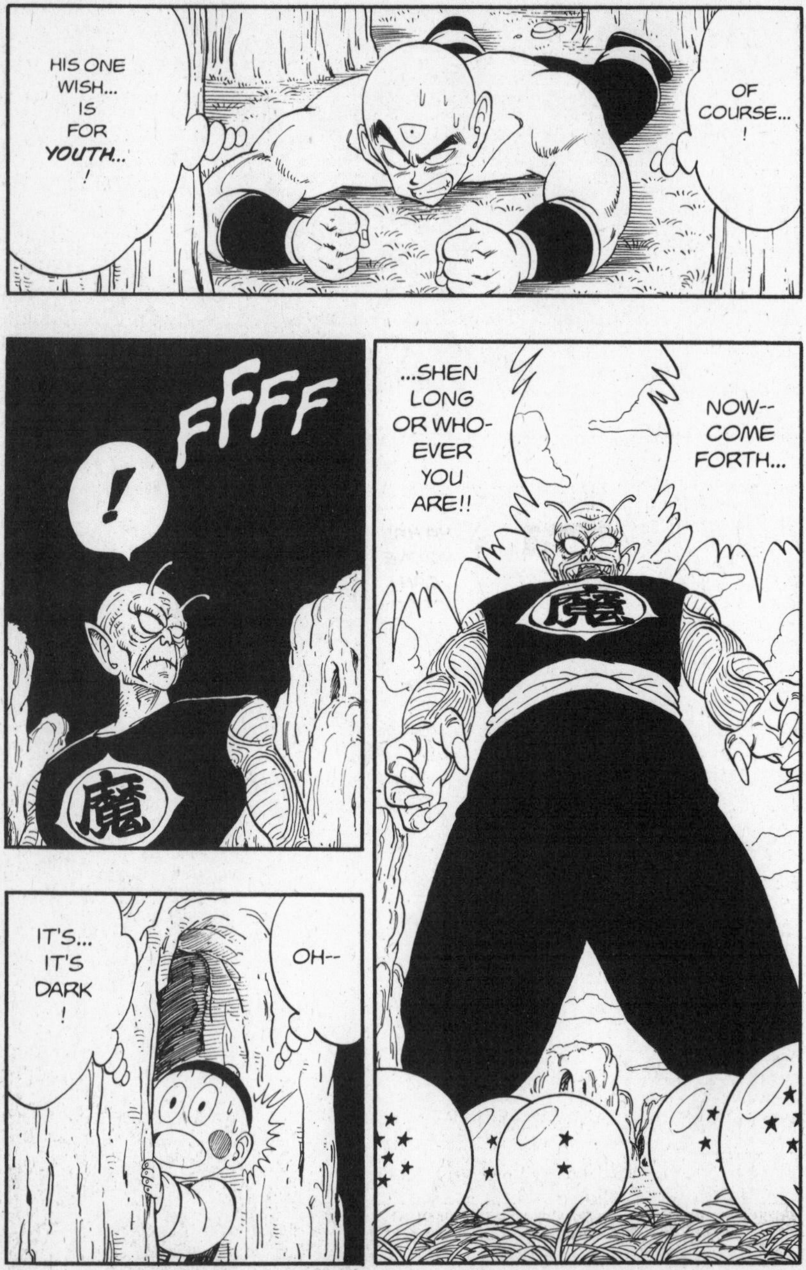

OF COURSE...!
HIS ONE WISH... IS FOR *YOUTH*...!
NOW-- COME FORTH...
...SHEN LONG OR WHO-EVER YOU ARE!!
FFFF
!
OH--
IT'S... IT'S DARK!

READ THIS WAY

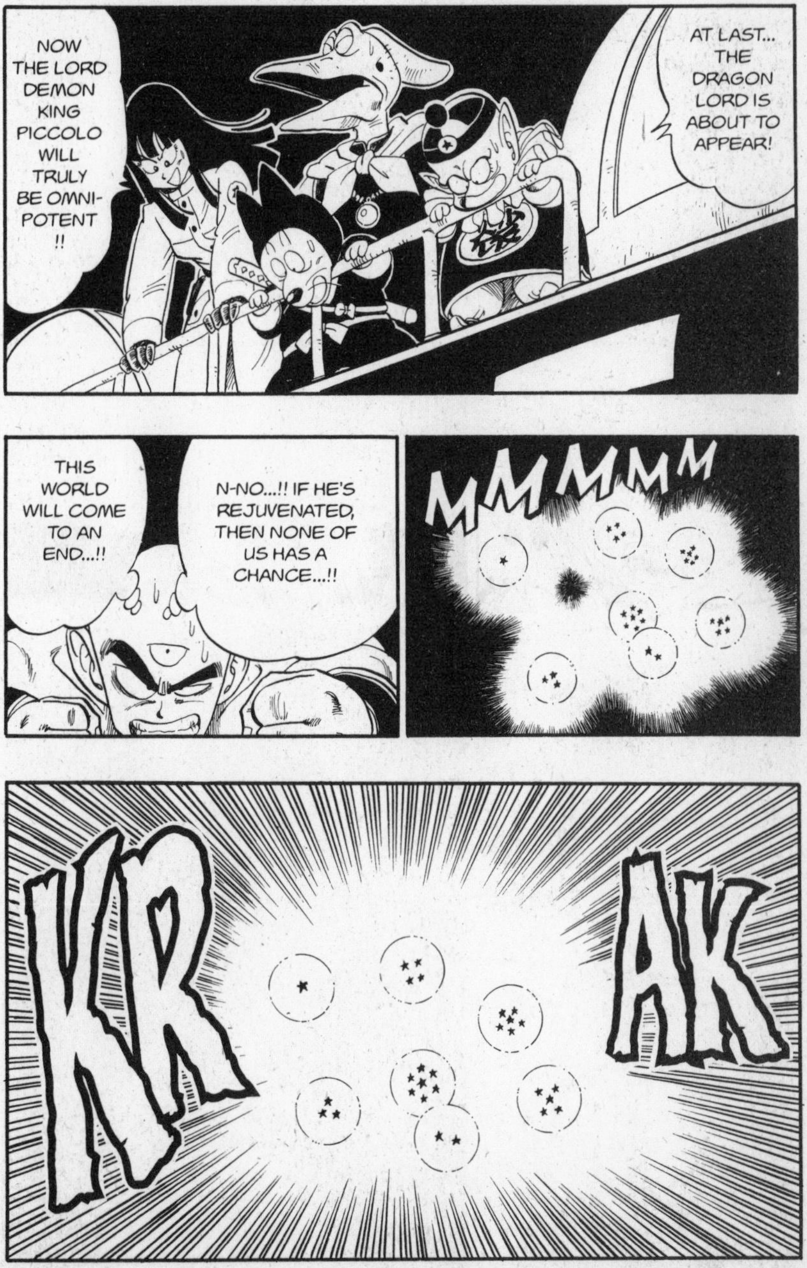
AT LAST... THE DRAGON LORD IS ABOUT TO APPEAR!
NOW THE LORD DEMON KING PICCOLO WILL TRULY BE OMNI-POTENT !!
MMMMMM
N-NO...!! IF HE'S REJUVENATED, THEN NONE OF US HAS A CHANCE...!!
THIS WORLD WILL COME TO AN END...!!
KR AK

READ THIS WAY

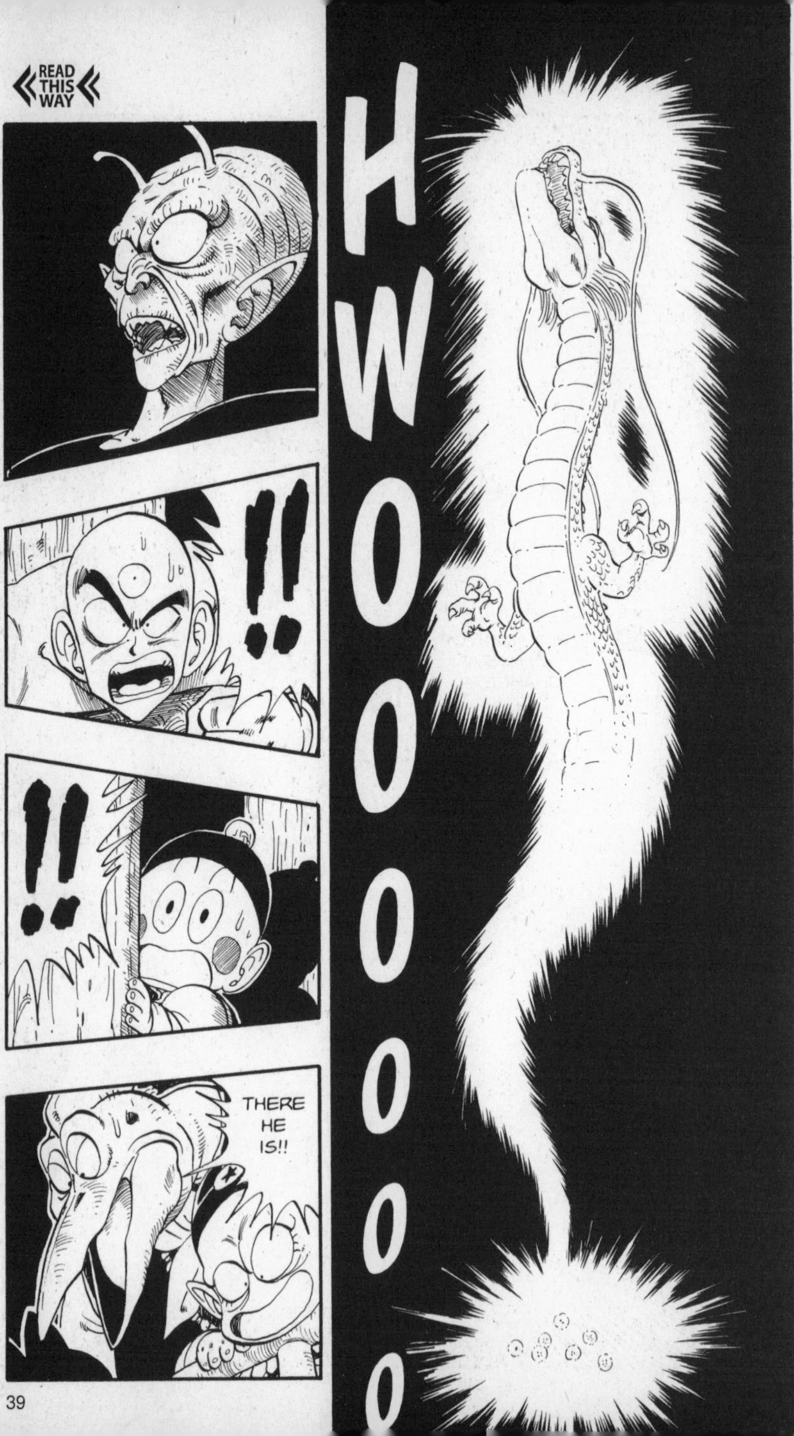

HWOOOOOO
!!
!!
THERE HE IS!!

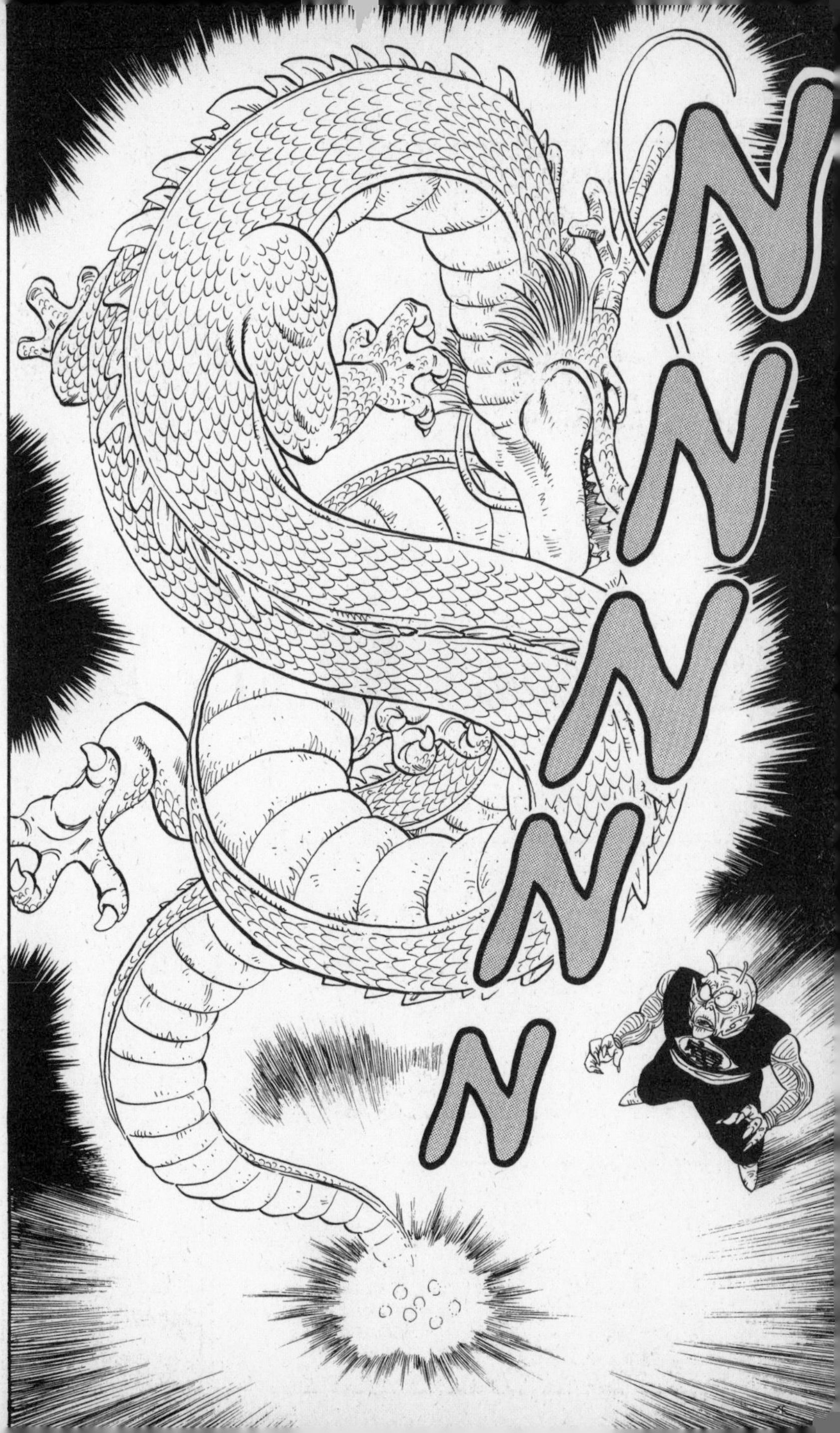
NNNNNNN

READ THIS WAY

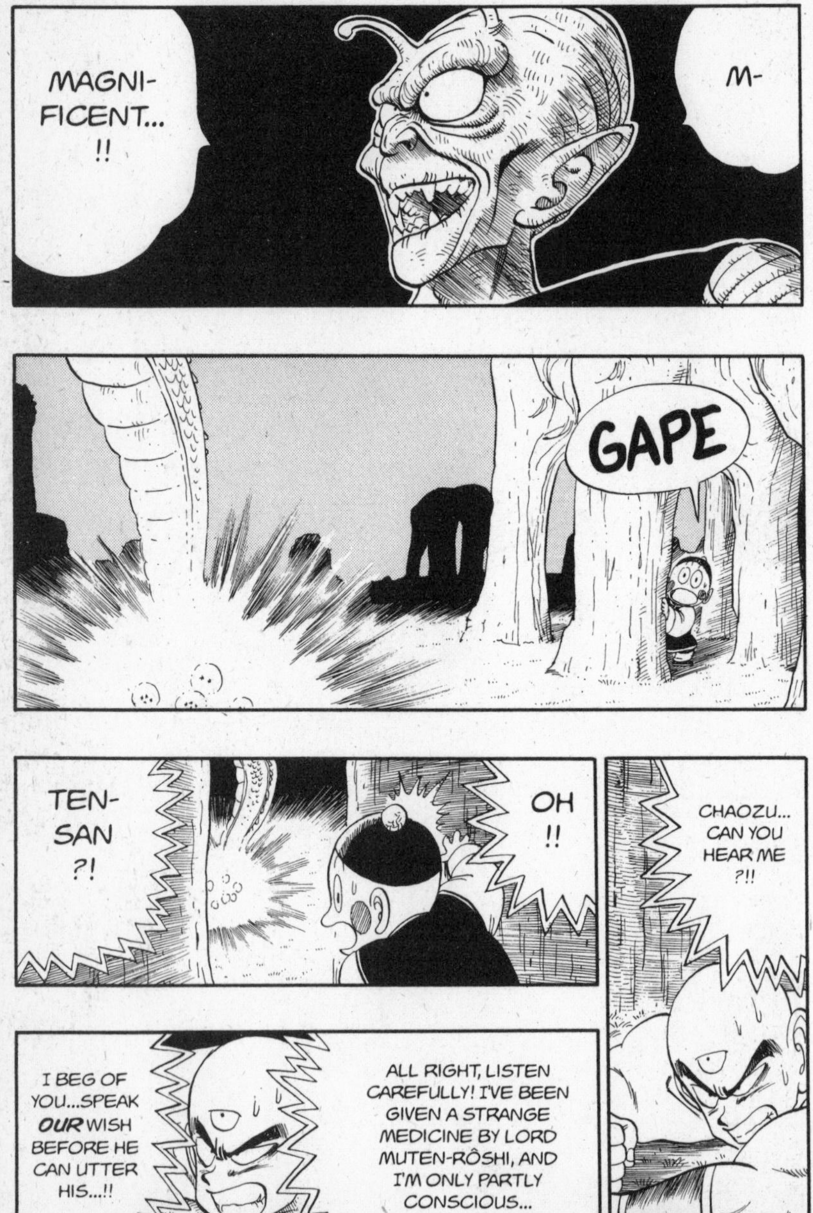
M-
MAGNI-FICENT...!!
GAPE
CHAOZU... CAN YOU HEAR ME ?!!
OH !!
TEN-SAN ?!
ALL RIGHT, LISTEN CAREFULLY! I'VE BEEN GIVEN A STRANGE MEDICINE BY LORD MUTEN-RÔSHI, AND I'M ONLY PARTLY CONSCIOUS...
I BEG OF YOU...SPEAK ***OUR*** WISH BEFORE HE CAN UTTER HIS...!!

READ THIS WAY

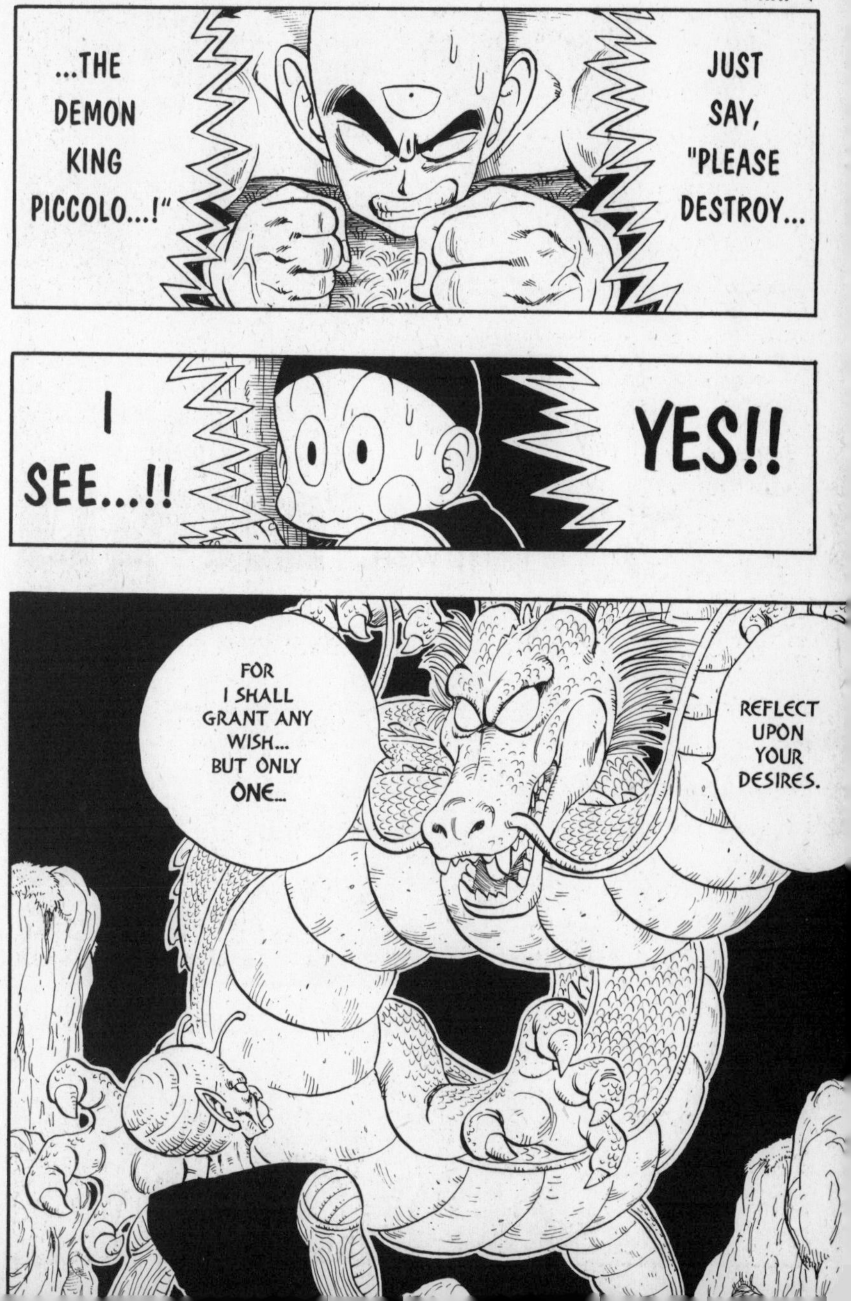
JUST SAY, "PLEASE DESTROY...
...THE DEMON KING PICCOLO...!"
YES!!
I SEE...!!
REFLECT UPON YOUR DESIRES.
FOR I SHALL GRANT ANY WISH... BUT ONLY ONE...

READ THIS WAY

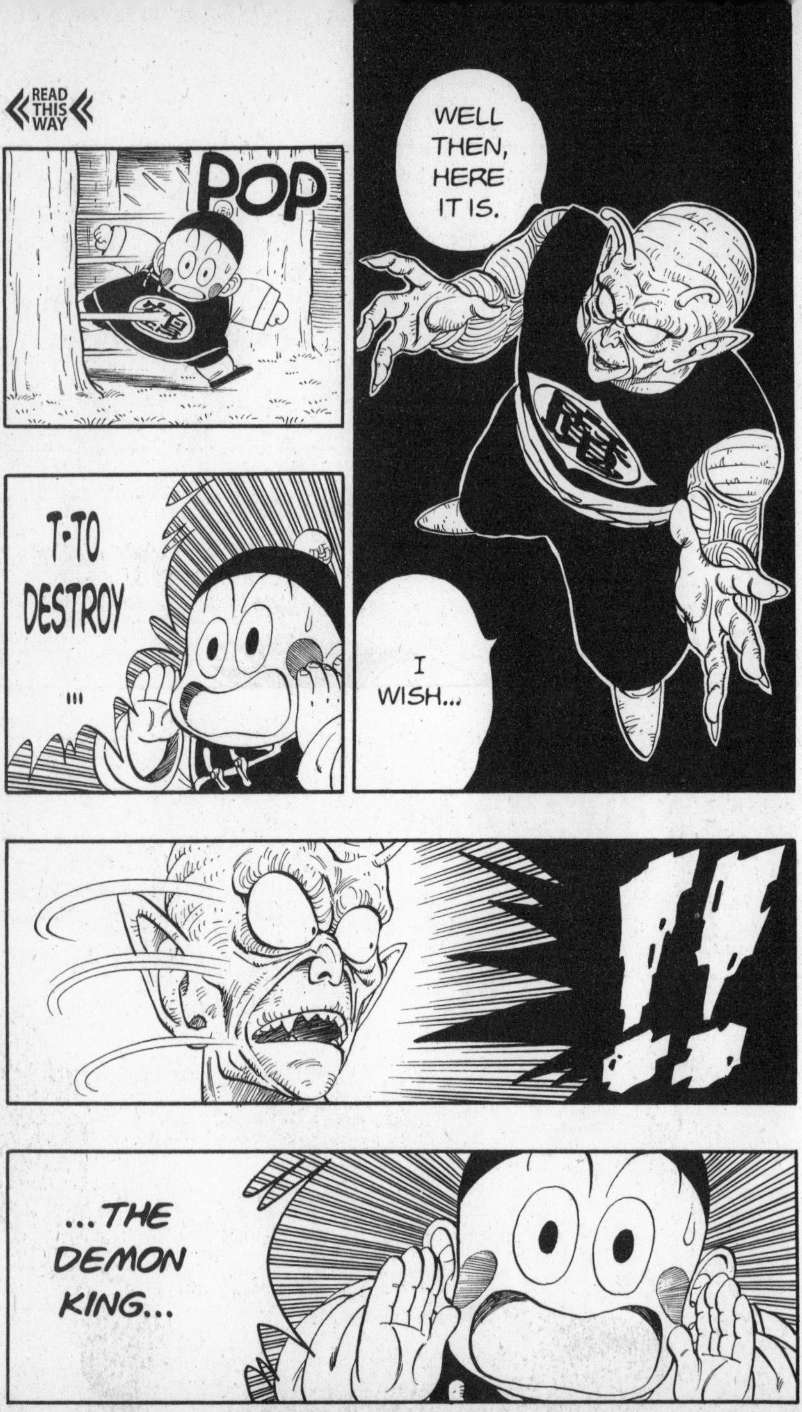

WELL THEN, HERE IT IS.
I WISH...
POP
T-TO DESTROY ...
!!
...THE DEMON KING...

READ THIS WAY

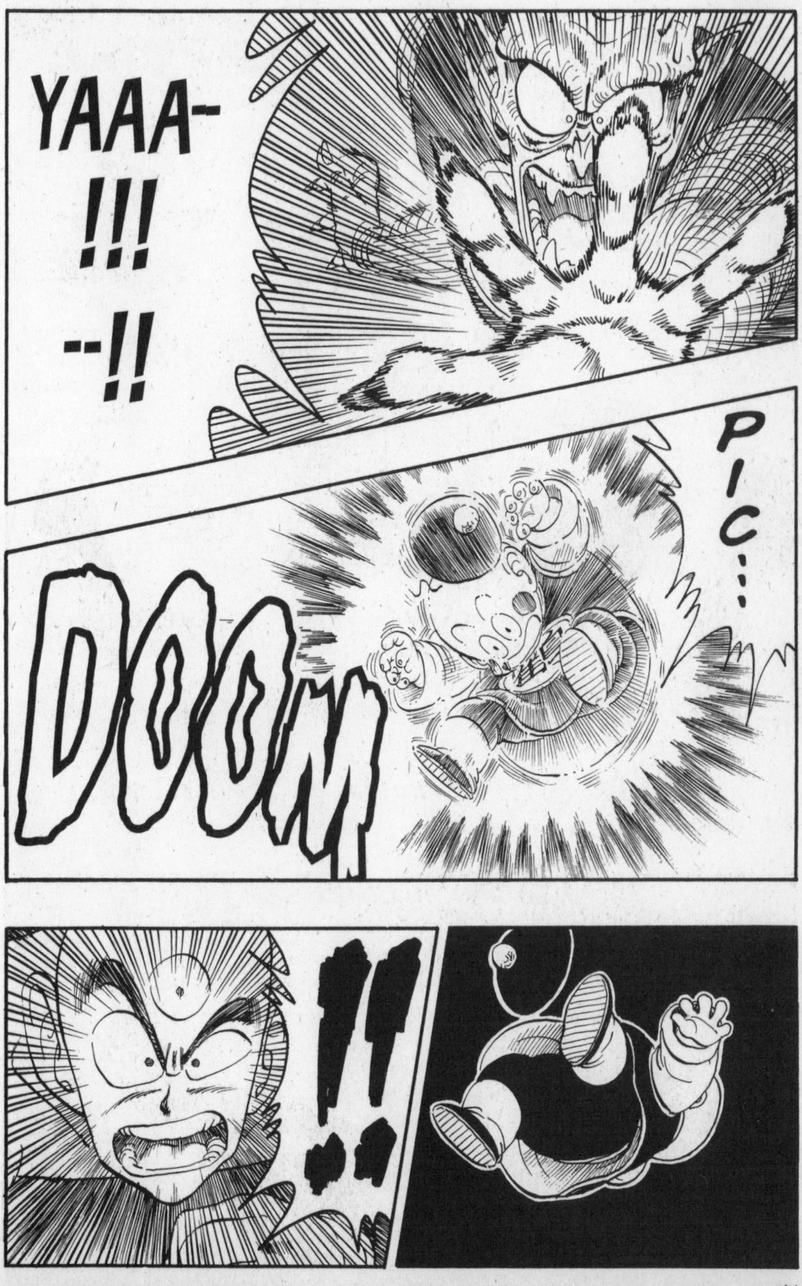
YAAA--
!!!
--!!
PIC...
DOOM
!!

READ THIS WAY

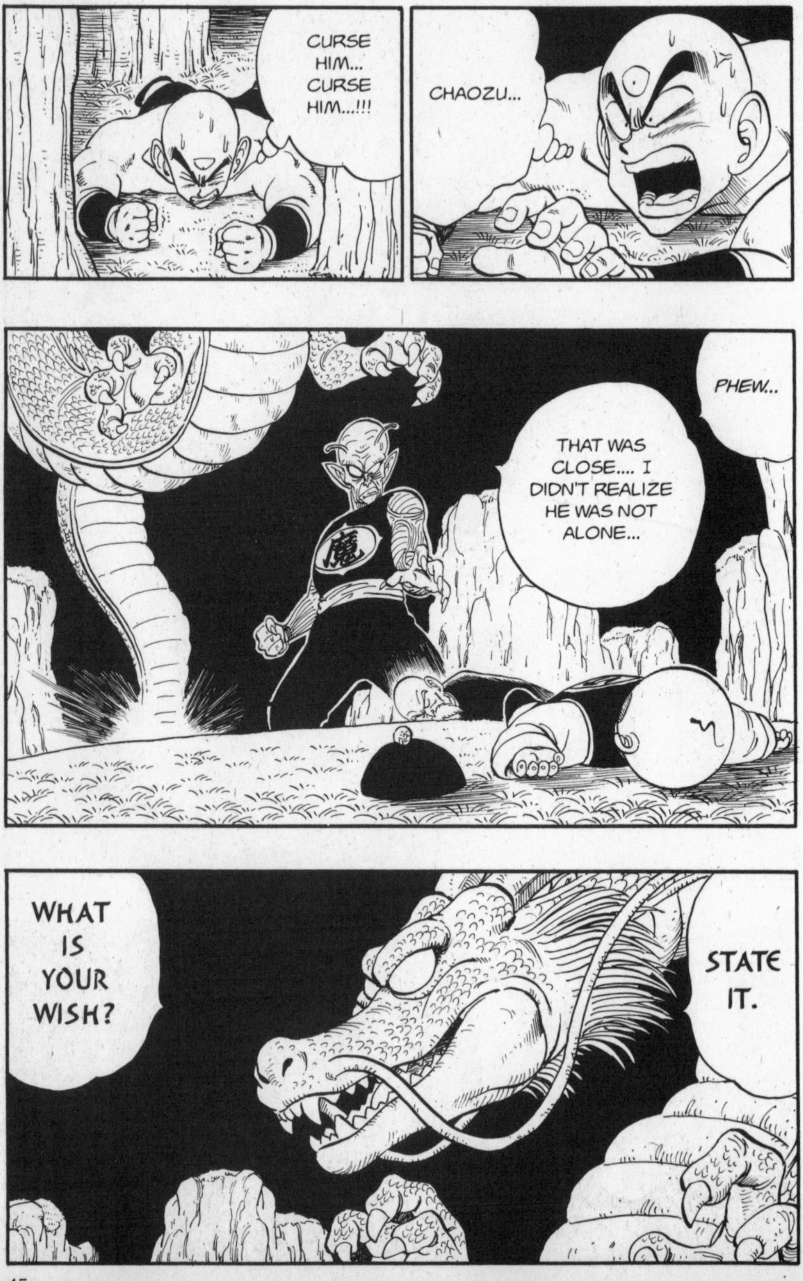
CHAOZU...
CURSE HIM... CURSE HIM...!!!
PHEW...
THAT WAS CLOSE.... I DIDN'T REALIZE HE WAS NOT ALONE...
WHAT IS YOUR WISH?
STATE IT.

READ THIS WAY

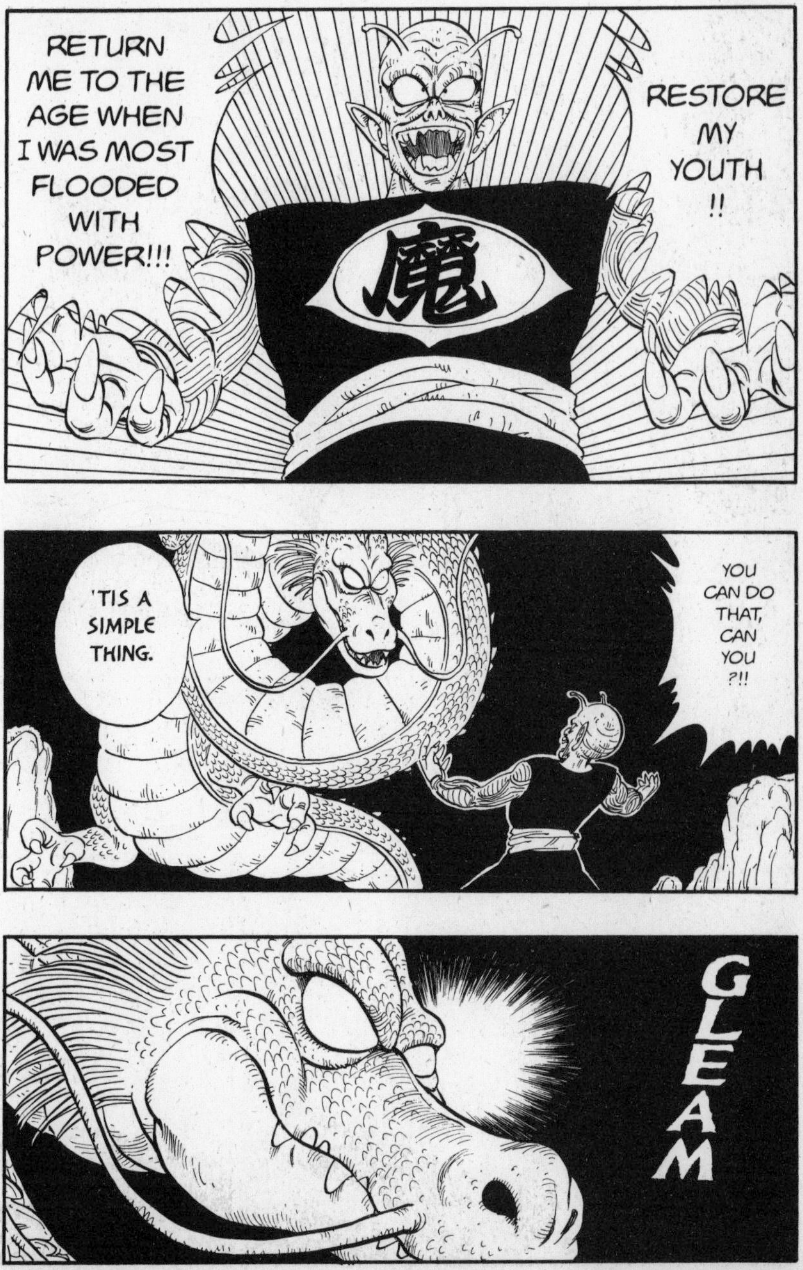
RESTORE MY YOUTH !!
RETURN ME TO THE AGE WHEN I WAS MOST FLOODED WITH POWER!!!
YOU CAN DO THAT, CAN YOU ?!!
'TIS A SIMPLE THING.
GLEAM

READ THIS WAY

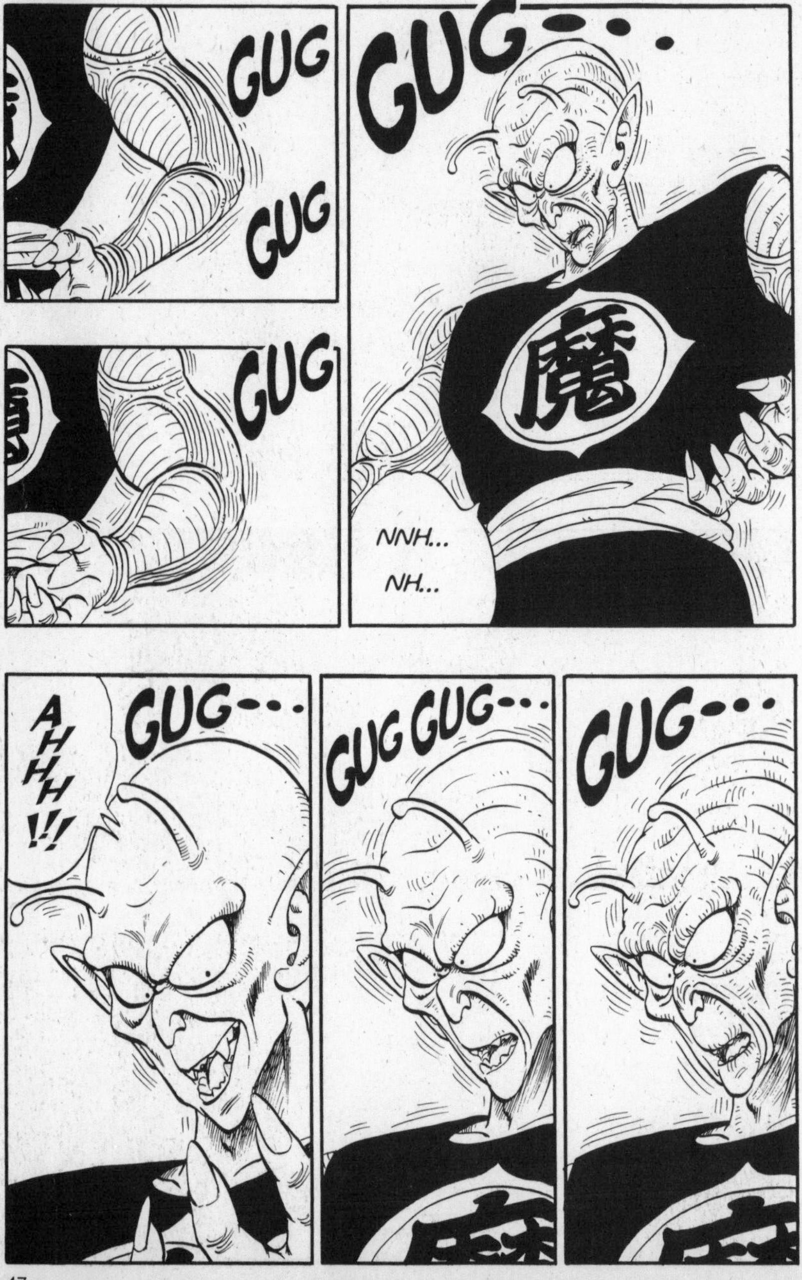
GUG...
魔
NNH...
NH...
GUG
GUG
GUG
GUG...
GUG GUG...
GUG...
AHHH!!!

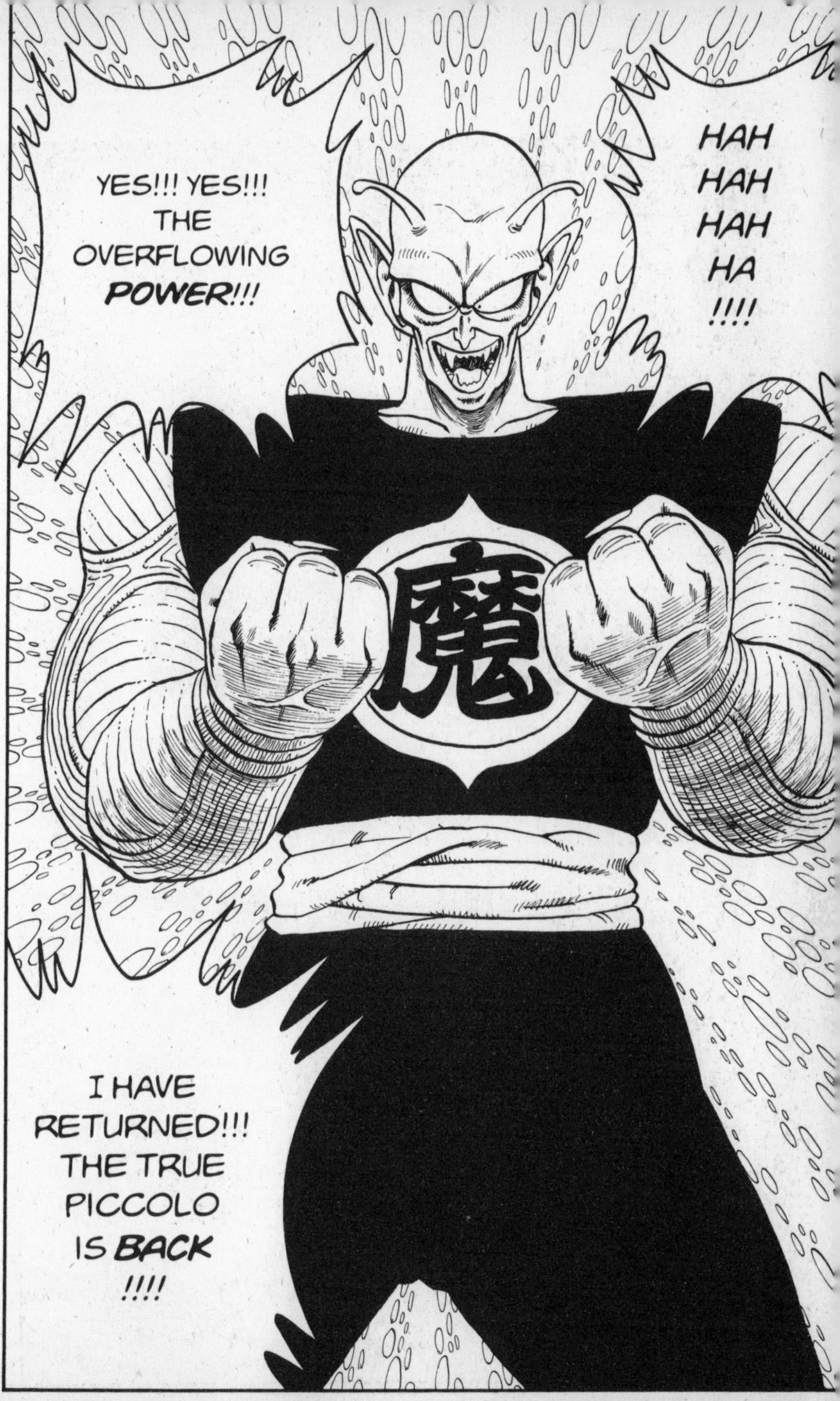
HAH HAH HAH HA !!!!
YES!!! YES!!! THE OVERFLOWING **POWER**!!!
I HAVE RETURNED!!! THE TRUE PICCOLO IS **BACK** !!!!

READ THIS WAY

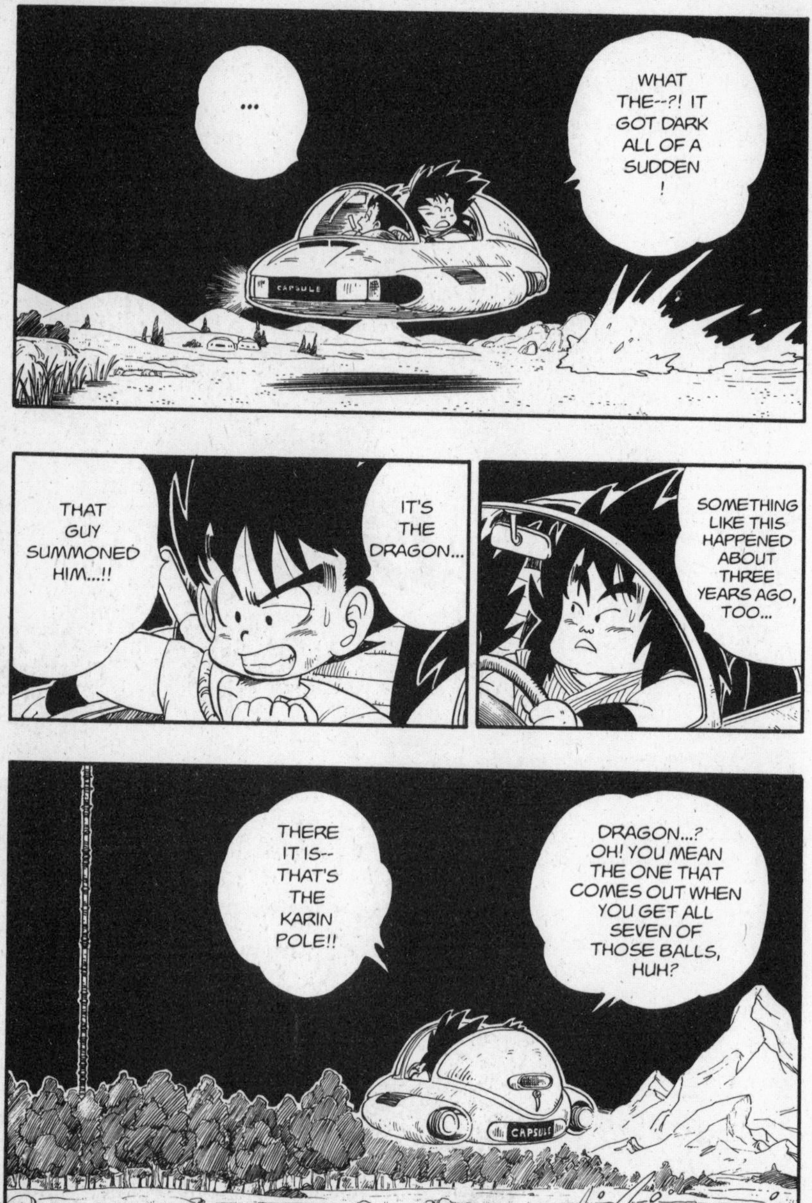
WHAT THE--?! IT GOT DARK ALL OF A SUDDEN!
...
SOMETHING LIKE THIS HAPPENED ABOUT THREE YEARS AGO, TOO...
IT'S THE DRAGON...
THAT GUY SUMMONED HIM...!!
DRAGON...? OH! YOU MEAN THE ONE THAT COMES OUT WHEN YOU GET ALL SEVEN OF THOSE BALLS, HUH?
THERE IT IS--THAT'S THE KARIN POLE!!
CAPSULE
CAPSULE

NEXT: No More Wishes

Tale 148 • Go Ask Karin!

READ THIS WAY

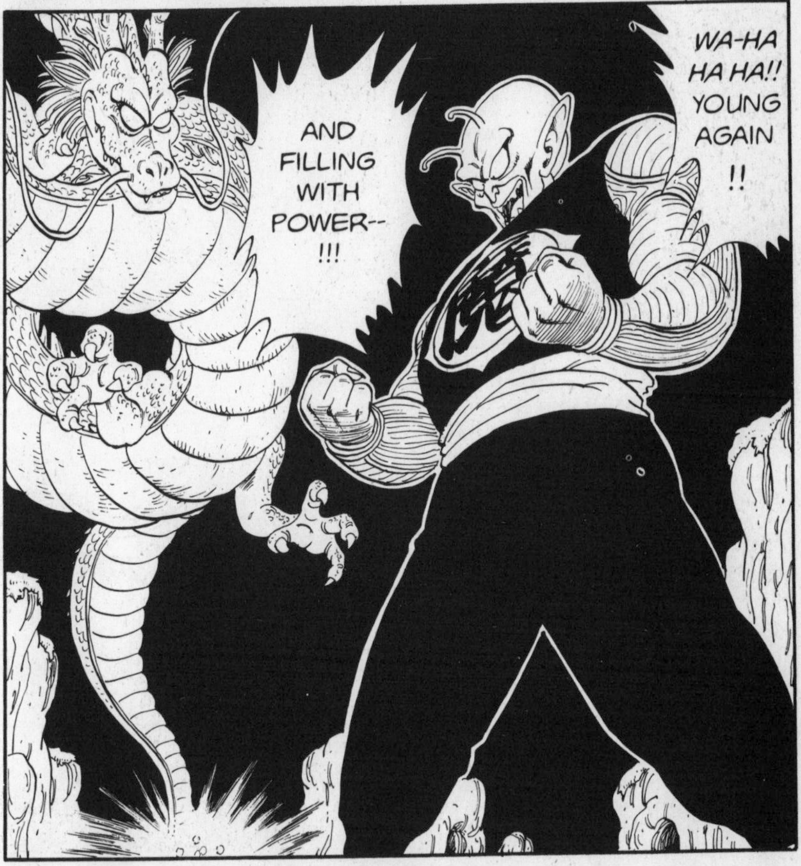
WA-HA HA HA!! YOUNG AGAIN !!
AND FILLING WITH POWER-- !!!

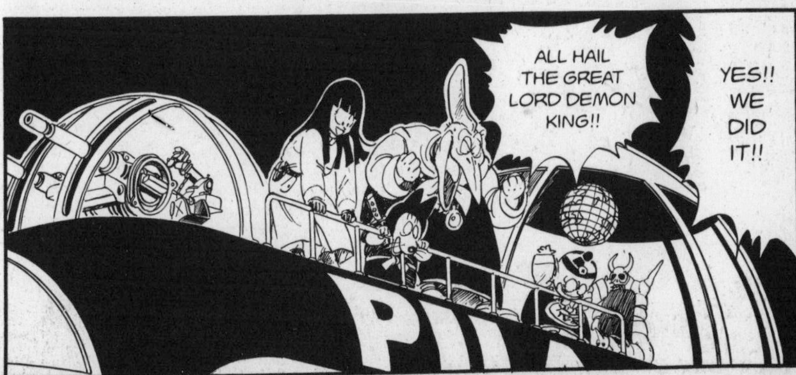
YES!! WE DID IT!!
ALL HAIL THE GREAT LORD DEMON KING!!
PIL

READ THIS WAY

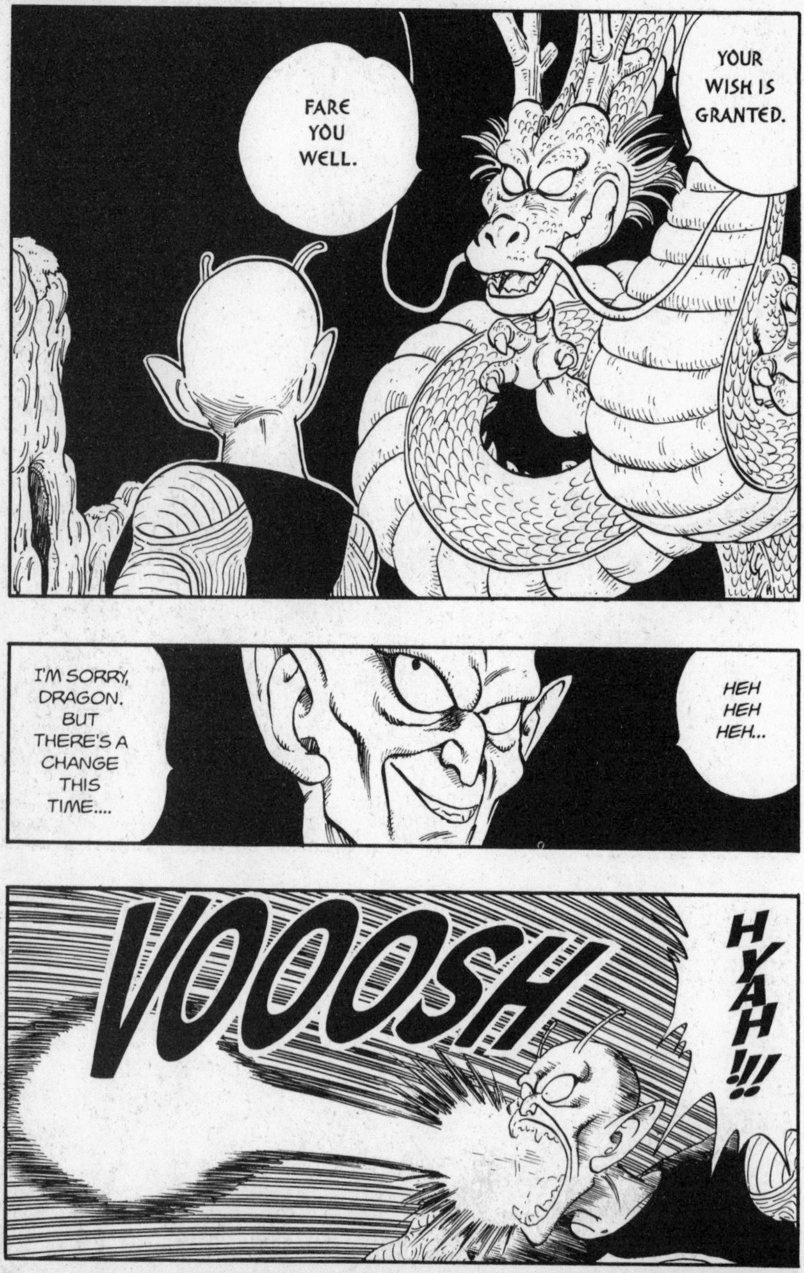
YOUR WISH IS GRANTED.
FARE YOU WELL.
HEH HEH HEH...
I'M SORRY, DRAGON. BUT THERE'S A CHANGE THIS TIME....
HYAH!!!
VOOOSH

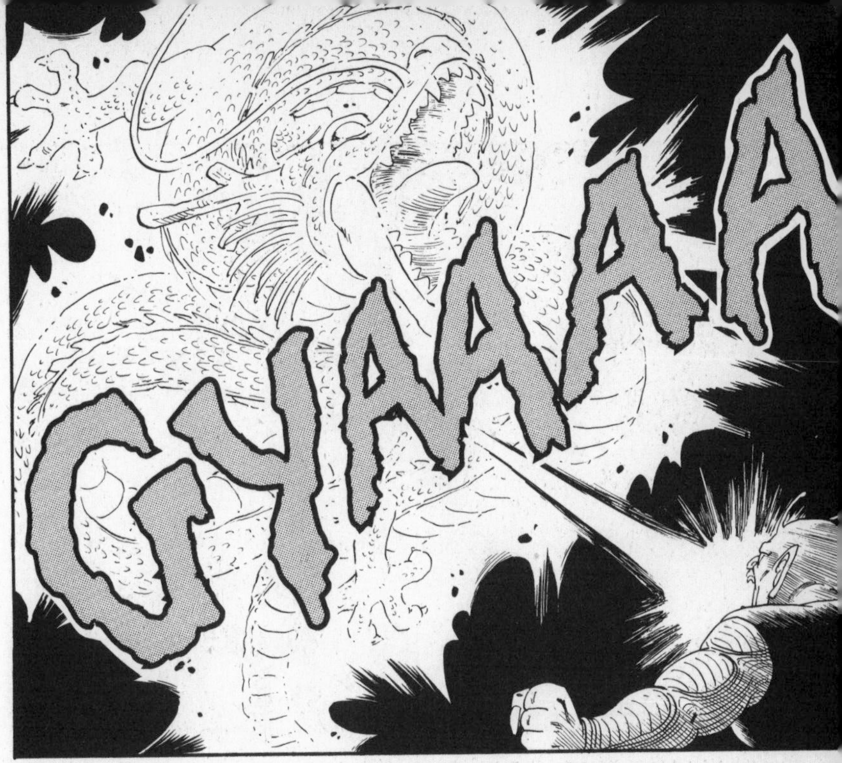
GYAAAA
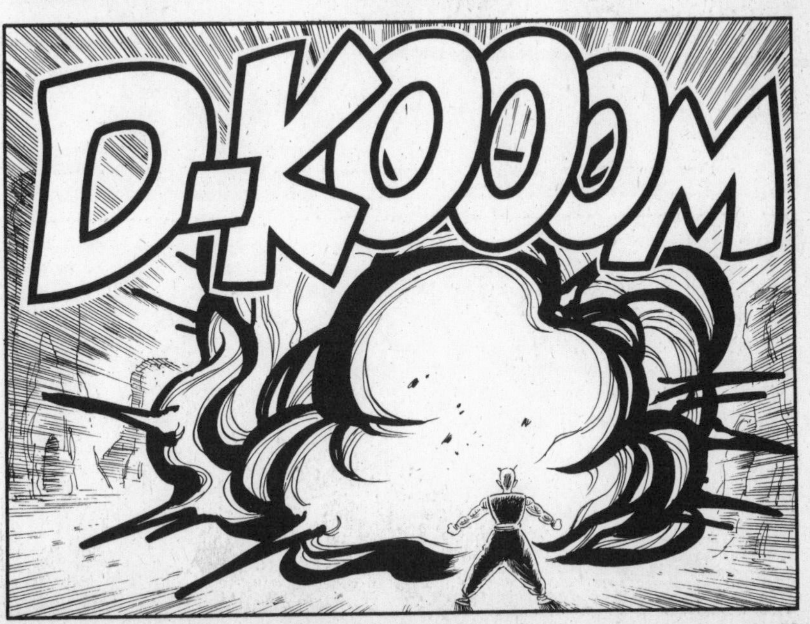
D-KOOOM

READ THIS WAY

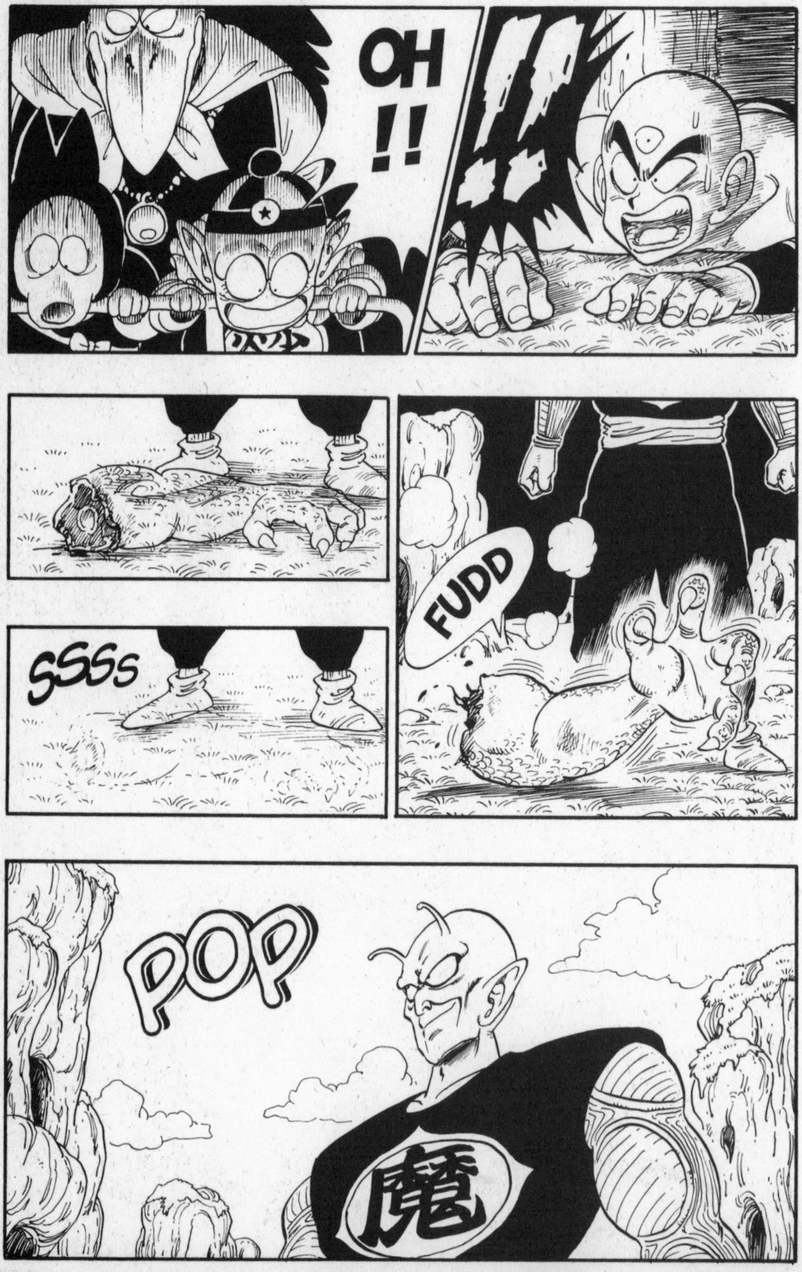
OH !!
FUDD
SSSs
POP
魔

READ THIS WAY

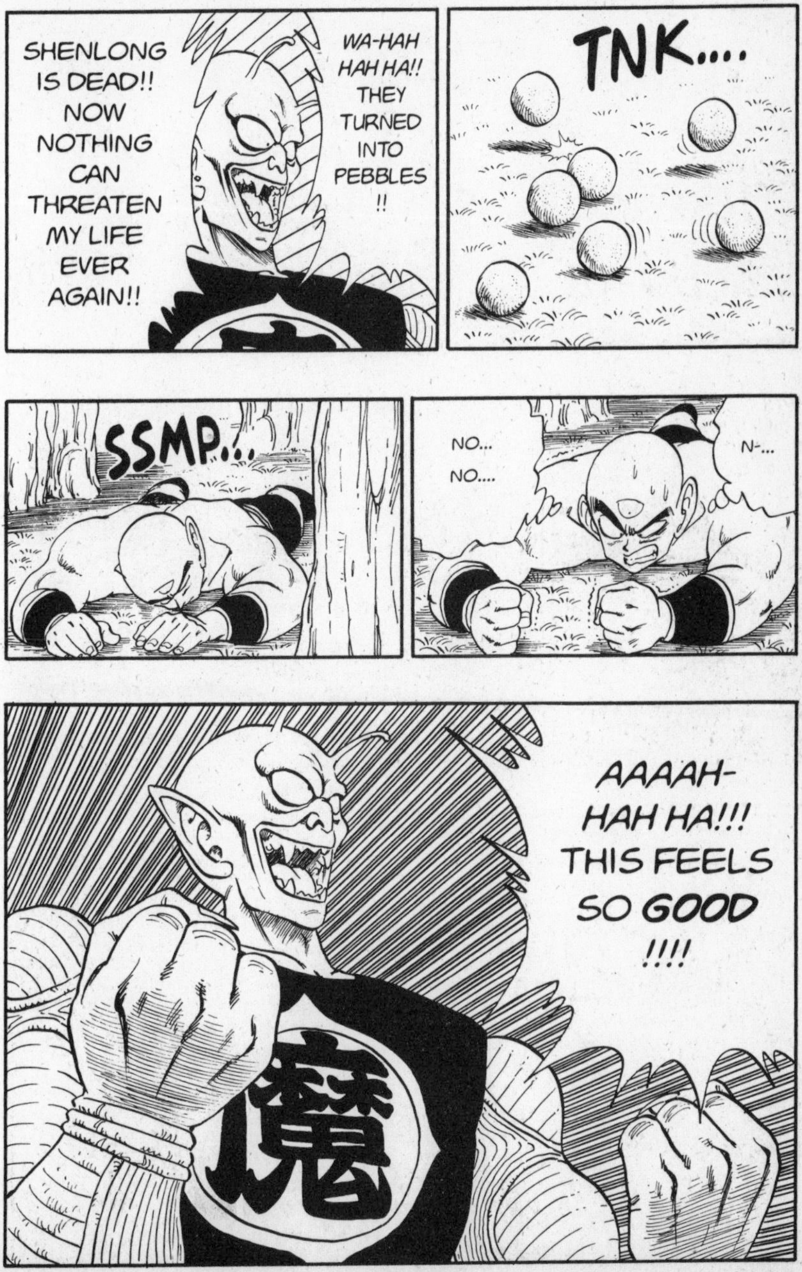
TNK....
WA-HAH HAH HA!! THEY TURNED INTO PEBBLES !!
SHENLONG IS DEAD!! NOW NOTHING CAN THREATEN MY LIFE EVER AGAIN!!
N-...
NO... NO....
SSMP...
AAAAH-HAH HA!!! THIS FEELS SO **GOOD** !!!!

READ THIS WAY

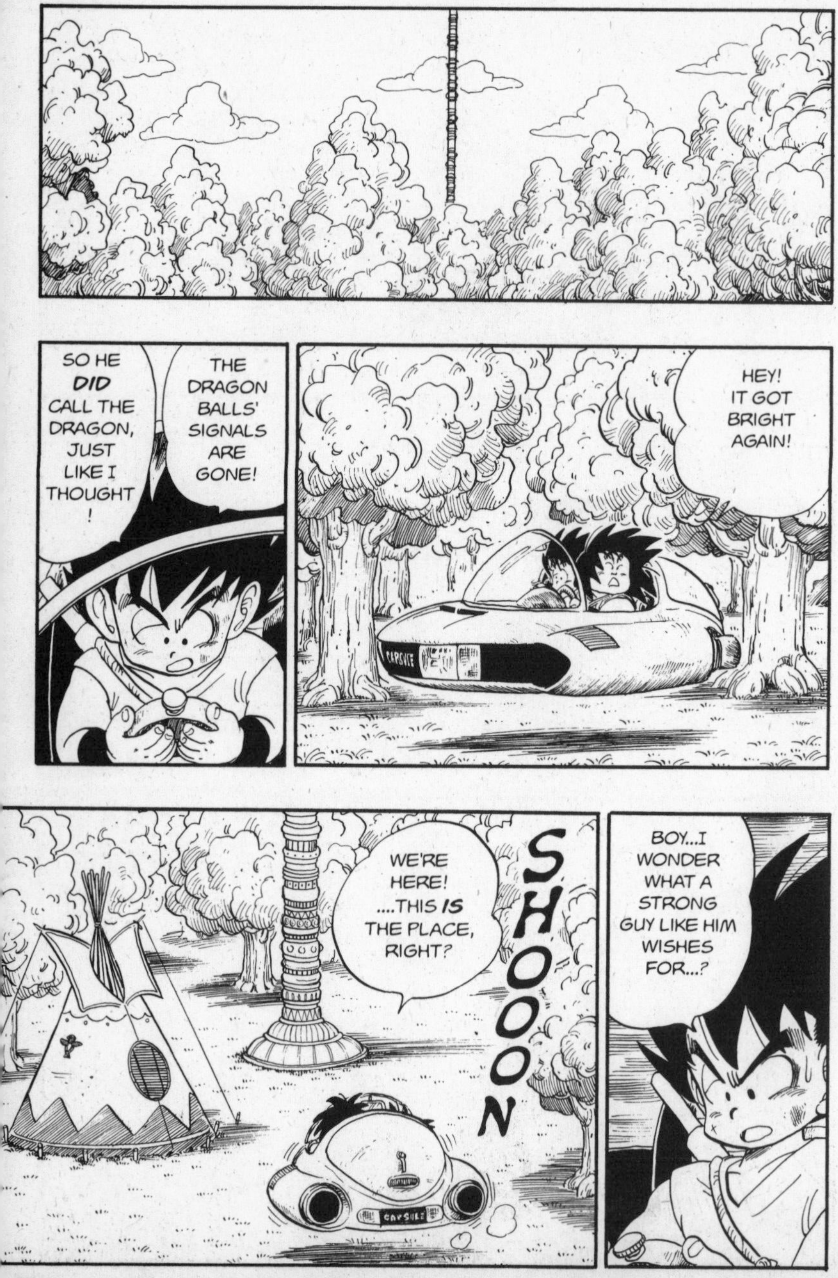

HEY! IT GOT BRIGHT AGAIN!
THE DRAGON BALLS' SIGNALS ARE GONE!
SO HE *DID* CALL THE DRAGON, JUST LIKE I THOUGHT!
BOY...I WONDER WHAT A STRONG GUY LIKE HIM WISHES FOR...?
SHOOOON
WE'RE HERE! ....THIS *IS* THE PLACE, RIGHT?

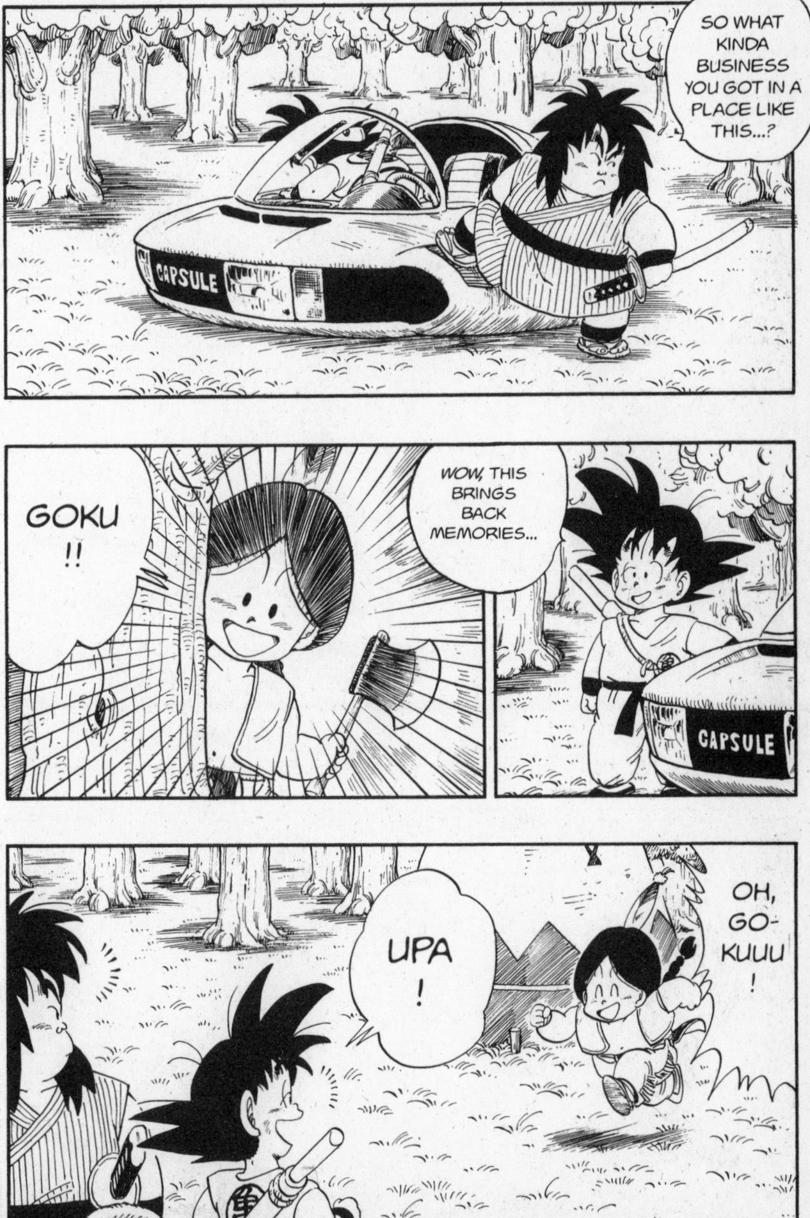
SO WHAT KINDA BUSINESS YOU GOT IN A PLACE LIKE THIS...?
WOW, THIS BRINGS BACK MEMORIES...
GOKU !!
OH, GO-KUUU !
UPA !
CAPSULE
CAPSULE

READ THIS WAY

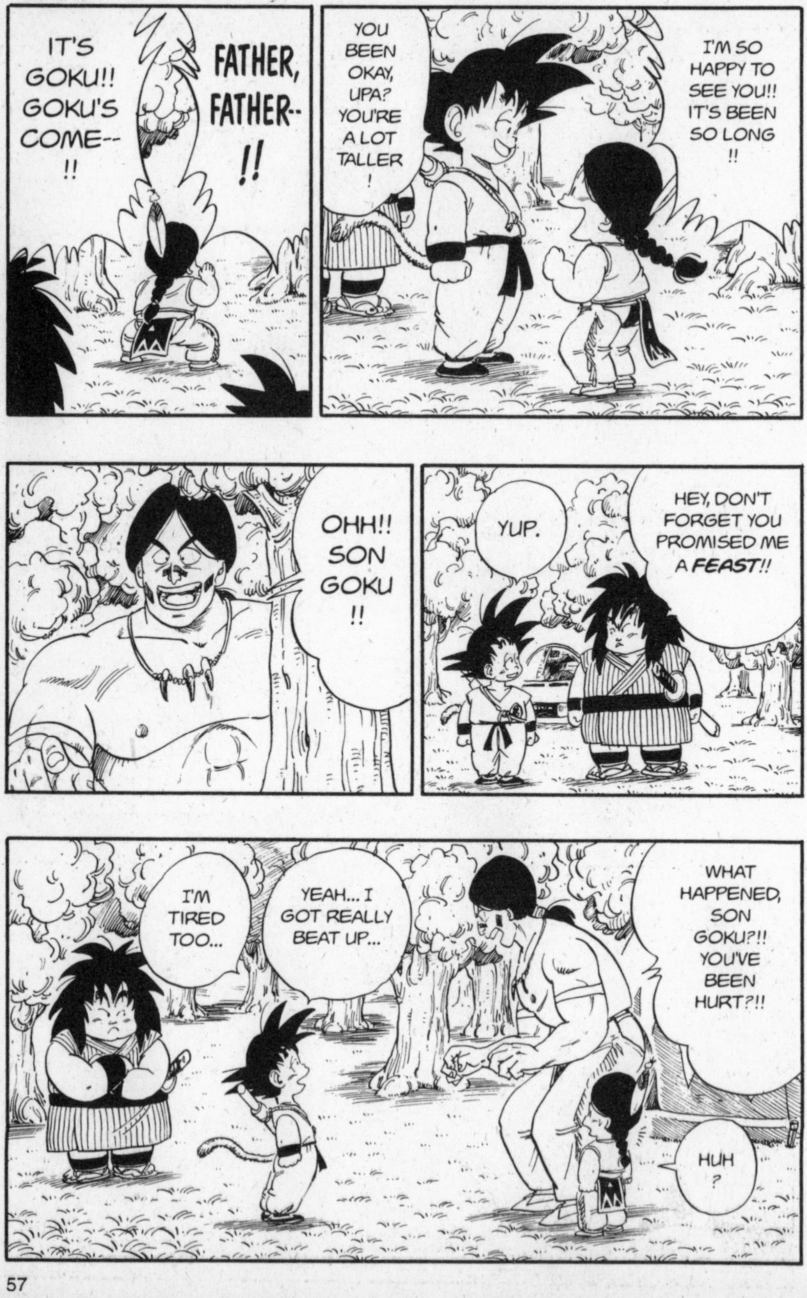
I'M SO HAPPY TO SEE YOU!! IT'S BEEN SO LONG !!
YOU BEEN OKAY, UPA? YOU'RE A LOT TALLER !
FATHER, FATHER-- !!
IT'S GOKU!! GOKU'S COME-- !!
HEY, DON'T FORGET YOU PROMISED ME A *FEAST*!!
YUP.
OHH!! SON GOKU !!
WHAT HAPPENED, SON GOKU?!! YOU'VE BEEN HURT?!!
HUH ?
YEAH... I GOT REALLY BEAT UP...
I'M TIRED TOO...

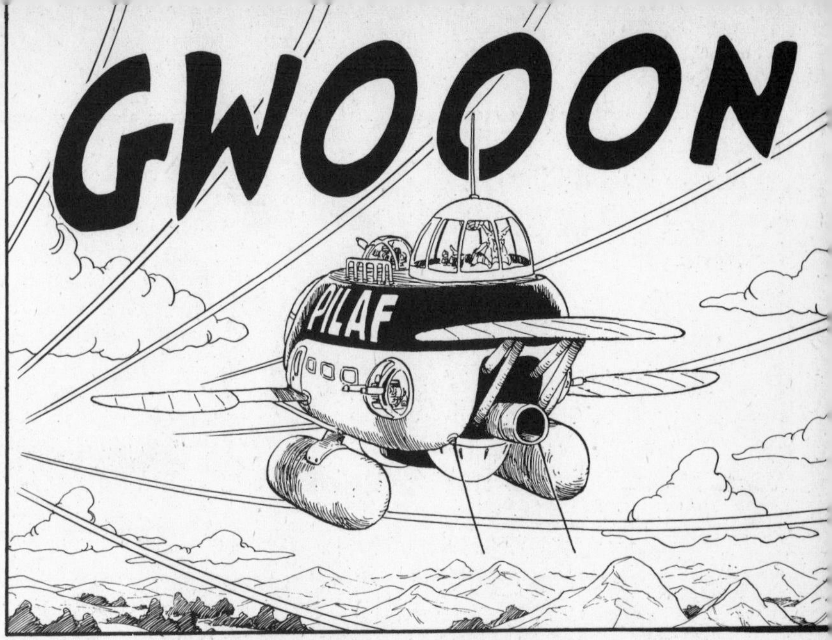
GWOOON
PILAF

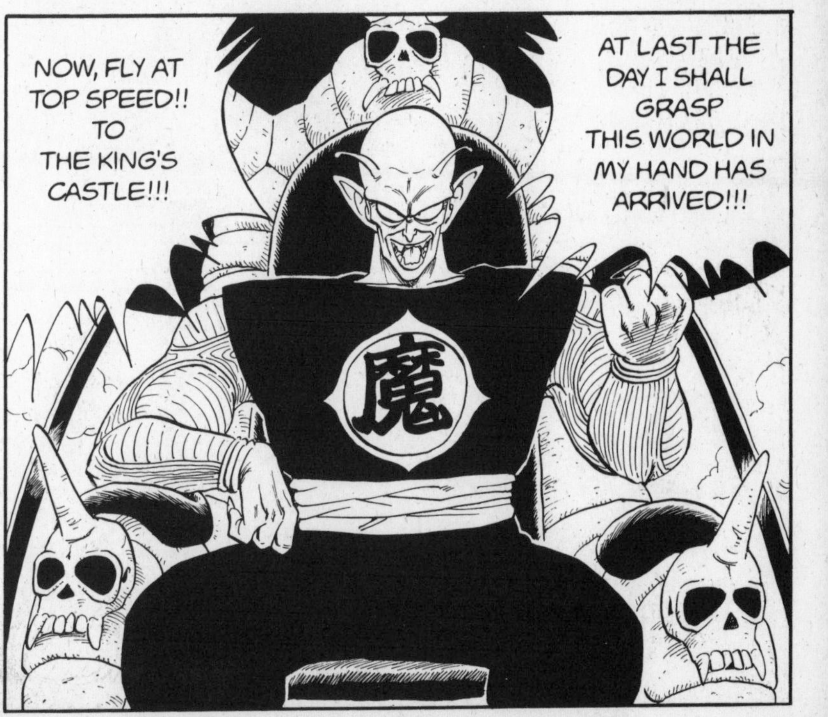
AT LAST THE DAY I SHALL GRASP THIS WORLD IN MY HAND HAS ARRIVED!!!
NOW, FLY AT TOP SPEED!! TO THE KING'S CASTLE!!!

READ THIS WAY

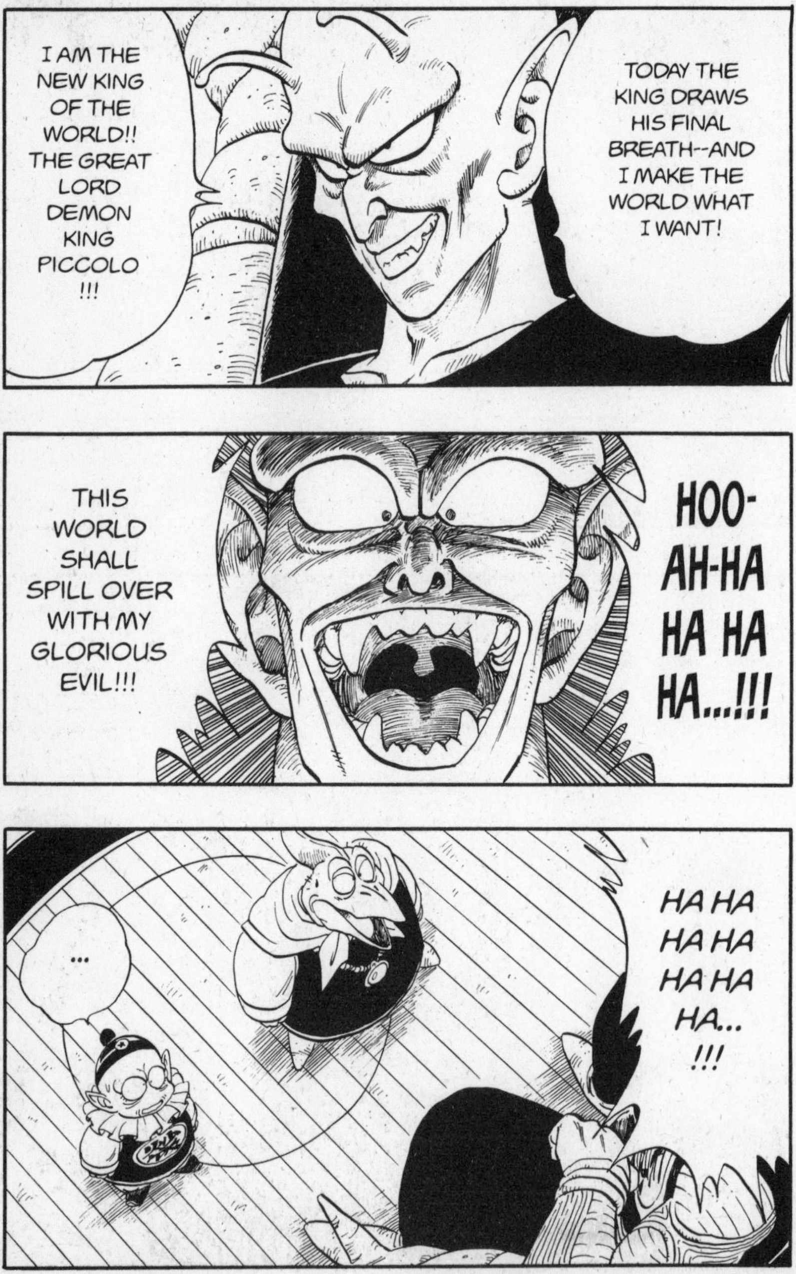
TODAY THE KING DRAWS HIS FINAL BREATH--AND I MAKE THE WORLD WHAT I WANT!
I AM THE NEW KING OF THE WORLD!! THE GREAT LORD DEMON KING PICCOLO !!!
HOO-AH-HA HA HA HA...!!!
THIS WORLD SHALL SPILL OVER WITH MY GLORIOUS EVIL!!!
HA HA HA HA HA HA HA... !!!
...

READ THIS WAY

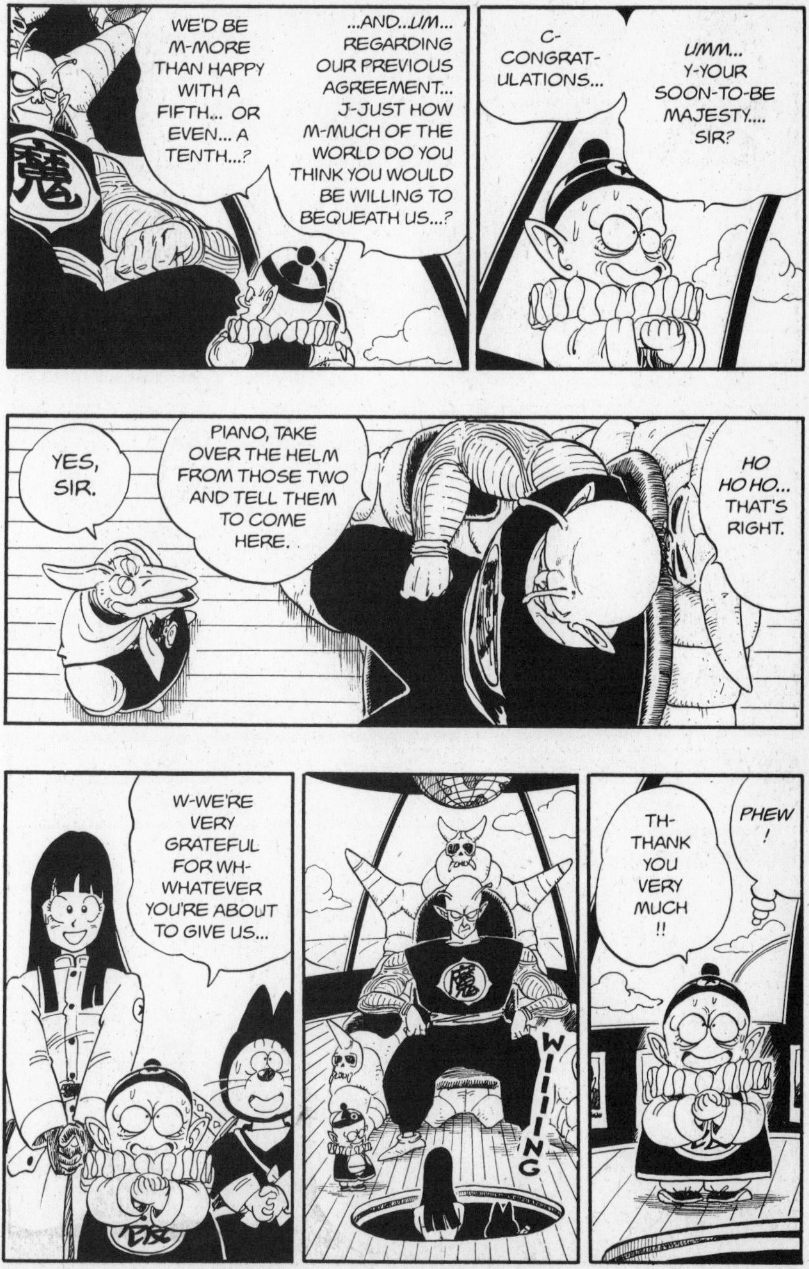
UMM... Y-YOUR SOON-TO-BE MAJESTY.... SIR?
C-CONGRATULATIONS...
...AND...UM... REGARDING OUR PREVIOUS AGREEMENT... J-JUST HOW M-MUCH OF THE WORLD DO YOU THINK YOU WOULD BE WILLING TO BEQUEATH US...?
WE'D BE M-MORE THAN HAPPY WITH A FIFTH... OR EVEN... A TENTH...?
HO HO HO... THAT'S RIGHT.
PIANO, TAKE OVER THE HELM FROM THOSE TWO AND TELL THEM TO COME HERE.
YES, SIR.
PHEW!
TH-THANK YOU VERY MUCH!!
WIIIIING
W-WE'RE VERY GRATEFUL FOR WH-WHATEVER YOU'RE ABOUT TO GIVE US...

READ THIS WAY

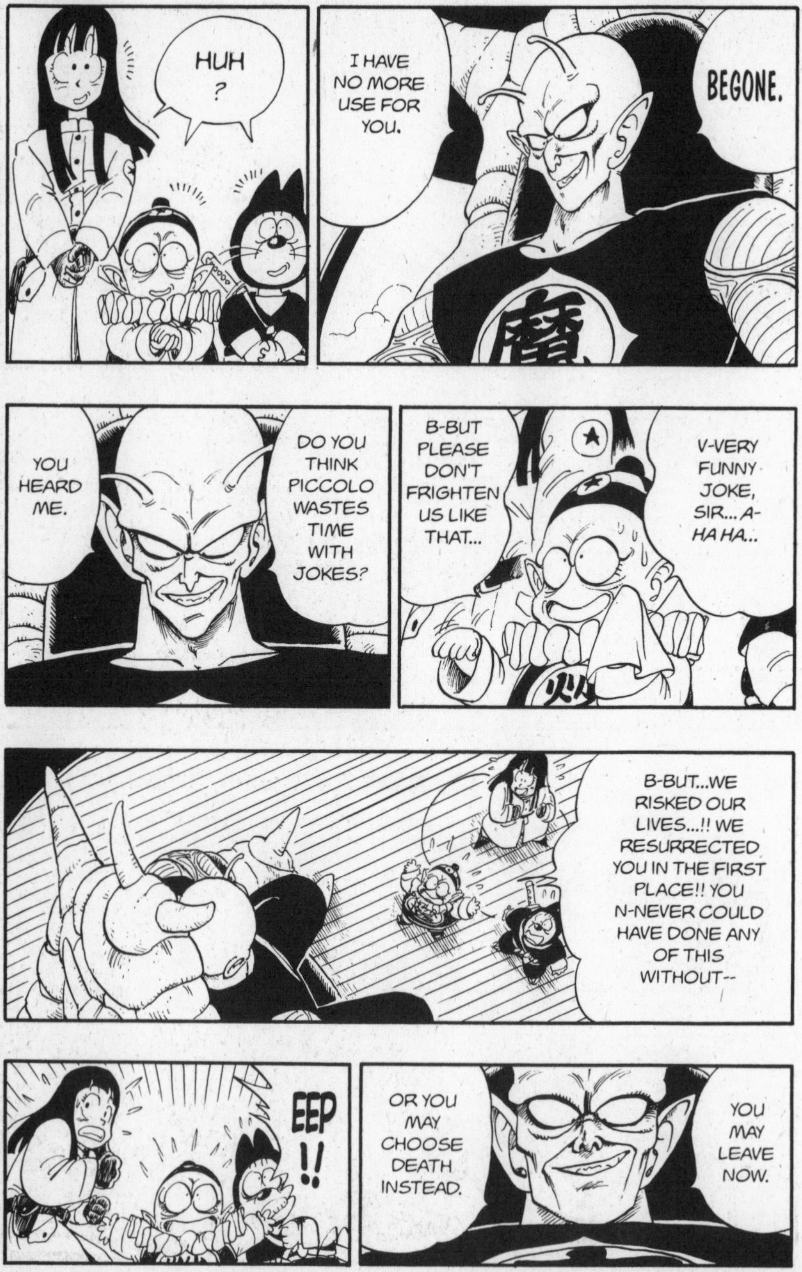
BEGONE.
I HAVE NO MORE USE FOR YOU.
HUH ?
V-VERY FUNNY JOKE, SIR... A-HA HA...
B-BUT PLEASE DON'T FRIGHTEN US LIKE THAT...
DO YOU THINK PICCOLO WASTES TIME WITH JOKES?
YOU HEARD ME.
B-BUT...WE RISKED OUR LIVES...!! WE RESURRECTED YOU IN THE FIRST PLACE!! YOU N-NEVER COULD HAVE DONE ANY OF THIS WITHOUT--
YOU MAY LEAVE NOW.
OR YOU MAY CHOOSE DEATH INSTEAD.
EEP !!

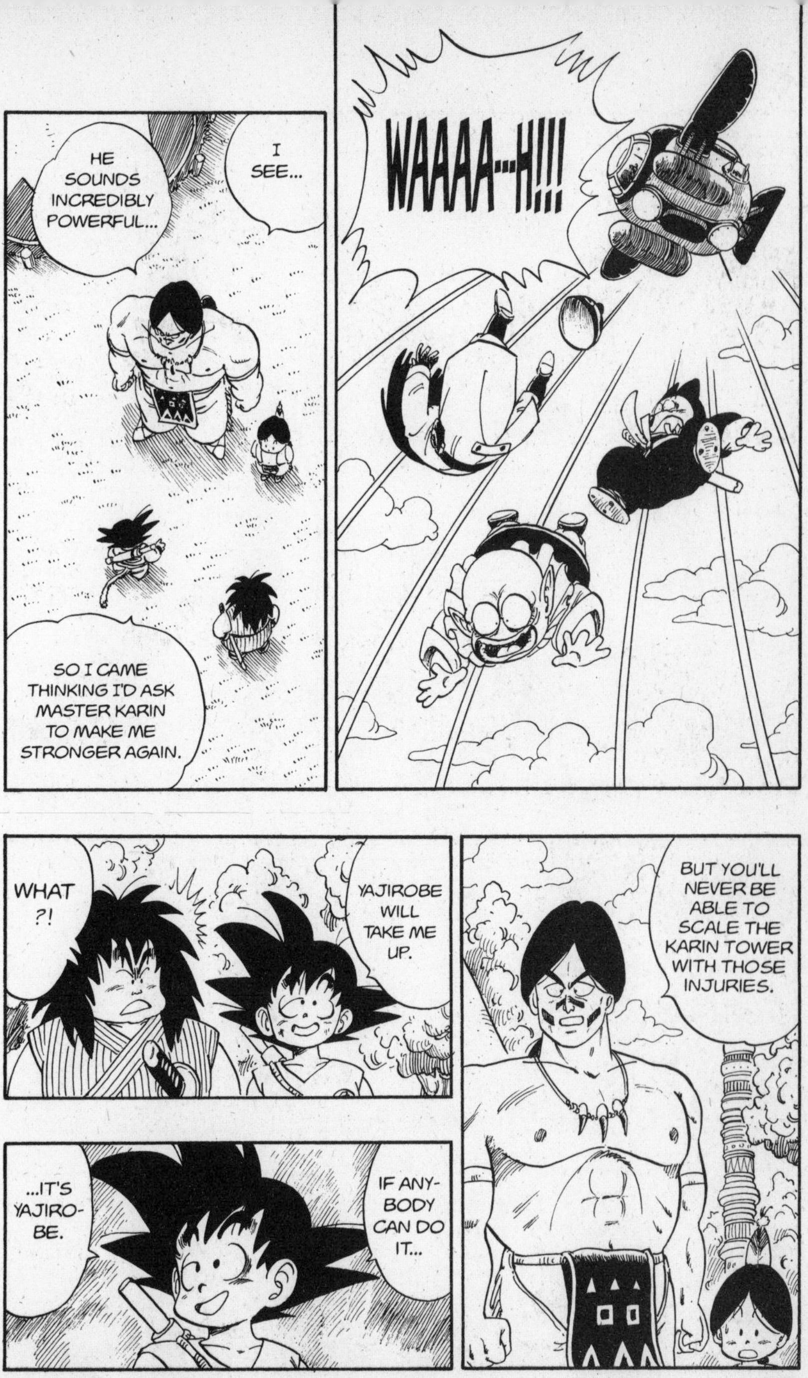
WAAAA-H!!!
I SEE...
HE SOUNDS INCREDIBLY POWERFUL...
SO I CAME THINKING I'D ASK MASTER KARIN TO MAKE ME STRONGER AGAIN.
BUT YOU'LL NEVER BE ABLE TO SCALE THE KARIN TOWER WITH THOSE INJURIES.
YAJIROBE WILL TAKE ME UP.
WHAT?!
IF ANY-BODY CAN DO IT...
...IT'S YAJIRO-BE.

READ THIS WAY

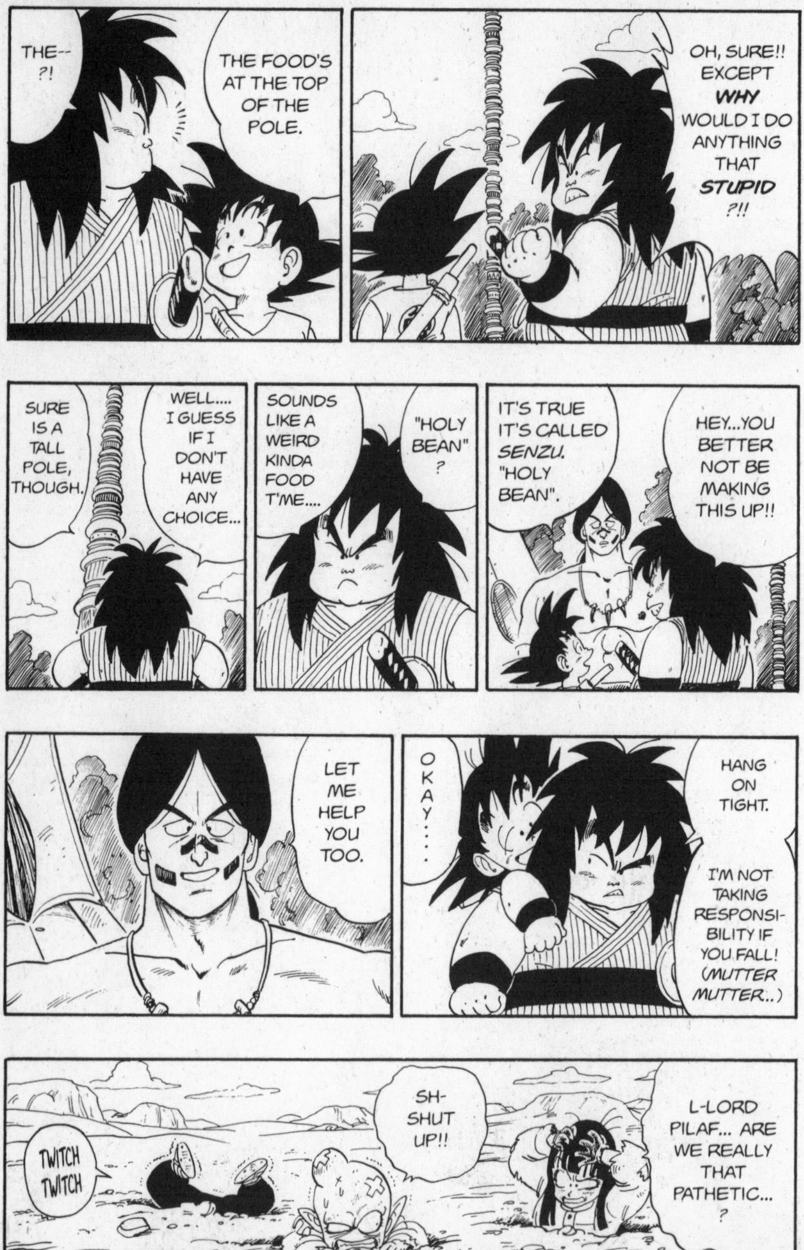

OH, SURE!! EXCEPT WHY WOULD I DO ANYTHING THAT STUPID ?!!
THE FOOD'S AT THE TOP OF THE POLE.
THE-- ?!
HEY...YOU BETTER NOT BE MAKING THIS UP!!
IT'S TRUE IT'S CALLED SENZU. "HOLY BEAN".
"HOLY BEAN" ?
SOUNDS LIKE A WEIRD KINDA FOOD T'ME....
WELL.... I GUESS IF I DON'T HAVE ANY CHOICE...
SURE IS A TALL POLE, THOUGH.
HANG ON TIGHT.
I'M NOT TAKING RESPONSI-BILITY IF YOU FALL! (MUTTER MUTTER...)
OKAY....
LET ME HELP YOU TOO.
L-LORD PILAF... ARE WE REALLY THAT PATHETIC... ?
SH-SHUT UP!!
TWITCH TWITCH

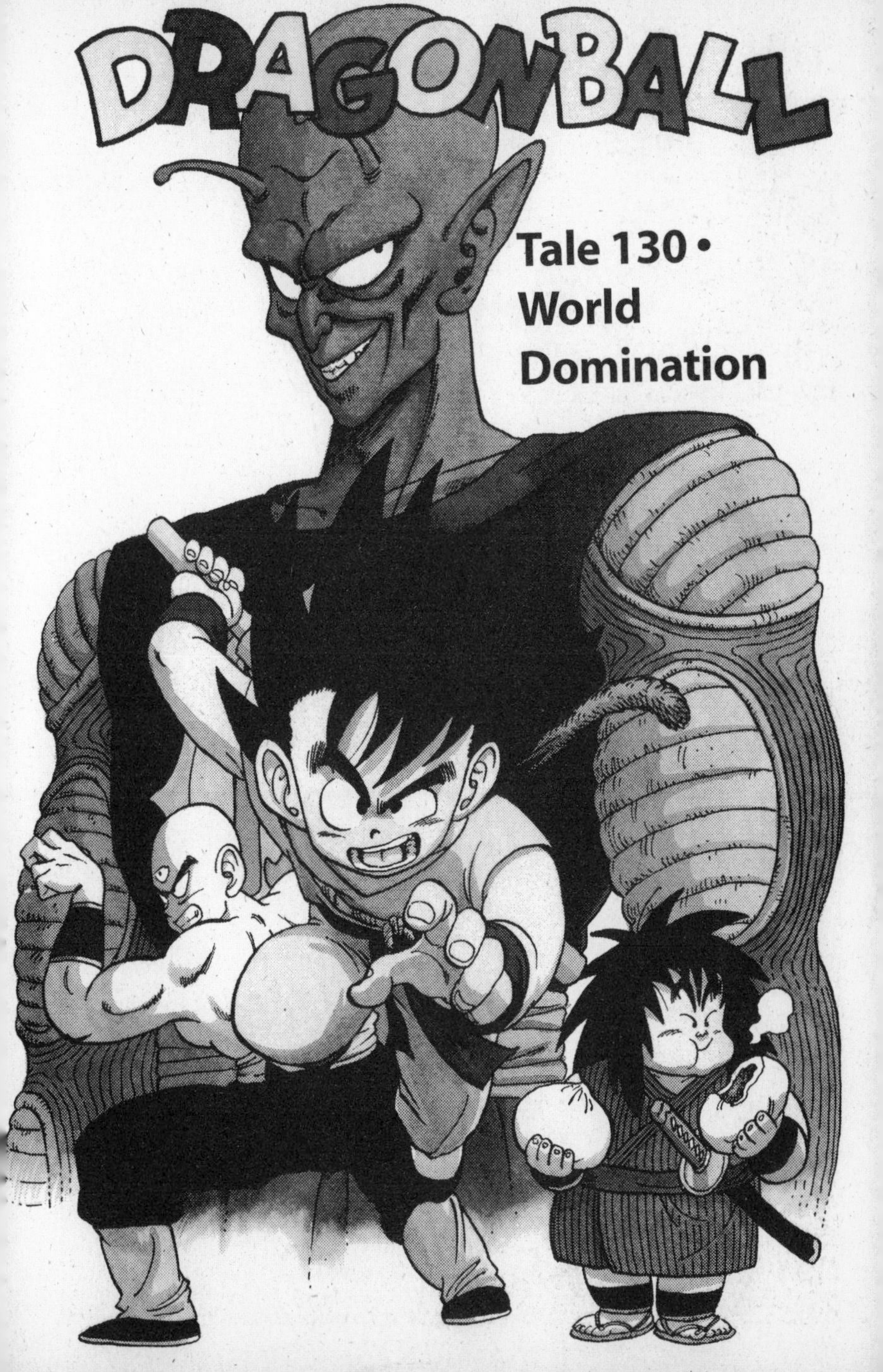

DRAGONBALL

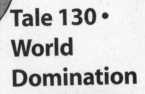

**Tale 130 •
World
Domination**

READ THIS WAY

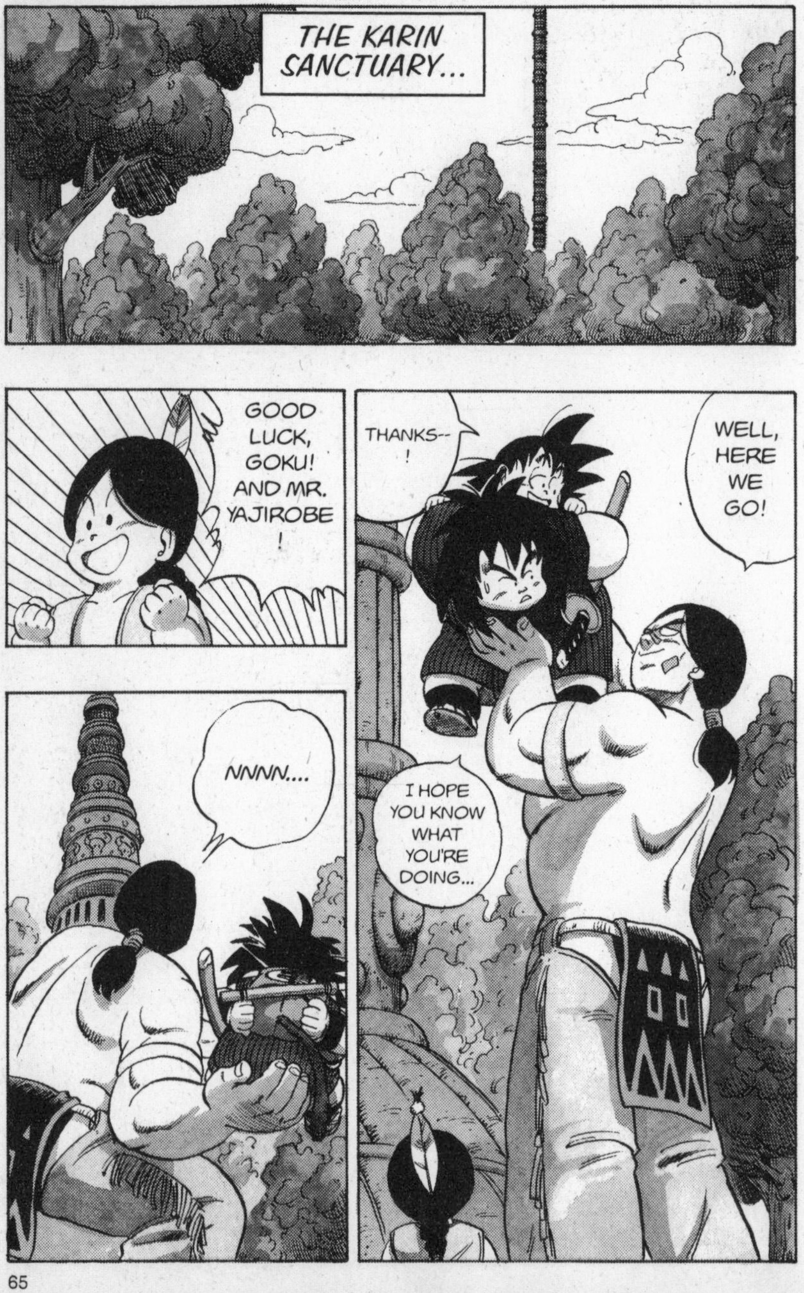
THE KARIN SANCTUARY...
WELL, HERE WE GO!
THANKS--!
I HOPE YOU KNOW WHAT YOU'RE DOING...
GOOD LUCK, GOKU! AND MR. YAJIROBE!
NNNN....

READ THIS WAY

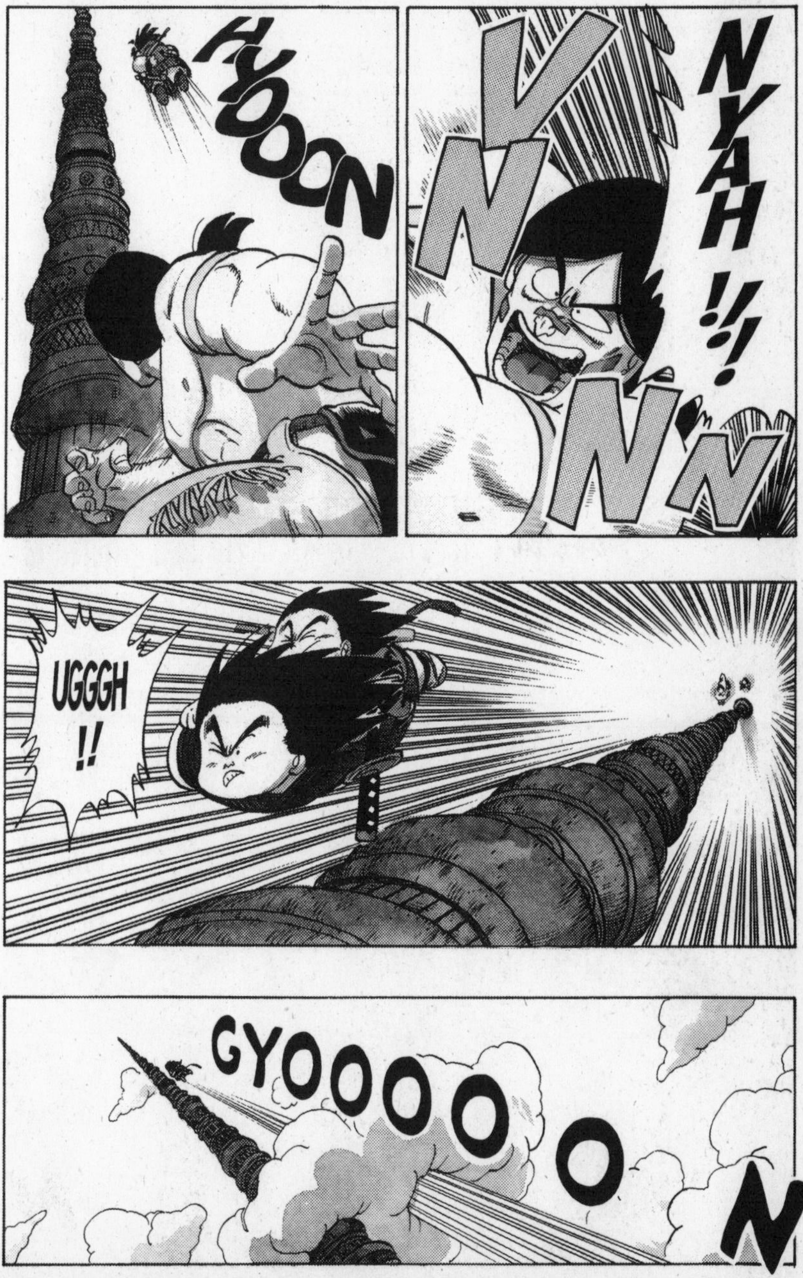
NYAH!!!
VNNNN
HYOOON
UGGGH!!
GYOOOOON

READ THIS WAY

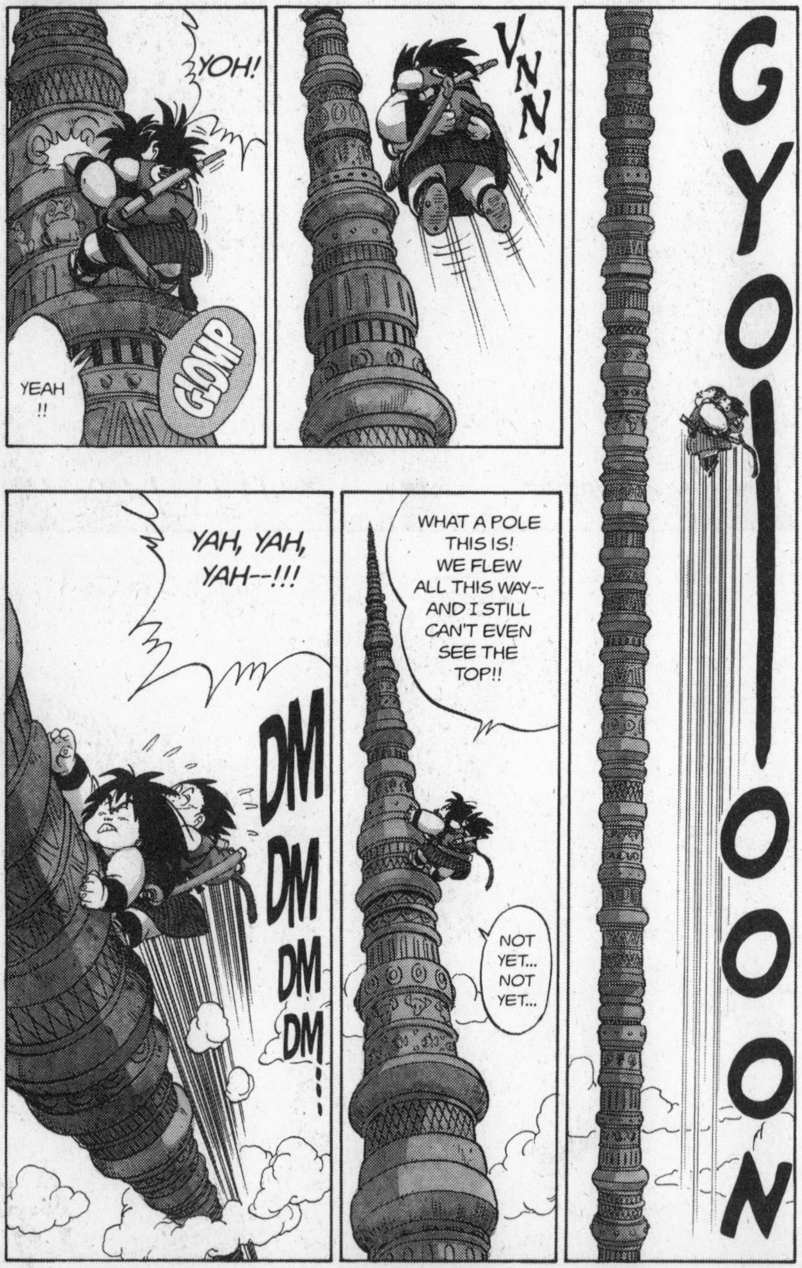
GYO—OOON
VNNN
YOH!
GLOMP
YEAH !!
WHAT A POLE THIS IS! WE FLEW ALL THIS WAY-- AND I STILL CAN'T EVEN SEE THE TOP!!
NOT YET... NOT YET...
YAH, YAH, YAH--!!!
DM DM DM DM...

READ THIS WAY

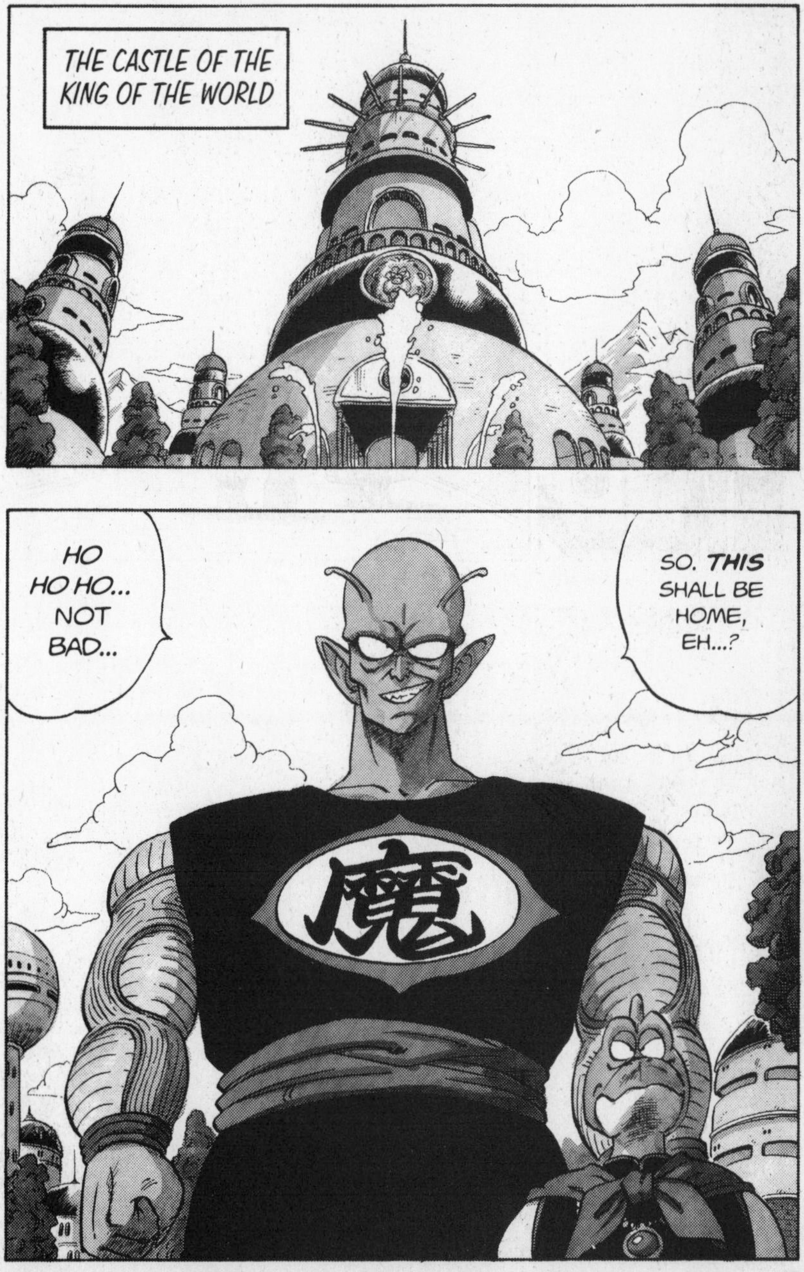
THE CASTLE OF THE KING OF THE WORLD
SO. THIS SHALL BE HOME, EH...?
HO HO HO... NOT BAD...
魔

READ THIS WAY

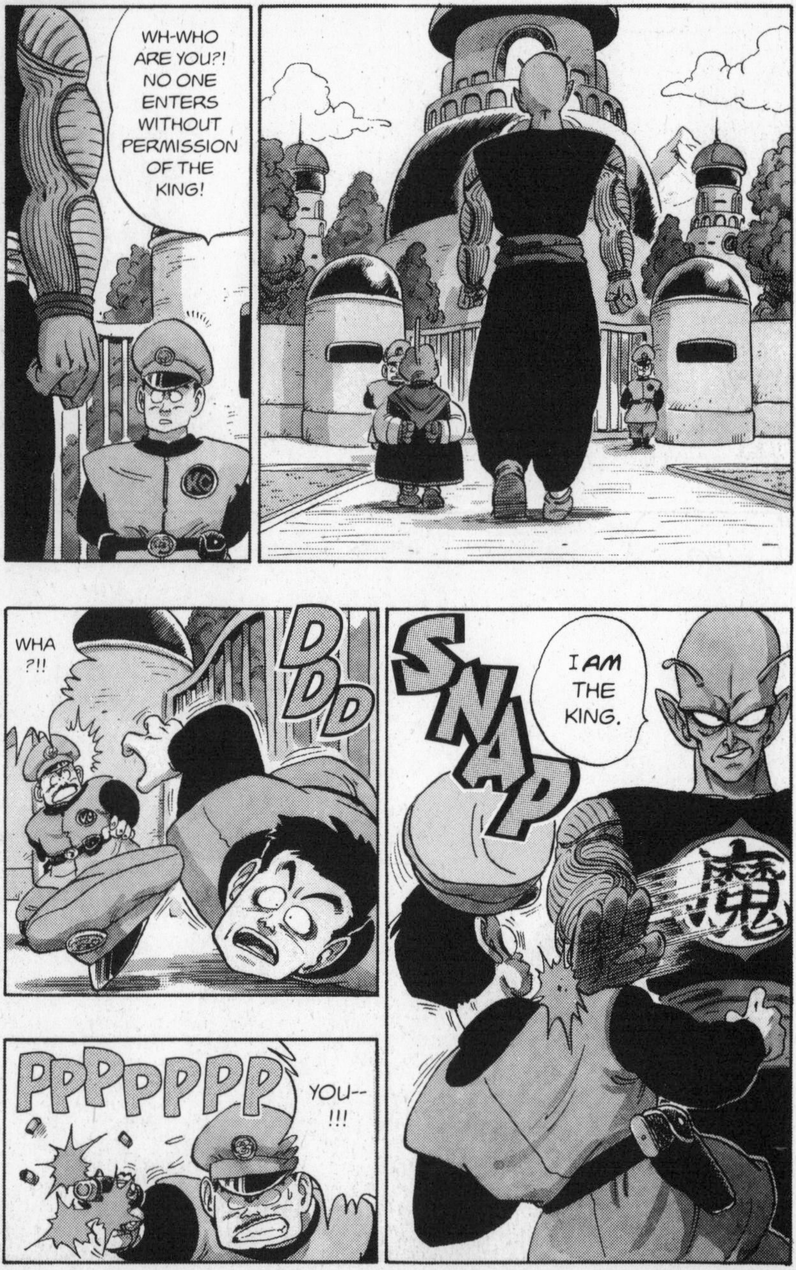
WH-WHO ARE YOU?! NO ONE ENTERS WITHOUT PERMISSION OF THE KING!
SNAP
I AM THE KING.
DDD
WHA ?!!
PPPPPPP
YOU-- !!!

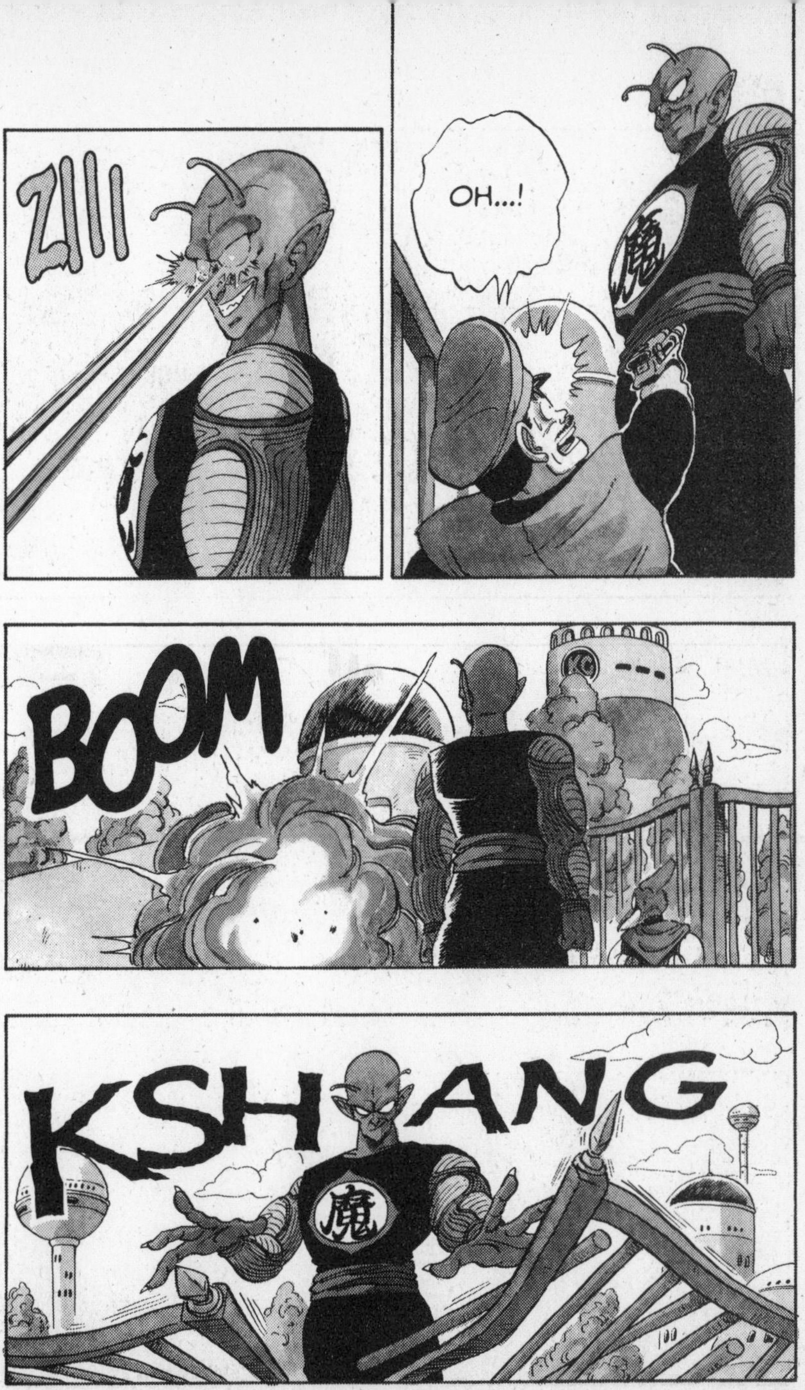
ZIII
OH...!
BOOM
KSHANG

READ THIS WAY

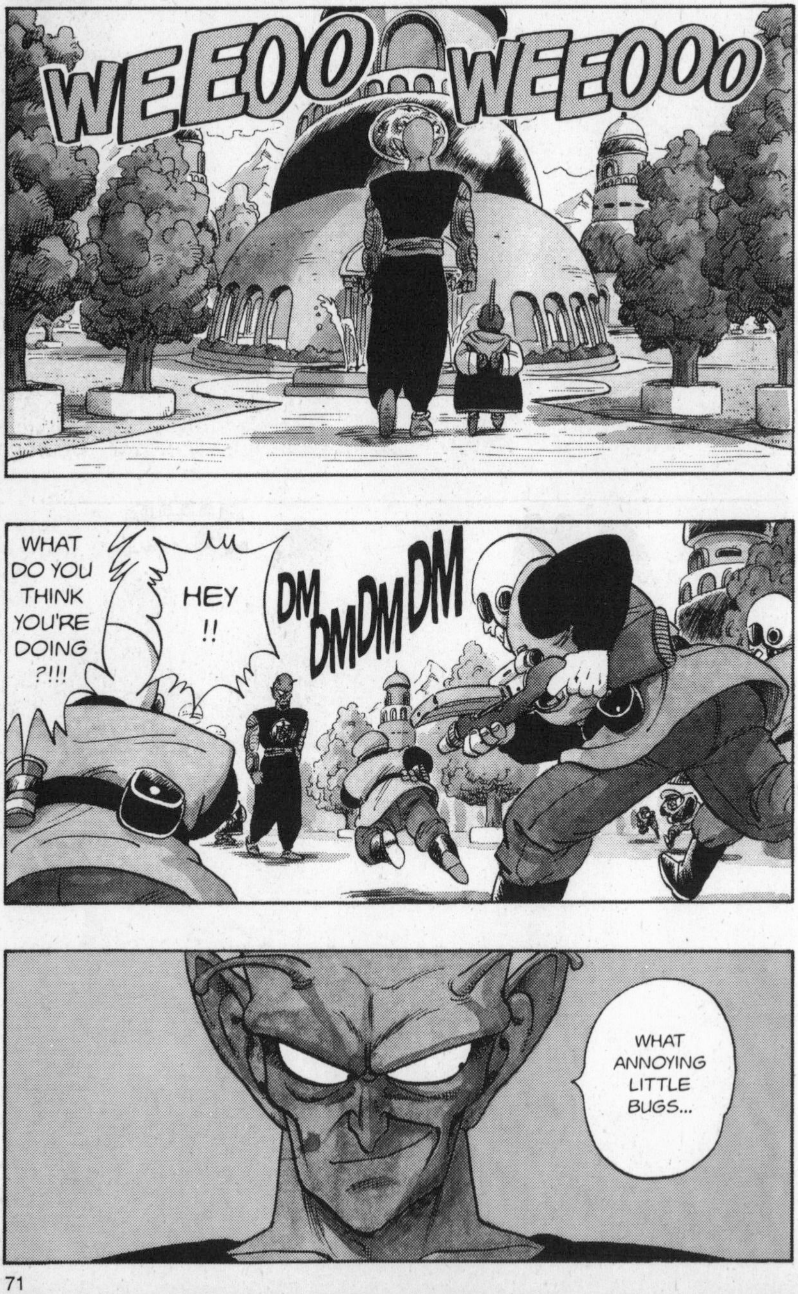
WEEOO WEEOOO
DM DMDMDM DM
HEY !!
WHAT DO YOU THINK YOU'RE DOING ?!!!
WHAT ANNOYING LITTLE BUGS...

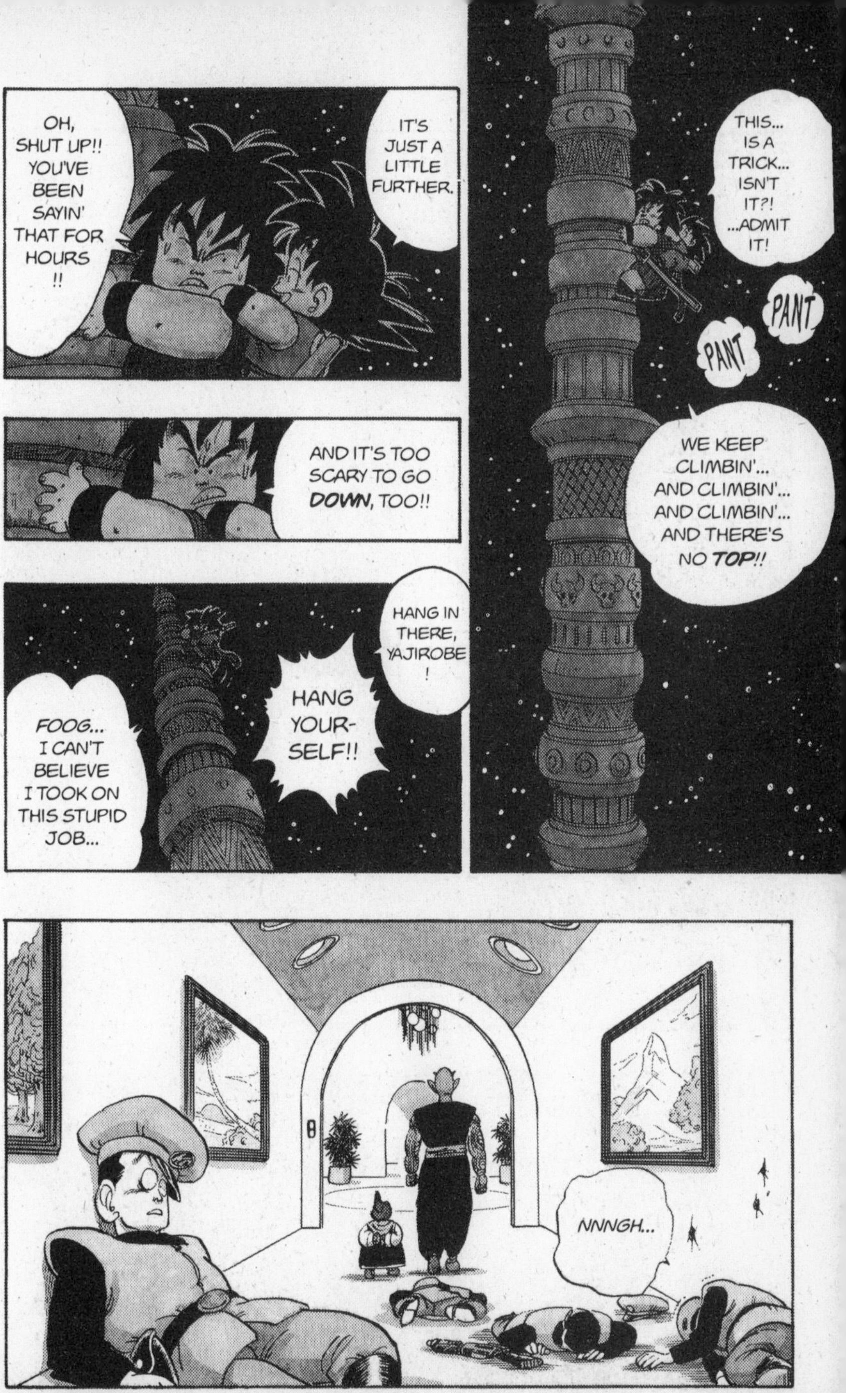
THIS... IS A TRICK... ISN'T IT?! ...ADMIT IT!
PANT
PANT
WE KEEP CLIMBIN'... AND CLIMBIN'... AND CLIMBIN'... AND THERE'S NO **TOP**!!
IT'S JUST A LITTLE FURTHER.
OH, SHUT UP!! YOU'VE BEEN SAYIN' THAT FOR HOURS !!
AND IT'S TOO SCARY TO GO **DOWN**, TOO!!
HANG IN THERE, YAJIROBE !
HANG YOUR-SELF!!
FOOG... I CAN'T BELIEVE I TOOK ON THIS STUPID JOB...
NNNGH...

READ THIS WAY

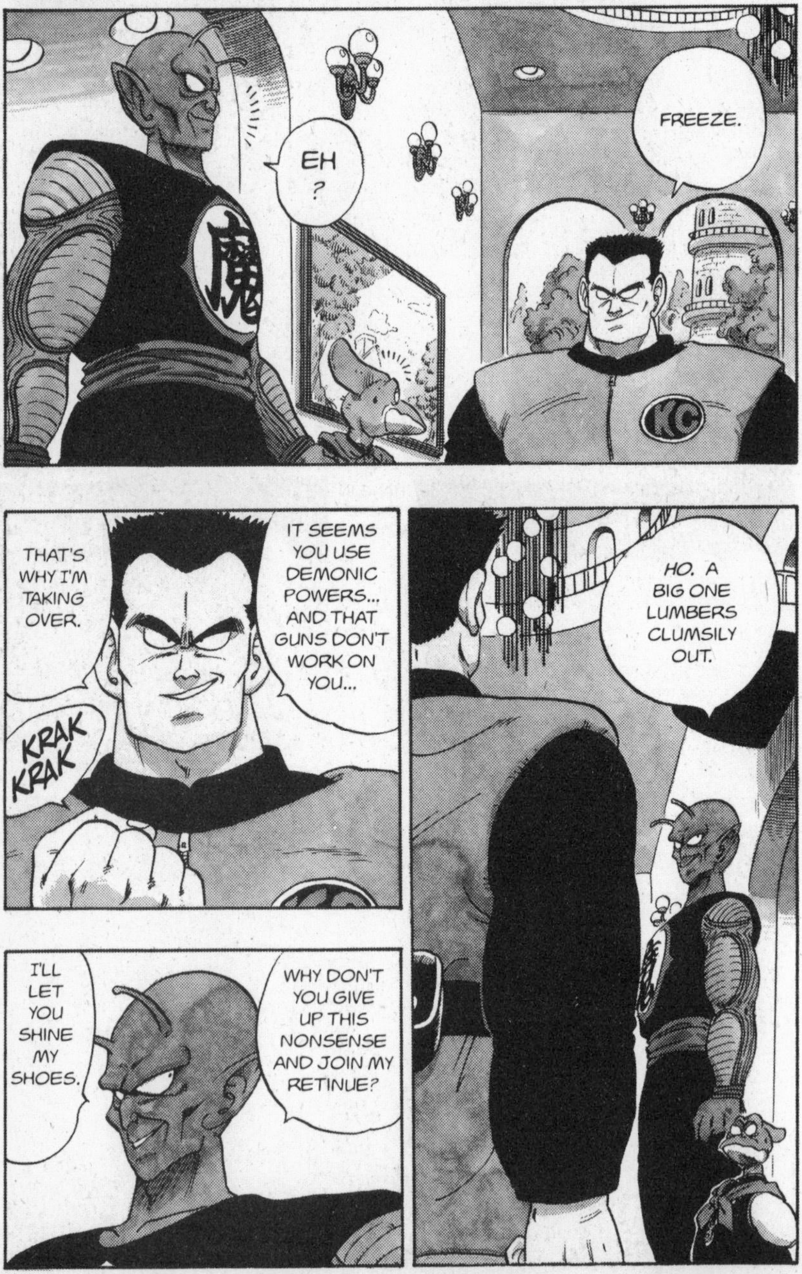
FREEZE.
EH ?
HO. A BIG ONE LUMBERS CLUMSILY OUT.
IT SEEMS YOU USE DEMONIC POWERS... AND THAT GUNS DON'T WORK ON YOU...
THAT'S WHY I'M TAKING OVER.
KRAK KRAK
WHY DON'T YOU GIVE UP THIS NONSENSE AND JOIN MY RETINUE?
I'LL LET YOU SHINE MY SHOES.

READ THIS WAY

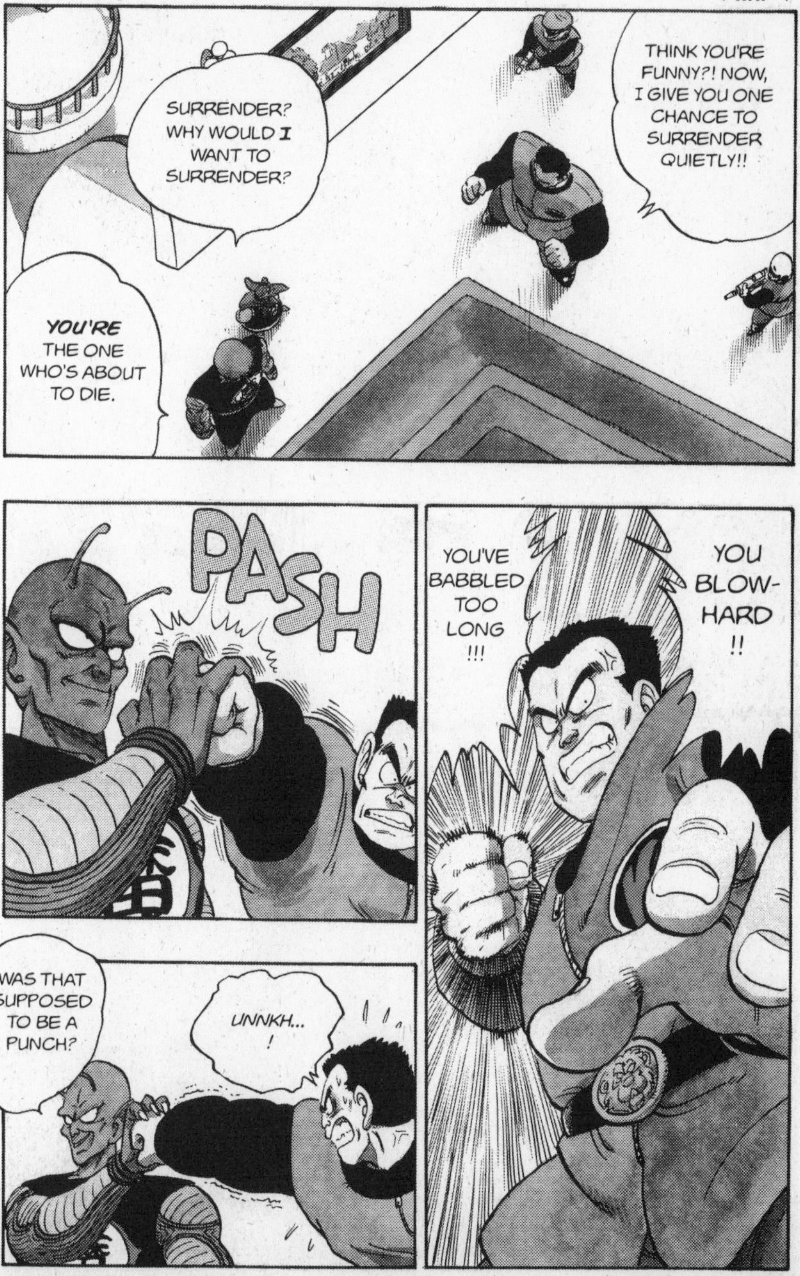
THINK YOU'RE FUNNY?! NOW, I GIVE YOU ONE CHANCE TO SURRENDER QUIETLY!!
SURRENDER? WHY WOULD *I* WANT TO SURRENDER?
YOU'RE THE ONE WHO'S ABOUT TO DIE.
YOU BLOW-HARD !!
YOU'VE BABBLED TOO LONG !!!
PASH
UNNKH... !
WAS THAT SUPPOSED TO BE A PUNCH?

READ THIS WAY

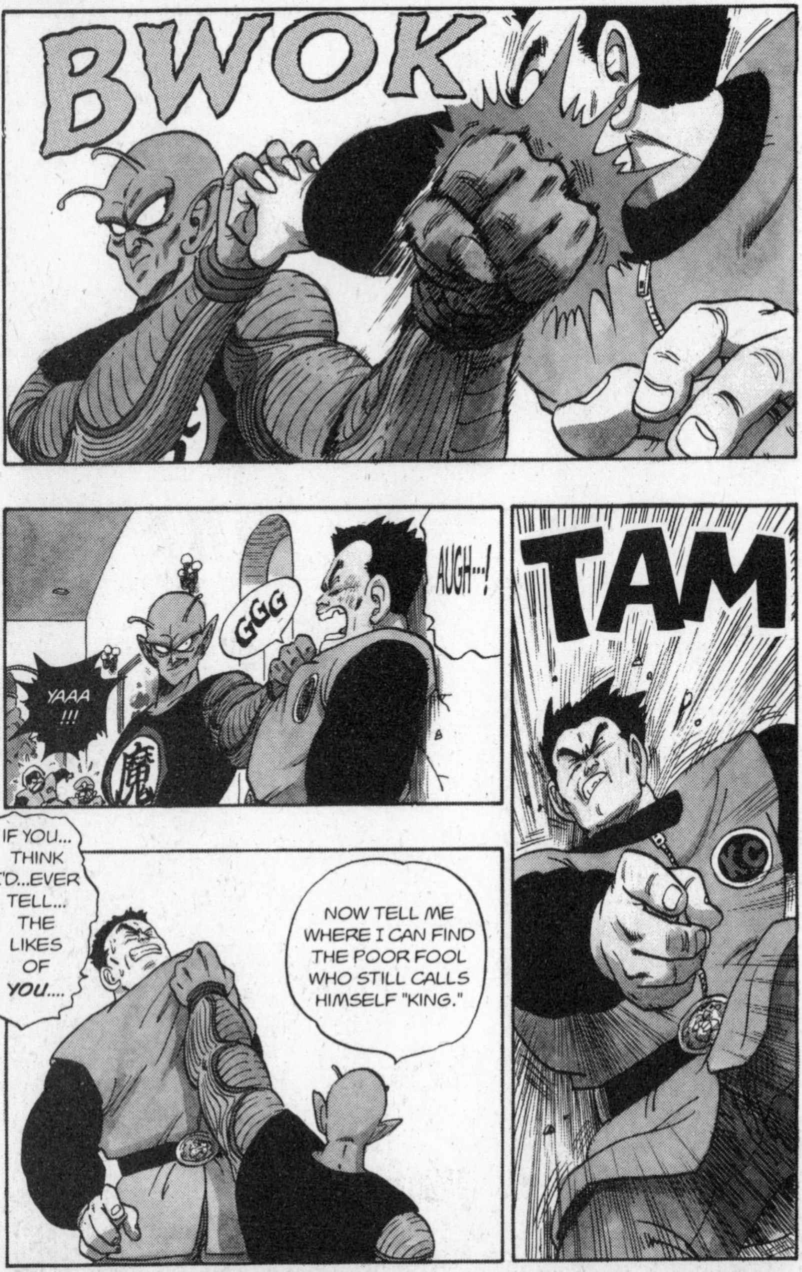
BWOK
TAM
AUGH...!
GGG
YAAA !!!
NOW TELL ME WHERE I CAN FIND THE POOR FOOL WHO STILL CALLS HIMSELF "KING."
IF YOU... THINK I'D...EVER TELL... THE LIKES OF *YOU*....

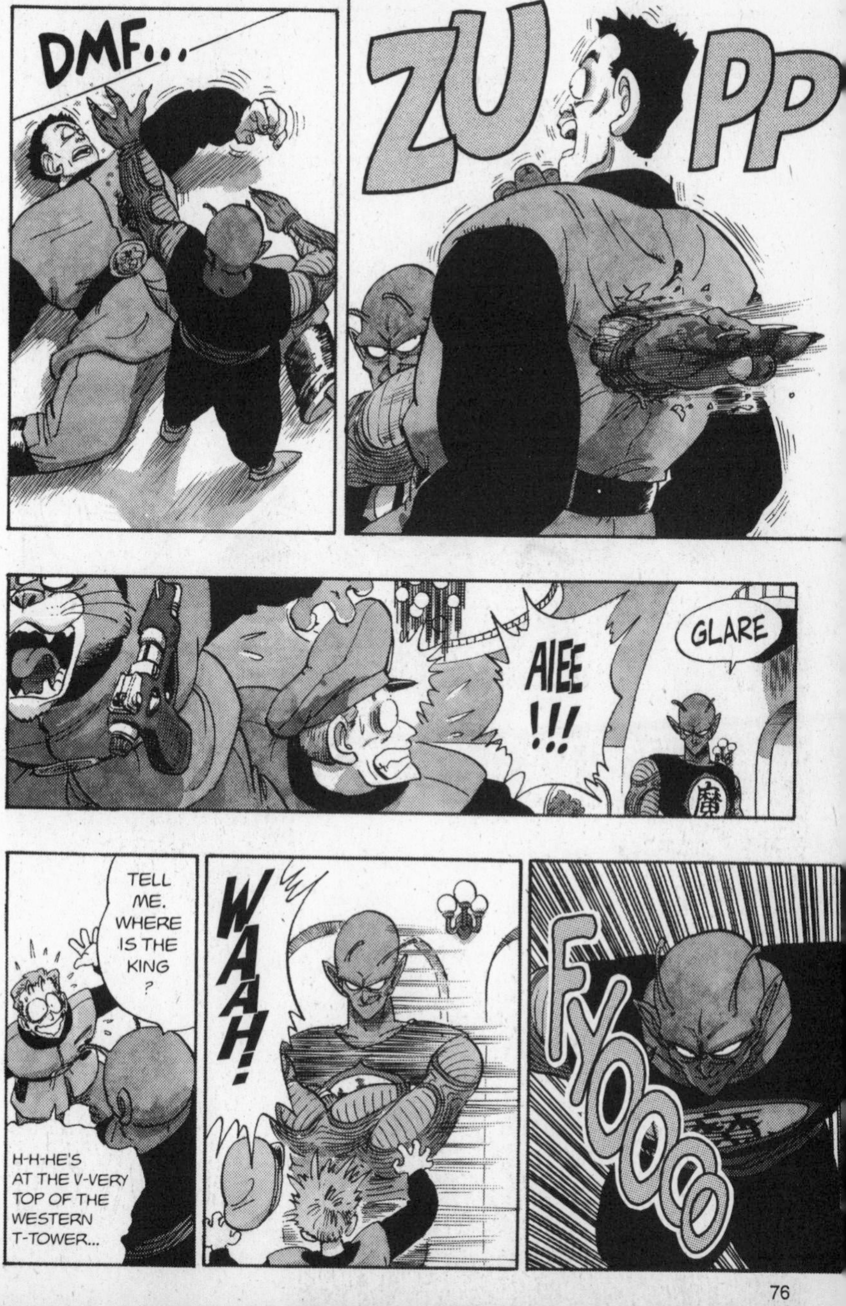
ZUPP
DMF...
GLARE
AIEE!!!
FYOOOO
WAAH!
TELL ME. WHERE IS THE KING?
H-H-HE'S AT THE V-VERY TOP OF THE WESTERN T-TOWER...

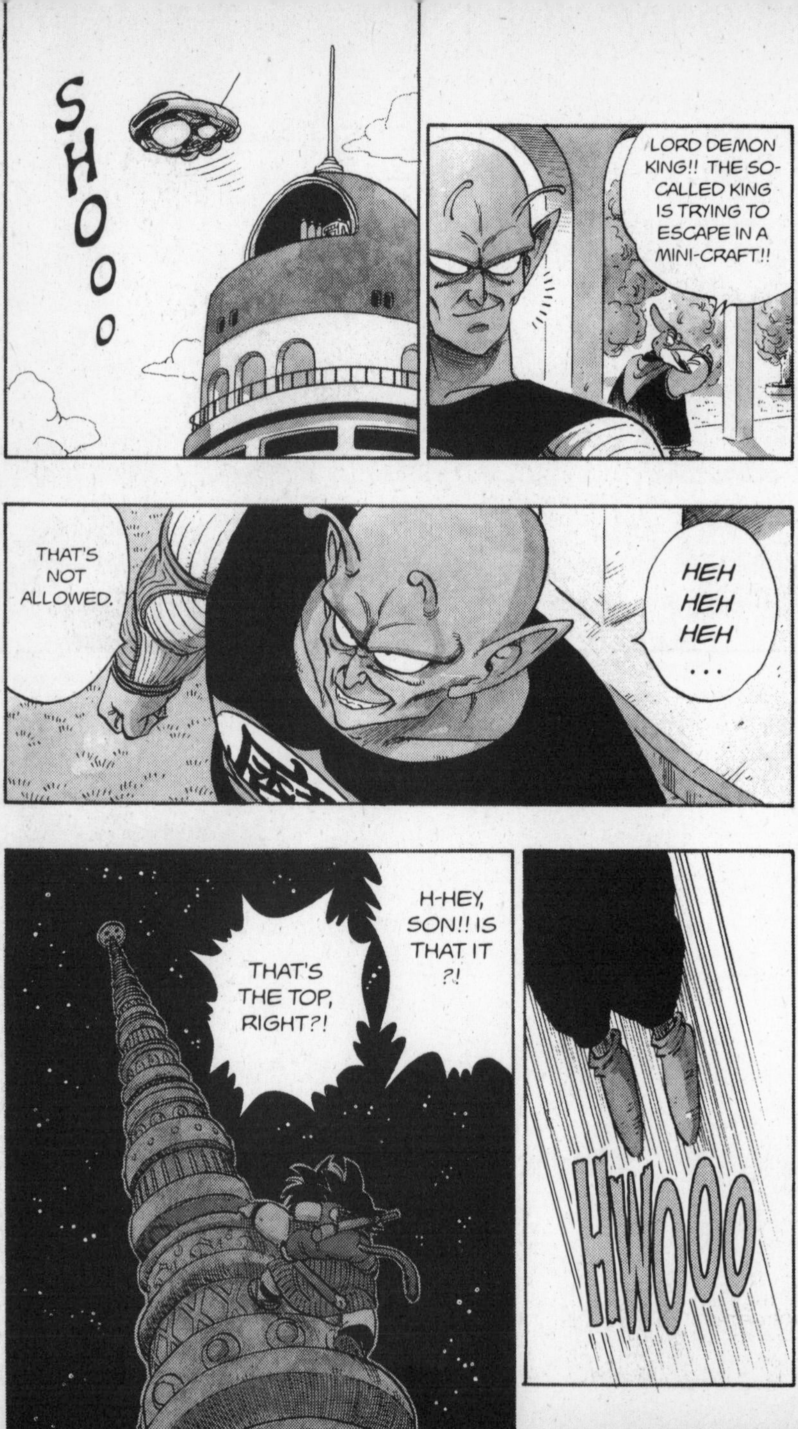
LORD DEMON KING!! THE SO-CALLED KING IS TRYING TO ESCAPE IN A MINI-CRAFT!!
SHOOOO
HEH HEH HEH ...
THAT'S NOT ALLOWED.
HWOOO
H-HEY, SON!! IS THAT IT ?!
THAT'S THE TOP, RIGHT?!

READ THIS WAY

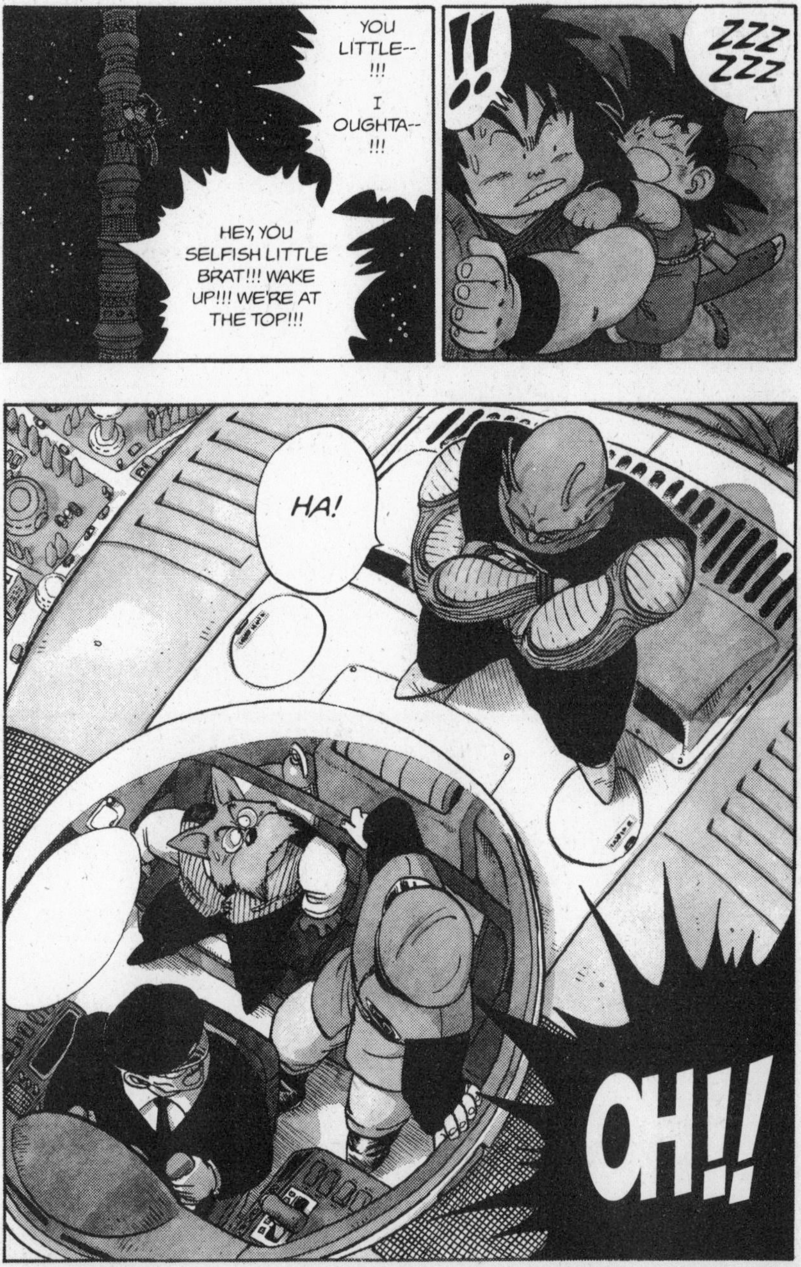
ZZZ ZZZ
!!
YOU LITTLE-- !!! I OUGHTA-- !!!
HEY, YOU SELFISH LITTLE BRAT!!! WAKE UP!!! WE'RE AT THE TOP!!!
HA!
OH!!

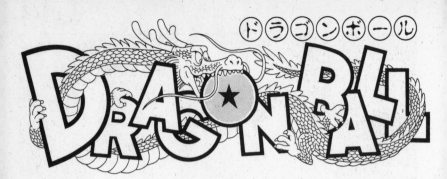

Tale 150 •
Karin's Quandary

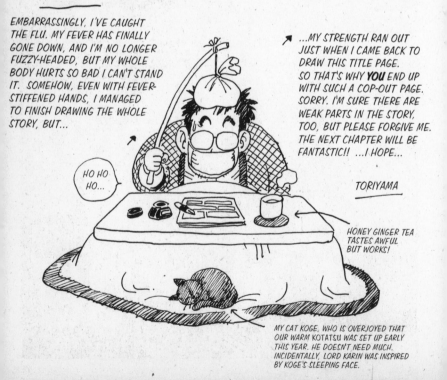

APOLOGIES

EMBARRASSINGLY, I'VE CAUGHT THE FLU. MY FEVER HAS FINALLY GONE DOWN, AND I'M NO LONGER FUZZY-HEADED, BUT MY WHOLE BODY HURTS SO BAD I CAN'T STAND IT. SOMEHOW, EVEN WITH FEVER-STIFFENED HANDS, I MANAGED TO FINISH DRAWING THE WHOLE STORY, BUT...

HO HO HO...

...MY STRENGTH RAN OUT JUST WHEN I CAME BACK TO DRAW THIS TITLE PAGE. SO THAT'S WHY **YOU** END UP WITH SUCH A COP-OUT PAGE. SORRY. I'M SURE THERE ARE WEAK PARTS IN THE STORY, TOO, BUT PLEASE FORGIVE ME. THE NEXT CHAPTER WILL BE FANTASTIC!! ...I HOPE...

TORIYAMA

HONEY GINGER TEA TASTES AWFUL BUT WORKS!

MY CAT KOGE, WHO IS OVERJOYED THAT OUR WARM KOTATSU WAS SET UP EARLY THIS YEAR. HE DOESN'T NEED MUCH. INCIDENTALLY, LORD KARIN WAS INSPIRED BY KOGE'S SLEEPING FACE.

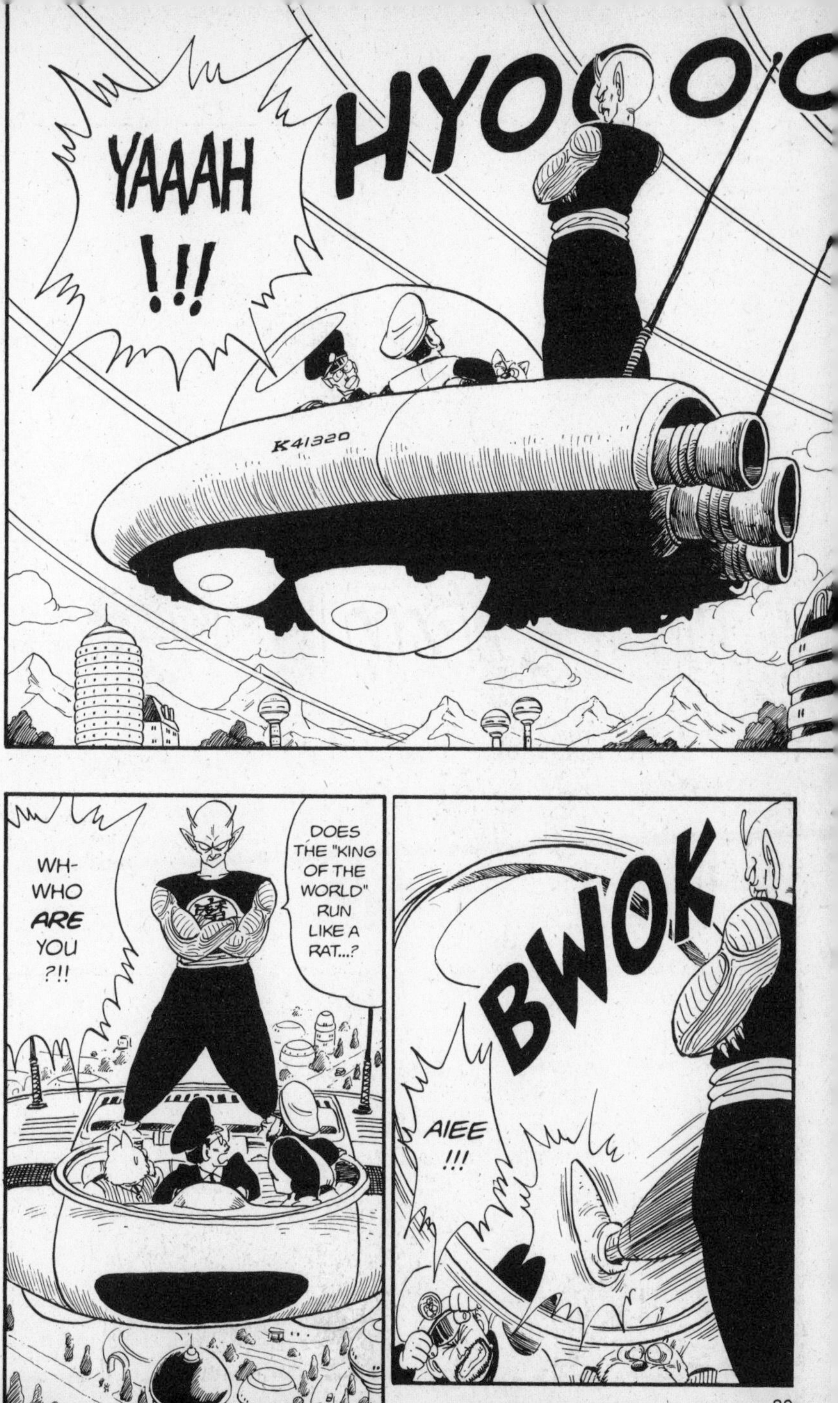
YAAAH !!!
HYOOOO
BWOK
AIEE !!!
DOES THE "KING OF THE WORLD" RUN LIKE A RAT...?
WH- WHO ARE YOU ?!!

READ THIS WAY

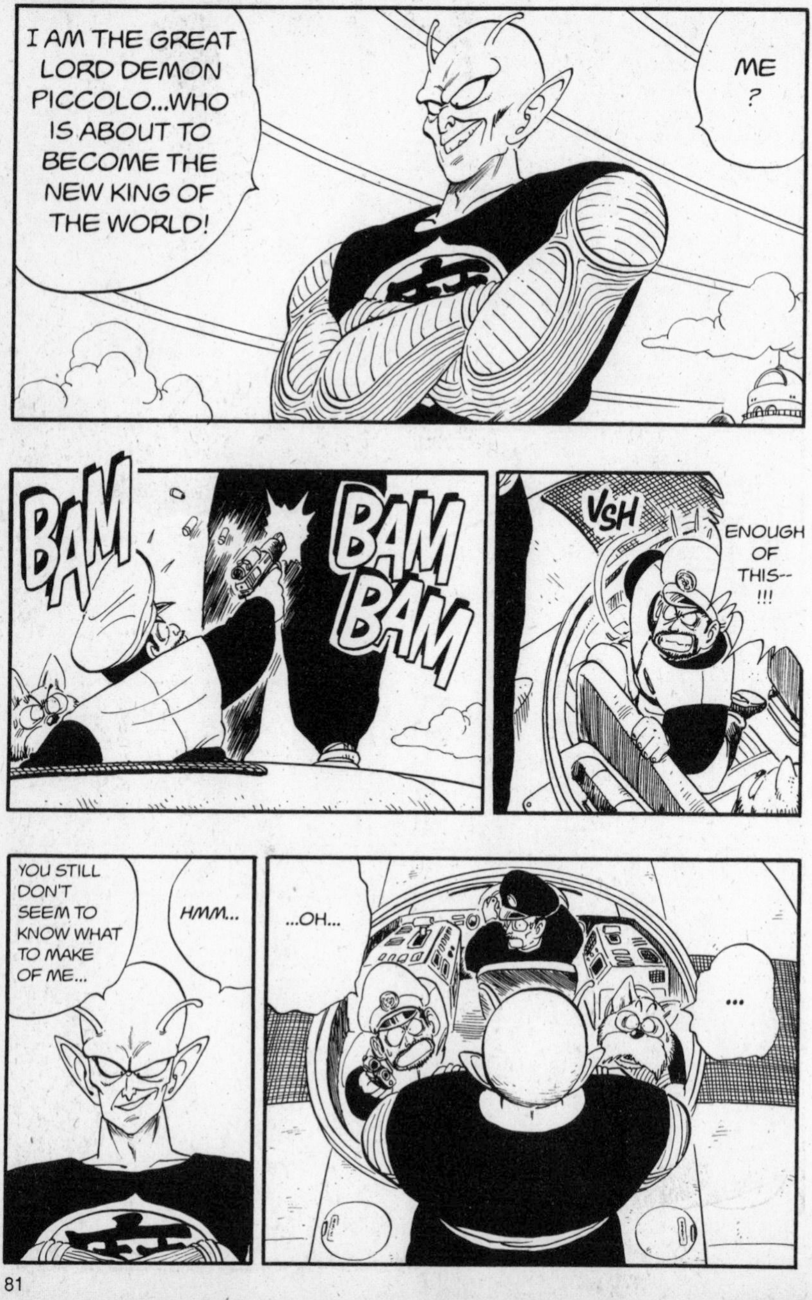
ME ?
I AM THE GREAT LORD DEMON PICCOLO...WHO IS ABOUT TO BECOME THE NEW KING OF THE WORLD!
VSH
ENOUGH OF THIS-- !!!
BAM BAM
BAM
BAM
...
...OH...
HMM...
YOU STILL DON'T SEEM TO KNOW WHAT TO MAKE OF ME...

READ THIS WAY

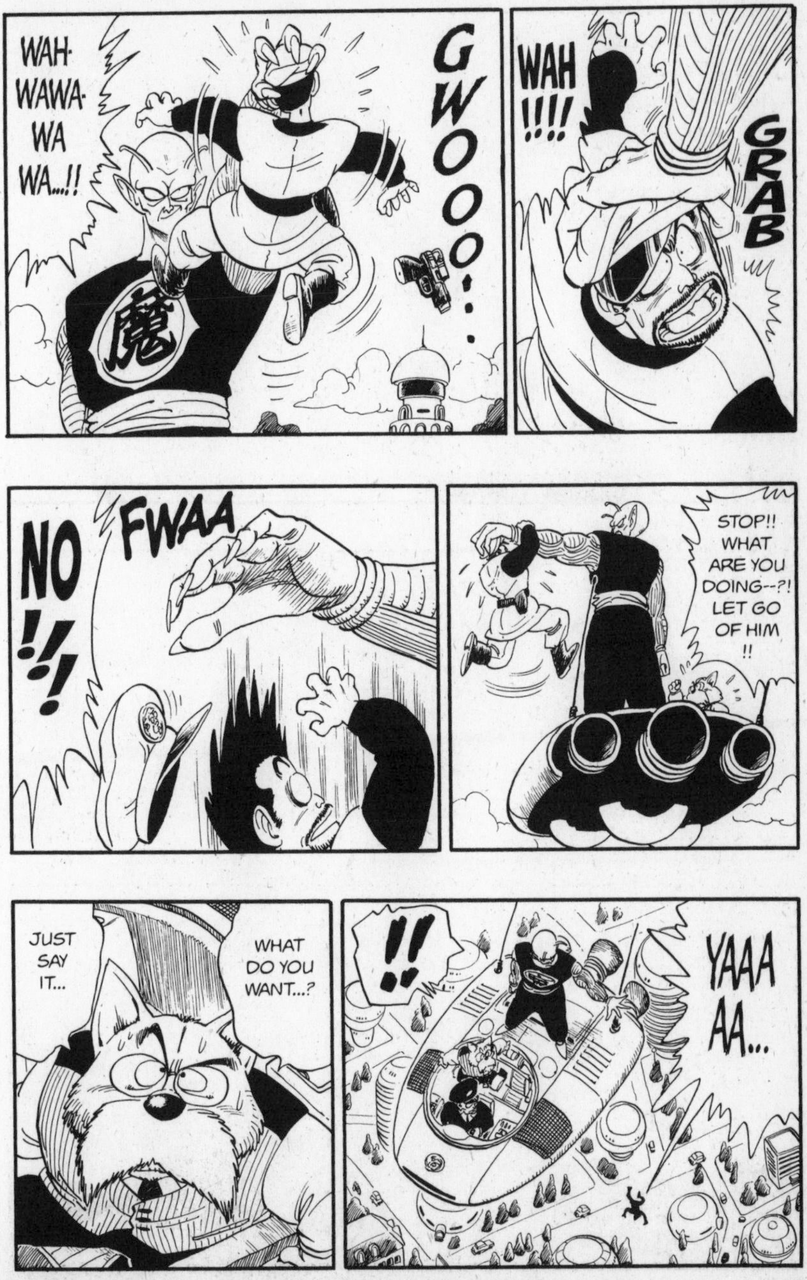

WAH !!!!
GRAB
GWOOOO...
WAH-WAWA-WA WA...!!
STOP!! WHAT ARE YOU DOING--?! LET GO OF HIM !!
FWAA
NO!!!
YAAAAA...
!!
WHAT DO YOU WANT...?
JUST SAY IT...

READ THIS WAY

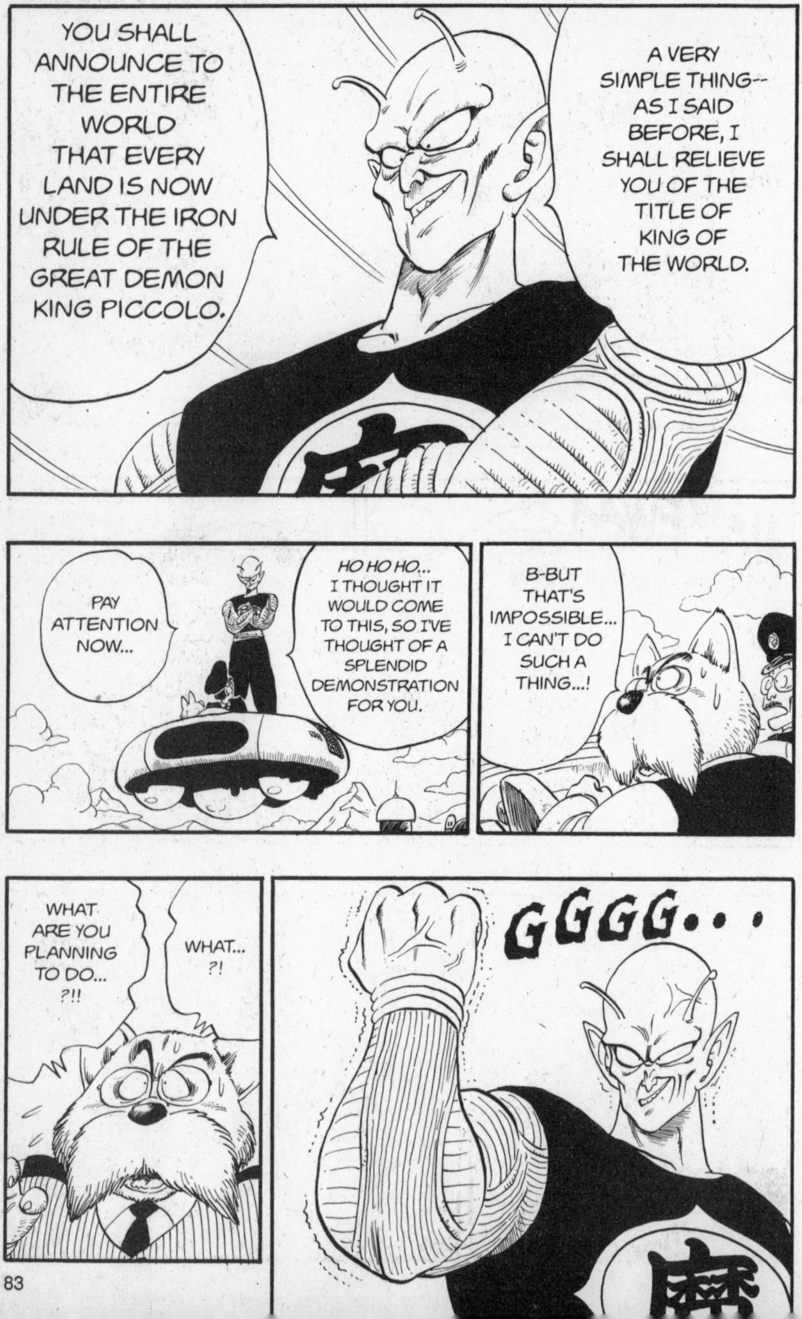
A VERY SIMPLE THING-- AS I SAID BEFORE, I SHALL RELIEVE YOU OF THE TITLE OF KING OF THE WORLD.
YOU SHALL ANNOUNCE TO THE ENTIRE WORLD THAT EVERY LAND IS NOW UNDER THE IRON RULE OF THE GREAT DEMON KING PICCOLO.
B-BUT THAT'S IMPOSSIBLE... I CAN'T DO SUCH A THING...!
HO HO HO... I THOUGHT IT WOULD COME TO THIS, SO I'VE THOUGHT OF A SPLENDID DEMONSTRATION FOR YOU.
PAY ATTENTION NOW...
GGGG...
WHAT... ?!
WHAT ARE YOU PLANNING TO DO... ?!!

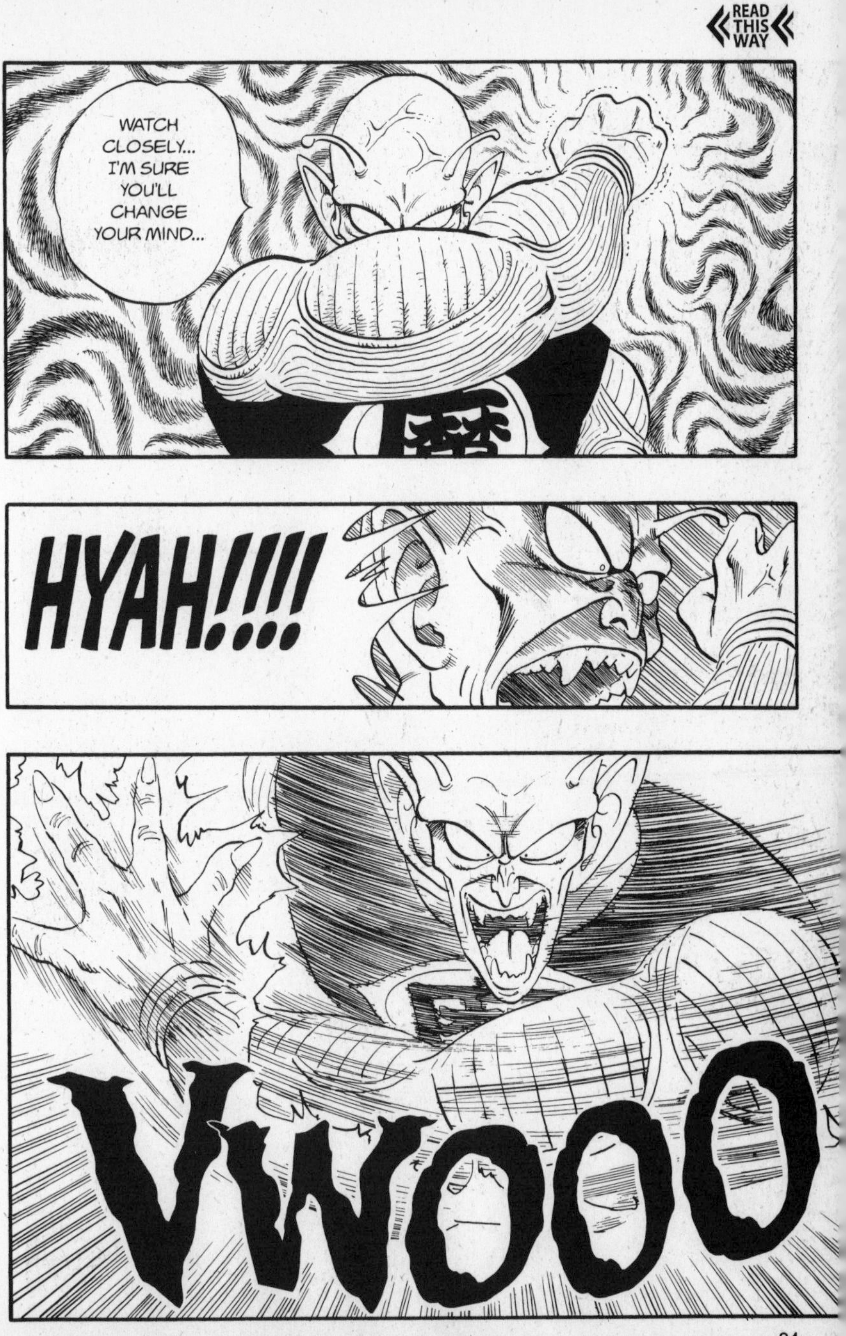
READ THIS WAY
WATCH CLOSELY... I'M SURE YOU'LL CHANGE YOUR MIND...
HYAH!!!!
VWOOO

READ THIS WAY

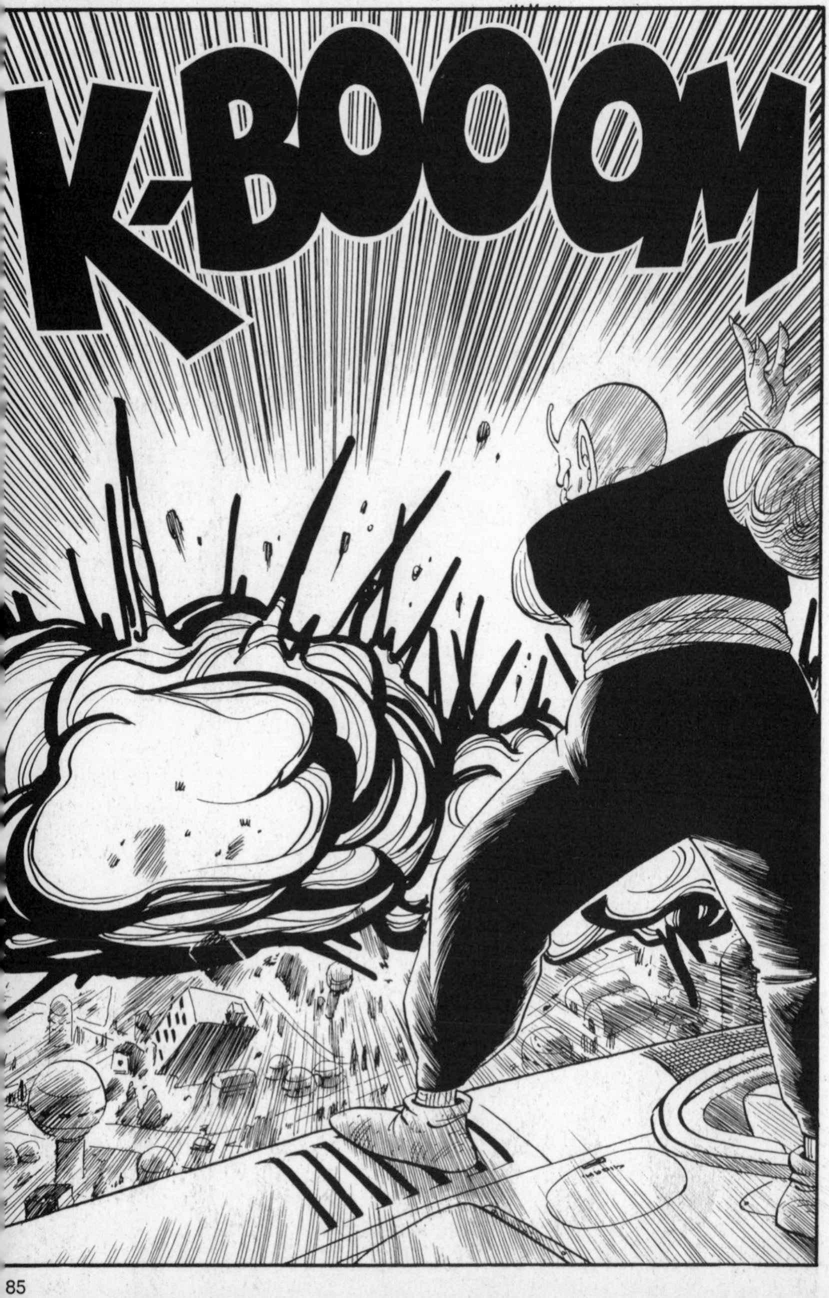
K-BOOOM

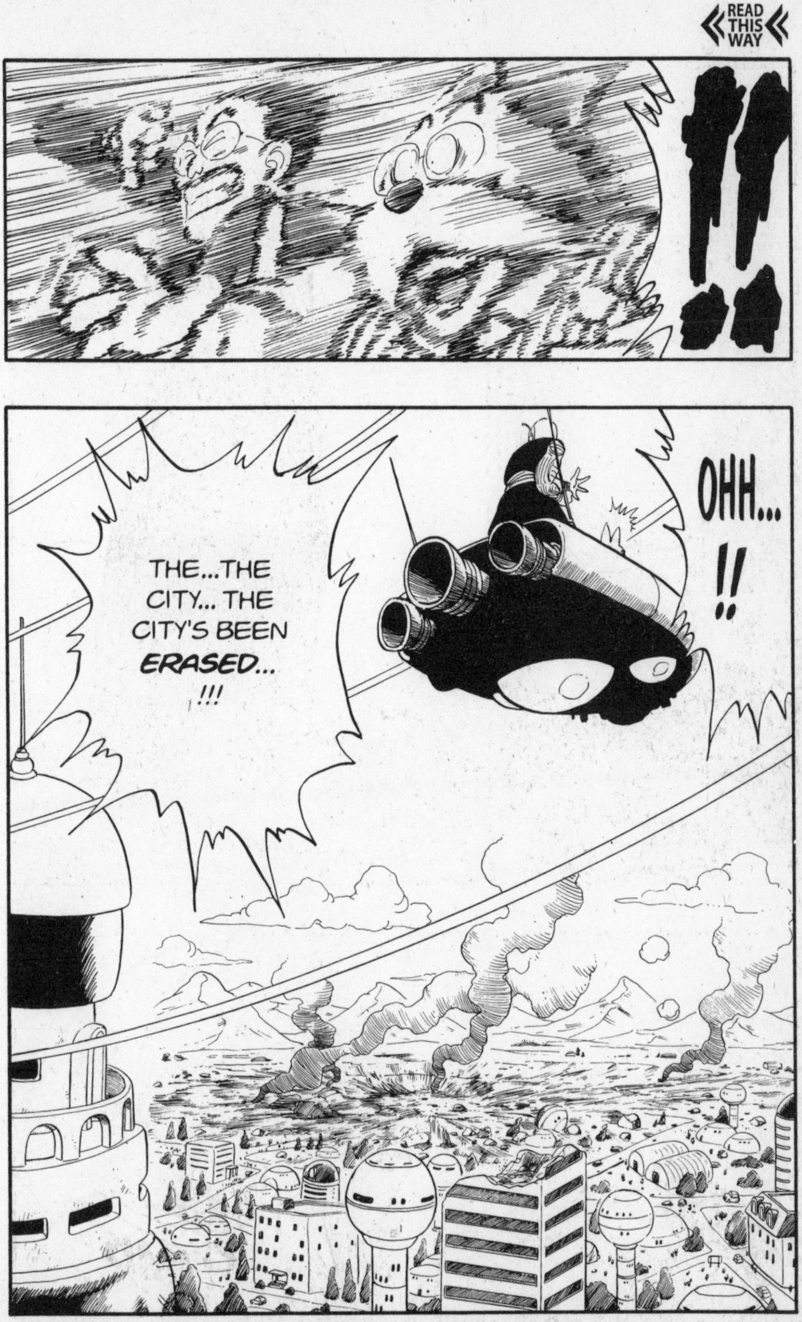
READ THIS WAY
!!
OHH... !!
THE...THE CITY... THE CITY'S BEEN ERASED... !!!

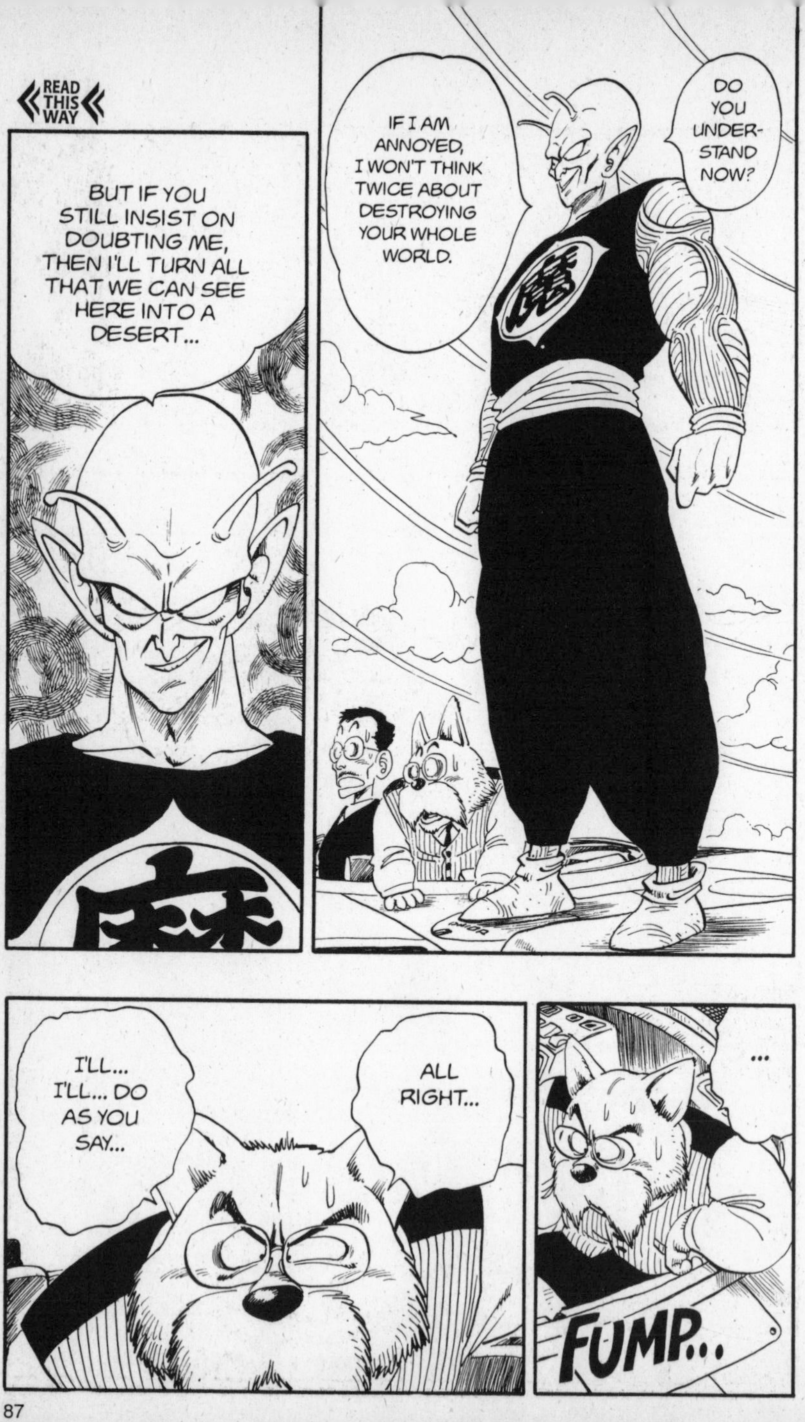
READ THIS WAY
DO YOU UNDER-STAND NOW?
IF I AM ANNOYED, I WON'T THINK TWICE ABOUT DESTROYING YOUR WHOLE WORLD.
BUT IF YOU STILL INSIST ON DOUBTING ME, THEN I'LL TURN ALL THAT WE CAN SEE HERE INTO A DESERT...
...
FUMP...
ALL RIGHT...
I'LL... I'LL... DO AS YOU SAY...

READ THIS WAY

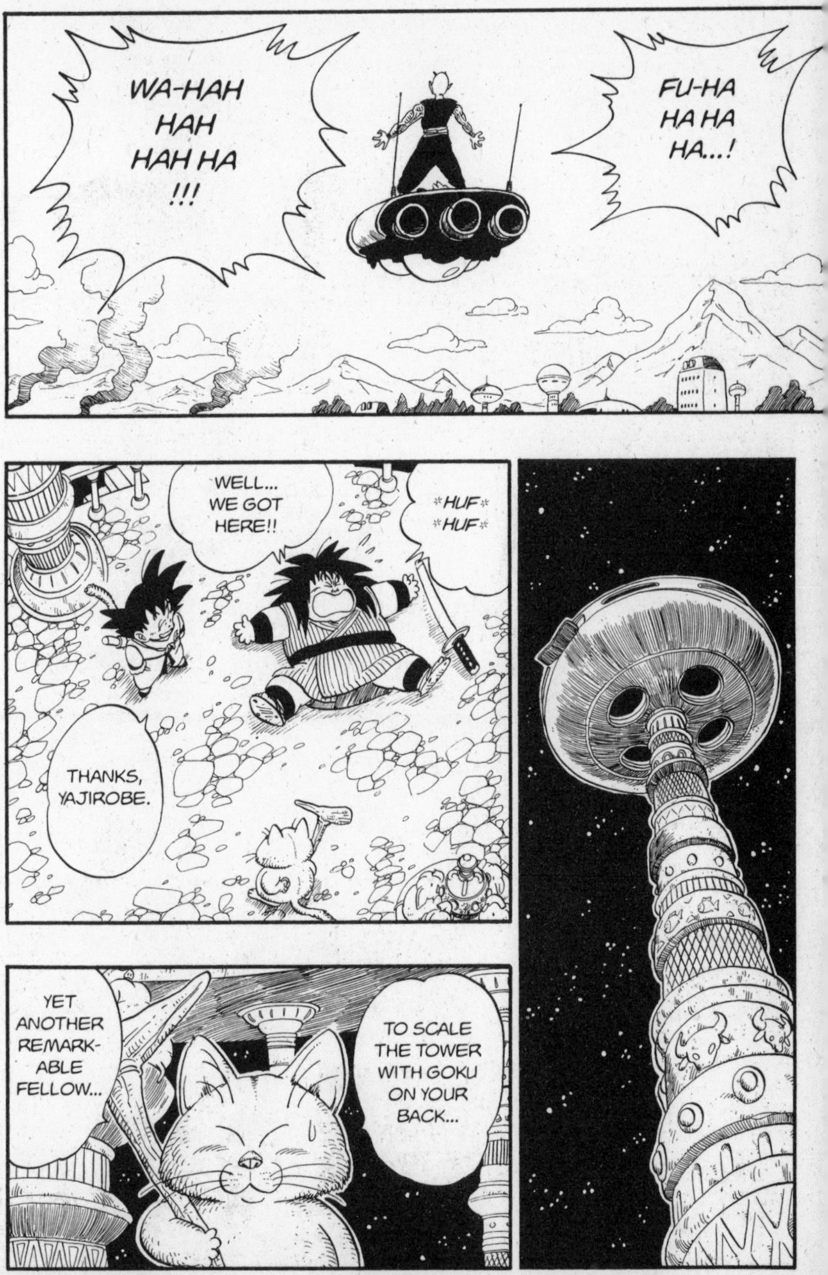

FU-HA HA HA HA...!
WA-HAH HAH HAH HA !!!
HUF *HUF*
WELL... WE GOT HERE!!
THANKS, YAJIROBE.
TO SCALE THE TOWER WITH GOKU ON YOUR BACK...
YET ANOTHER REMARK-ABLE FELLOW...

READ THIS WAY

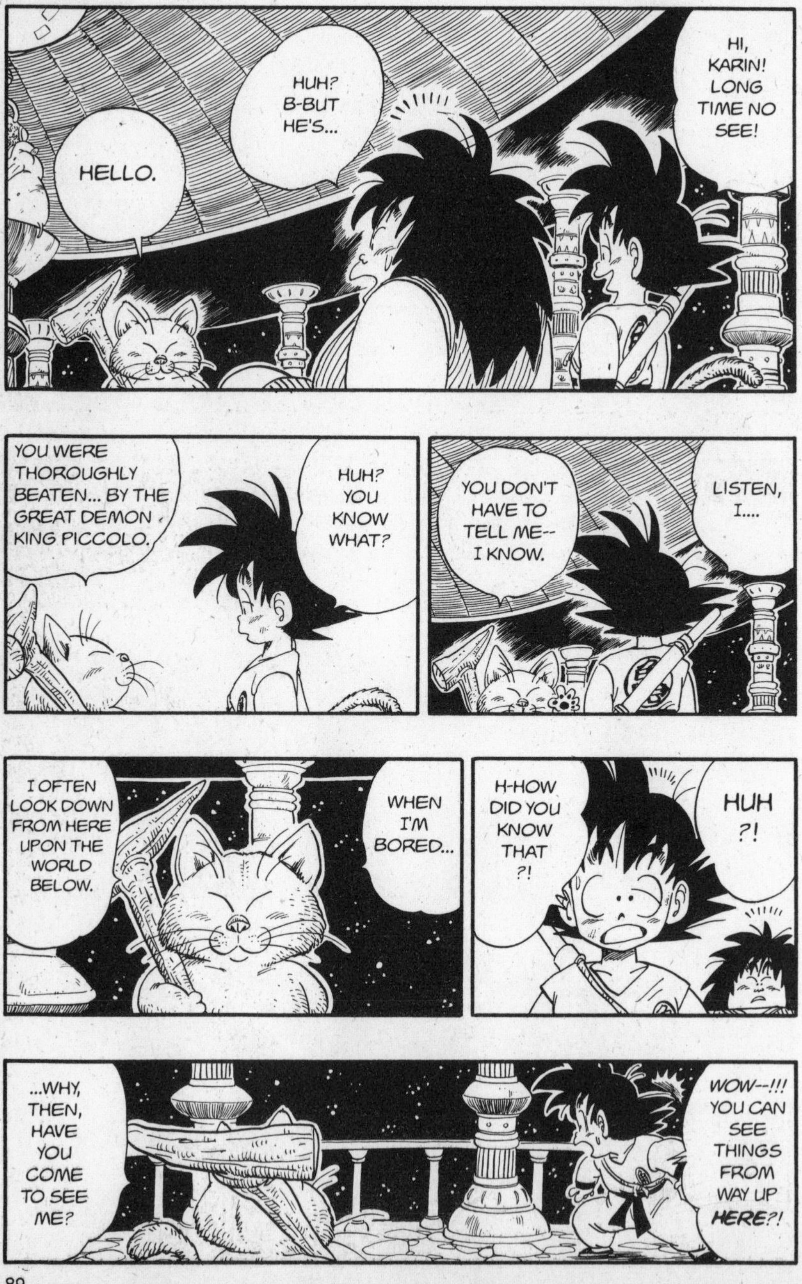
HI, KARIN! LONG TIME NO SEE!
HUH? B-BUT HE'S...
HELLO.
LISTEN, I....
YOU DON'T HAVE TO TELL ME-- I KNOW.
HUH? YOU KNOW WHAT?
YOU WERE THOROUGHLY BEATEN... BY THE GREAT DEMON KING PICCOLO.
HUH ?!
H-HOW DID YOU KNOW THAT ?!
WHEN I'M BORED...
I OFTEN LOOK DOWN FROM HERE UPON THE WORLD BELOW.
WOW--!!! YOU CAN SEE THINGS FROM WAY UP ***HERE***?!
...WHY, THEN, HAVE YOU COME TO SEE ME?

READ THIS WAY

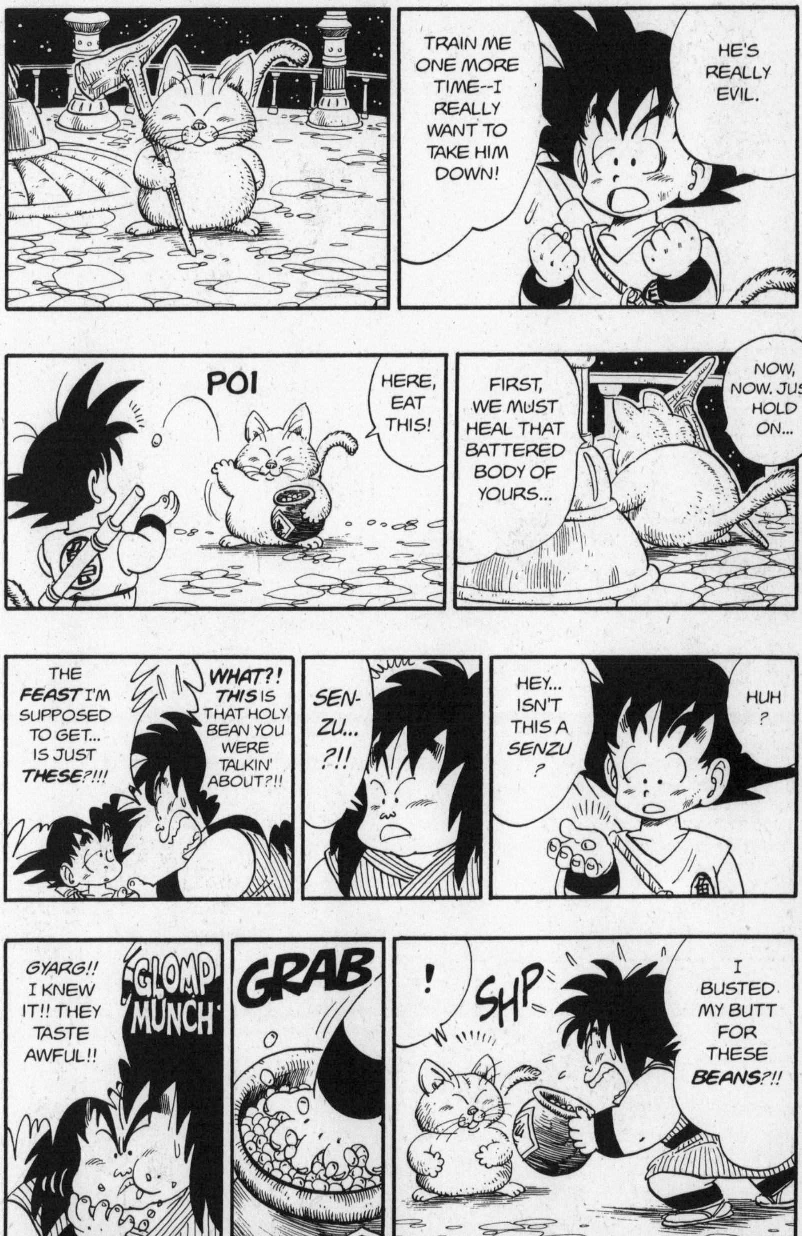
HE'S REALLY EVIL.
TRAIN ME ONE MORE TIME--I REALLY WANT TO TAKE HIM DOWN!
NOW, NOW. JUST HOLD ON...
FIRST, WE MUST HEAL THAT BATTERED BODY OF YOURS...
HERE, EAT THIS!
POI
HUH ?
HEY... ISN'T THIS A SENZU ?
SEN-ZU... ?!!
WHAT?! THIS IS THAT HOLY BEAN YOU WERE TALKIN' ABOUT?!!
THE FEAST I'M SUPPOSED TO GET... IS JUST THESE?!!!
I BUSTED MY BUTT FOR THESE BEANS?!!
SHP
!
GRAB
GLOMP MUNCH
GYARG!! I KNEW IT!! THEY TASTE AWFUL!!

READ THIS WAY

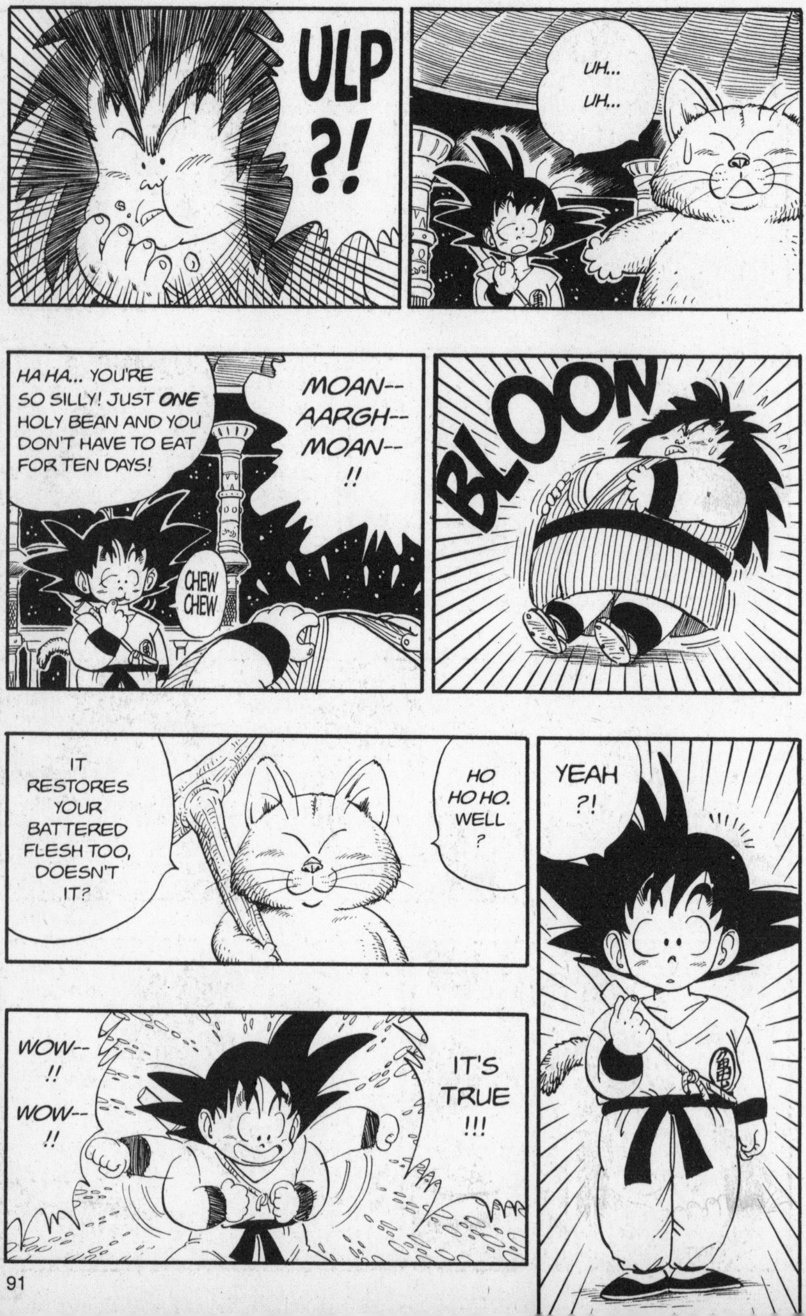
UH...
UH...
ULP
?!
BLOON
MOAN--
AARGH--
MOAN--
!!
HA HA... YOU'RE SO SILLY! JUST **ONE** HOLY BEAN AND YOU DON'T HAVE TO EAT FOR TEN DAYS!
CHEW
CHEW
YEAH
?!
HO
HO HO.
WELL
?
IT RESTORES YOUR BATTERED FLESH TOO, DOESN'T IT?
IT'S
TRUE
!!!
WOW--
!!
WOW--
!!

READ THIS WAY

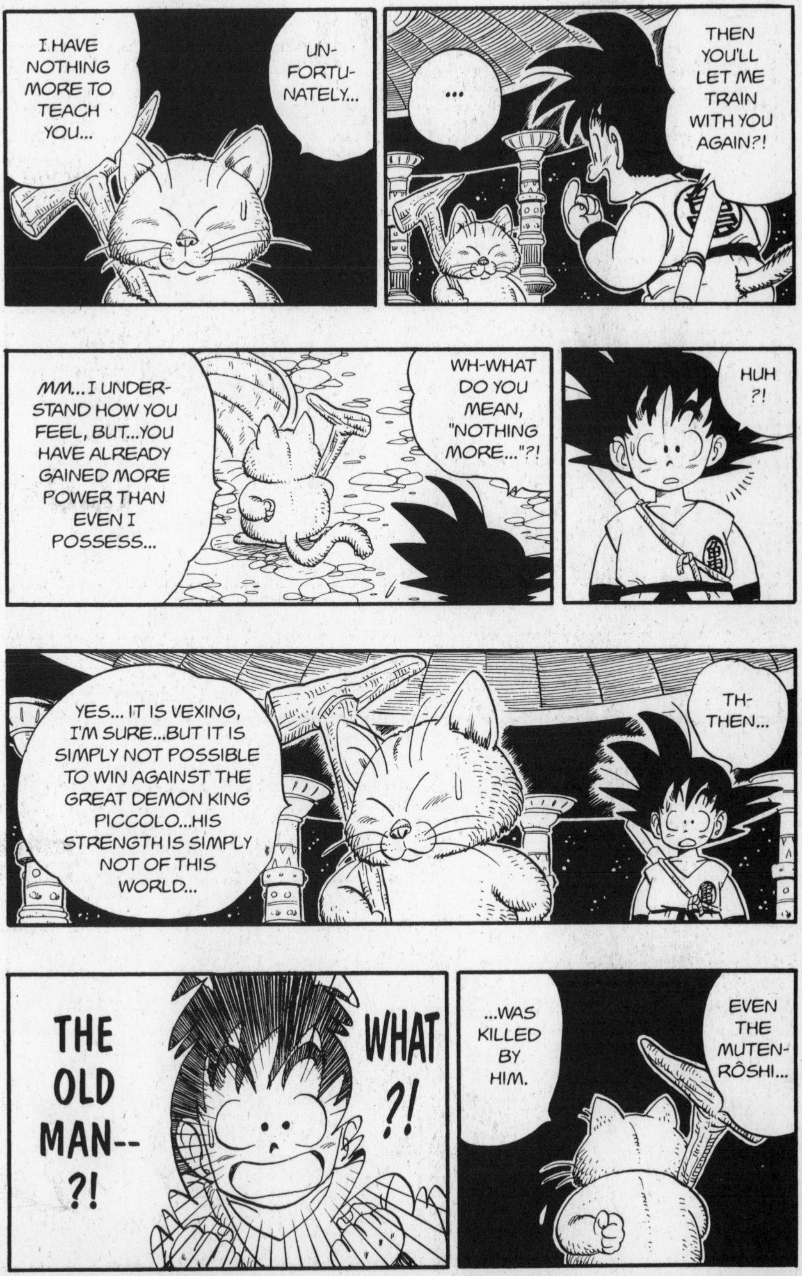
THEN YOU'LL LET ME TRAIN WITH YOU AGAIN?!
...
UN-FORTU-NATELY...
I HAVE NOTHING MORE TO TEACH YOU...
HUH ?!
WH-WHAT DO YOU MEAN, "NOTHING MORE..."?!
MM...I UNDER-STAND HOW YOU FEEL, BUT...YOU HAVE ALREADY GAINED MORE POWER THAN EVEN I POSSESS...
TH-THEN...
YES... IT IS VEXING, I'M SURE...BUT IT IS SIMPLY NOT POSSIBLE TO WIN AGAINST THE GREAT DEMON KING PICCOLO...HIS STRENGTH IS SIMPLY NOT OF THIS WORLD...
EVEN THE MUTEN-RÔSHI...
...WAS KILLED BY HIM.
WHAT ?!
THE OLD MAN-- ?!

READ THIS WAY

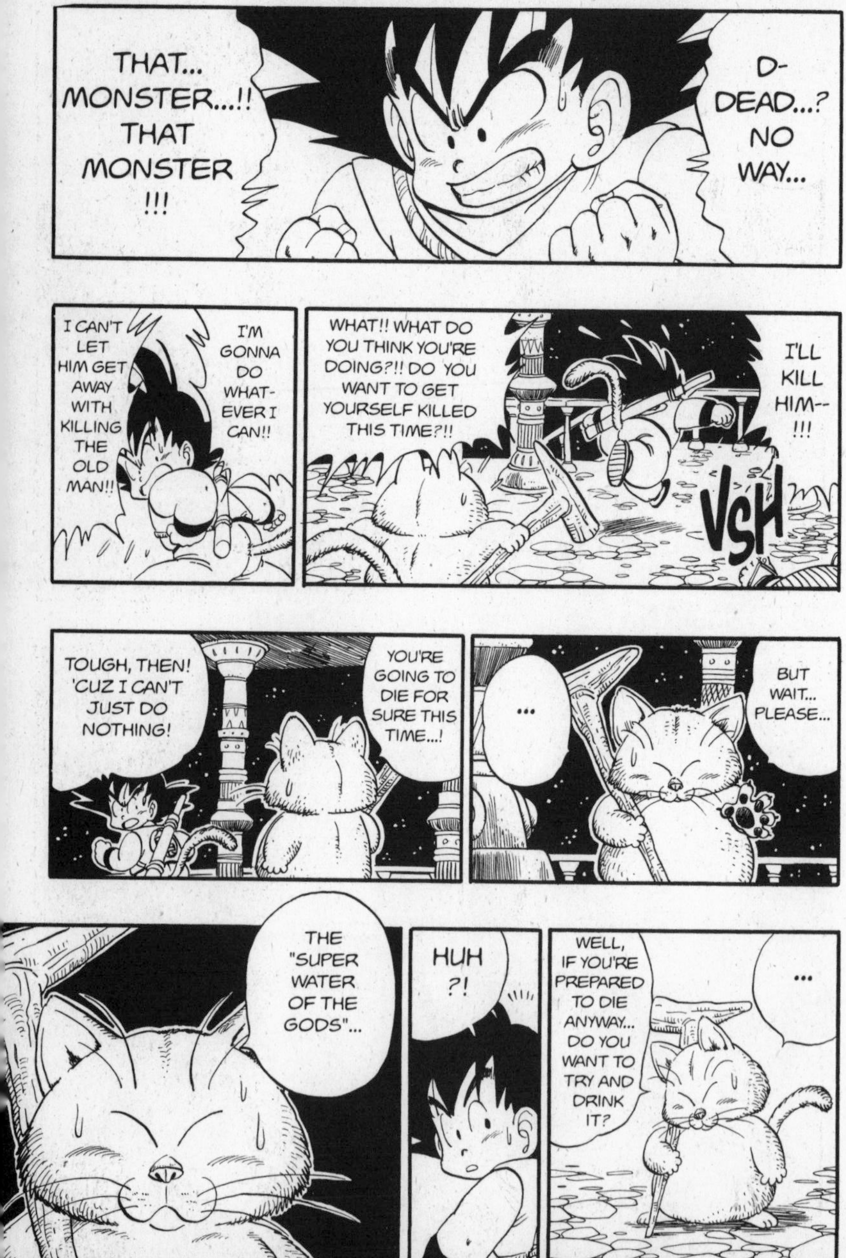

D- DEAD...? NO WAY...
THAT... MONSTER...!! THAT MONSTER !!!
I'LL KILL HIM-- !!!
WHAT!! WHAT DO YOU THINK YOU'RE DOING?!! DO YOU WANT TO GET YOURSELF KILLED THIS TIME?!!
VSH
I'M GONNA DO WHATEVER I CAN!!
I CAN'T LET HIM GET AWAY WITH KILLING THE OLD MAN!!
BUT WAIT... PLEASE...
...
YOU'RE GOING TO DIE FOR SURE THIS TIME...!
TOUGH, THEN! 'CUZ I CAN'T JUST DO NOTHING!
...
WELL, IF YOU'RE PREPARED TO DIE ANYWAY... DO YOU WANT TO TRY AND DRINK IT?
HUH ?!
THE "SUPER WATER OF THE GODS"...

NEXT: The Superest Super Water!!!

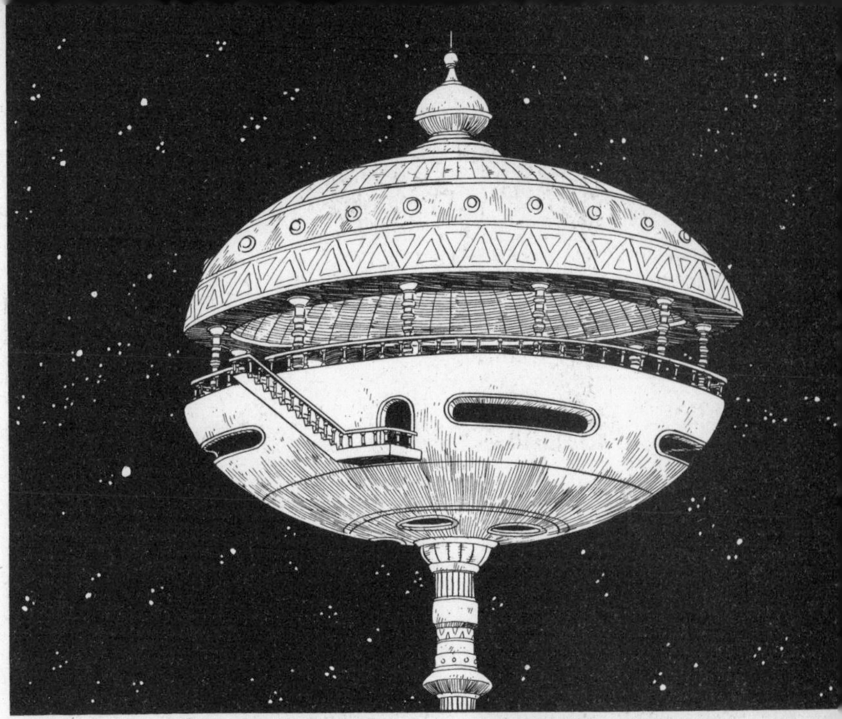

Tale 151 • The Superest Super Water!!!

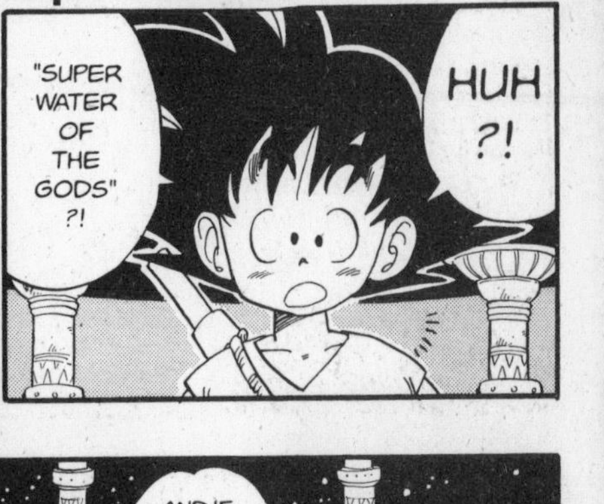
HUH ?!
"SUPER WATER OF THE GODS" ?!

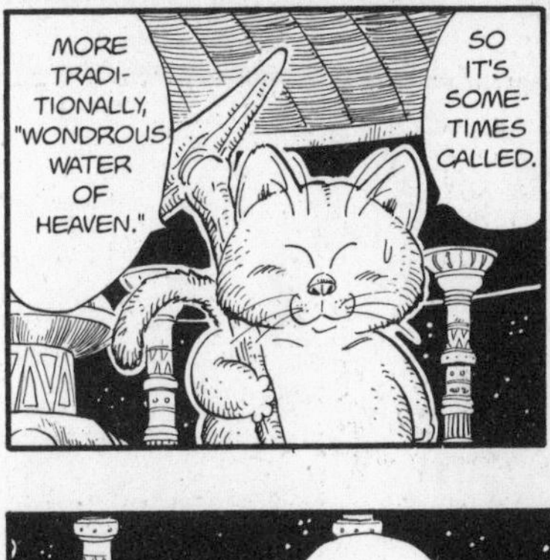
SO IT'S SOME-TIMES CALLED.
MORE TRADI-TIONALLY, "WONDROUS WATER OF HEAVEN."

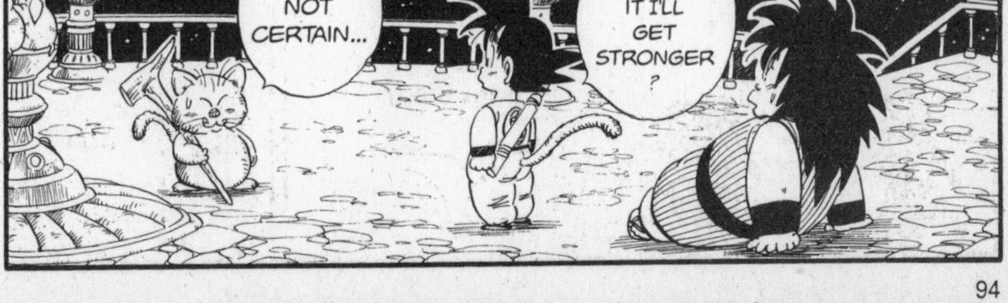
AND IF I DRINK IT I'LL GET STRONGER ?
I'M NOT CERTAIN...

READ THIS WAY

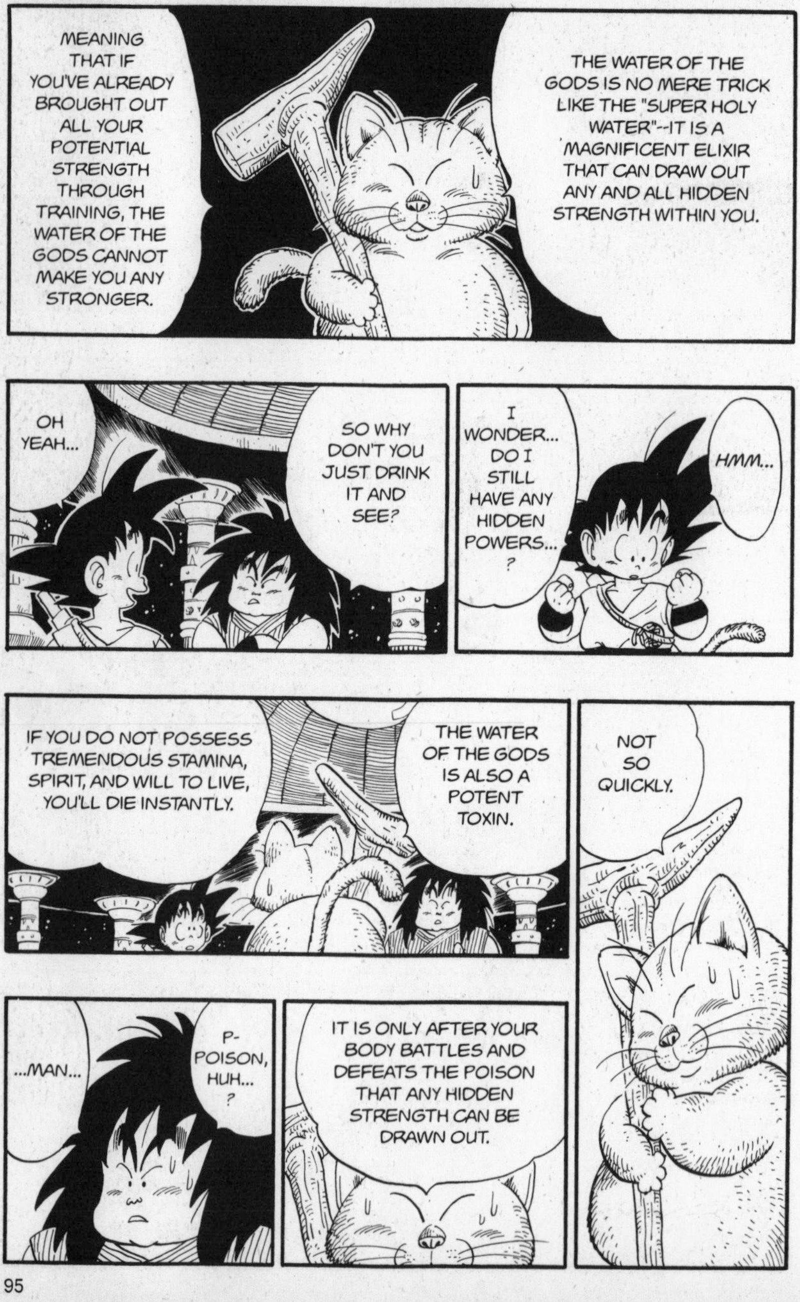

THE WATER OF THE GODS IS NO MERE TRICK LIKE THE "SUPER HOLY WATER"--IT IS A MAGNIFICENT ELIXIR THAT CAN DRAW OUT ANY AND ALL HIDDEN STRENGTH WITHIN YOU.
MEANING THAT IF YOU'VE ALREADY BROUGHT OUT ALL YOUR POTENTIAL STRENGTH THROUGH TRAINING, THE WATER OF THE GODS CANNOT MAKE YOU ANY STRONGER.
HMM...
I WONDER... DO I STILL HAVE ANY HIDDEN POWERS...?
SO WHY DON'T YOU JUST DRINK IT AND SEE?
OH YEAH...
NOT SO QUICKLY.
THE WATER OF THE GODS IS ALSO A POTENT TOXIN.
IF YOU DO NOT POSSESS TREMENDOUS STAMINA, SPIRIT, AND WILL TO LIVE, YOU'LL DIE INSTANTLY.
IT IS ONLY AFTER YOUR BODY BATTLES AND DEFEATS THE POISON THAT ANY HIDDEN STRENGTH CAN BE DRAWN OUT.
P-POISON, HUH...?
...MAN...

READ THIS WAY

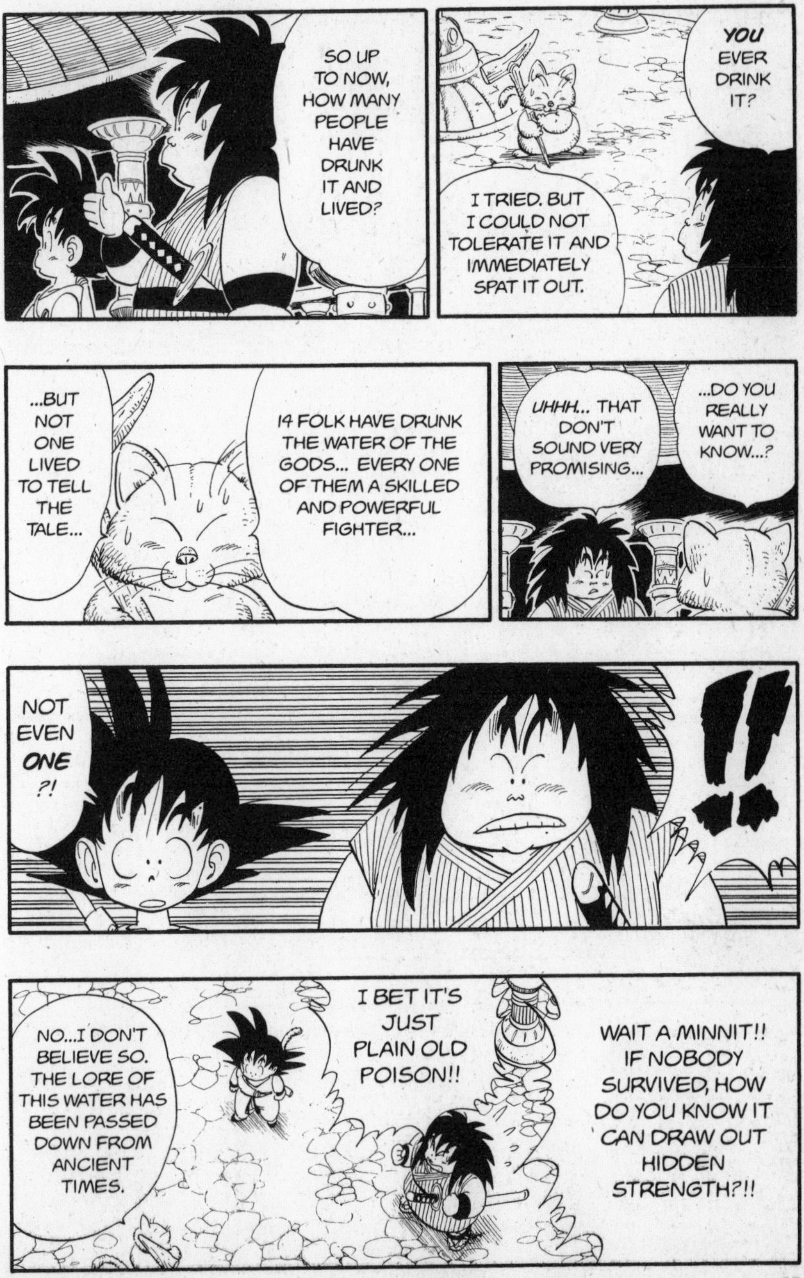
YOU EVER DRINK IT?
I TRIED. BUT I COULD NOT TOLERATE IT AND IMMEDIATELY SPAT IT OUT.
SO UP TO NOW, HOW MANY PEOPLE HAVE DRUNK IT AND LIVED?
...DO YOU REALLY WANT TO KNOW...?
UHHH... THAT DON'T SOUND VERY PROMISING...
14 FOLK HAVE DRUNK THE WATER OF THE GODS... EVERY ONE OF THEM A SKILLED AND POWERFUL FIGHTER...
...BUT NOT ONE LIVED TO TELL THE TALE...
NOT EVEN ONE ?!
WAIT A MINNIT!! IF NOBODY SURVIVED, HOW DO YOU KNOW IT CAN DRAW OUT HIDDEN STRENGTH?!!
I BET IT'S JUST PLAIN OLD POISON!!
NO...I DON'T BELIEVE SO. THE LORE OF THIS WATER HAS BEEN PASSED DOWN FROM ANCIENT TIMES.

READ THIS WAY

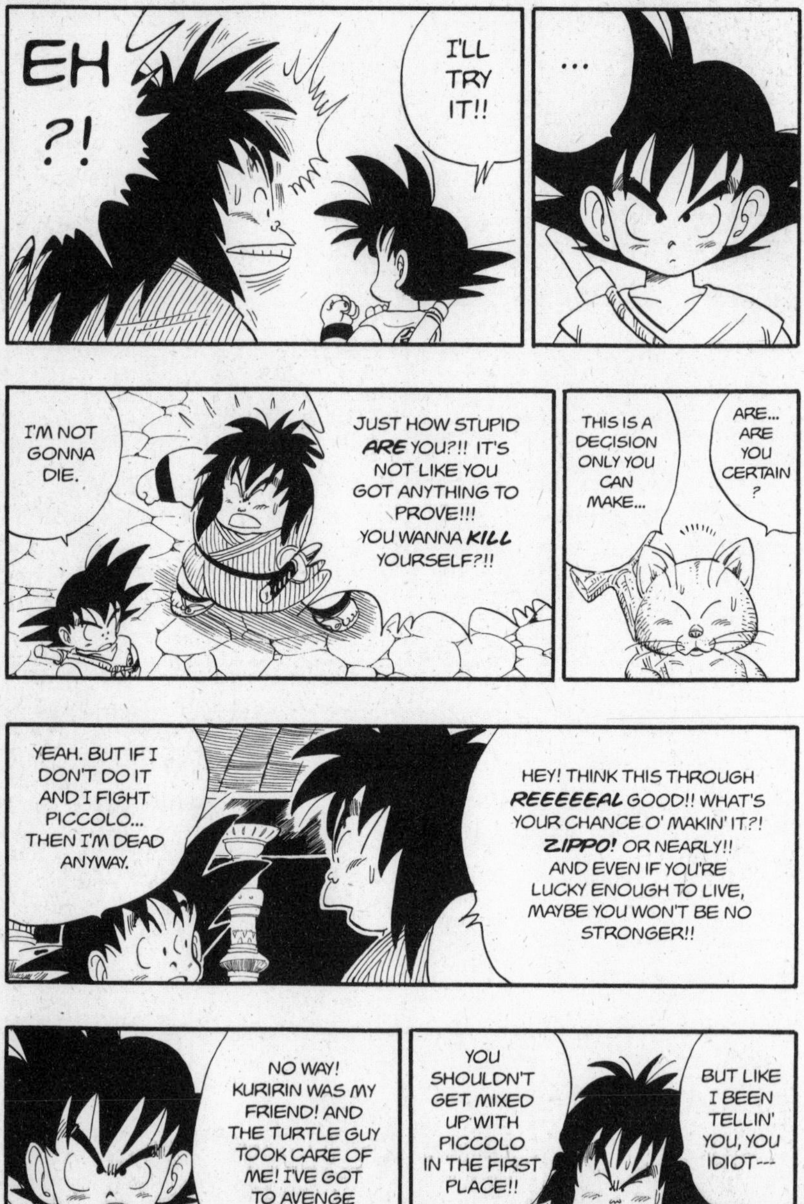
...
I'LL TRY IT!!
EH ?!
ARE... ARE YOU CERTAIN?
THIS IS A DECISION ONLY YOU CAN MAKE...
JUST HOW STUPID **ARE** YOU?!! IT'S NOT LIKE YOU GOT ANYTHING TO PROVE!!! YOU WANNA **KILL** YOURSELF?!!
I'M NOT GONNA DIE.
HEY! THINK THIS THROUGH **REEEEEAL** GOOD!! WHAT'S YOUR CHANCE O' MAKIN' IT?! **ZIPPO!** OR NEARLY!! AND EVEN IF YOU'RE LUCKY ENOUGH TO LIVE, MAYBE YOU WON'T BE NO STRONGER!!
YEAH. BUT IF I DON'T DO IT AND I FIGHT PICCOLO... THEN I'M DEAD ANYWAY.
BUT LIKE I BEEN TELLIN' YOU, YOU IDIOT---
YOU SHOULDN'T GET MIXED UP WITH PICCOLO IN THE FIRST PLACE!!
NO WAY! KURIRIN WAS MY FRIEND! AND THE TURTLE GUY TOOK CARE OF ME! I'VE GOT TO AVENGE THEM!

READ THIS WAY

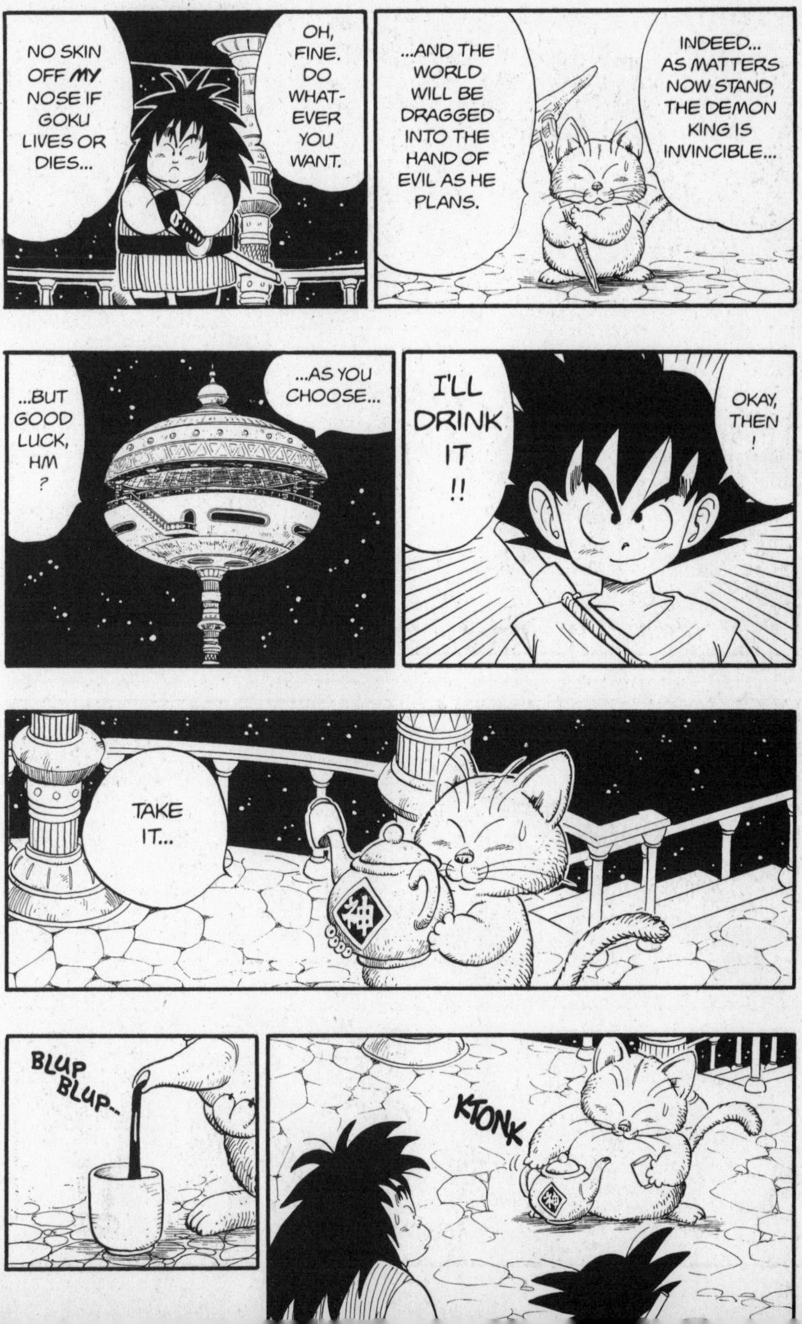
INDEED... AS MATTERS NOW STAND, THE DEMON KING IS INVINCIBLE...
...AND THE WORLD WILL BE DRAGGED INTO THE HAND OF EVIL AS HE PLANS.
OH, FINE. DO WHATEVER YOU WANT.
NO SKIN OFF MY NOSE IF GOKU LIVES OR DIES...
OKAY, THEN!
I'LL DRINK IT!!
...AS YOU CHOOSE...
...BUT GOOD LUCK, HM?
TAKE IT...
KTONK
BLUP BLUP...

READ THIS WAY

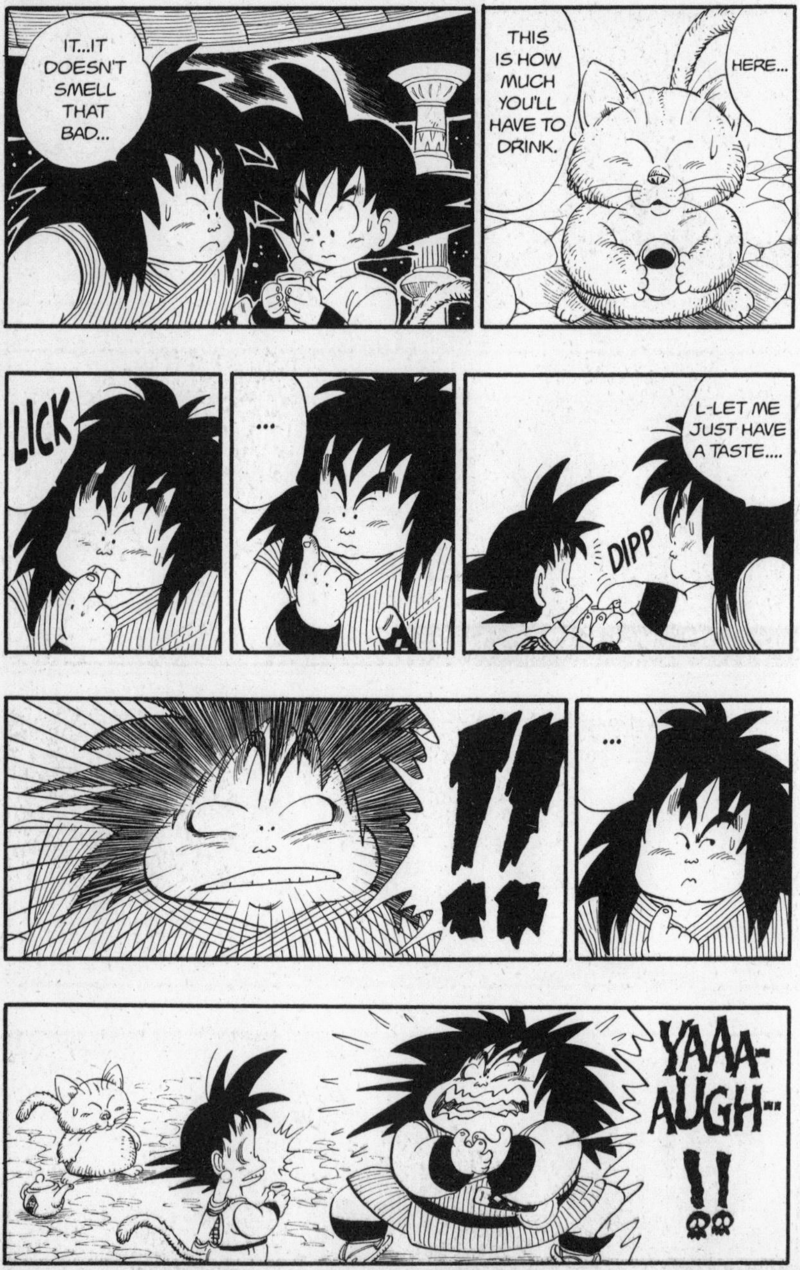
HERE...
THIS IS HOW MUCH YOU'LL HAVE TO DRINK.
IT...IT DOESN'T SMELL THAT BAD...
L-LET ME JUST HAVE A TASTE....
DIPP
...
LICK
...
!!
YAAA-AUGH--!!

READ THIS WAY

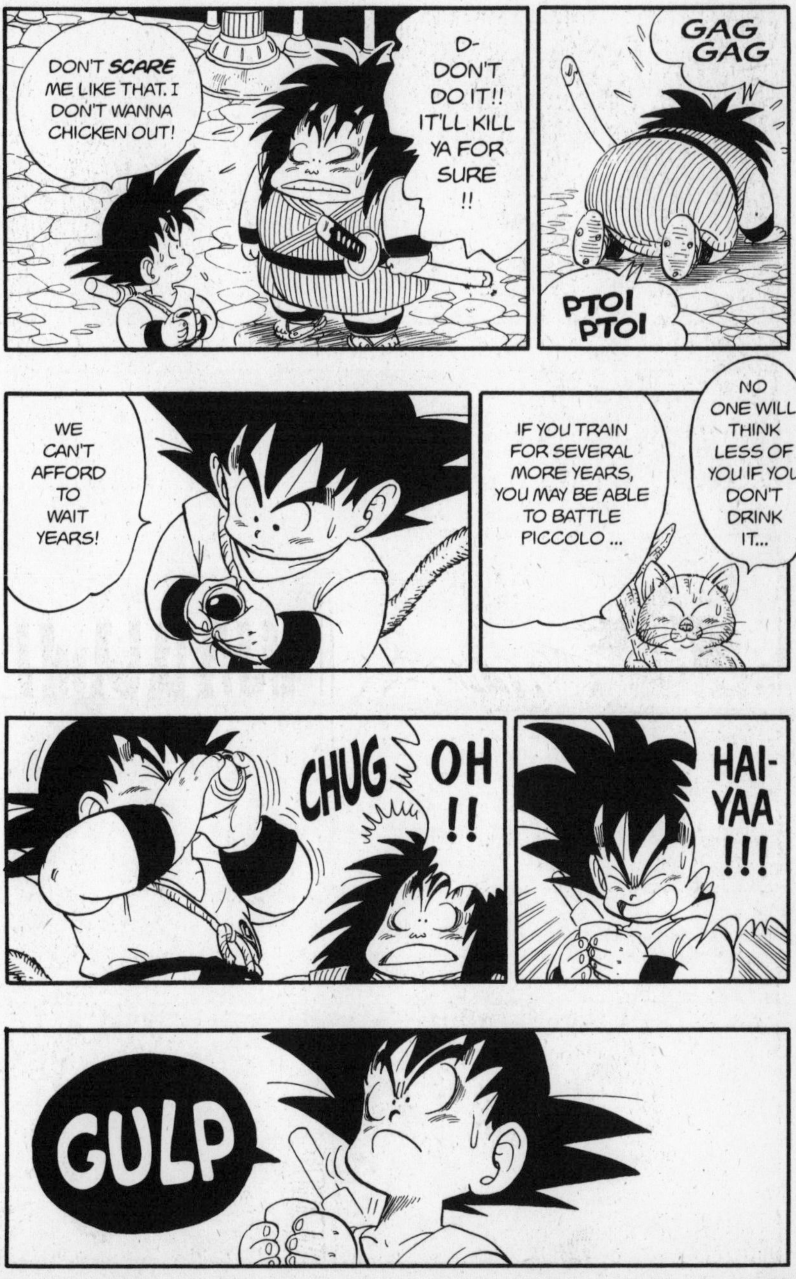
GAG GAG
PTOI PTOI
D- DON'T DO IT!! IT'LL KILL YA FOR SURE !!
DON'T SCARE ME LIKE THAT. I DON'T WANNA CHICKEN OUT!
NO ONE WILL THINK LESS OF YOU IF YOU DON'T DRINK IT...
IF YOU TRAIN FOR SEVERAL MORE YEARS, YOU MAY BE ABLE TO BATTLE PICCOLO ...
WE CAN'T AFFORD TO WAIT YEARS!
HAI-YAA !!!
OH !!
CHUG
GULP

READ THIS WAY

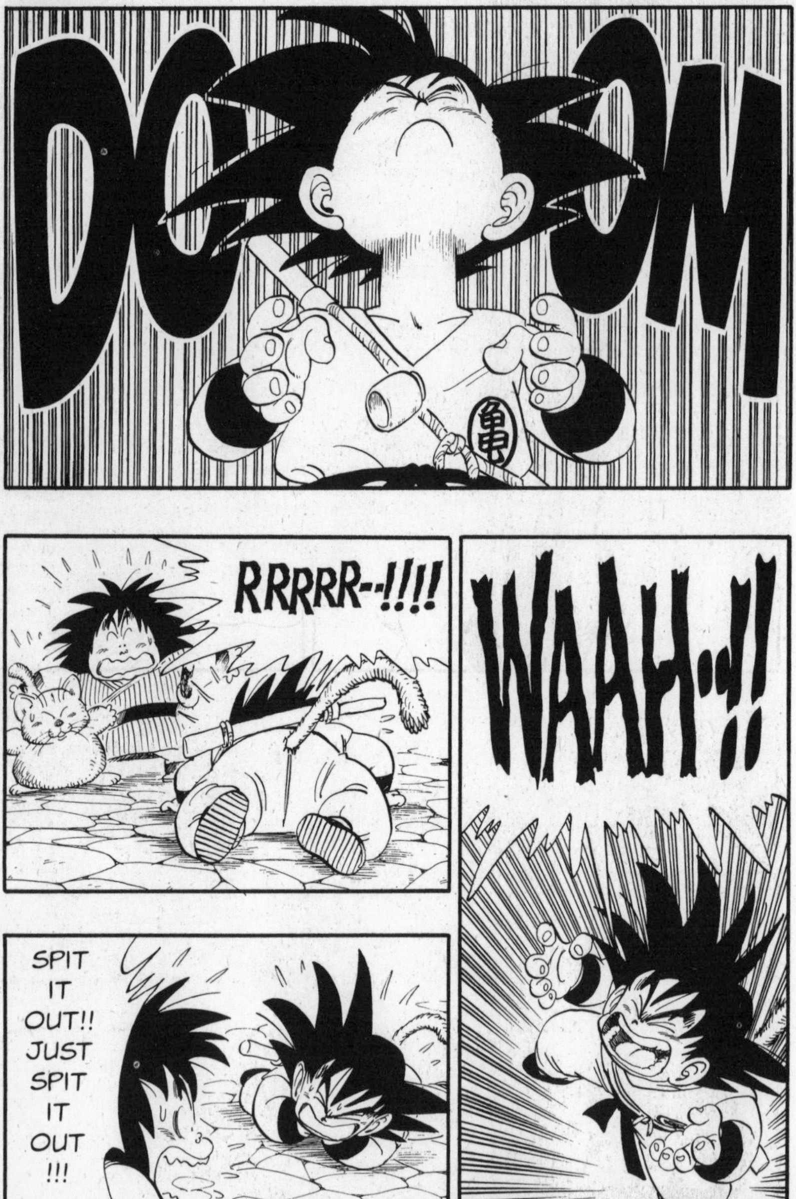

DOOM!
WAAH--!!
RRRRR--!!!!
SPIT IT OUT!! JUST SPIT IT OUT!!!

READ THIS WAY

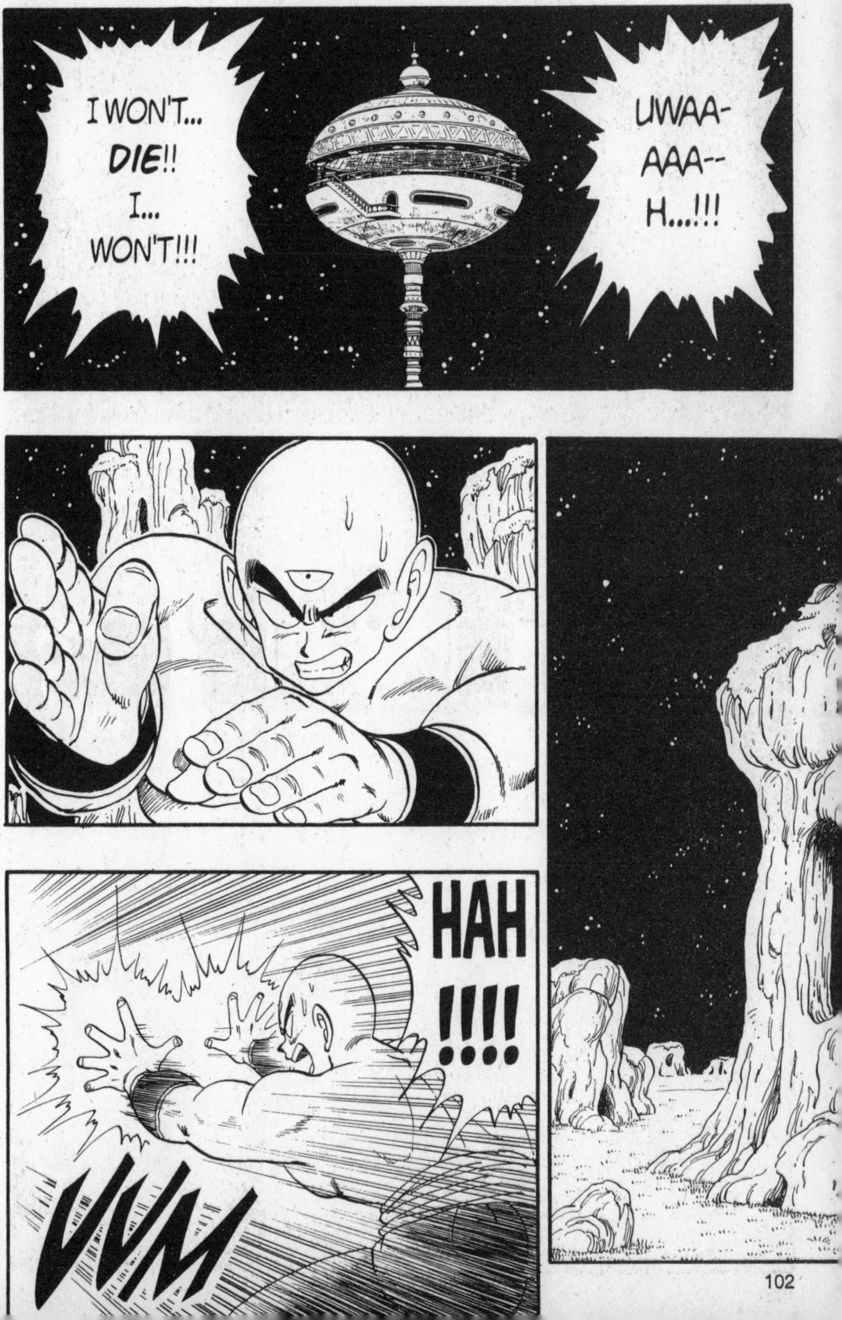
UWAA-AAA--H...!!!
I WON'T... DIE!! I... WON'T!!!
HAH!!!!
VVM

READ THIS WAY

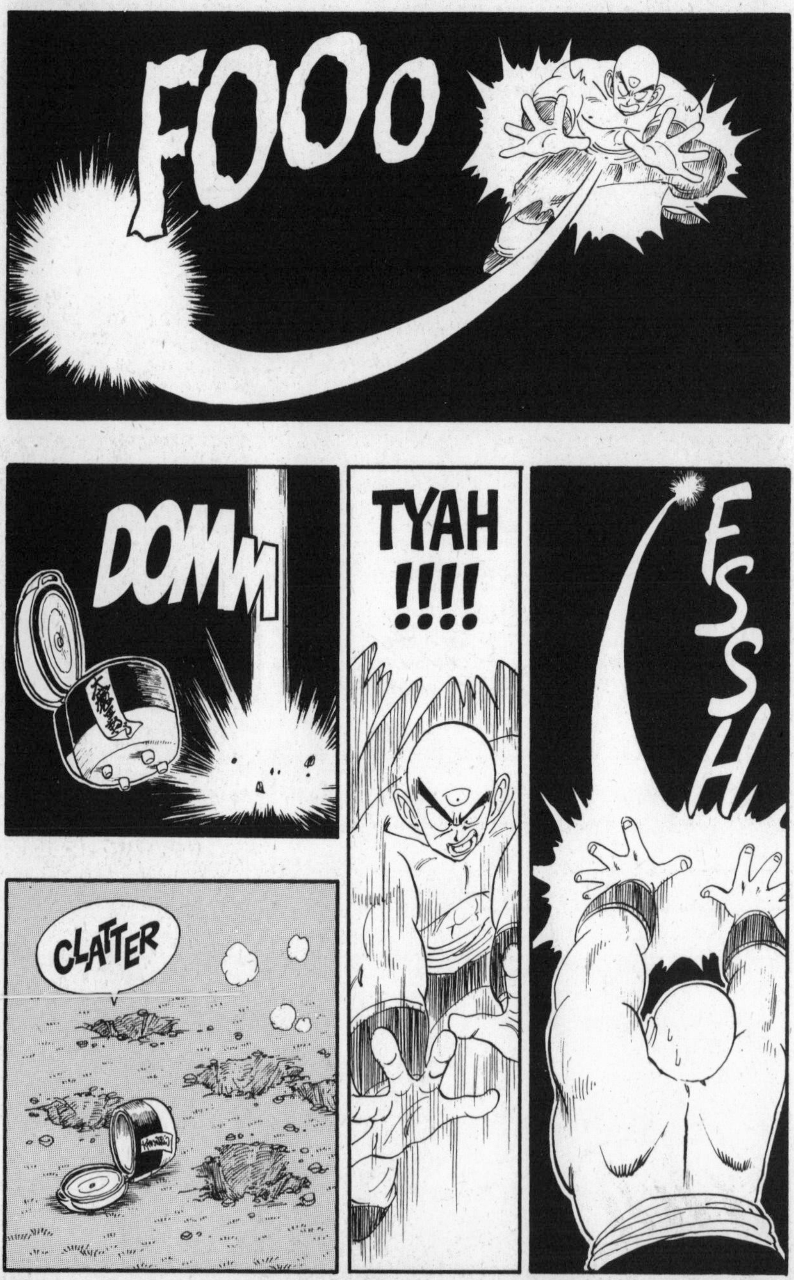

FOOO
FSSH
TYAH !!!!
DOMM
CLATTER

READ THIS WAY

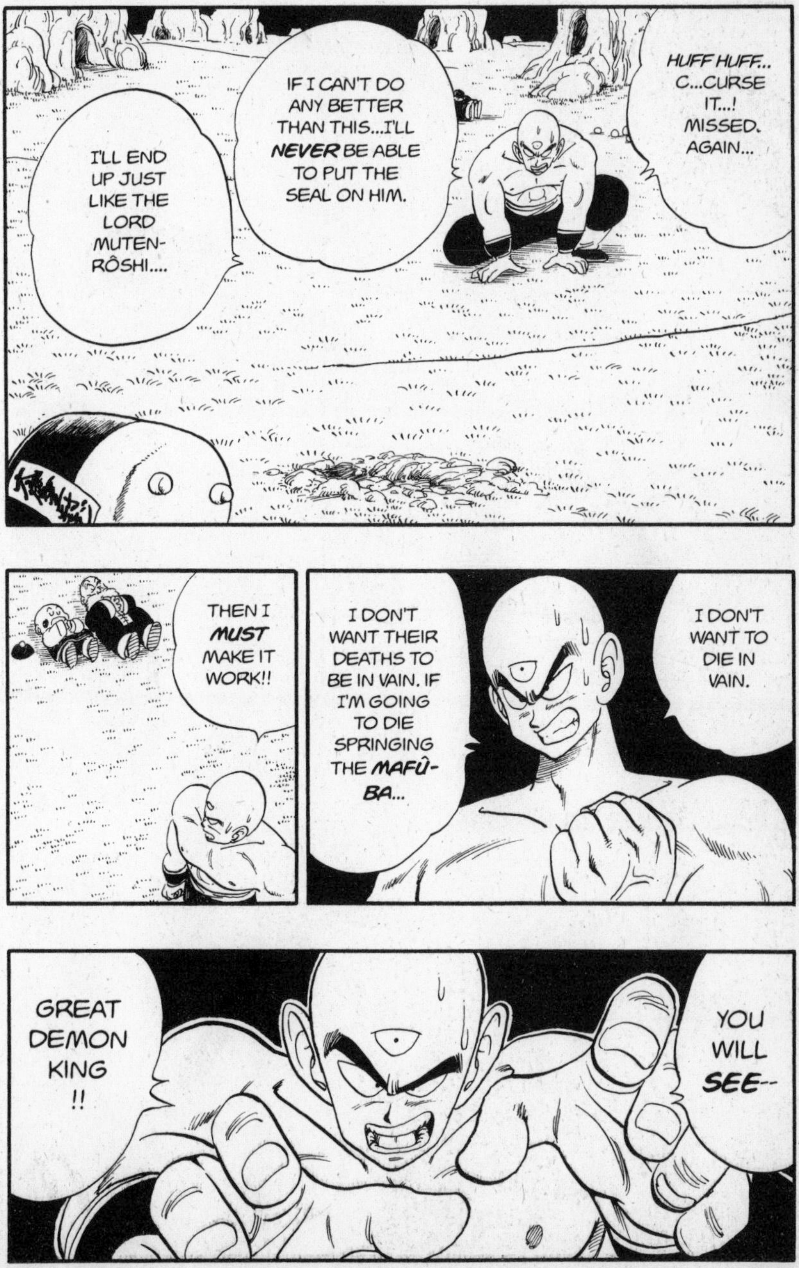
HUFF HUFF... C...CURSE IT...! MISSED. AGAIN...
IF I CAN'T DO ANY BETTER THAN THIS...I'LL NEVER BE ABLE TO PUT THE SEAL ON HIM.
I'LL END UP JUST LIKE THE LORD MUTEN-RÔSHI....
I DON'T WANT TO DIE IN VAIN.
I DON'T WANT THEIR DEATHS TO BE IN VAIN. IF I'M GOING TO DIE SPRINGING THE MAFÛ-BA...
THEN I MUST MAKE IT WORK!!
YOU WILL SEE--
GREAT DEMON KING !!

READ THIS WAY

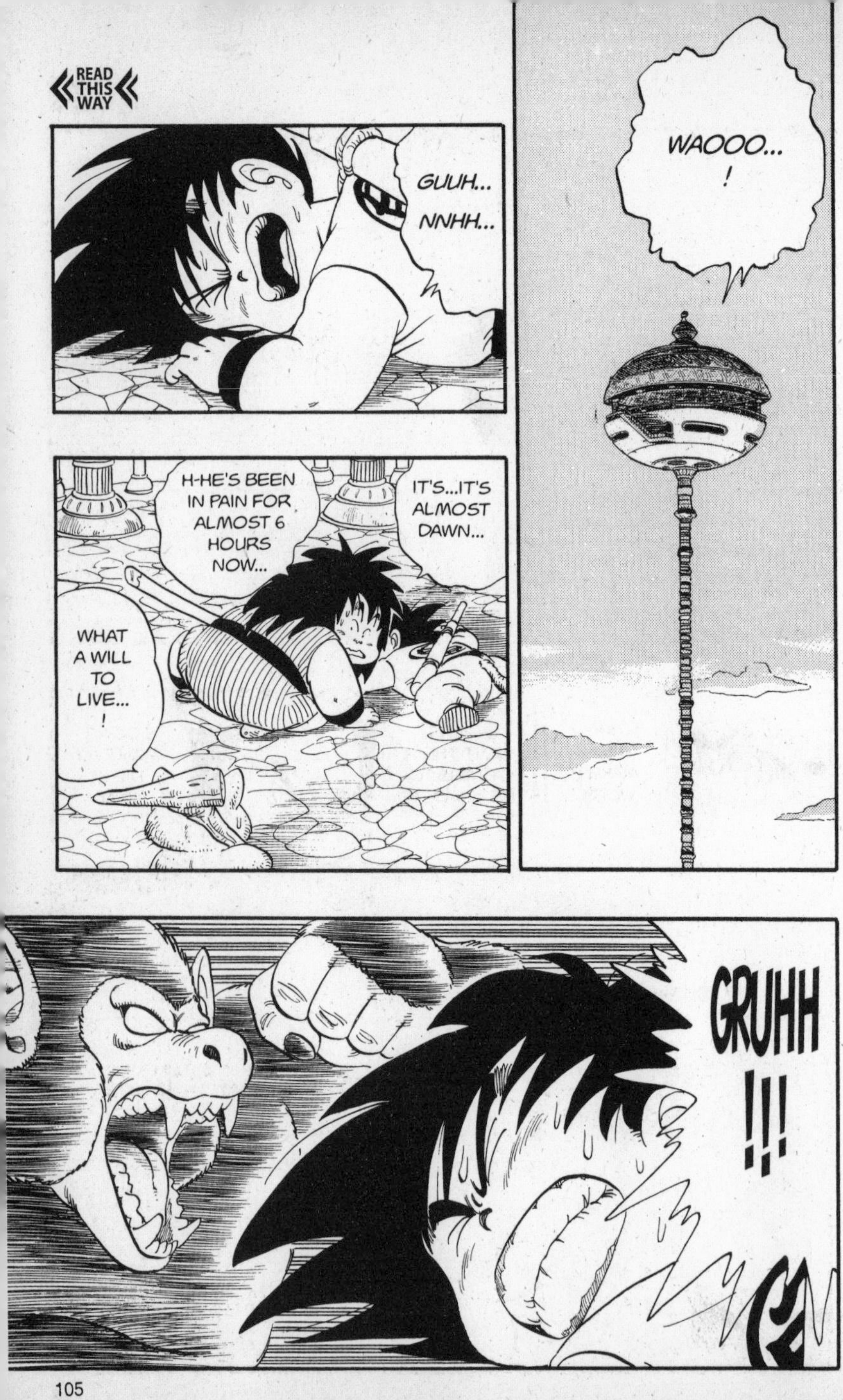
WAOOO... !
GUUH... NNHH...
IT'S...IT'S ALMOST DAWN...
H-HE'S BEEN IN PAIN FOR ALMOST 6 HOURS NOW...
WHAT A WILL TO LIVE... !
GRUHH !!!

READ THIS WAY

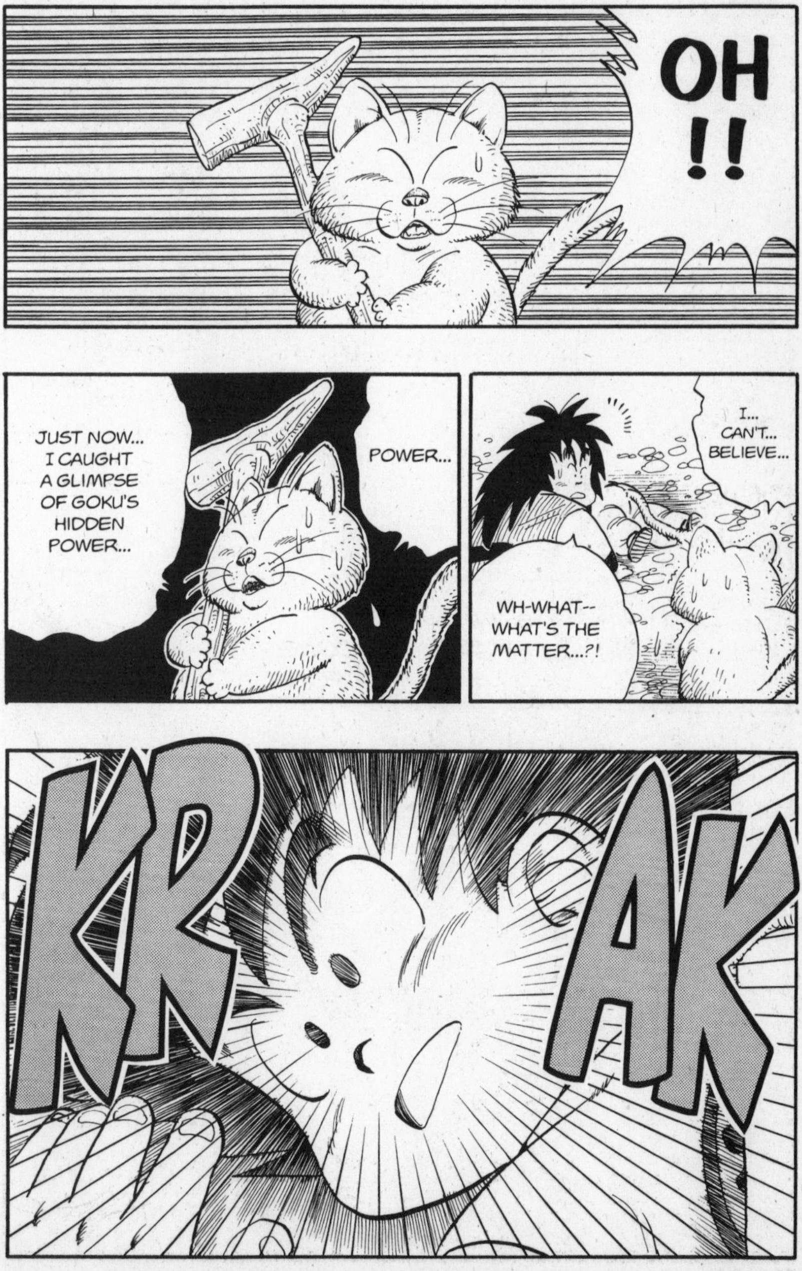
OH !!
I... CAN'T... BELIEVE...
WH-WHAT-- WHAT'S THE MATTER...?!
JUST NOW... I CAUGHT A GLIMPSE OF GOKU'S HIDDEN POWER...
POWER...
KRAK

READ THIS WAY

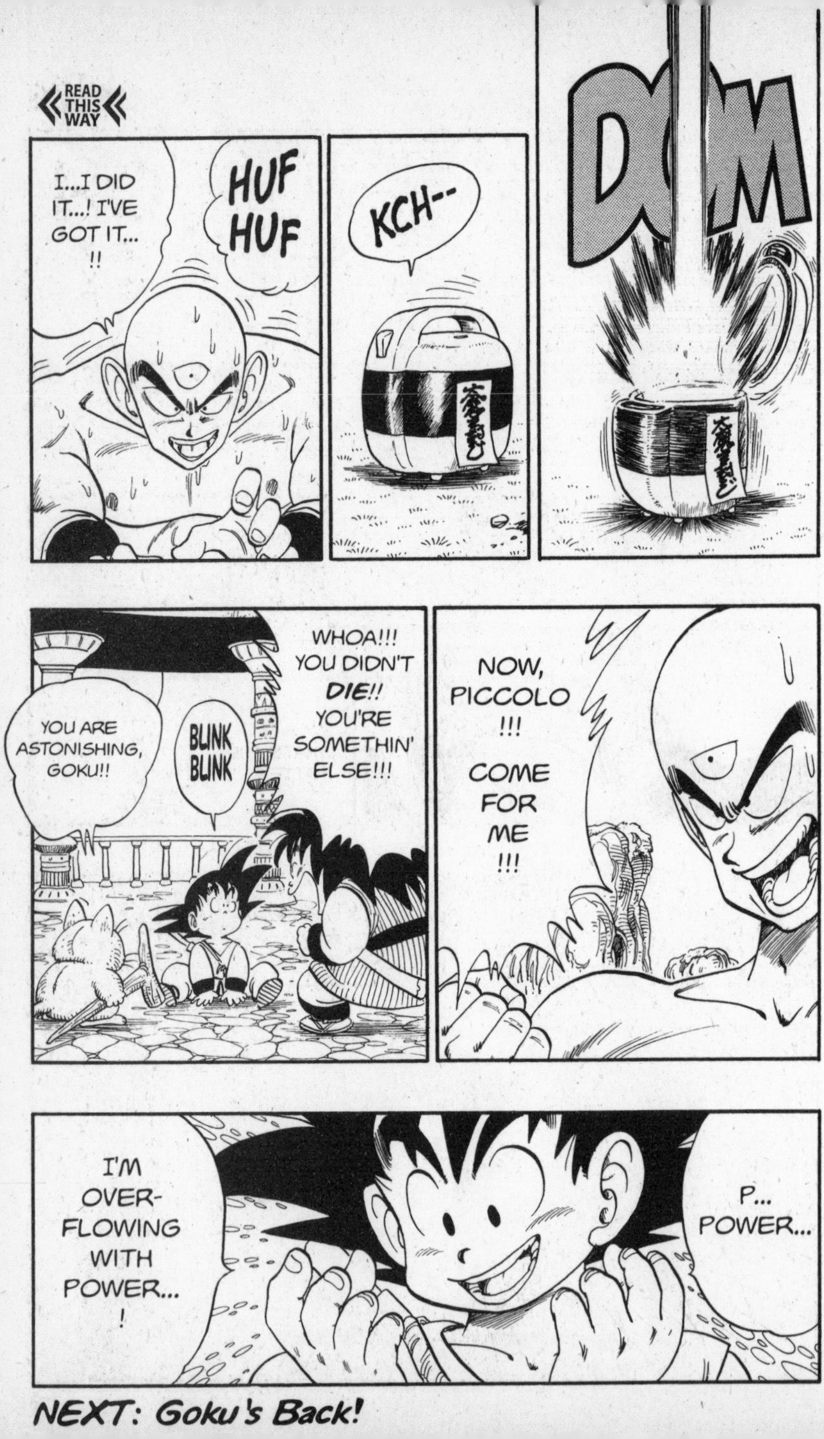
DOM
KCH--
HUF HUF
I...I DID IT...! I'VE GOT IT... !!
NOW, PICCOLO !!! COME FOR ME !!!
WHOA!!! YOU DIDN'T DIE!! YOU'RE SOMETHIN' ELSE!!!
BLINK BLINK
YOU ARE ASTONISHING, GOKU!!
P... POWER...
I'M OVER-FLOWING WITH POWER... !

NEXT: Goku's Back!

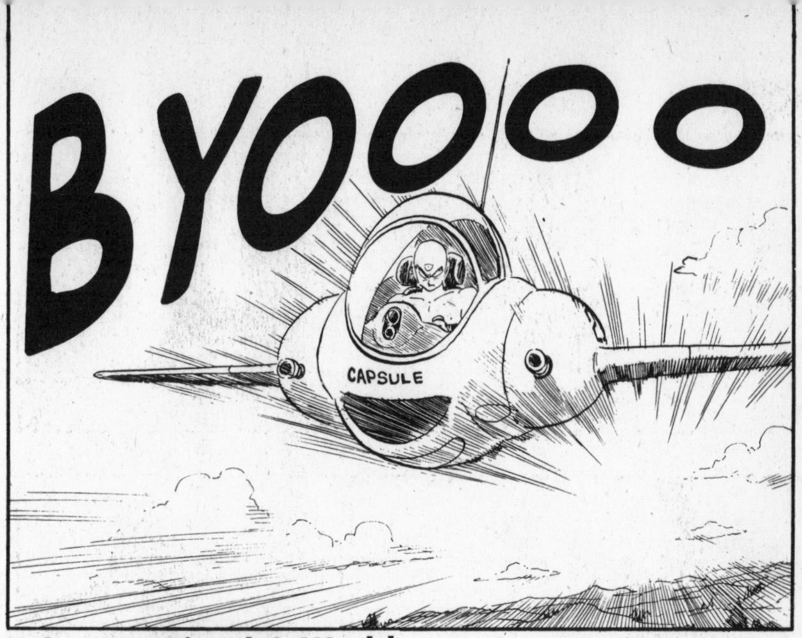
BYOOOO
CAPSULE

Tale 152 • Piccolo's World

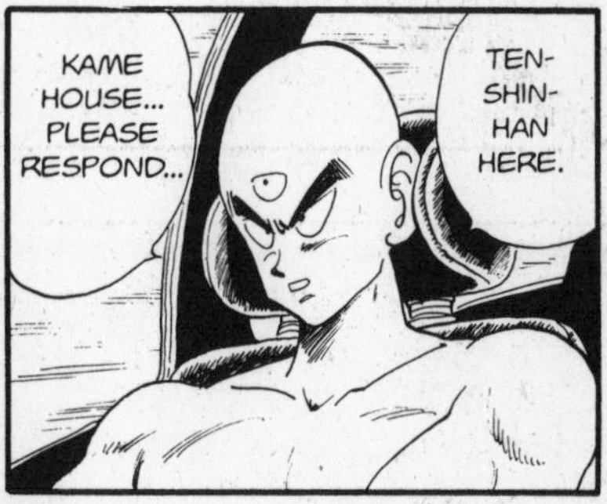
TEN-SHIN-HAN HERE.
KAME HOUSE... PLEASE RESPOND...

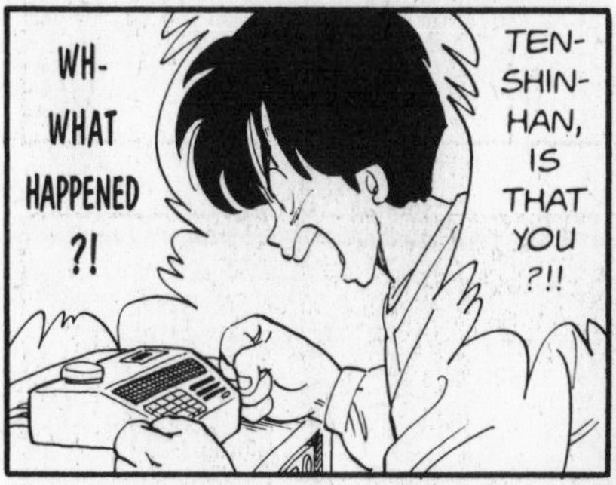
TEN-SHIN-HAN, IS THAT YOU ?!!
WH-WHAT HAPPENED ?!

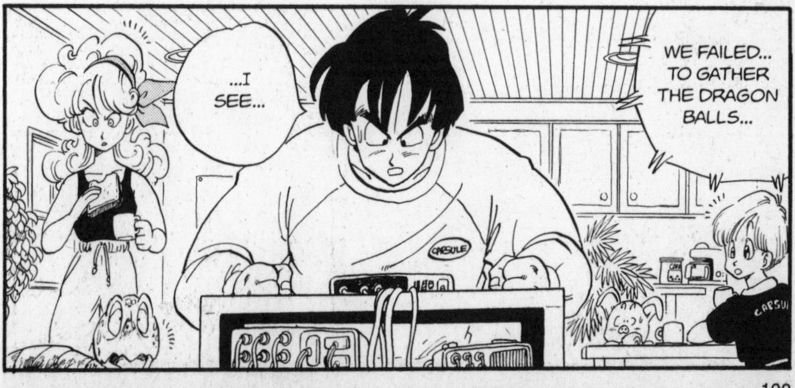
WE FAILED... TO GATHER THE DRAGON BALLS...
...I SEE...
CAPSULE

READ THIS WAY

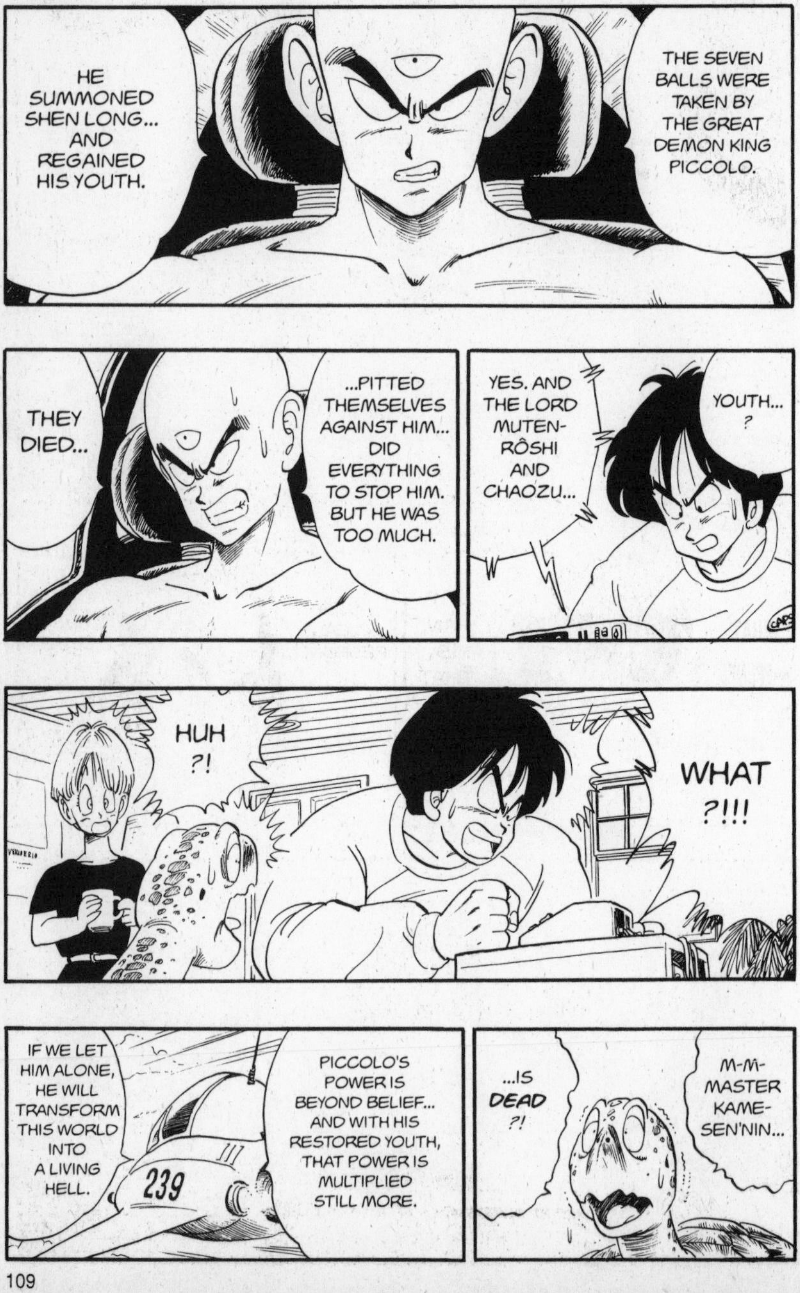
THE SEVEN BALLS WERE TAKEN BY THE GREAT DEMON KING PICCOLO.
HE SUMMONED SHEN LONG... AND REGAINED HIS YOUTH.
YOUTH... ?
YES. AND THE LORD MUTEN-RÔSHI AND CHAOZU...
...PITTED THEMSELVES AGAINST HIM... DID EVERYTHING TO STOP HIM. BUT HE WAS TOO MUCH.
THEY DIED...
WHAT ?!!!
HUH ?!
M-M-MASTER KAME-SEN'NIN...
...IS DEAD ?!
PICCOLO'S POWER IS BEYOND BELIEF... AND WITH HIS RESTORED YOUTH, THAT POWER IS MULTIPLIED STILL MORE.
IF WE LET HIM ALONE, HE WILL TRANSFORM THIS WORLD INTO A LIVING HELL.
239

READ THIS WAY

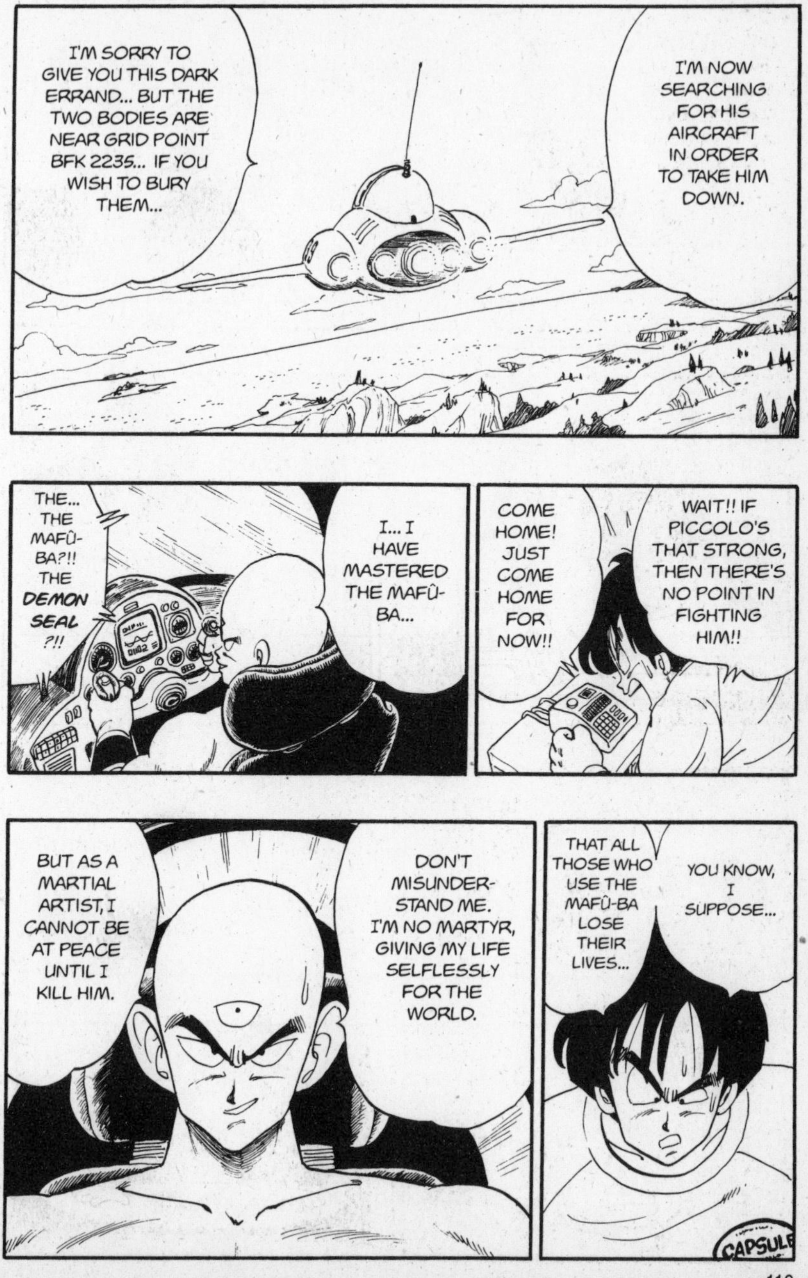

I'M NOW SEARCHING FOR HIS AIRCRAFT IN ORDER TO TAKE HIM DOWN.
I'M SORRY TO GIVE YOU THIS DARK ERRAND... BUT THE TWO BODIES ARE NEAR GRID POINT BFK 2235... IF YOU WISH TO BURY THEM...
WAIT!! IF PICCOLO'S THAT STRONG, THEN THERE'S NO POINT IN FIGHTING HIM!!
COME HOME! JUST COME HOME FOR NOW!!
I... I HAVE MASTERED THE MAFÛ-BA...
THE... THE MAFÛ-BA?!! THE **DEMON SEAL** ?!!
YOU KNOW, I SUPPOSE...
THAT ALL THOSE WHO USE THE MAFÛ-BA LOSE THEIR LIVES...
DON'T MISUNDER-STAND ME. I'M NO MARTYR, GIVING MY LIFE SELFLESSLY FOR THE WORLD.
BUT AS A MARTIAL ARTIST, I CANNOT BE AT PEACE UNTIL I KILL HIM.
CAPSULE

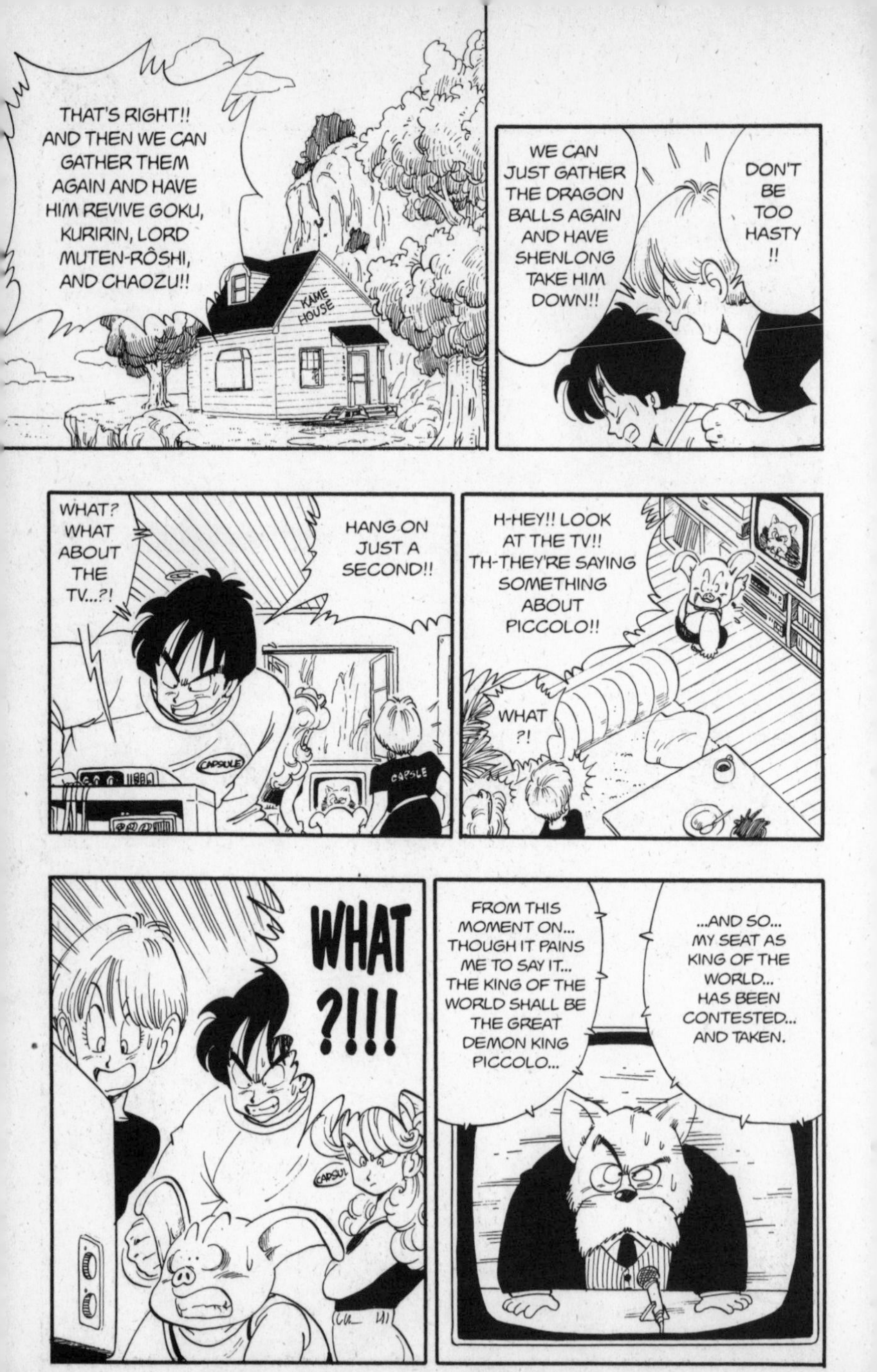
DON'T BE TOO HASTY !!
WE CAN JUST GATHER THE DRAGON BALLS AGAIN AND HAVE SHENLONG TAKE HIM DOWN!!
THAT'S RIGHT!! AND THEN WE CAN GATHER THEM AGAIN AND HAVE HIM REVIVE GOKU, KURIRIN, LORD MUTEN-RÔSHI, AND CHAOZU!!
KAME HOUSE
H-HEY!! LOOK AT THE TV!! TH-THEY'RE SAYING SOMETHING ABOUT PICCOLO!!
WHAT ?!
HANG ON JUST A SECOND!!
WHAT? WHAT ABOUT THE TV...?!
CAPSULE
CAPSLE
...AND SO... MY SEAT AS KING OF THE WORLD... HAS BEEN CONTESTED... AND TAKEN.
FROM THIS MOMENT ON... THOUGH IT PAINS ME TO SAY IT... THE KING OF THE WORLD SHALL BE THE GREAT DEMON KING PICCOLO...
WHAT ?!!!
CAPSUL

READ THIS WAY

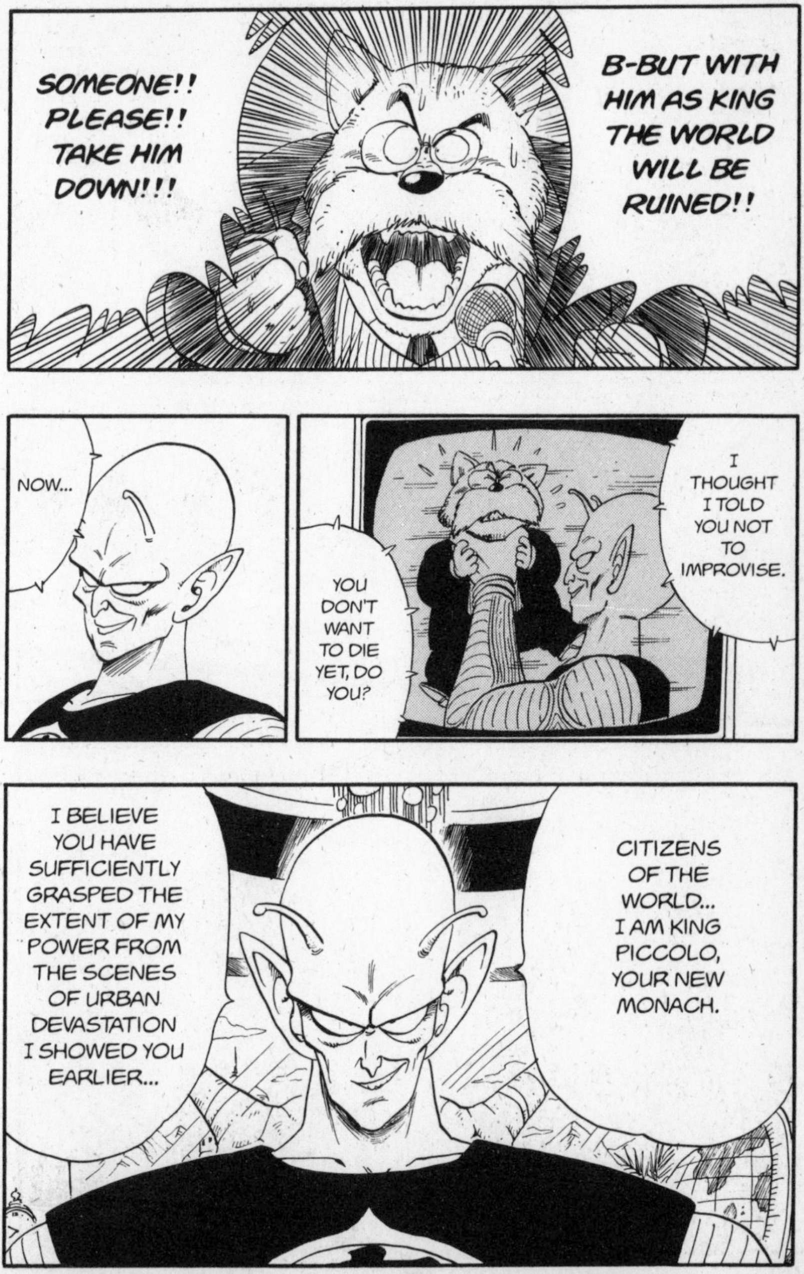
B-BUT WITH HIM AS KING THE WORLD WILL BE RUINED!!
SOMEONE!! PLEASE!! TAKE HIM DOWN!!!
I THOUGHT I TOLD YOU NOT TO IMPROVISE.
YOU DON'T WANT TO DIE YET, DO YOU?
NOW...
CITIZENS OF THE WORLD... I AM KING PICCOLO, YOUR NEW MONACH.
I BELIEVE YOU HAVE SUFFICIENTLY GRASPED THE EXTENT OF MY POWER FROM THE SCENES OF URBAN DEVASTATION I SHOWED YOU EARLIER...

READ THIS WAY

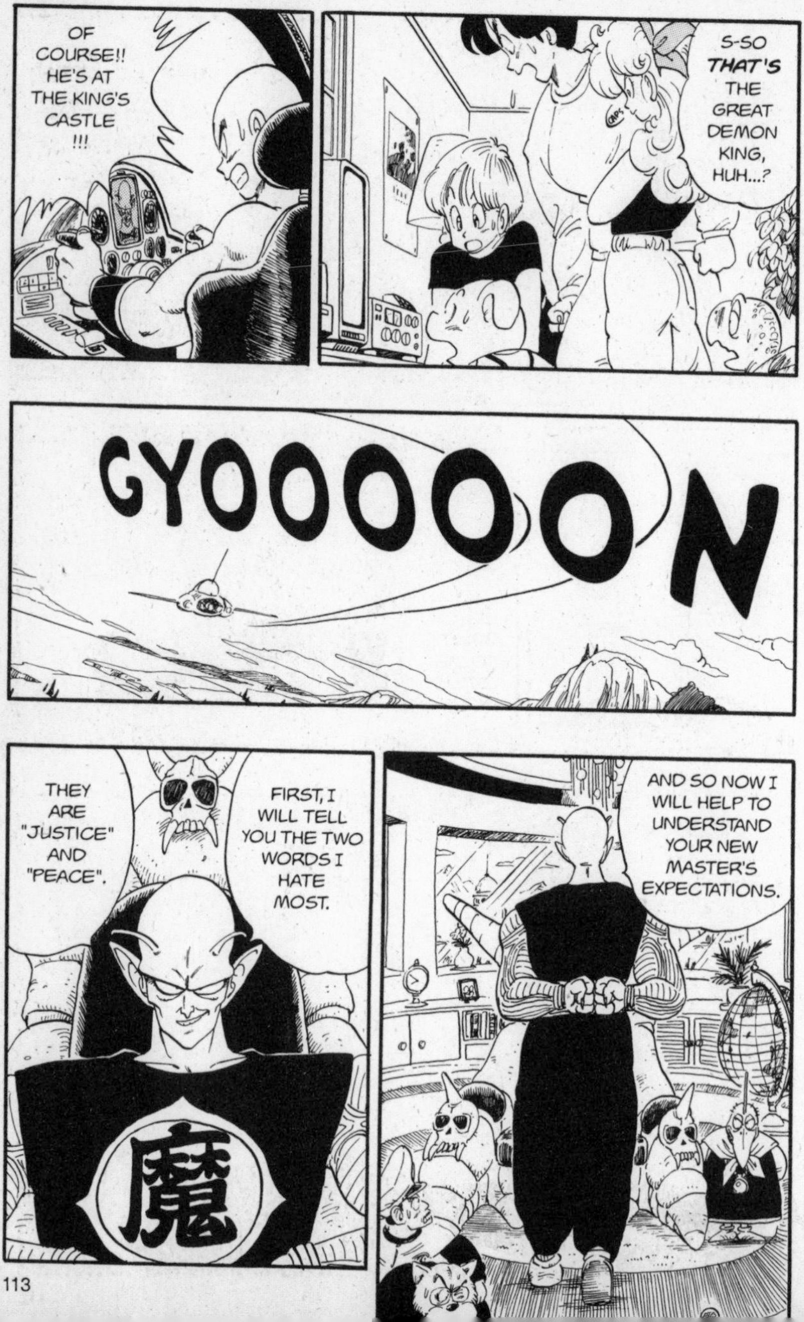
S-SO *THAT'S* THE GREAT DEMON KING, HUH...?
OF COURSE!! HE'S AT THE KING'S CASTLE!!!
GYOOOOON
AND SO NOW I WILL HELP TO UNDERSTAND YOUR NEW MASTER'S EXPECTATIONS.
FIRST, I WILL TELL YOU THE TWO WORDS I HATE MOST.
THEY ARE "JUSTICE" AND "PEACE".
魔

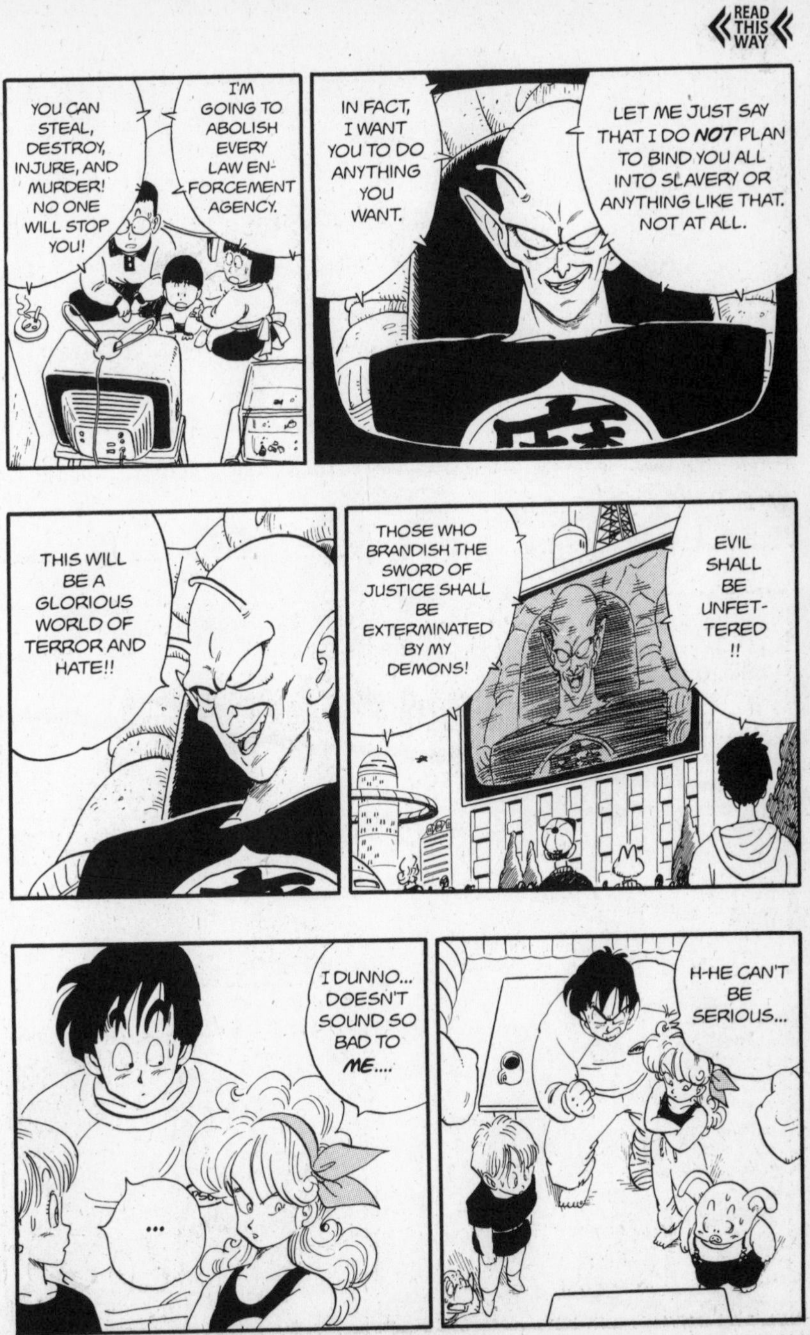
READ THIS WAY
LET ME JUST SAY THAT I DO ***NOT*** PLAN TO BIND YOU ALL INTO SLAVERY OR ANYTHING LIKE THAT. NOT AT ALL.
IN FACT, I WANT YOU TO DO ANYTHING YOU WANT.
I'M GOING TO ABOLISH EVERY LAW EN-FORCEMENT AGENCY.
YOU CAN STEAL, DESTROY, INJURE, AND MURDER! NO ONE WILL STOP YOU!
EVIL SHALL BE UNFET-TERED !!
THOSE WHO BRANDISH THE SWORD OF JUSTICE SHALL BE EXTERMINATED BY MY DEMONS!
THIS WILL BE A GLORIOUS WORLD OF TERROR AND HATE!!
H-HE CAN'T BE SERIOUS...
I DUNNO... DOESN'T SOUND SO BAD TO ***ME***....
...

READ THIS WAY

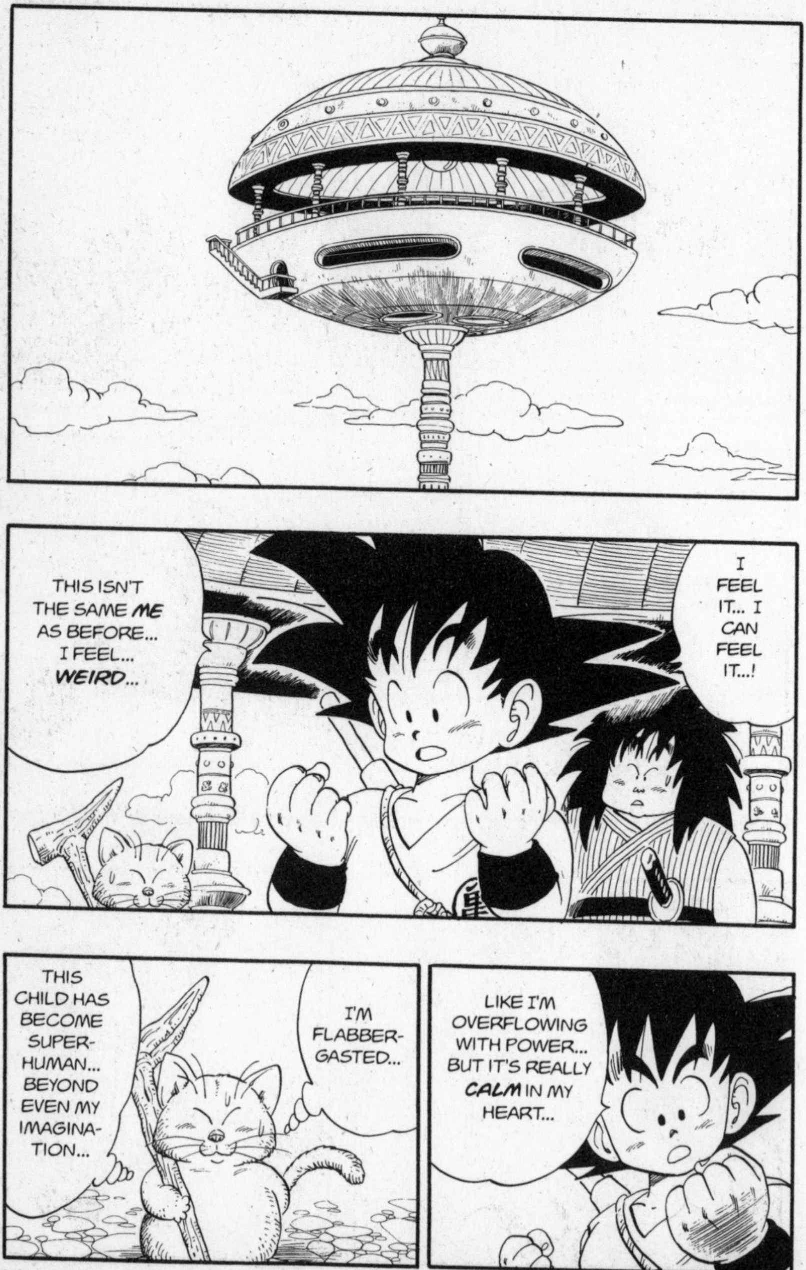
I FEEL IT... I CAN FEEL IT...!
THIS ISN'T THE SAME *ME* AS BEFORE... I FEEL... ***WEIRD***...
LIKE I'M OVERFLOWING WITH POWER... BUT IT'S REALLY ***CALM*** IN MY HEART...
I'M FLABBERGASTED...
THIS CHILD HAS BECOME SUPER-HUMAN... BEYOND EVEN MY IMAGINATION...

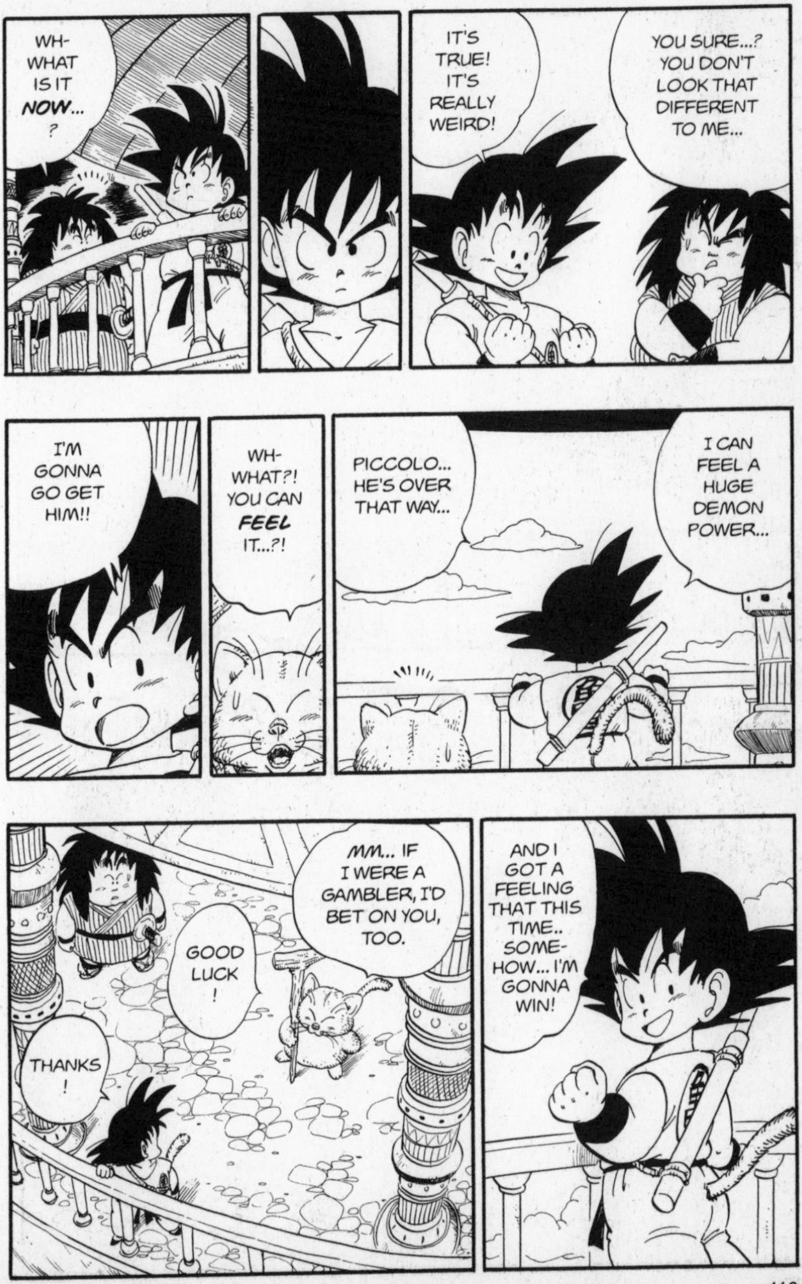
YOU SURE...? YOU DON'T LOOK THAT DIFFERENT TO ME...
IT'S TRUE! IT'S REALLY WEIRD!
WH- WHAT IS IT *NOW*... ?
I CAN FEEL A HUGE DEMON POWER...
PICCOLO... HE'S OVER THAT WAY...
WH- WHAT?! YOU CAN *FEEL* IT...?!
I'M GONNA GO GET HIM!!
AND I GOT A FEELING THAT THIS TIME.. SOME-HOW... I'M GONNA WIN!
MM... IF I WERE A GAMBLER, I'D BET ON YOU, TOO.
GOOD LUCK !
THANKS !

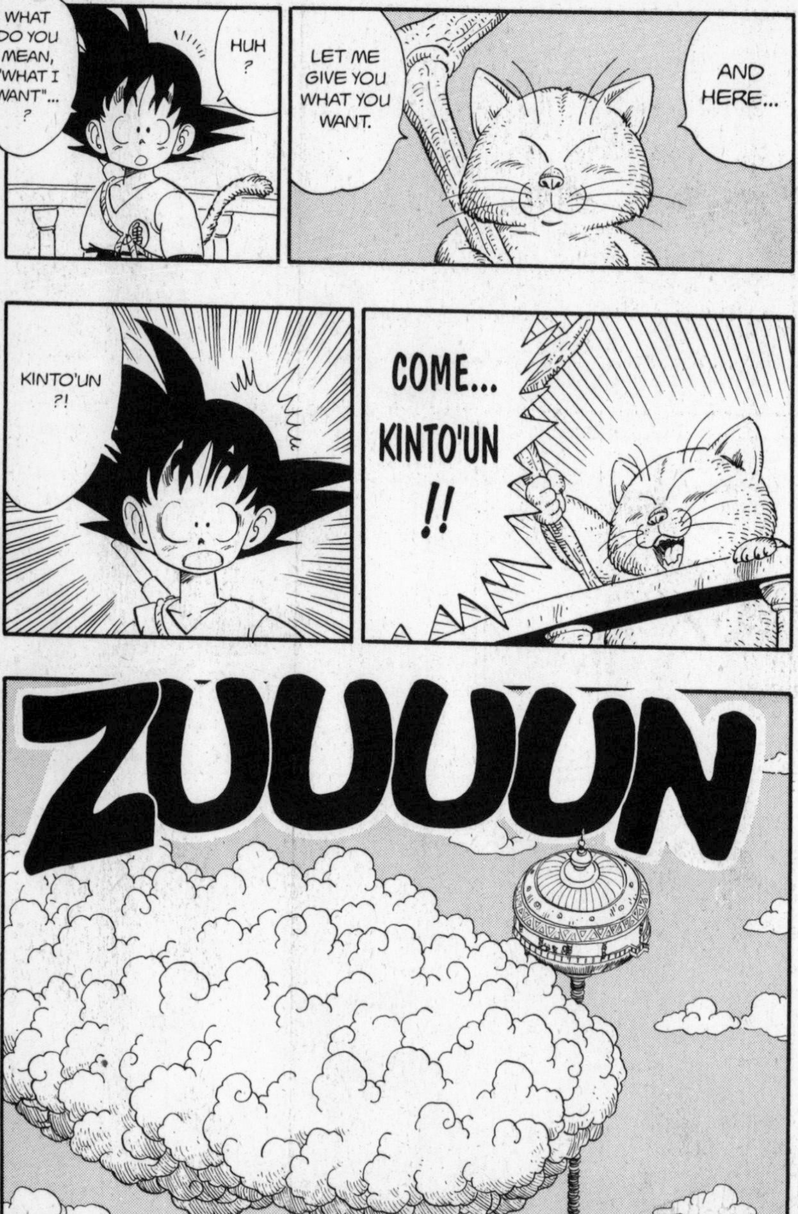
AND HERE...
LET ME GIVE YOU WHAT YOU WANT.
HUH ?
WHAT DO YOU MEAN, "WHAT I WANT"... ?
COME... KINTO'UN !!
KINTO'UN ?!
ZUUUUN

READ THIS WAY

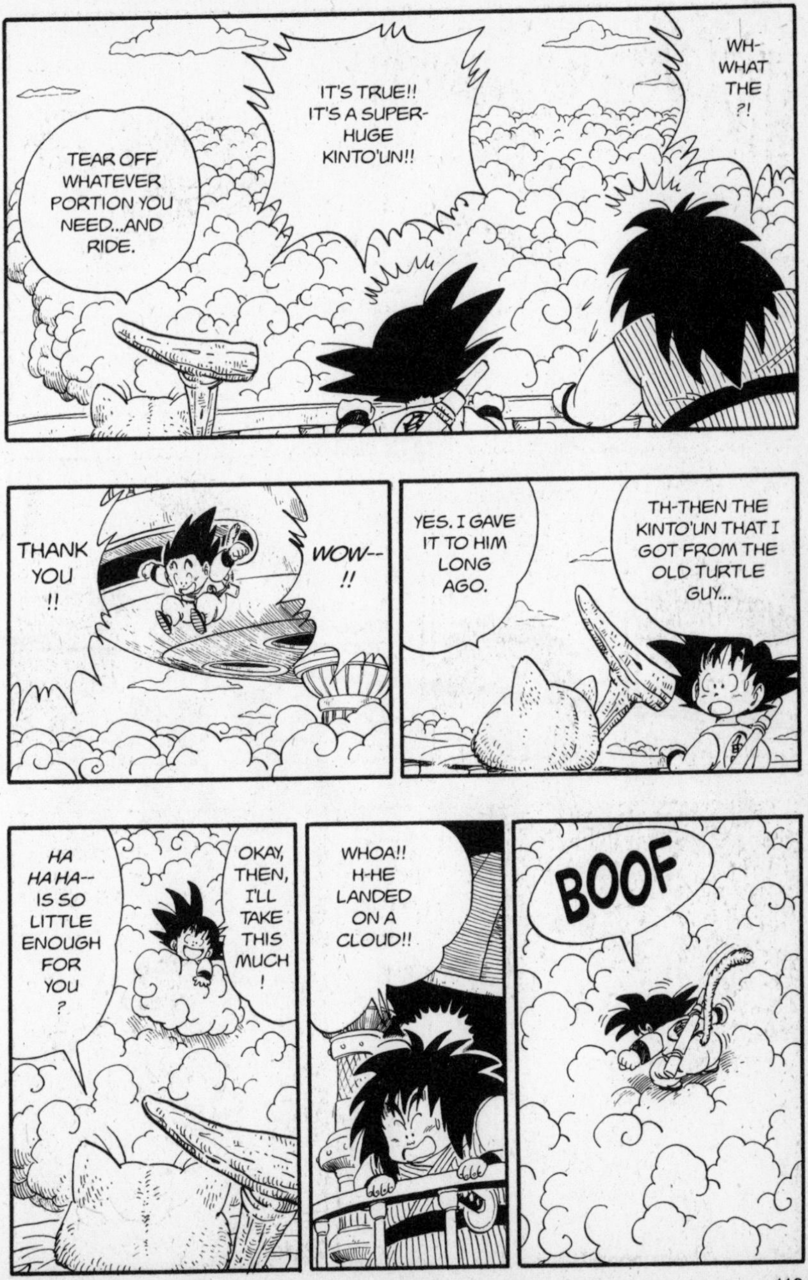
WH- WHAT THE ?!
IT'S TRUE!! IT'S A SUPER-HUGE KINTO'UN!!
TEAR OFF WHATEVER PORTION YOU NEED...AND RIDE.
TH-THEN THE KINTO'UN THAT I GOT FROM THE OLD TURTLE GUY...
YES. I GAVE IT TO HIM LONG AGO.
WOW--!!
THANK YOU!!
BOOF
WHOA!! H-HE LANDED ON A CLOUD!!
OKAY, THEN, I'LL TAKE THIS MUCH!
HA HA HA-- IS SO LITTLE ENOUGH FOR YOU?

READ THIS WAY

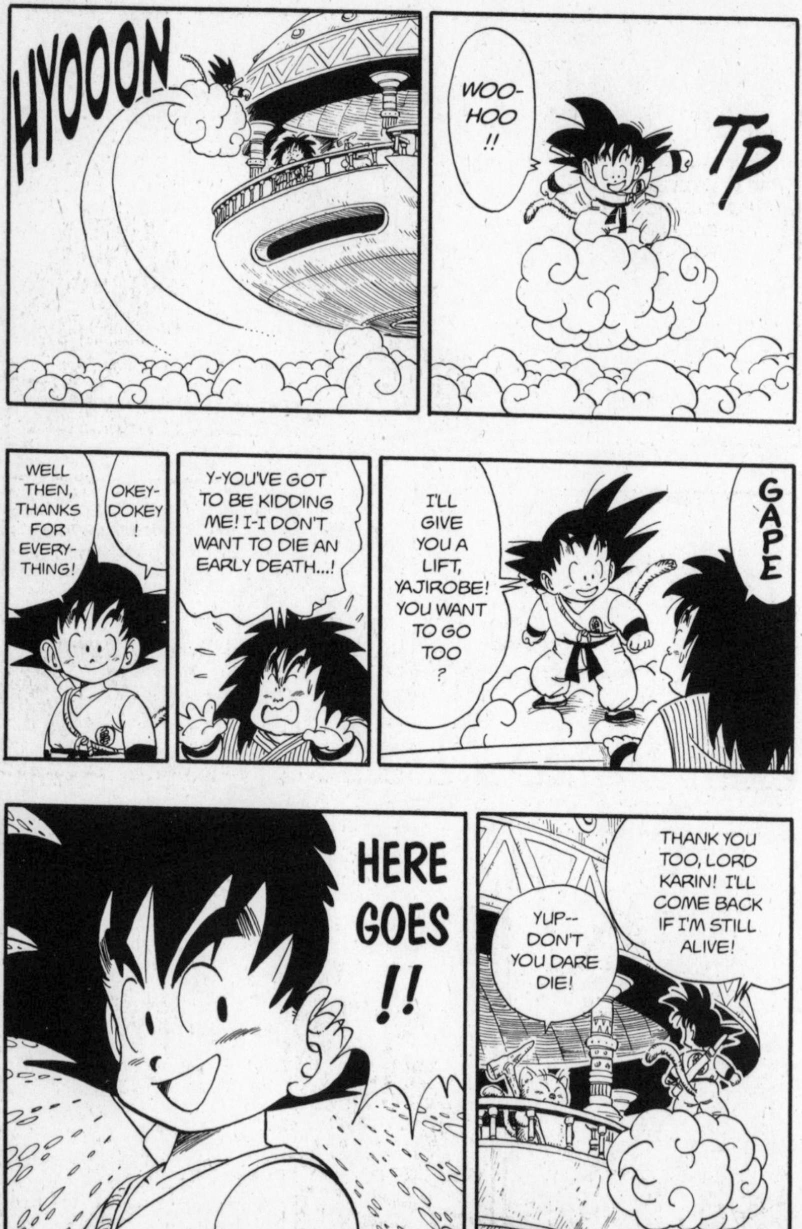
WOO-HOO !!
Tp
HYOOON
GAPE
I'LL GIVE YOU A LIFT, YAJIROBE! YOU WANT TO GO TOO ?
Y-YOU'VE GOT TO BE KIDDING ME! I-I DON'T WANT TO DIE AN EARLY DEATH...!
OKEY-DOKEY !
WELL THEN, THANKS FOR EVERY-THING!
THANK YOU TOO, LORD KARIN! I'LL COME BACK IF I'M STILL ALIVE!
YUP-- DON'T YOU DARE DIE!
HERE GOES !!

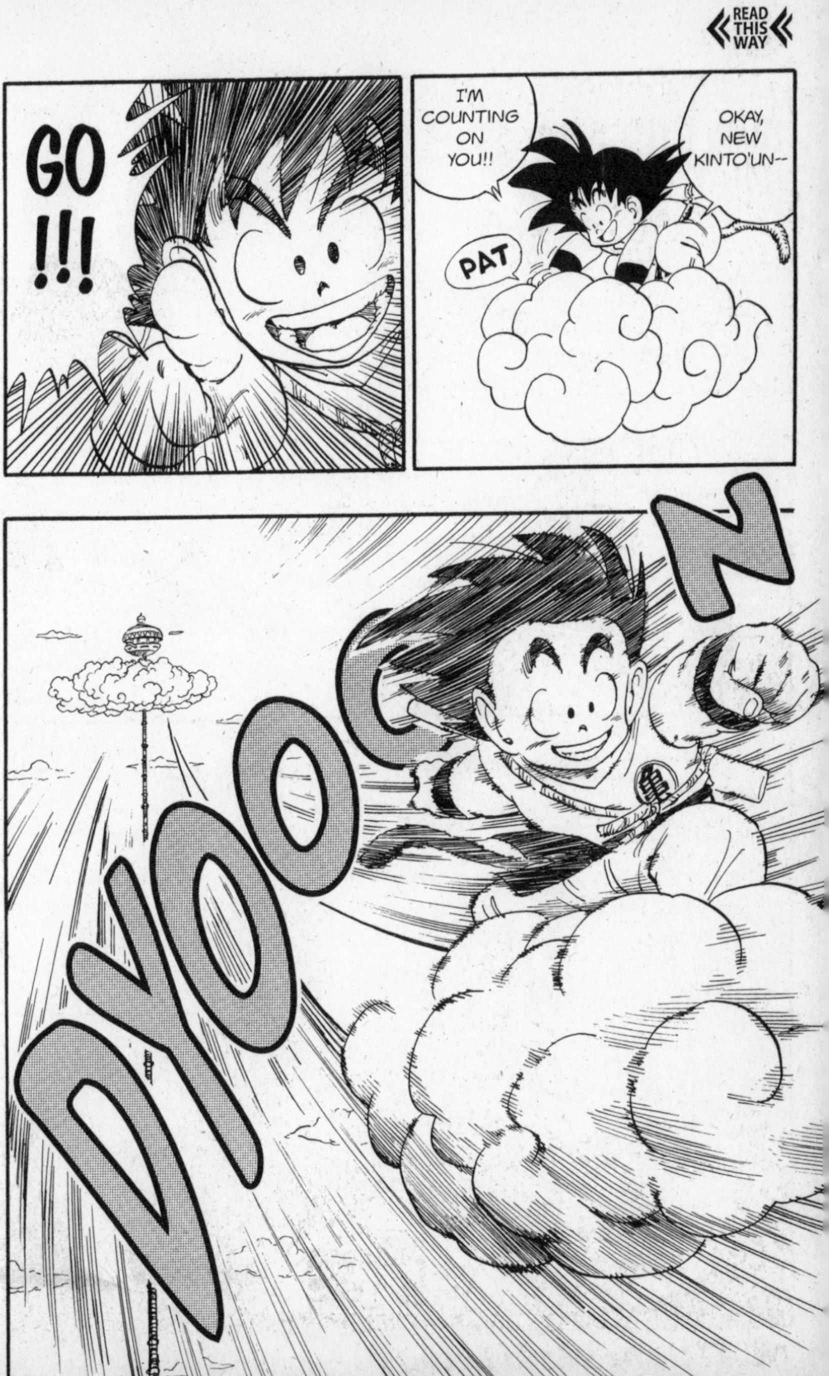
READ THIS WAY
OKAY, NEW KINTO'UN--
I'M COUNTING ON YOU!!
PAT
GO !!!
DYOOON

READ THIS WAY

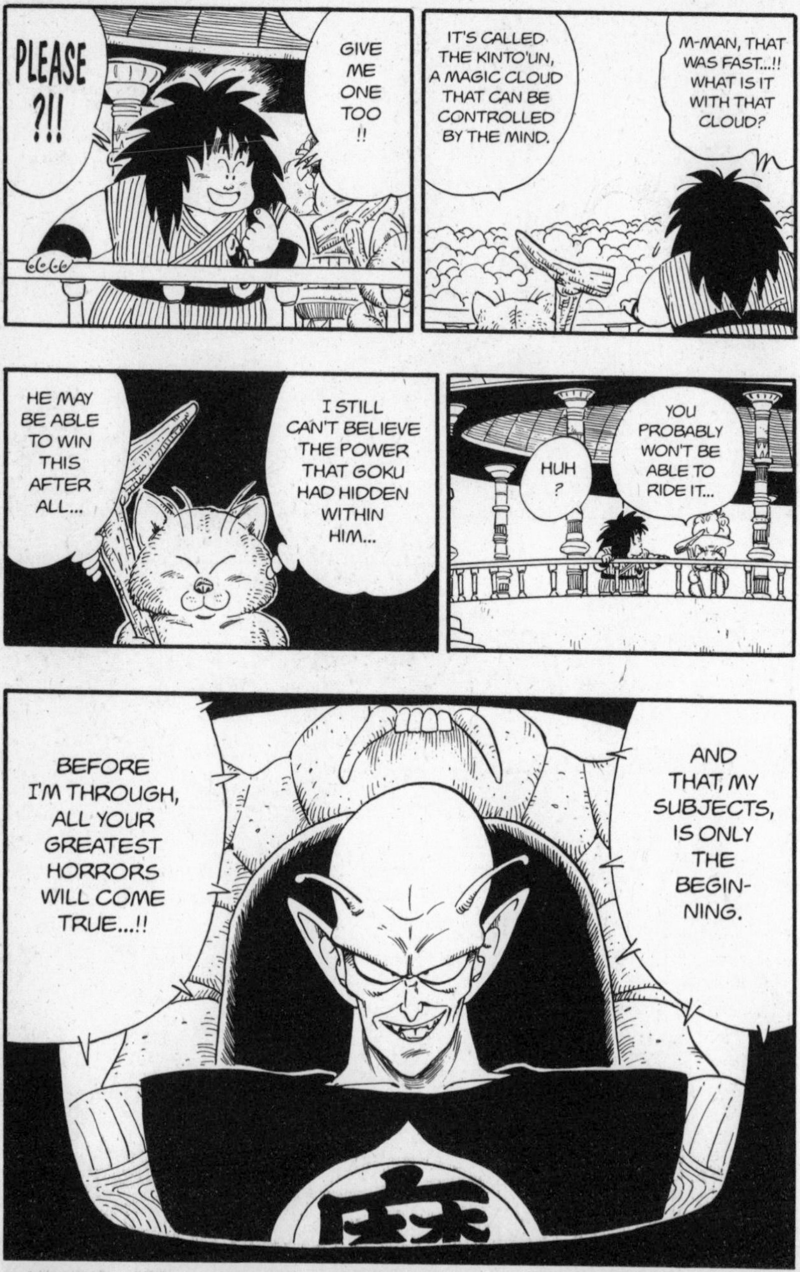
M-MAN, THAT WAS FAST...!! WHAT IS IT WITH THAT CLOUD?
IT'S CALLED THE KINTO'UN, A MAGIC CLOUD THAT CAN BE CONTROLLED BY THE MIND.
GIVE ME ONE TOO !!
PLEASE ?!!
YOU PROBABLY WON'T BE ABLE TO RIDE IT...
HUH ?
I STILL CAN'T BELIEVE THE POWER THAT GOKU HAD HIDDEN WITHIN HIM...
HE MAY BE ABLE TO WIN THIS AFTER ALL...
AND THAT, MY SUBJECTS, IS ONLY THE BEGIN-NING.
BEFORE I'M THROUGH, ALL YOUR GREATEST HORRORS WILL COME TRUE...!!

NEXT: The World Lottery

READ THIS WAY

Tale 153 • Tenshinhan's Decision!!

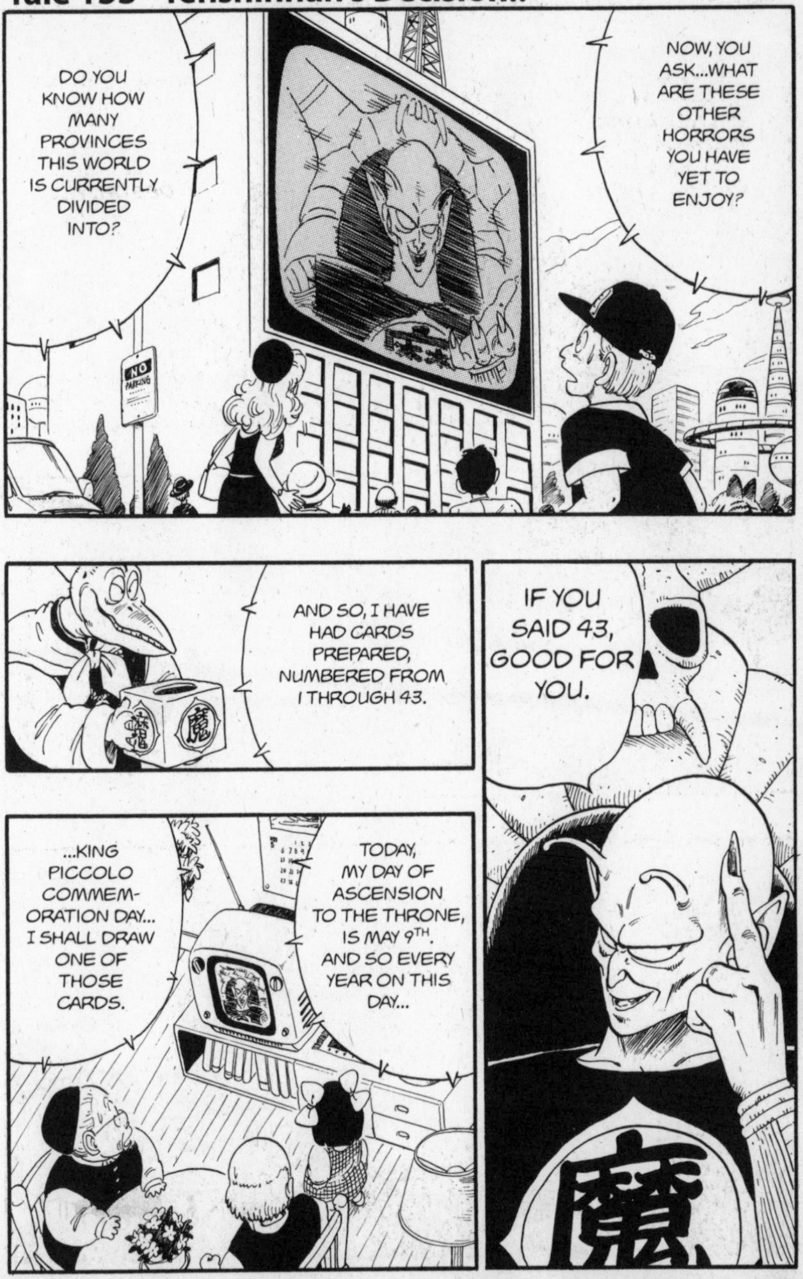
NOW, YOU ASK...WHAT ARE THESE OTHER HORRORS YOU HAVE YET TO ENJOY?
DO YOU KNOW HOW MANY PROVINCES THIS WORLD IS CURRENTLY DIVIDED INTO?
NO PARKING
IF YOU SAID 43, GOOD FOR YOU.
AND SO, I HAVE HAD CARDS PREPARED, NUMBERED FROM 1 THROUGH 43.
TODAY, MY DAY OF ASCENSION TO THE THRONE, IS MAY 9TH. AND SO EVERY YEAR ON THIS DAY...
...KING PICCOLO COMMEMORATION DAY... I SHALL DRAW ONE OF THOSE CARDS.

READ THIS WAY

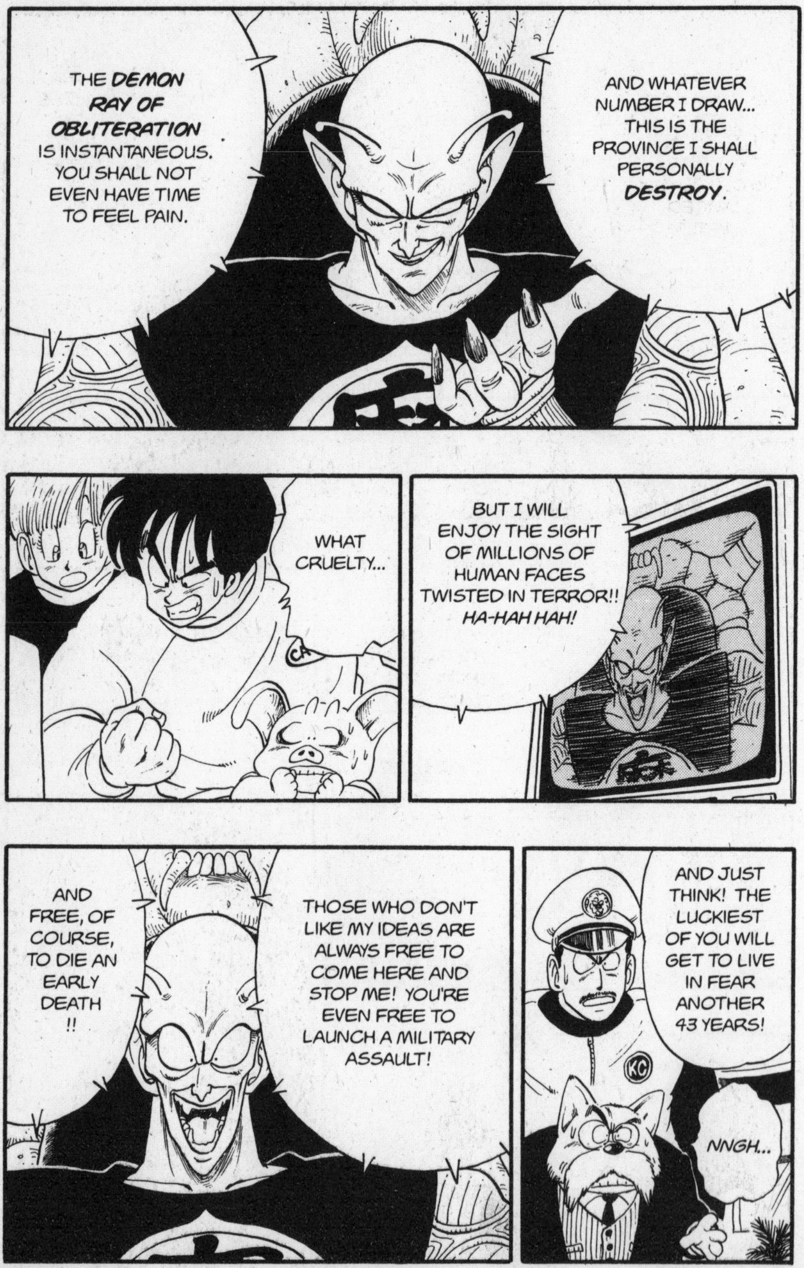

AND WHATEVER NUMBER I DRAW... THIS IS THE PROVINCE I SHALL PERSONALLY DESTROY.
THE DEMON RAY OF OBLITERATION IS INSTANTANEOUS. YOU SHALL NOT EVEN HAVE TIME TO FEEL PAIN.
BUT I WILL ENJOY THE SIGHT OF MILLIONS OF HUMAN FACES TWISTED IN TERROR!! HA-HAH HAH!
WHAT CRUELTY...
AND JUST THINK! THE LUCKIEST OF YOU WILL GET TO LIVE IN FEAR ANOTHER 43 YEARS!
NNGH...
THOSE WHO DON'T LIKE MY IDEAS ARE ALWAYS FREE TO COME HERE AND STOP ME! YOU'RE EVEN FREE TO LAUNCH A MILITARY ASSAULT!
AND FREE, OF COURSE, TO DIE AN EARLY DEATH !!

READ THIS WAY

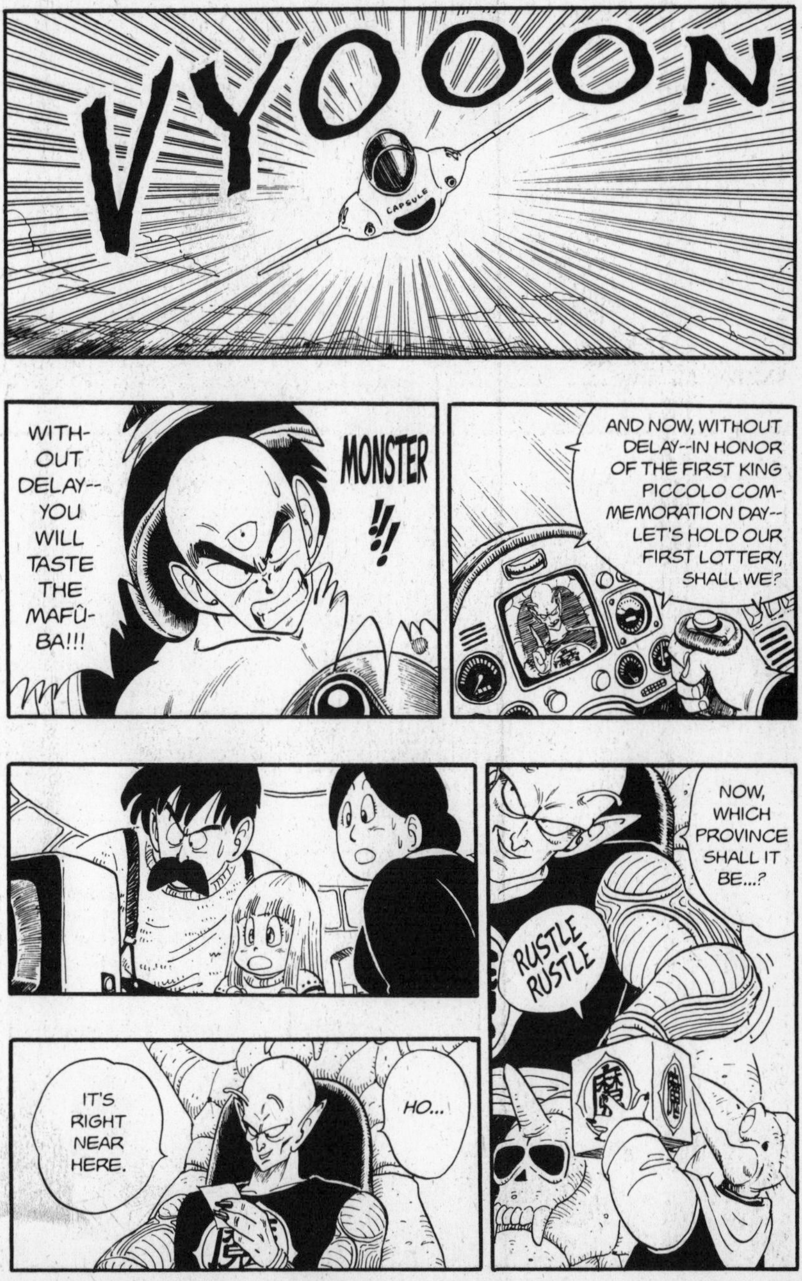

VYOOON
CAPSULE
AND NOW, WITHOUT DELAY--IN HONOR OF THE FIRST KING PICCOLO COMMEMORATION DAY--LET'S HOLD OUR FIRST LOTTERY, SHALL WE?
WITHOUT DELAY--YOU WILL TASTE THE MAFÛBA!!!
MONSTER !!!
NOW, WHICH PROVINCE SHALL IT BE...?
RUSTLE RUSTLE
HO...
IT'S RIGHT NEAR HERE.

READ THIS WAY

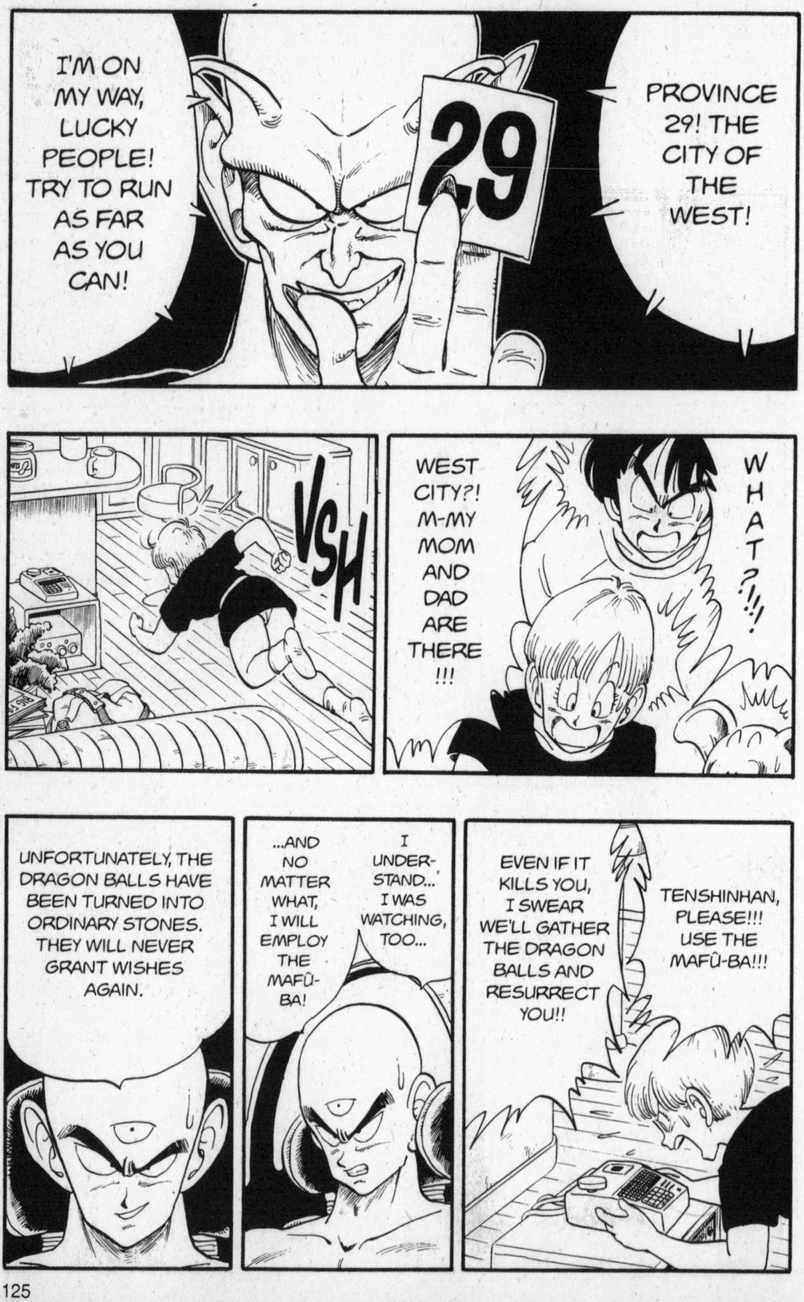
PROVINCE 29! THE CITY OF THE WEST!
I'M ON MY WAY, LUCKY PEOPLE! TRY TO RUN AS FAR AS YOU CAN!
29
WHAT?!!!
WEST CITY?! M-MY MOM AND DAD ARE THERE!!!
VSH
TENSHINHAN, PLEASE!!! USE THE MAFÛ-BA!!!
EVEN IF IT KILLS YOU, I SWEAR WE'LL GATHER THE DRAGON BALLS AND RESURRECT YOU!!
I UNDERSTAND... I WAS WATCHING, TOO...
...AND NO MATTER WHAT, I WILL EMPLOY THE MAFÛ-BA!
UNFORTUNATELY, THE DRAGON BALLS HAVE BEEN TURNED INTO ORDINARY STONES. THEY WILL NEVER GRANT WISHES AGAIN.

READ THIS WAY

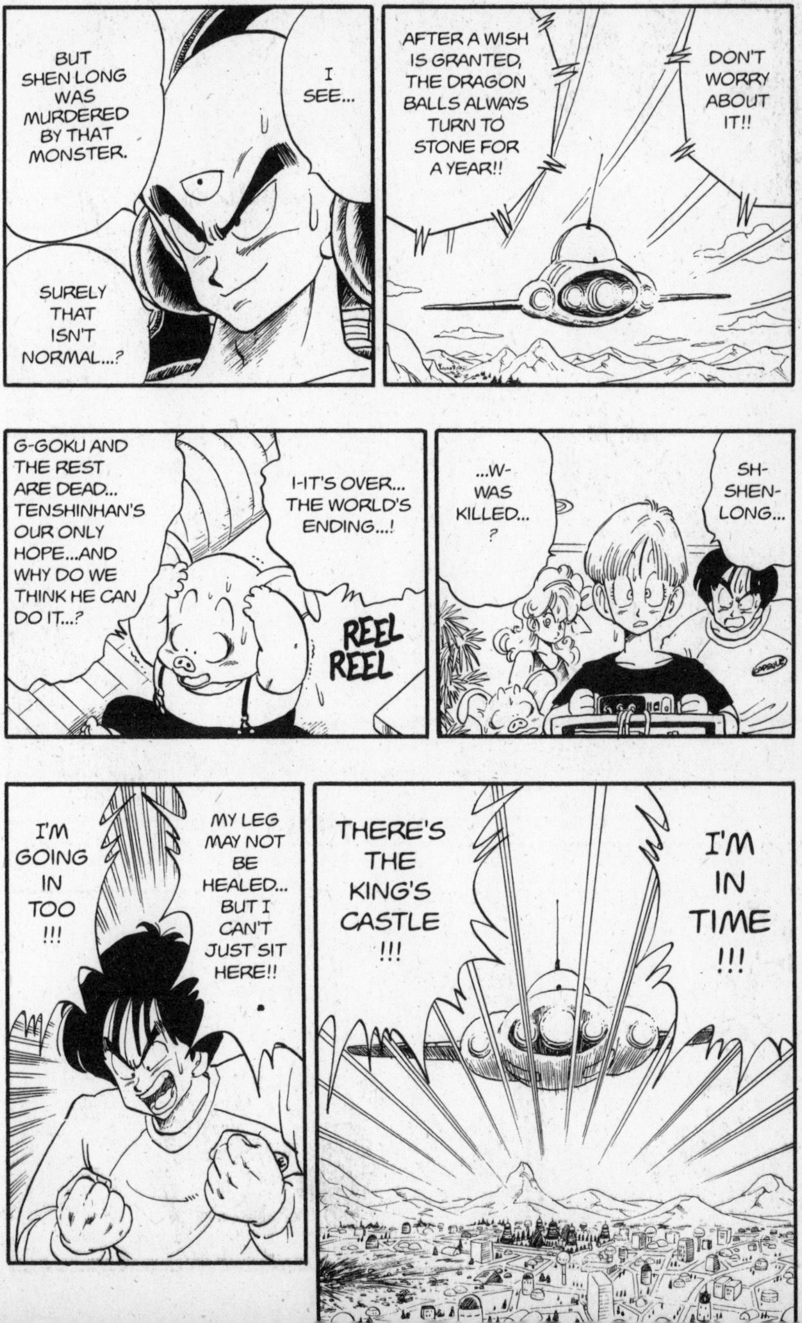
DON'T WORRY ABOUT IT!!
AFTER A WISH IS GRANTED, THE DRAGON BALLS ALWAYS TURN TO STONE FOR A YEAR!!
I SEE...
BUT SHEN LONG WAS MURDERED BY THAT MONSTER.
SURELY THAT ISN'T NORMAL...?
SH-SHEN-LONG...
...W-WAS KILLED...?
I-IT'S OVER... THE WORLD'S ENDING...!
G-GOKU AND THE REST ARE DEAD... TENSHINHAN'S OUR ONLY HOPE...AND WHY DO WE THINK HE CAN DO IT...?
REEL REEL
I'M IN TIME!!!
THERE'S THE KING'S CASTLE!!!
MY LEG MAY NOT BE HEALED... BUT I CAN'T JUST SIT HERE!!
I'M GOING IN TOO!!!

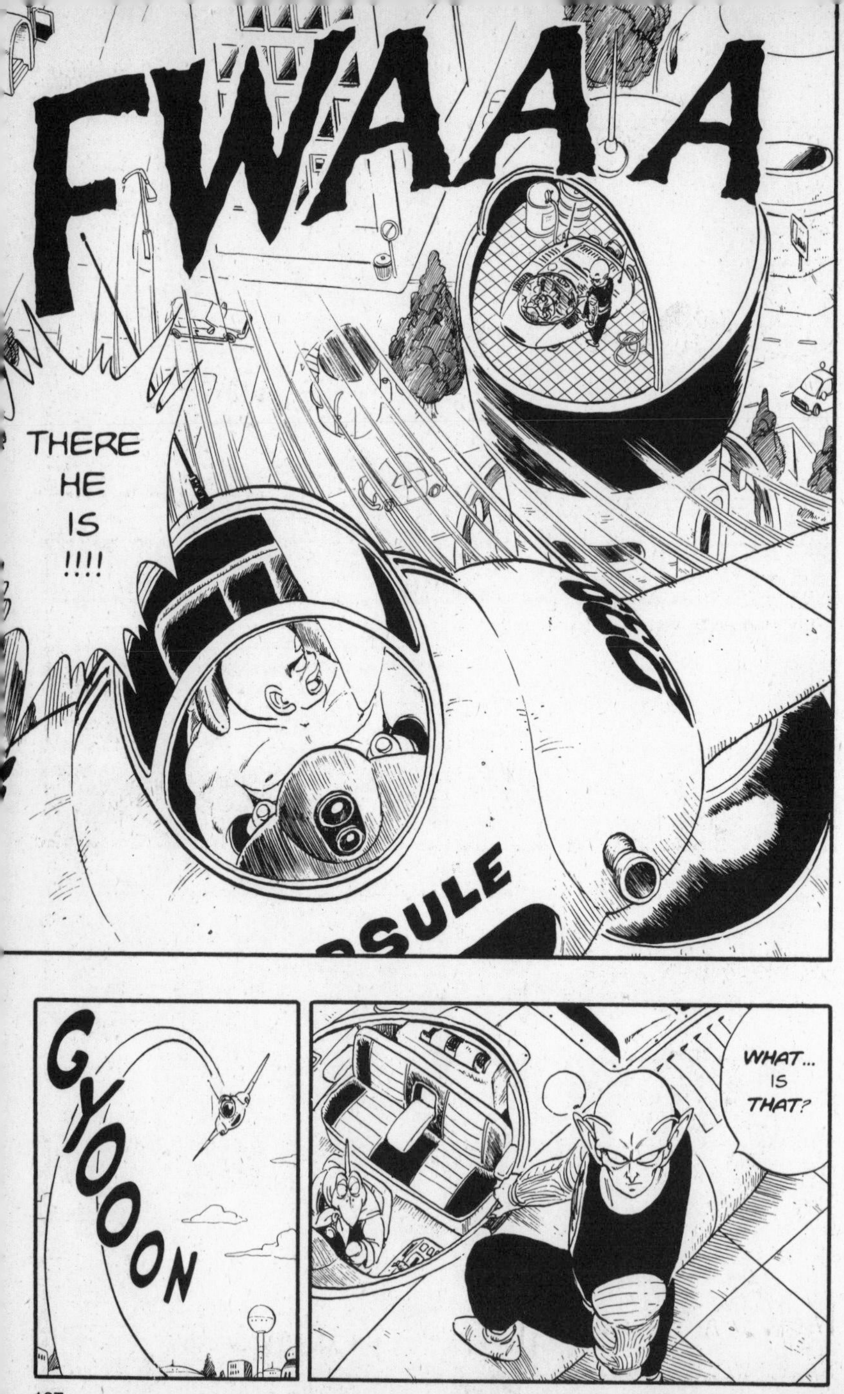
FWAAA
THERE HE IS!!!!
WHAT... IS THAT?
GYOOOON

READ THIS WAY

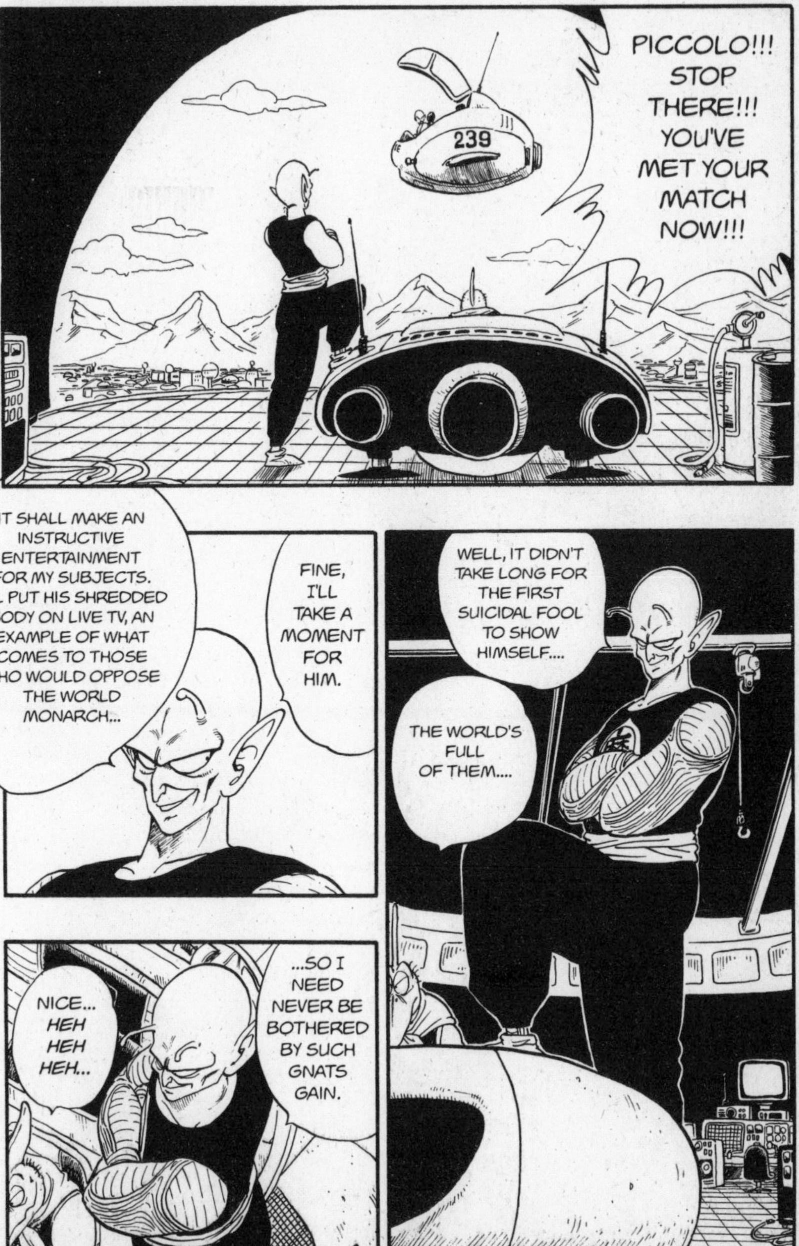

PICCOLO!!! STOP THERE!!! YOU'VE MET YOUR MATCH NOW!!!
239
WELL, IT DIDN'T TAKE LONG FOR THE FIRST SUICIDAL FOOL TO SHOW HIMSELF....
THE WORLD'S FULL OF THEM....
FINE, I'LL TAKE A MOMENT FOR HIM.
IT SHALL MAKE AN INSTRUCTIVE ENTERTAINMENT FOR MY SUBJECTS. I'LL PUT HIS SHREDDED BODY ON LIVE TV, AN EXAMPLE OF WHAT COMES TO THOSE WHO WOULD OPPOSE THE WORLD MONARCH...
...SO I NEED NEVER BE BOTHERED BY SUCH GNATS GAIN.
NICE... HEH HEH HEH...

READ THIS WAY

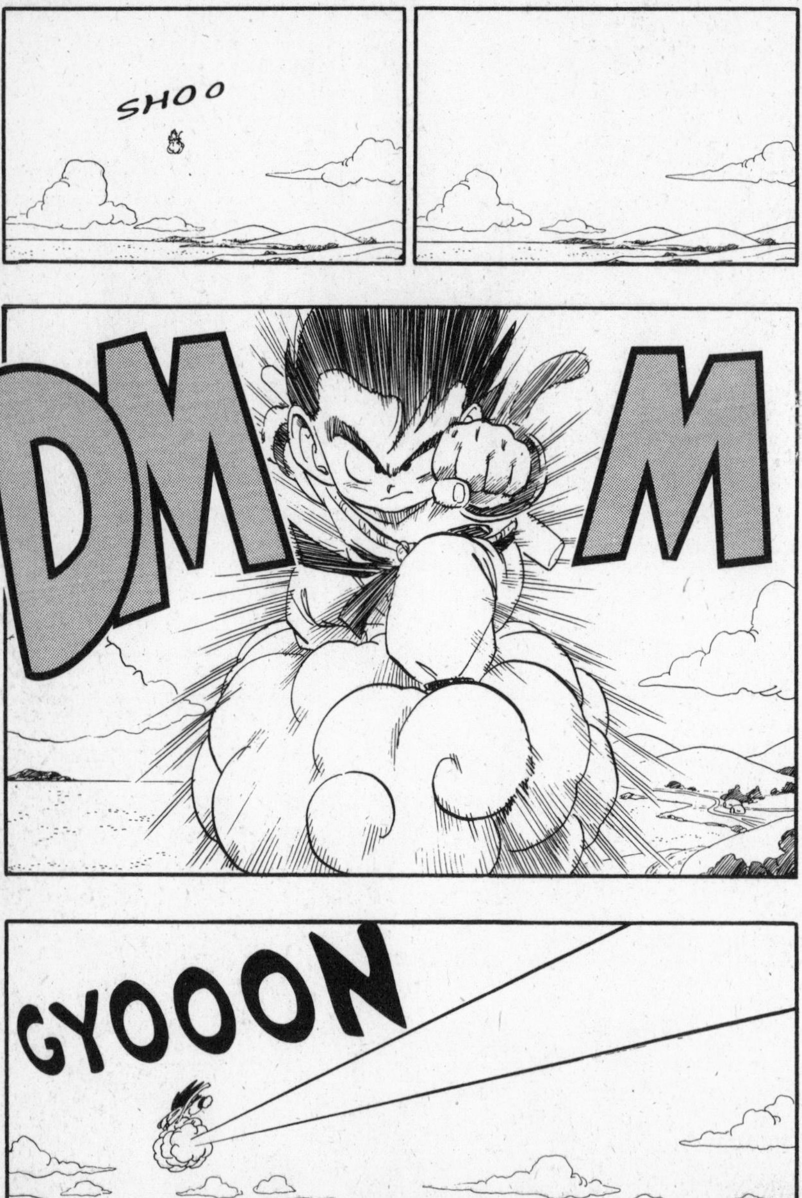
SHOO
DM M
GYOOON

READ THIS WAY

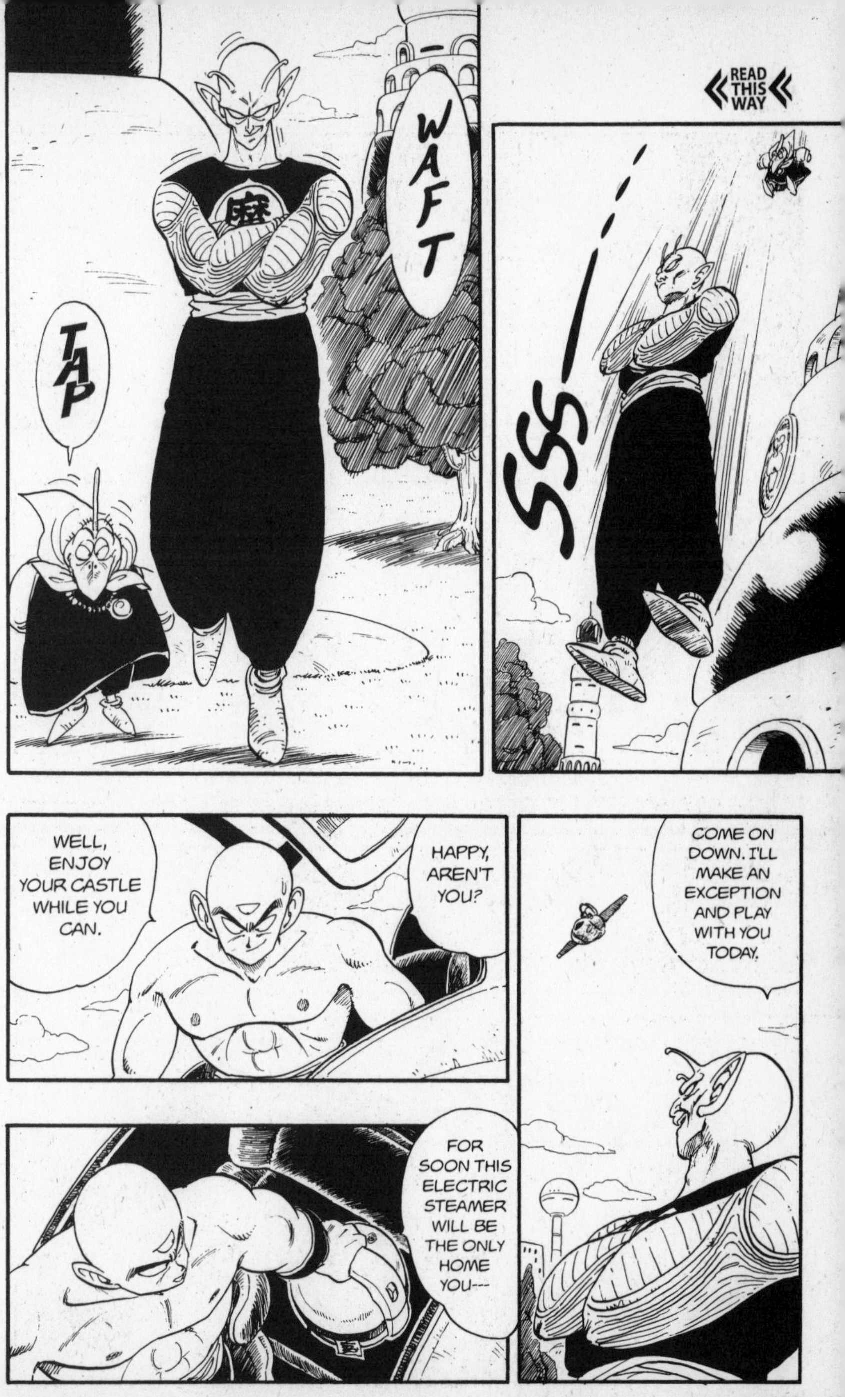
SSS—
WAFT
TAP
COME ON DOWN. I'LL MAKE AN EXCEPTION AND PLAY WITH YOU TODAY.
HAPPY, AREN'T YOU?
WELL, ENJOY YOUR CASTLE WHILE YOU CAN.
FOR SOON THIS ELECTRIC STEAMER WILL BE THE ONLY HOME YOU--

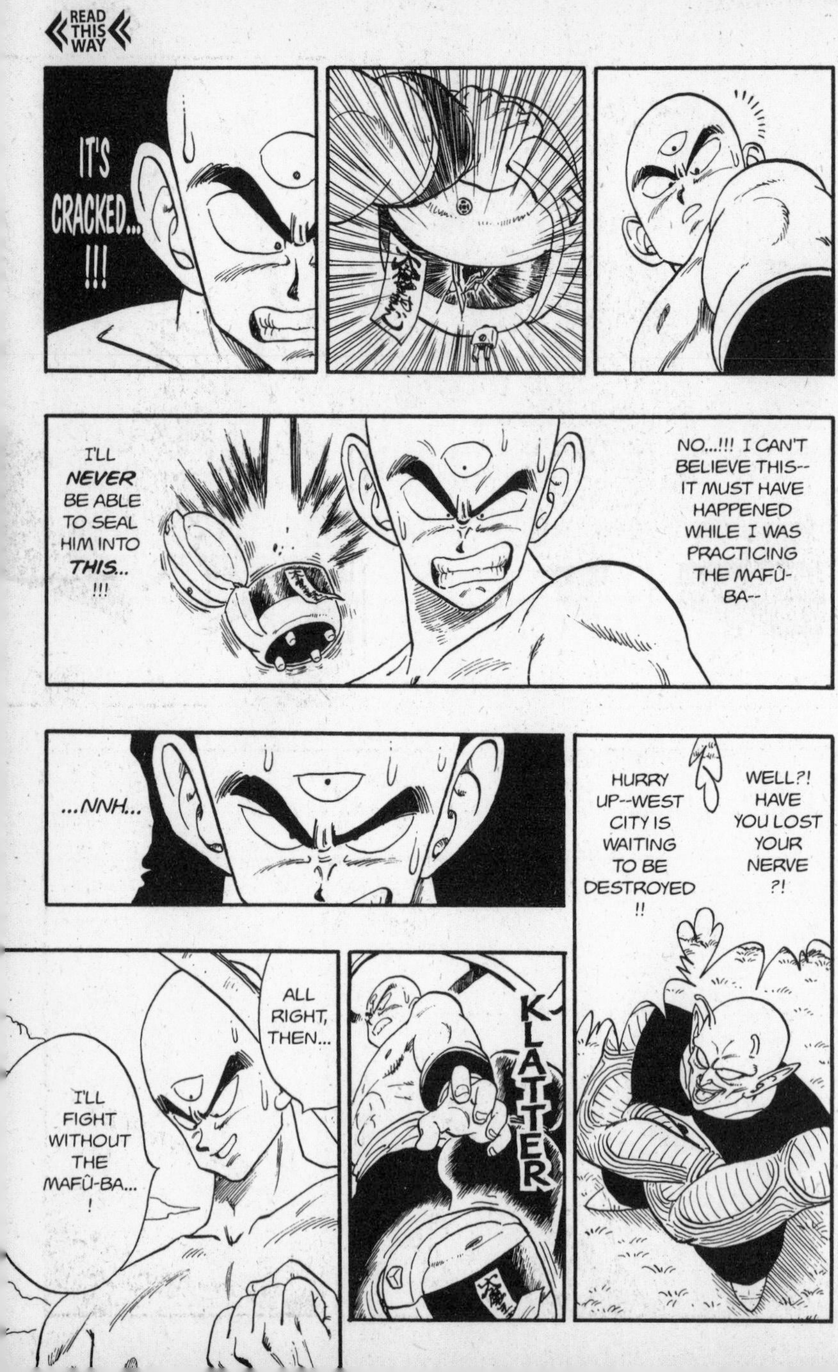

READ THIS WAY
IT'S CRACKED... !!!
NO...!!! I CAN'T BELIEVE THIS-- IT MUST HAVE HAPPENED WHILE I WAS PRACTICING THE MAFÛ-BA--
I'LL NEVER BE ABLE TO SEAL HIM INTO THIS... !!!
WELL?! HAVE YOU LOST YOUR NERVE ?!
HURRY UP--WEST CITY IS WAITING TO BE DESTROYED !!
...NNH...
KLATTER
ALL RIGHT, THEN...
I'LL FIGHT WITHOUT THE MAFÛ-BA... !

READ THIS WAY

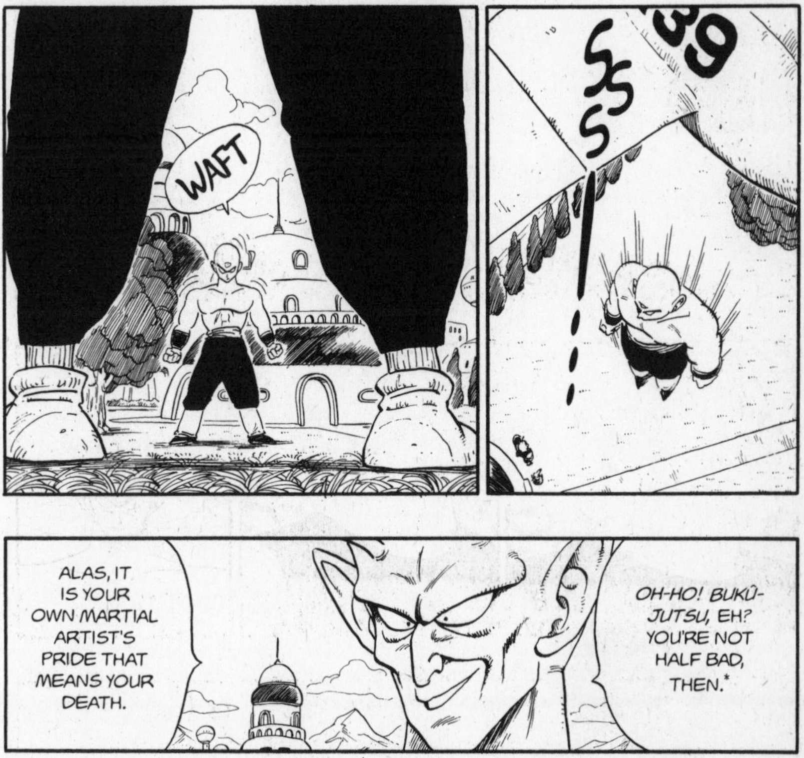
WAFT
OH-HO! BUKÛ-JUTSU, EH? YOU'RE NOT HALF BAD, THEN.*
ALAS, IT IS YOUR OWN MARTIAL ARTIST'S PRIDE THAT MEANS YOUR DEATH.

* *BUKÛ-JUTSU* = "THE TECHNIQUE OF HOVERING IN THE AIR"

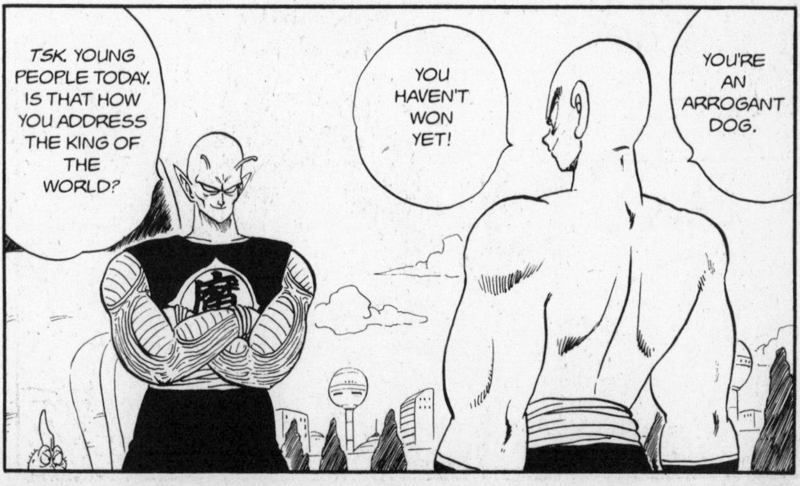
YOU'RE AN ARROGANT DOG.
YOU HAVEN'T WON YET!
TSK. YOUNG PEOPLE TODAY. IS THAT HOW YOU ADDRESS THE KING OF THE WORLD?

READ THIS WAY

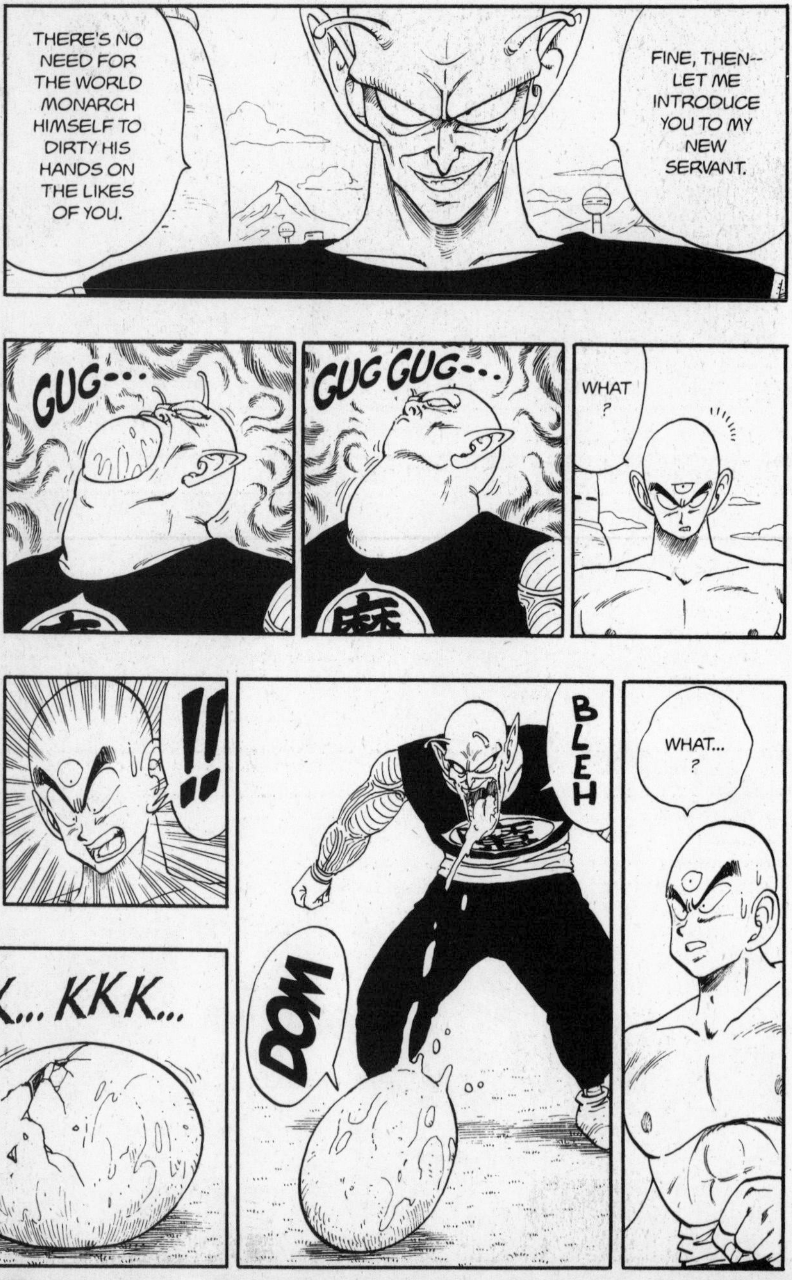
FINE, THEN-- LET ME INTRODUCE YOU TO MY NEW SERVANT.
THERE'S NO NEED FOR THE WORLD MONARCH HIMSELF TO DIRTY HIS HANDS ON THE LIKES OF YOU.
WHAT ?
GUG GUG--...
GUG--...
WHAT... ?
BLEH
DOM
!!
K... KKK...

READ THIS WAY

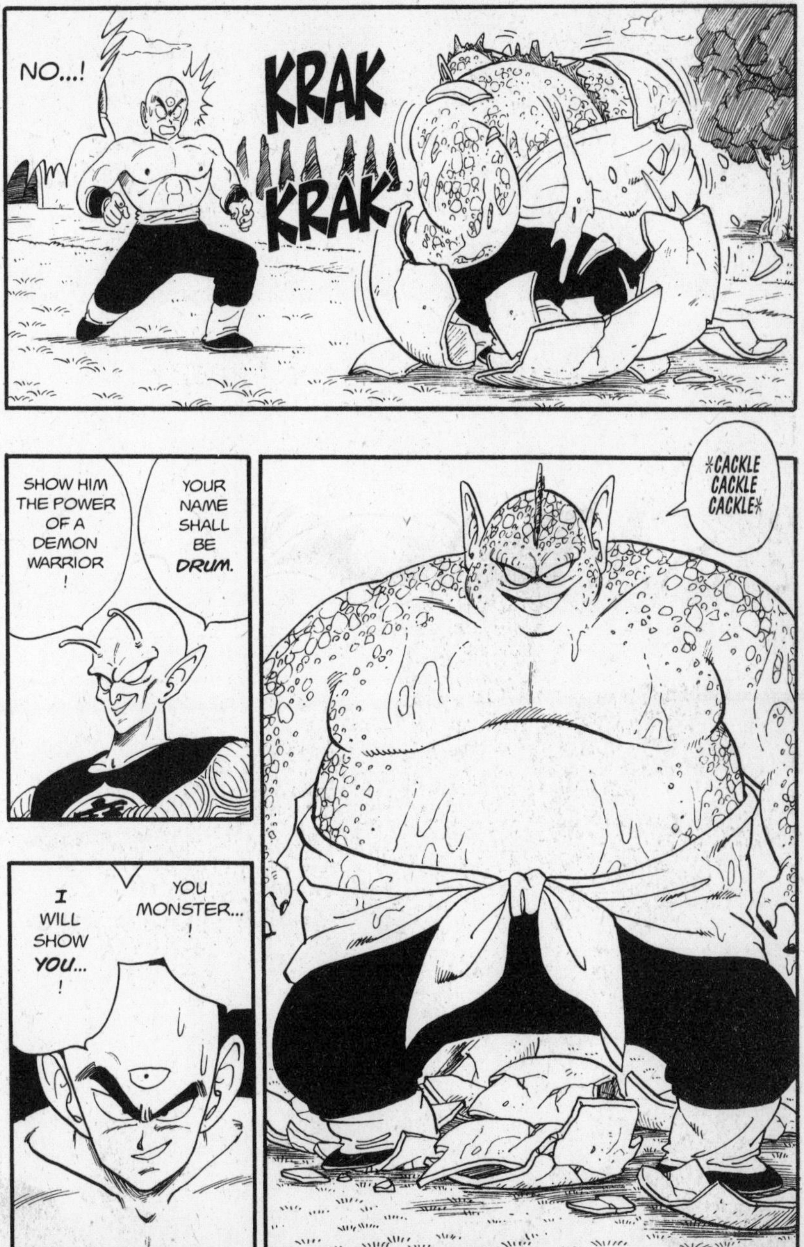
KRAK KRAK
NO...!
CACKLE CACKLE CACKLE
YOUR NAME SHALL BE **DRUM**.
SHOW HIM THE POWER OF A DEMON WARRIOR!
YOU MONSTER...!
I WILL SHOW **YOU**...!

Tale 154 • Tenshinhan vs. Drum

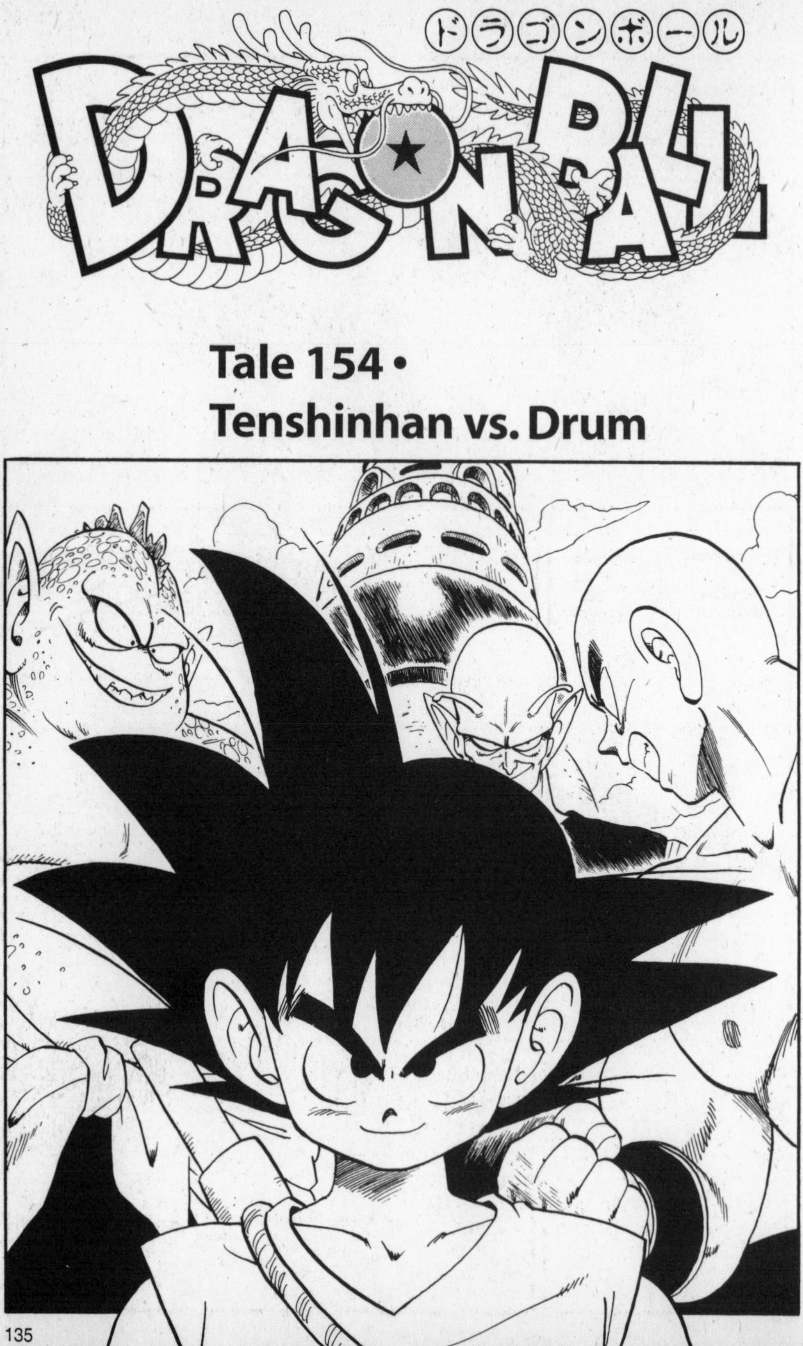

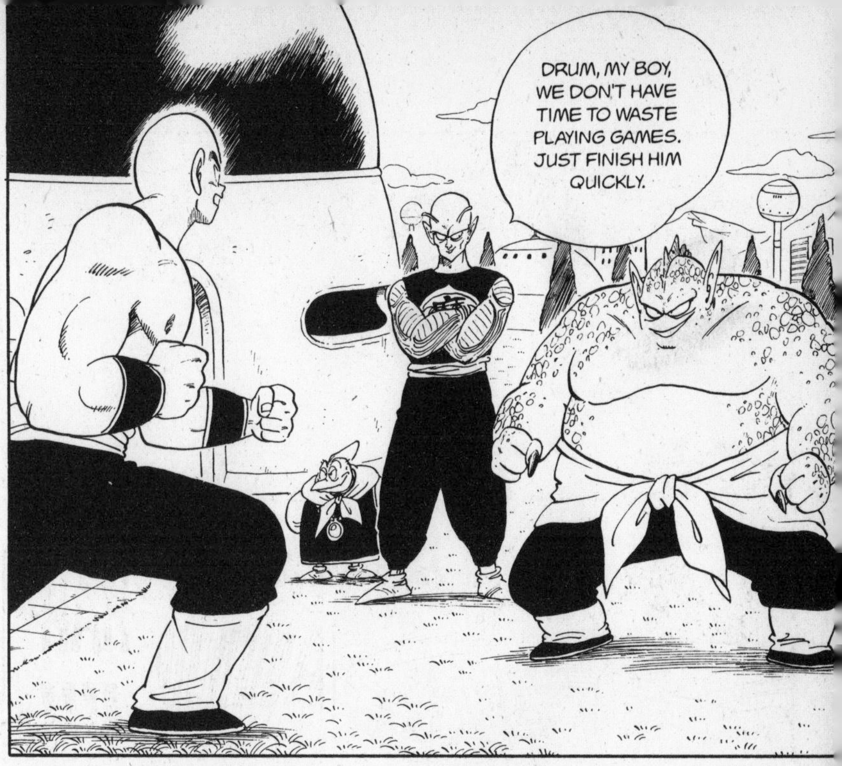
DRUM, MY BOY, WE DON'T HAVE TIME TO WASTE PLAYING GAMES. JUST FINISH HIM QUICKLY.

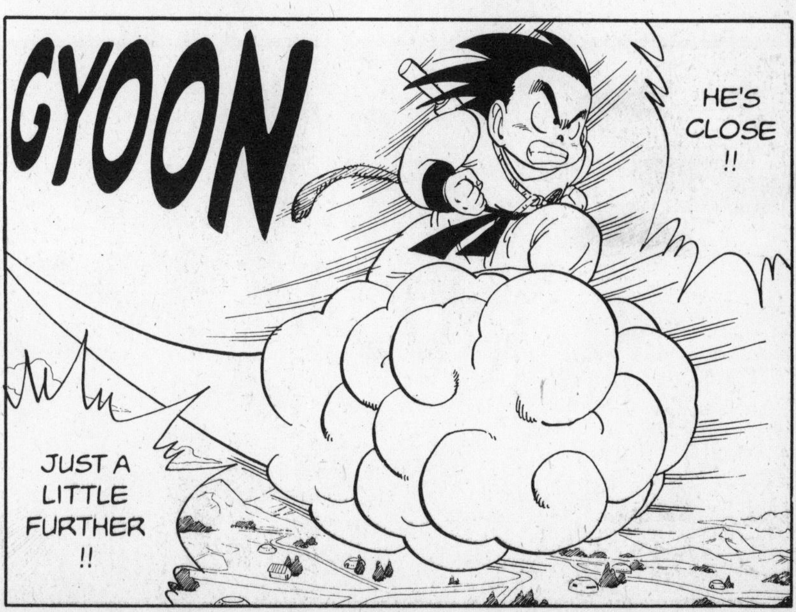
GYOON
HE'S CLOSE !!
JUST A LITTLE FURTHER !!

READ THIS WAY

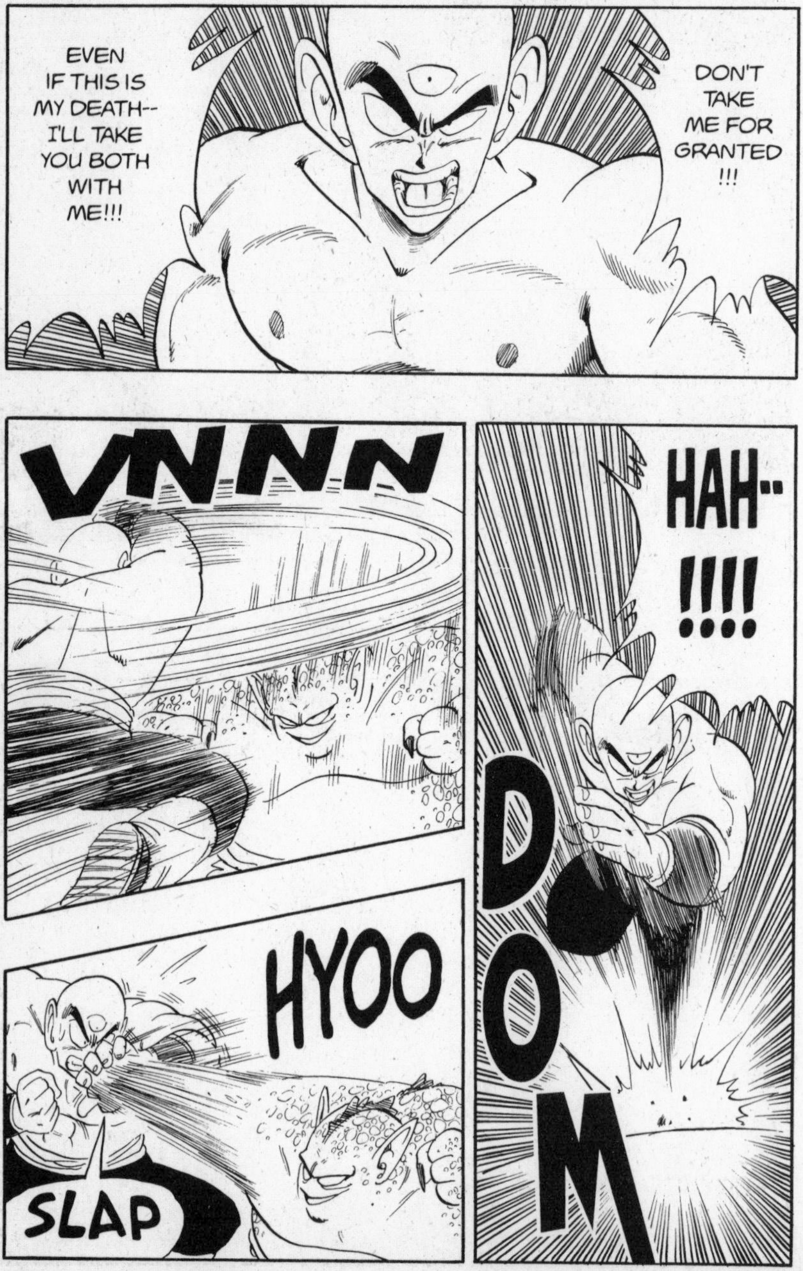
DON'T TAKE ME FOR GRANTED !!!
EVEN IF THIS IS MY DEATH-- I'LL TAKE YOU BOTH WITH ME!!!
HAH-- !!!!
DOM
VNNN
HYOO
SLAP

READ THIS WAY

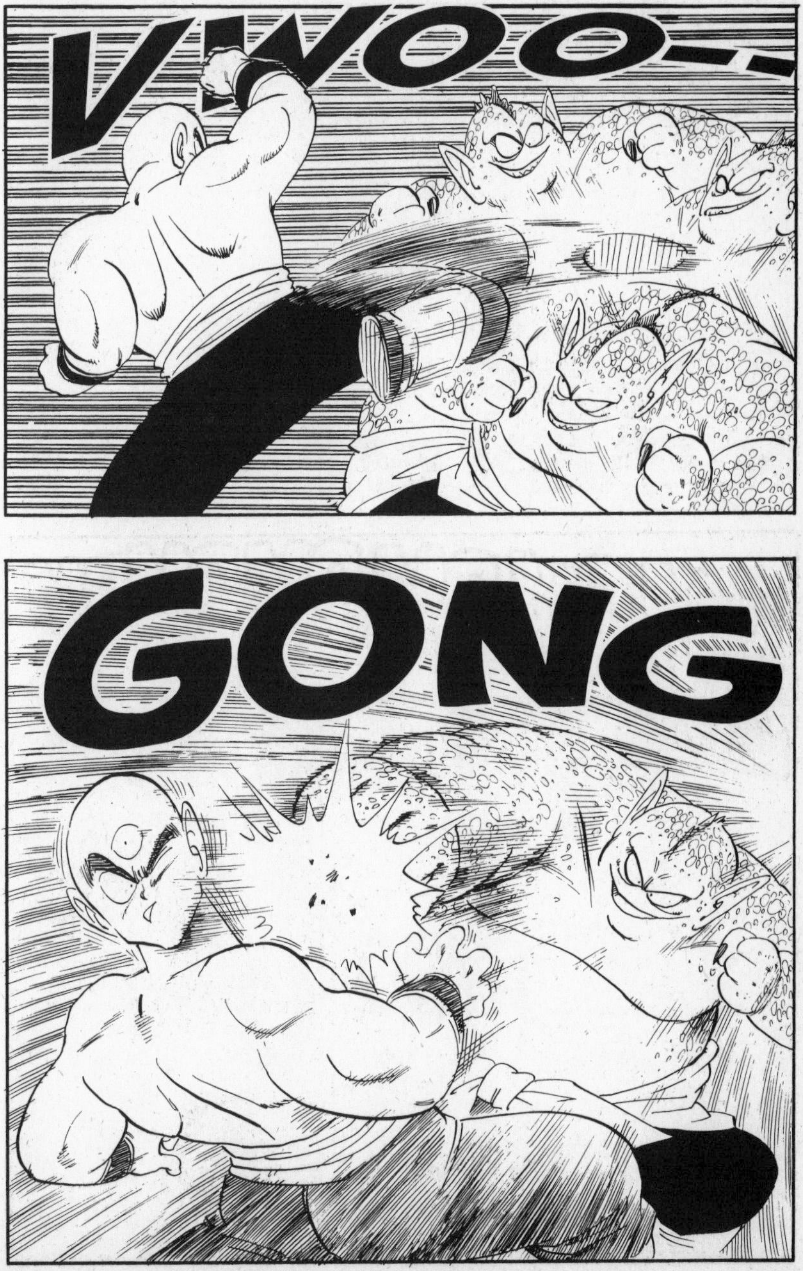
VWOO--
GONG

READ THIS WAY

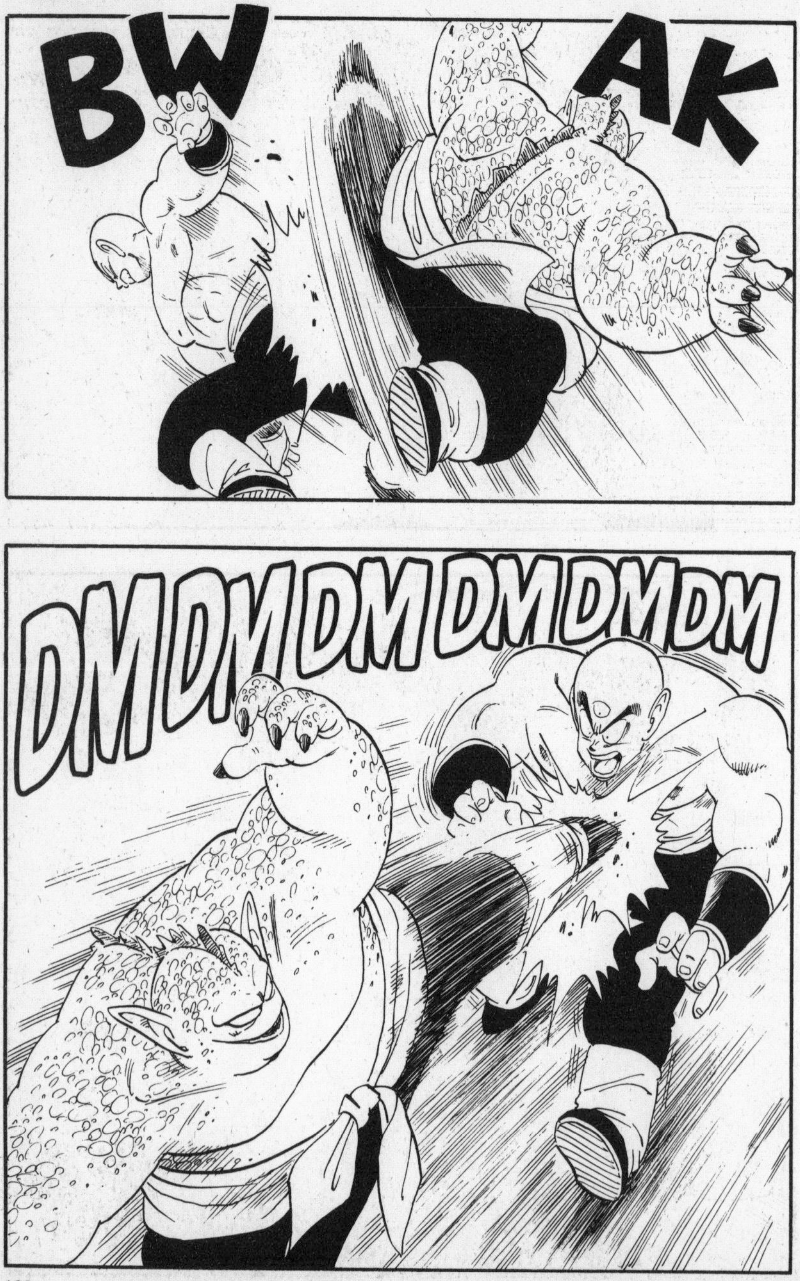
BWAK
DMDMDMDMDMDM

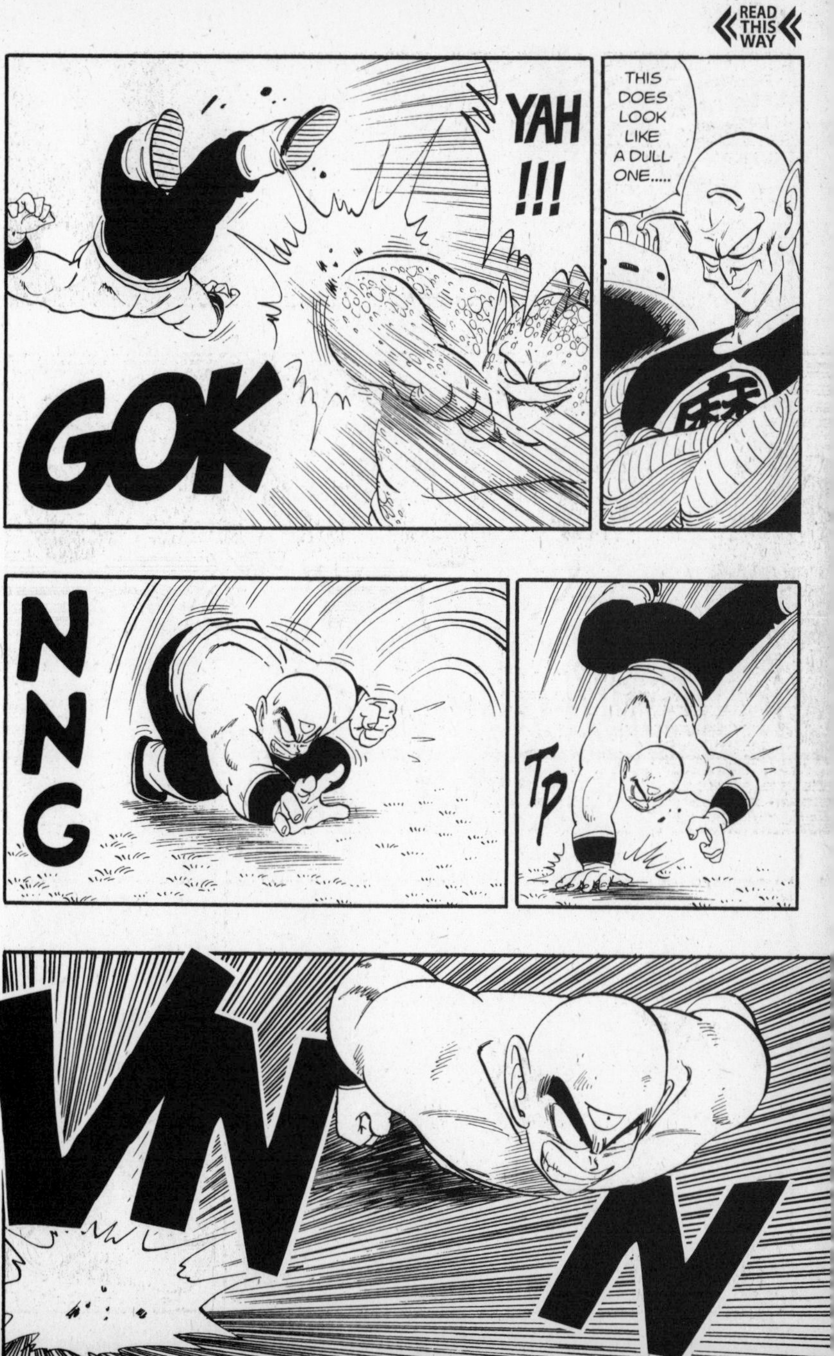
READ THIS WAY
THIS DOES LOOK LIKE A DULL ONE.....
YAH !!!
GOK
TP
NNG
VWN

READ THIS WAY

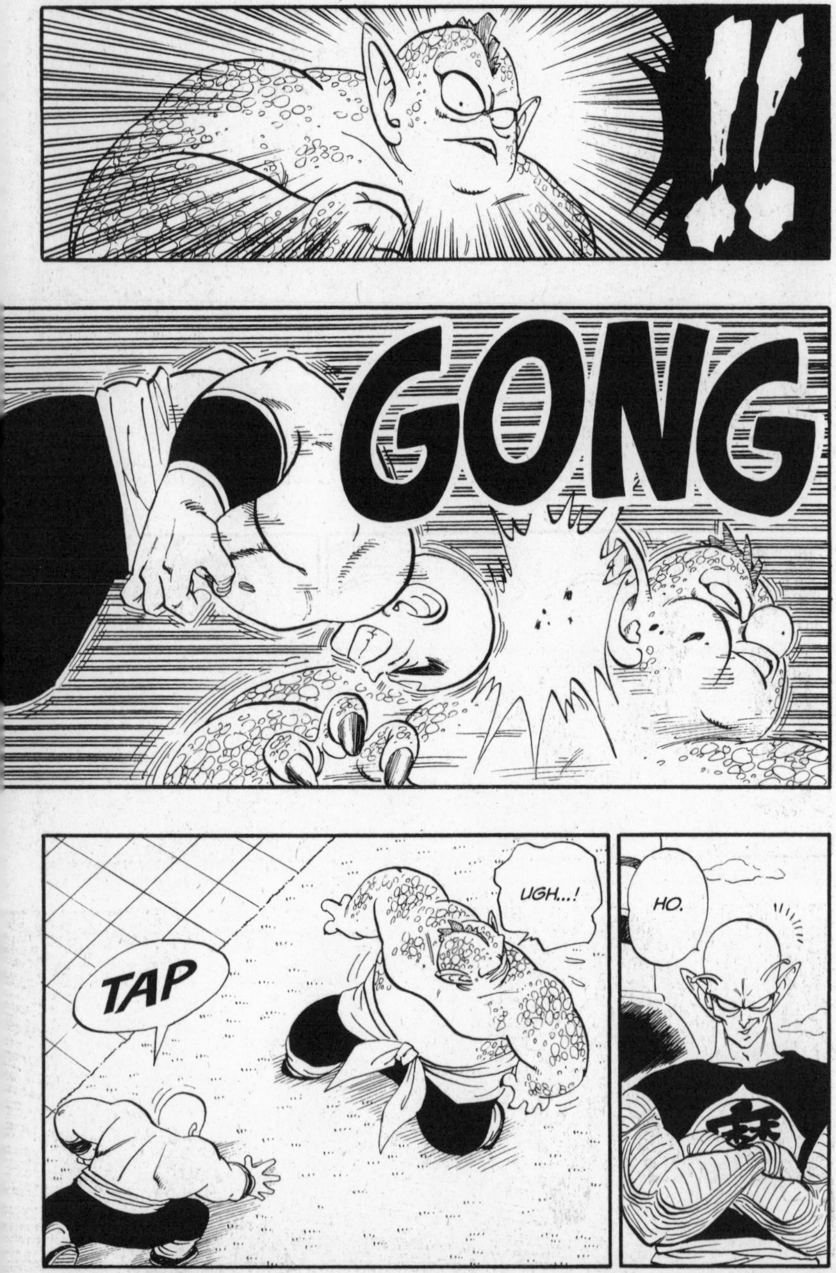
!!
GONG
HO.
UGH...!
TAP

READ THIS WAY

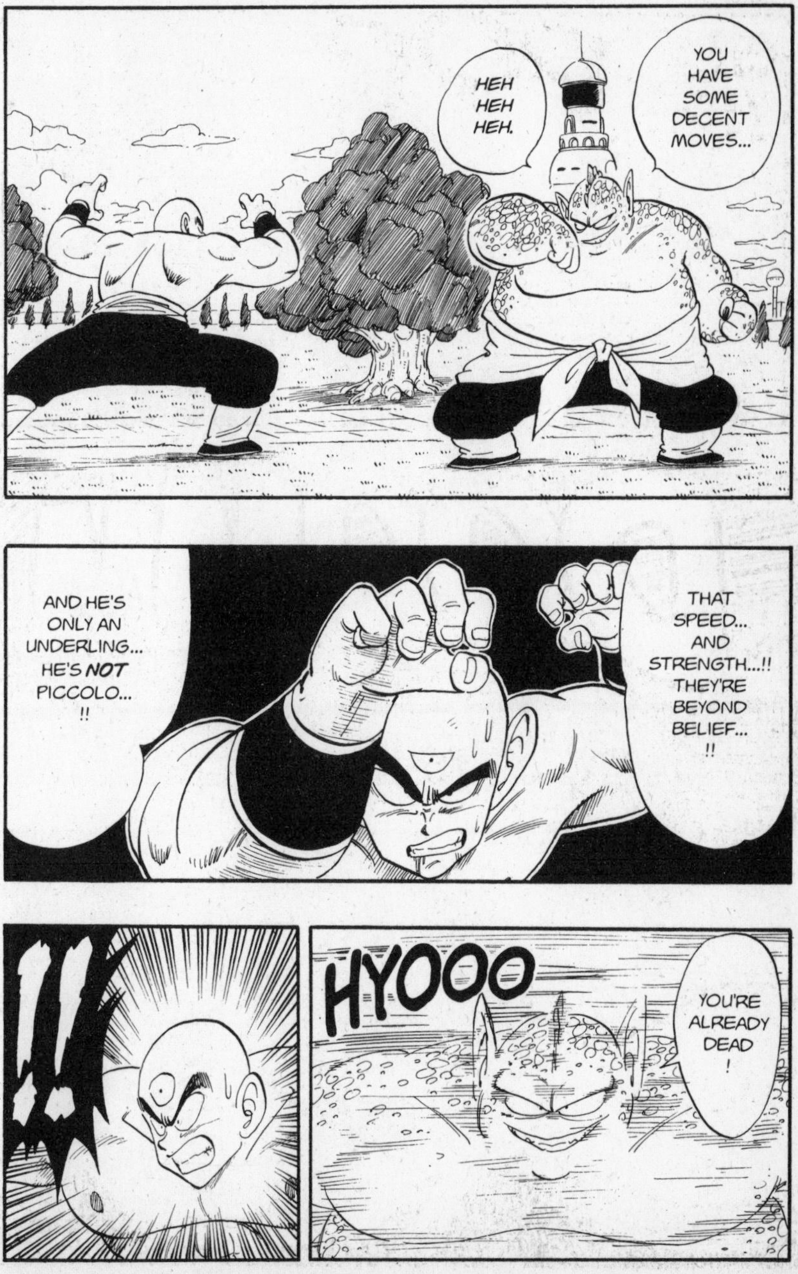
YOU HAVE SOME DECENT MOVES...
HEH HEH HEH.
THAT SPEED... AND STRENGTH...!! THEY'RE BEYOND BELIEF... !!
AND HE'S ONLY AN UNDERLING... HE'S ***NOT*** PICCOLO... !!
HYOOO
YOU'RE ALREADY DEAD !
!!

READ THIS WAY

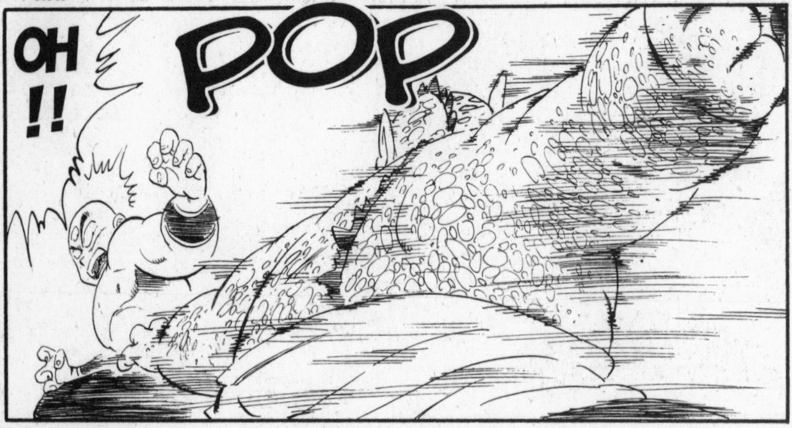
POP
OH !!

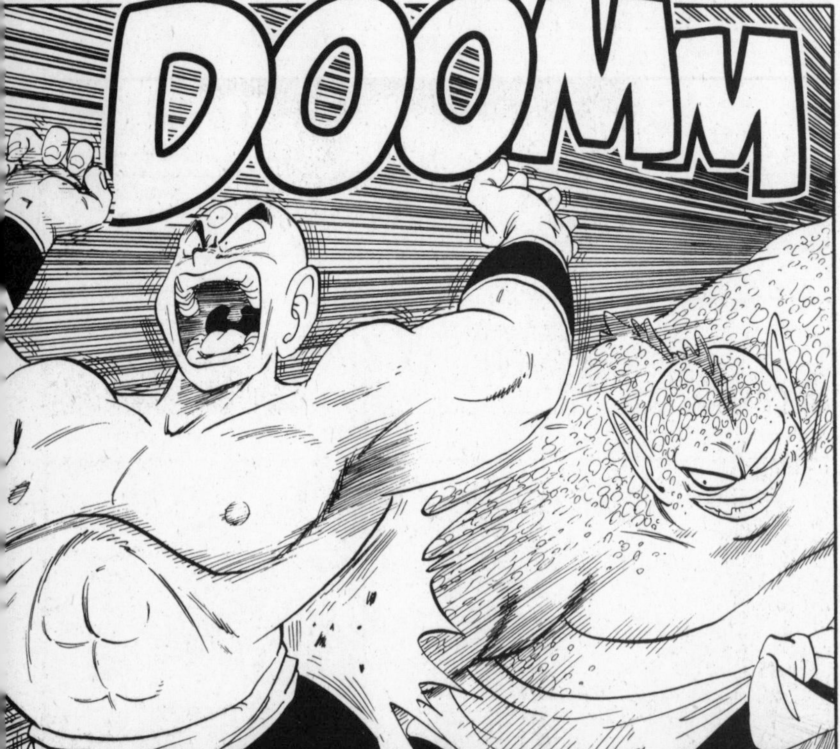
DOOMM

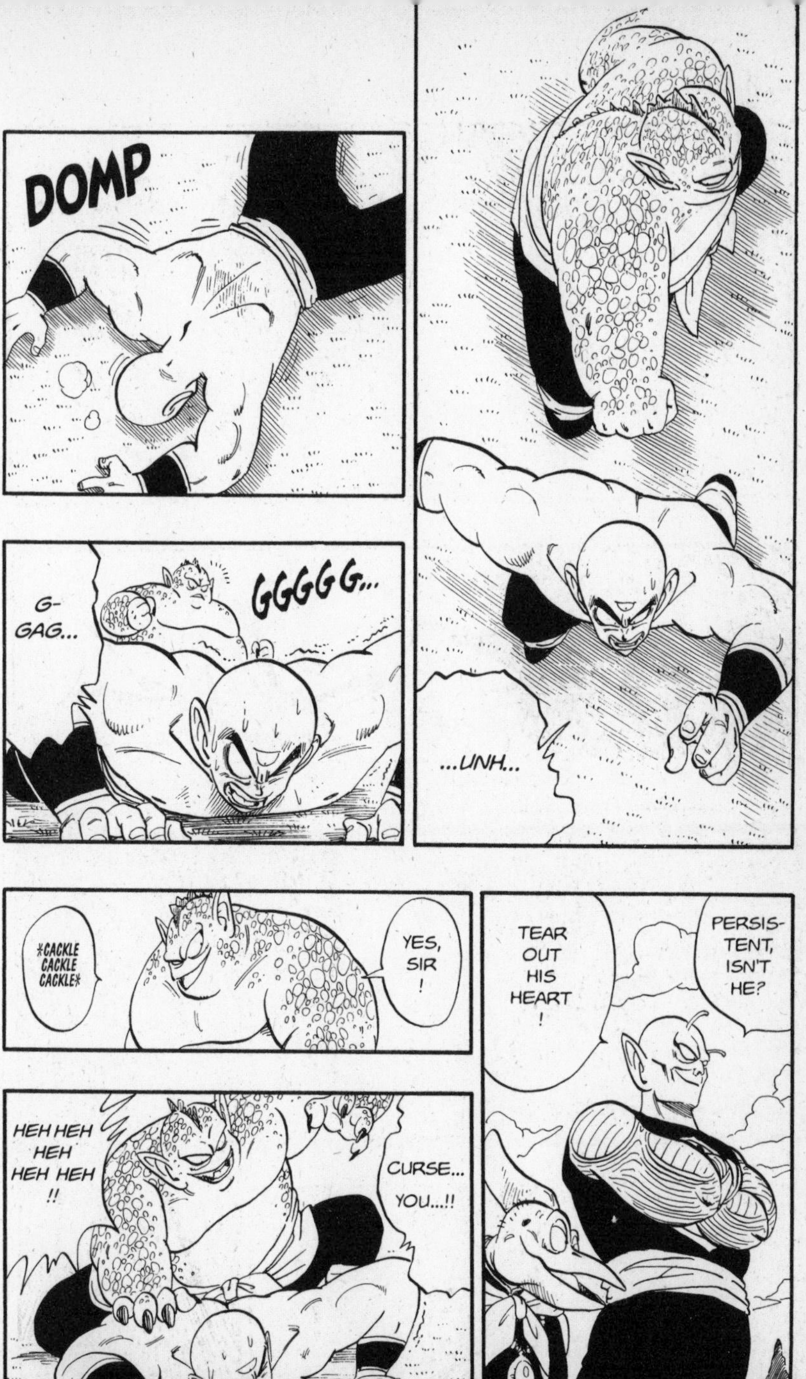
...UNH...
DOMP
GGGGG...
G-GAG...
PERSIS-TENT, ISN'T HE?
TEAR OUT HIS HEART!
YES, SIR!
CACKLE CACKLE CACKLE
CURSE... YOU...!!
HEH HEH HEH HEH HEH!!

READ THIS WAY

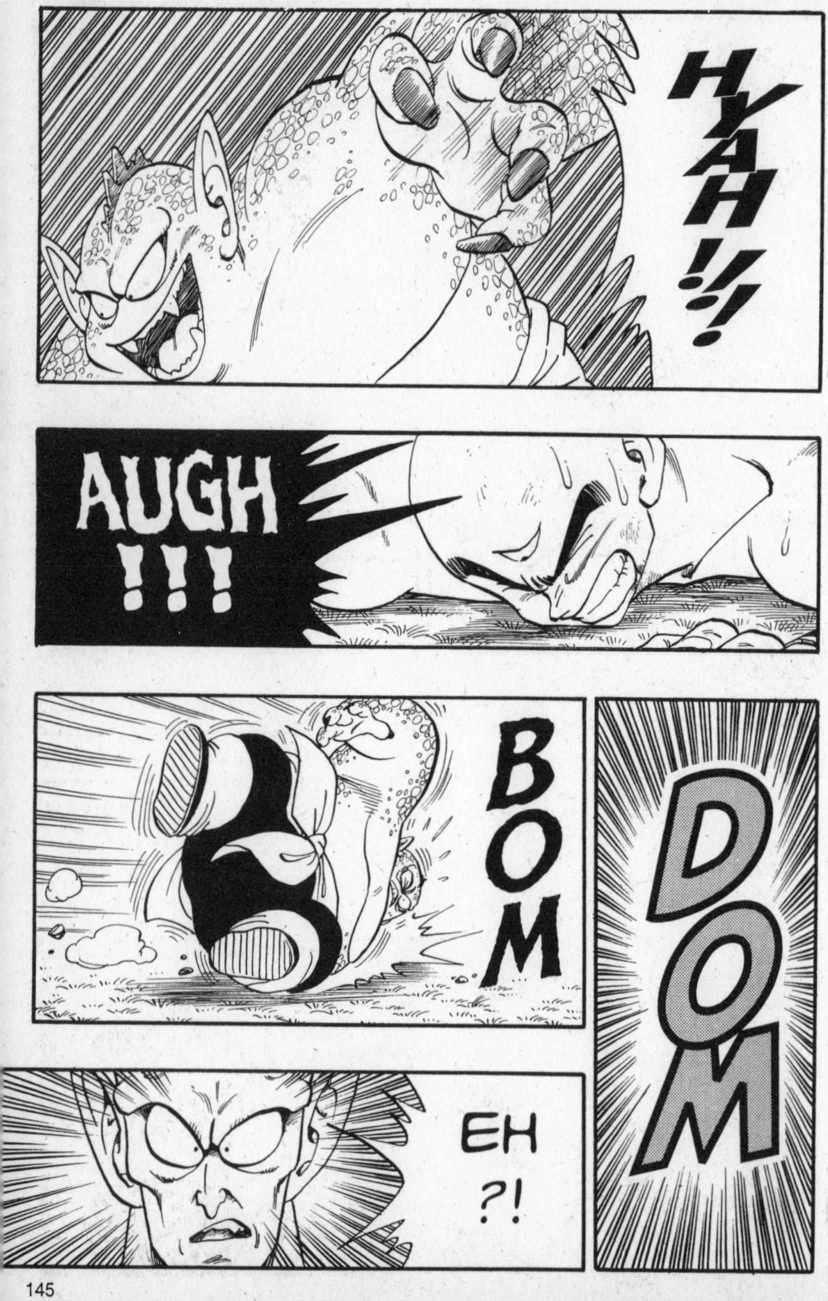
HYAH!!!
AUGH!!!
DOM
BOM
EH ?!

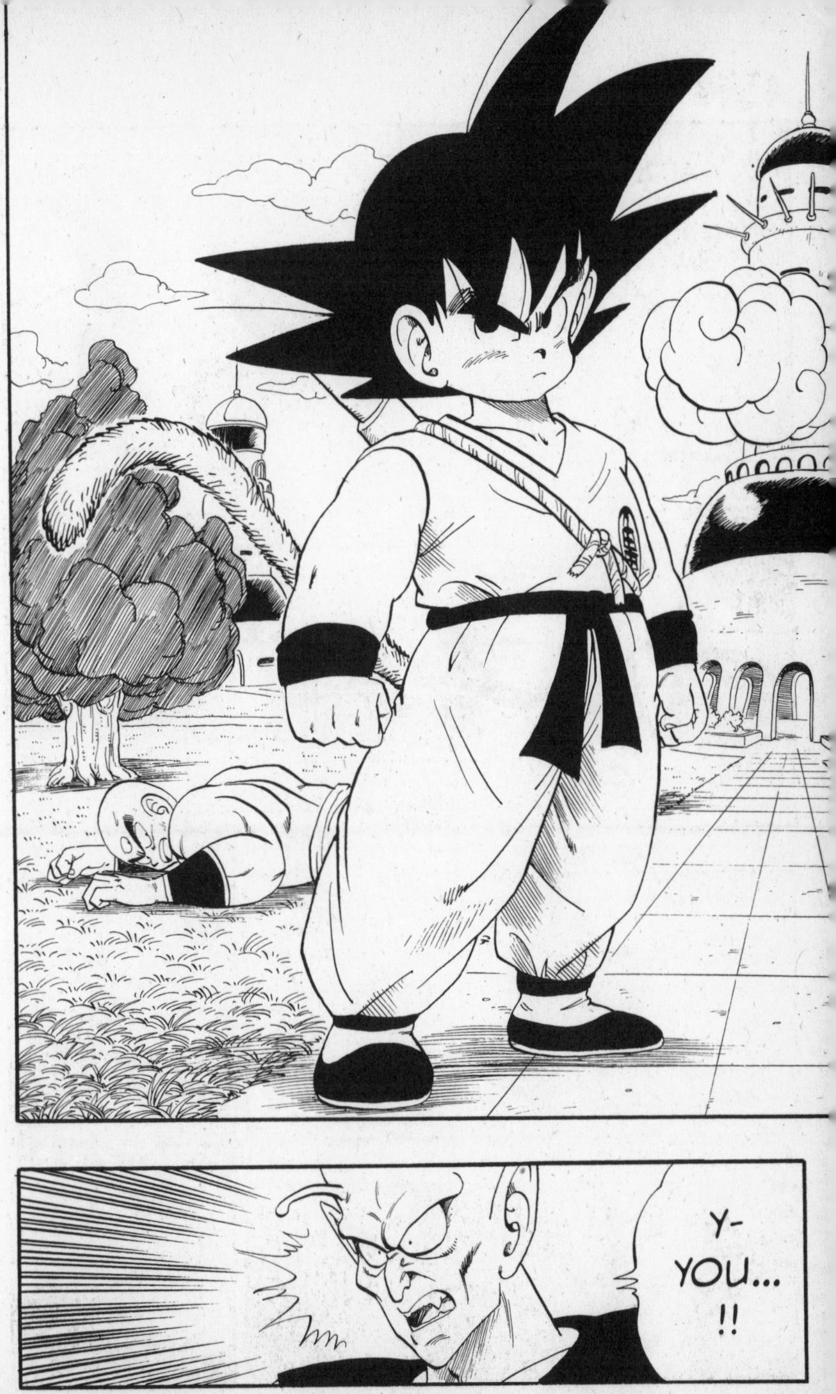
Y-
YOU...
!!

READ THIS WAY

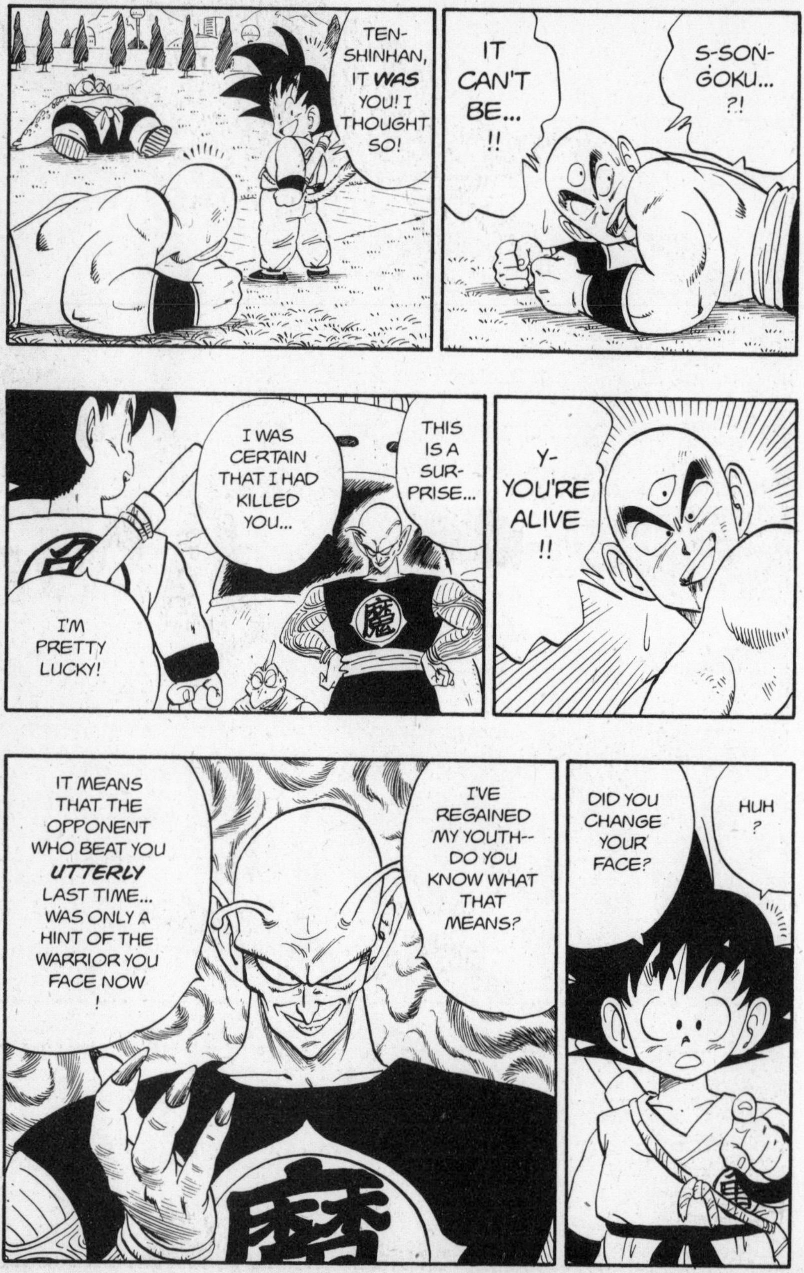
S-SON-GOKU...?!
IT CAN'T BE...!!
TEN-SHINHAN, IT WAS YOU! I THOUGHT SO!
Y-YOU'RE ALIVE!!
THIS IS A SURPRISE...
I WAS CERTAIN THAT I HAD KILLED YOU...
I'M PRETTY LUCKY!
HUH?
DID YOU CHANGE YOUR FACE?
I'VE REGAINED MY YOUTH-- DO YOU KNOW WHAT THAT MEANS?
IT MEANS THAT THE OPPONENT WHO BEAT YOU UTTERLY LAST TIME... WAS ONLY A HINT OF THE WARRIOR YOU FACE NOW!

READ THIS WAY

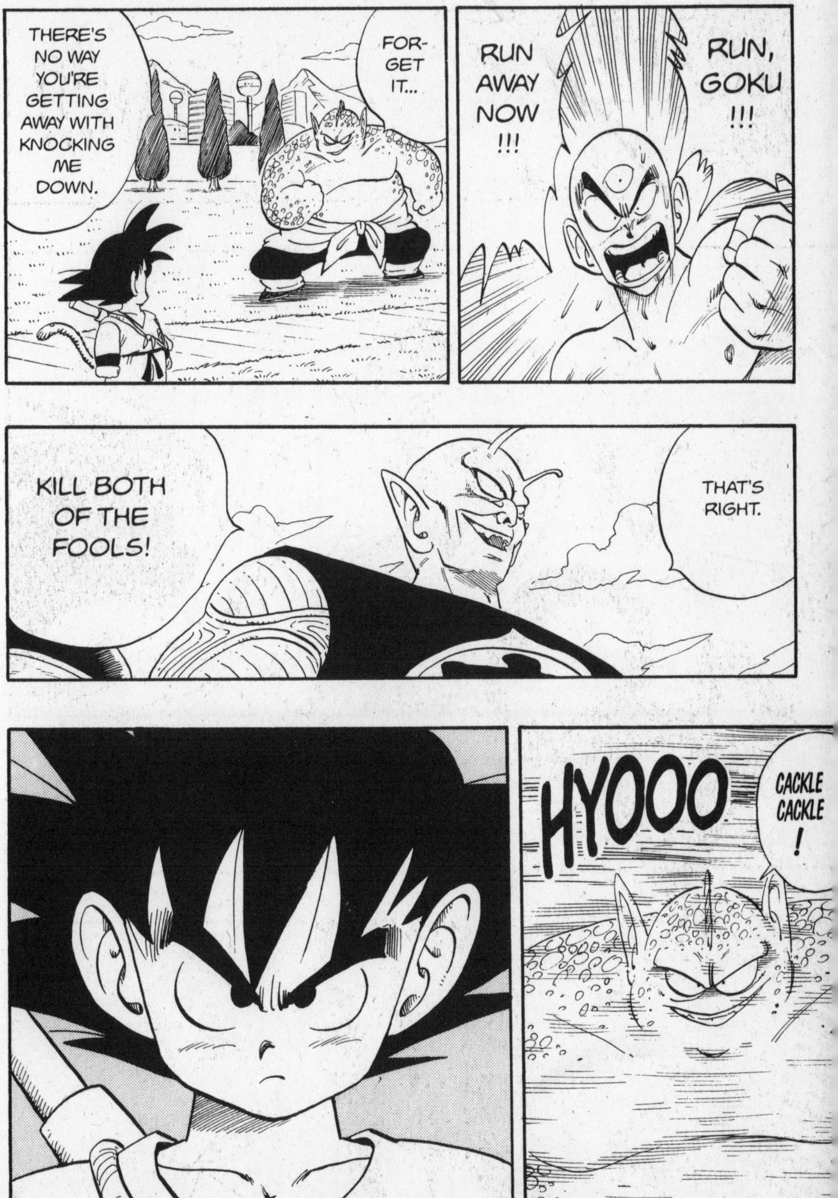
RUN, GOKU !!!
RUN AWAY NOW !!!
FOR-GET IT...
THERE'S NO WAY YOU'RE GETTING AWAY WITH KNOCKING ME DOWN.
THAT'S RIGHT.
KILL BOTH OF THE FOOLS!
CACKLE CACKLE !
HYOOO

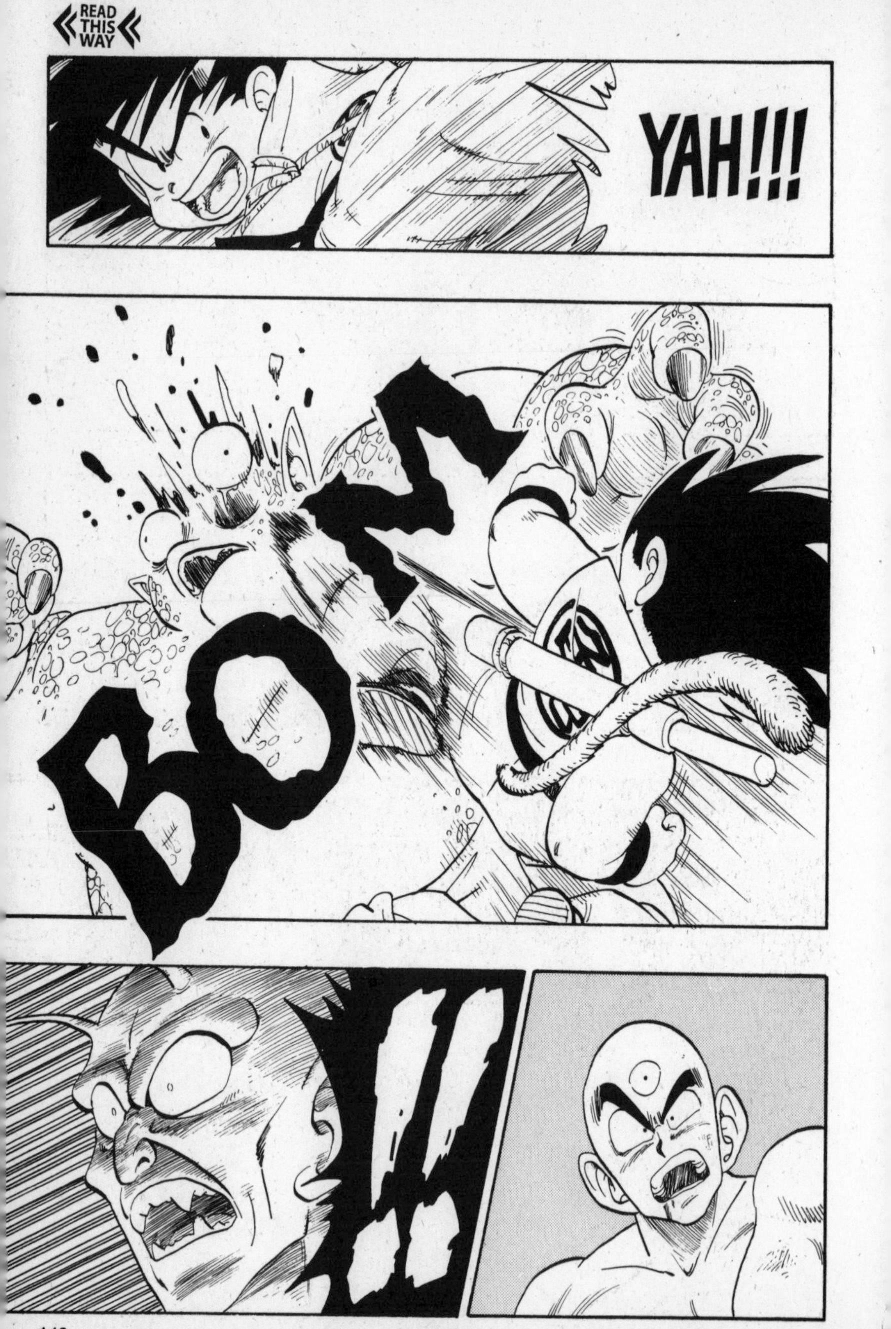
READ THIS WAY
YAH!!!
BOM
!!

Tale 155
Guess Who's Back?

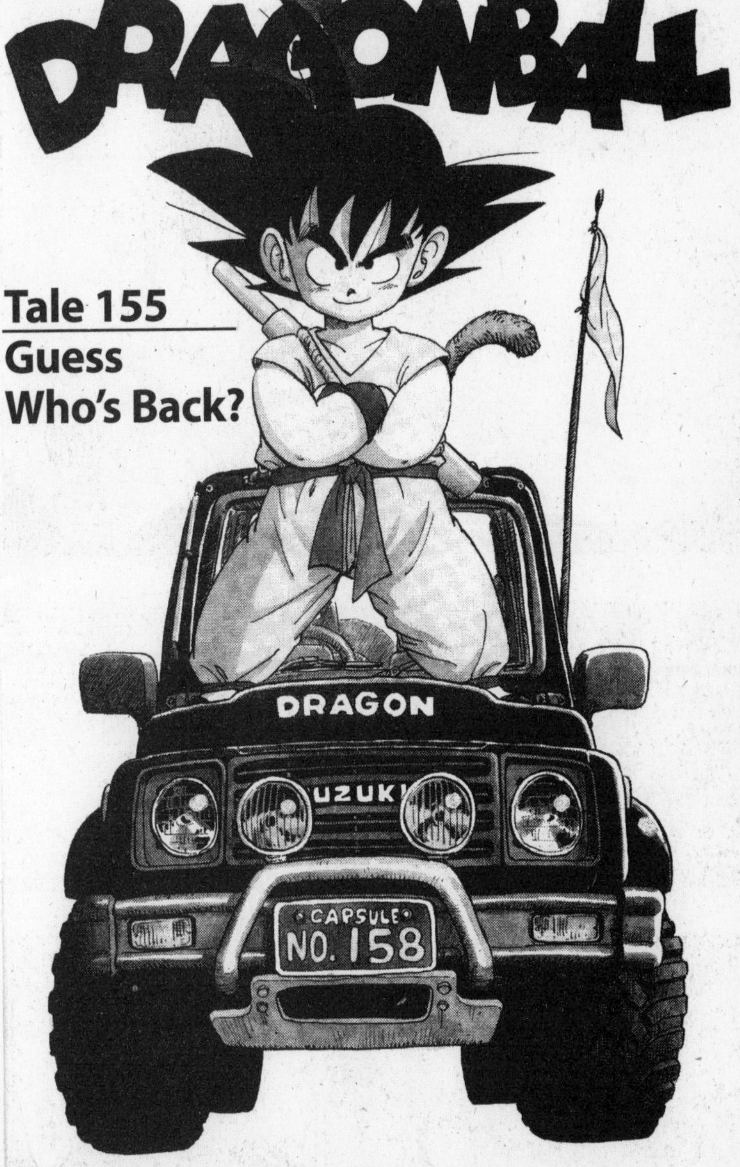
DRAGONBALL
DRAGON
UZUKI
CAPSULE
NO. 158

READ THIS WAY

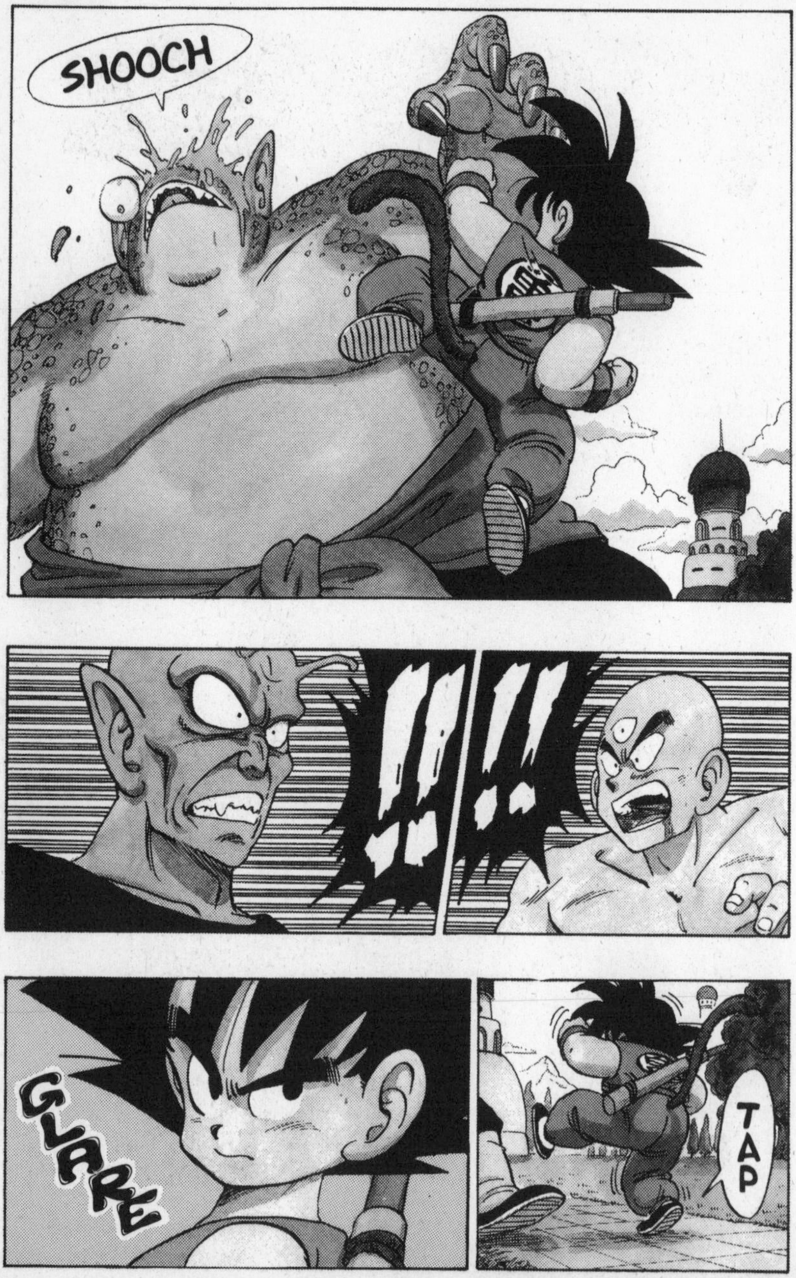
SHOOCH
!!
!!
TAP
GLARE

READ THIS WAY

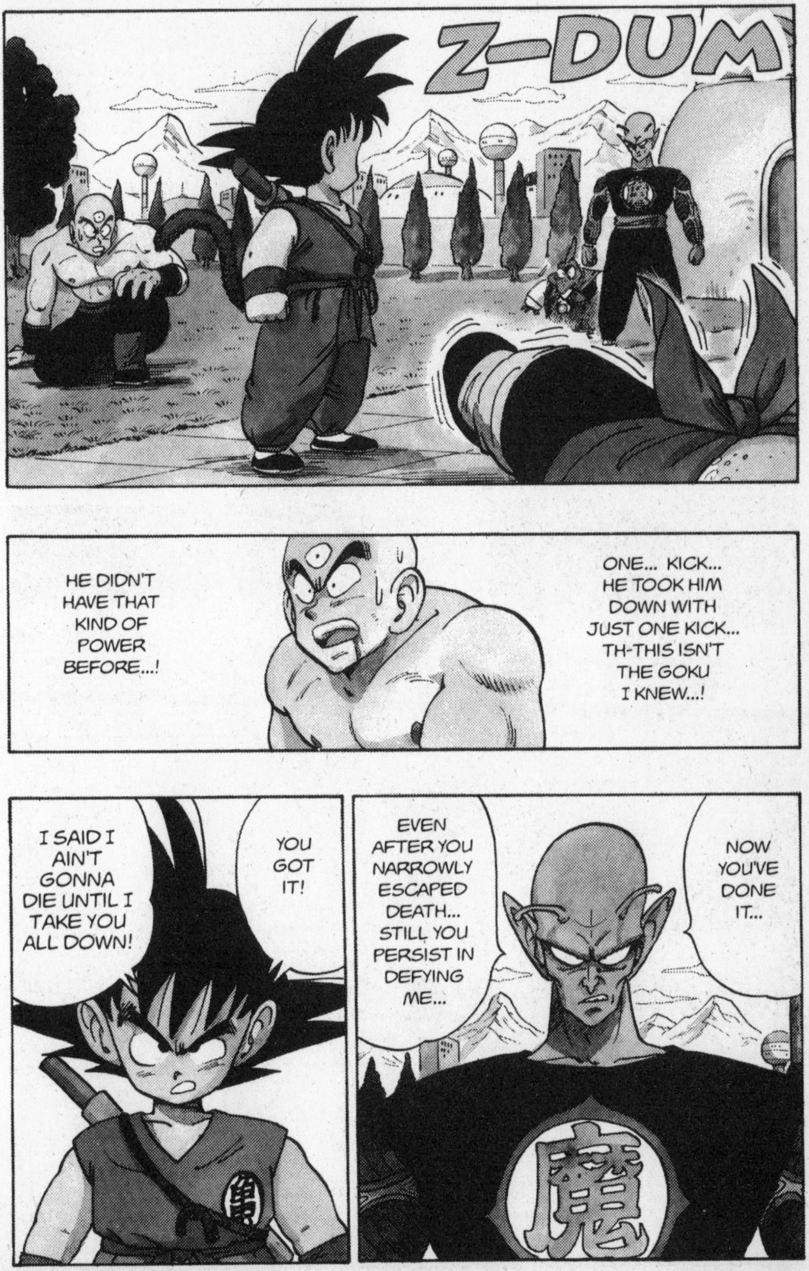
Z-DUM
ONE... KICK... HE TOOK HIM DOWN WITH JUST ONE KICK... TH-THIS ISN'T THE GOKU I KNEW...!
HE DIDN'T HAVE THAT KIND OF POWER BEFORE...!
NOW YOU'VE DONE IT...
EVEN AFTER YOU NARROWLY ESCAPED DEATH... STILL, YOU PERSIST IN DEFYING ME...
YOU GOT IT!
I SAID I AIN'T GONNA DIE UNTIL I TAKE YOU ALL DOWN!

READ THIS WAY

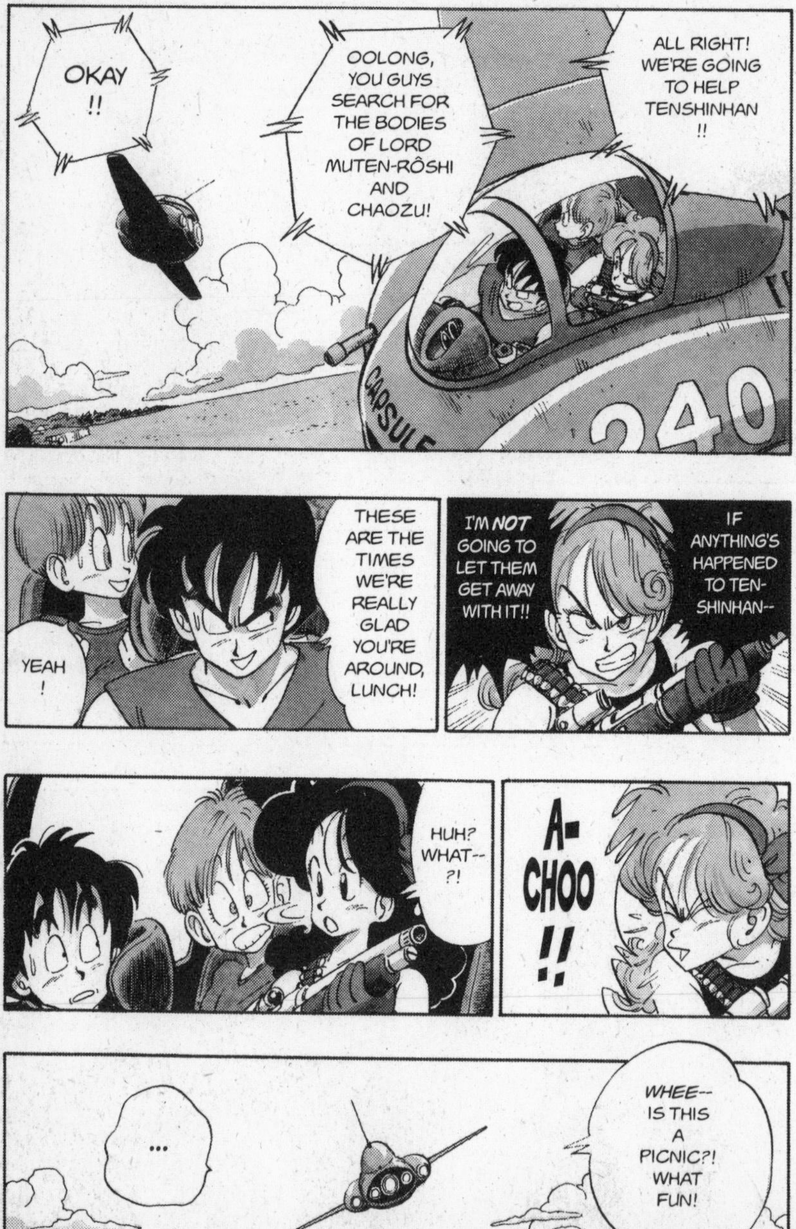
ALL RIGHT! WE'RE GOING TO HELP TENSHINHAN !!
OOLONG, YOU GUYS SEARCH FOR THE BODIES OF LORD MUTEN-RÔSHI AND CHAOZU!
OKAY !!
CAPSULE 240
IF ANYTHING'S HAPPENED TO TEN-SHINHAN--
I'M **NOT** GOING TO LET THEM GET AWAY WITH IT!!
THESE ARE THE TIMES WE'RE REALLY GLAD YOU'RE AROUND, LUNCH!
YEAH !
A-CHOO !!
HUH? WHAT--?!
WHEE-- IS THIS A PICNIC?! WHAT FUN!
...

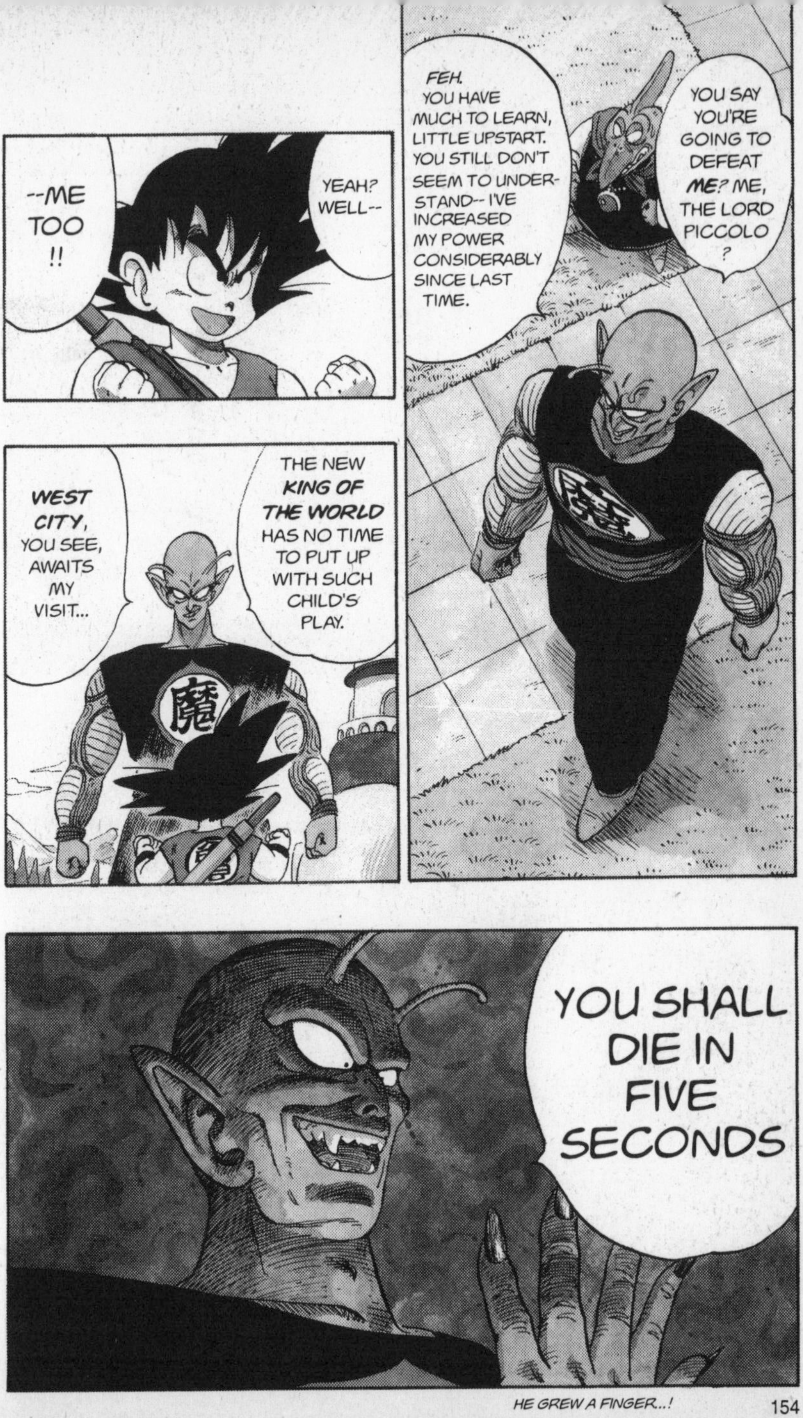
YOU SAY YOU'RE GOING TO DEFEAT ME? ME, THE LORD PICCOLO?
FEH. YOU HAVE MUCH TO LEARN, LITTLE UPSTART. YOU STILL DON'T SEEM TO UNDER-STAND-- I'VE INCREASED MY POWER CONSIDERABLY SINCE LAST TIME.
YEAH? WELL--
--ME TOO !!
THE NEW KING OF THE WORLD HAS NO TIME TO PUT UP WITH SUCH CHILD'S PLAY.
WEST CITY, YOU SEE, AWAITS MY VISIT...
YOU SHALL DIE IN FIVE SECONDS

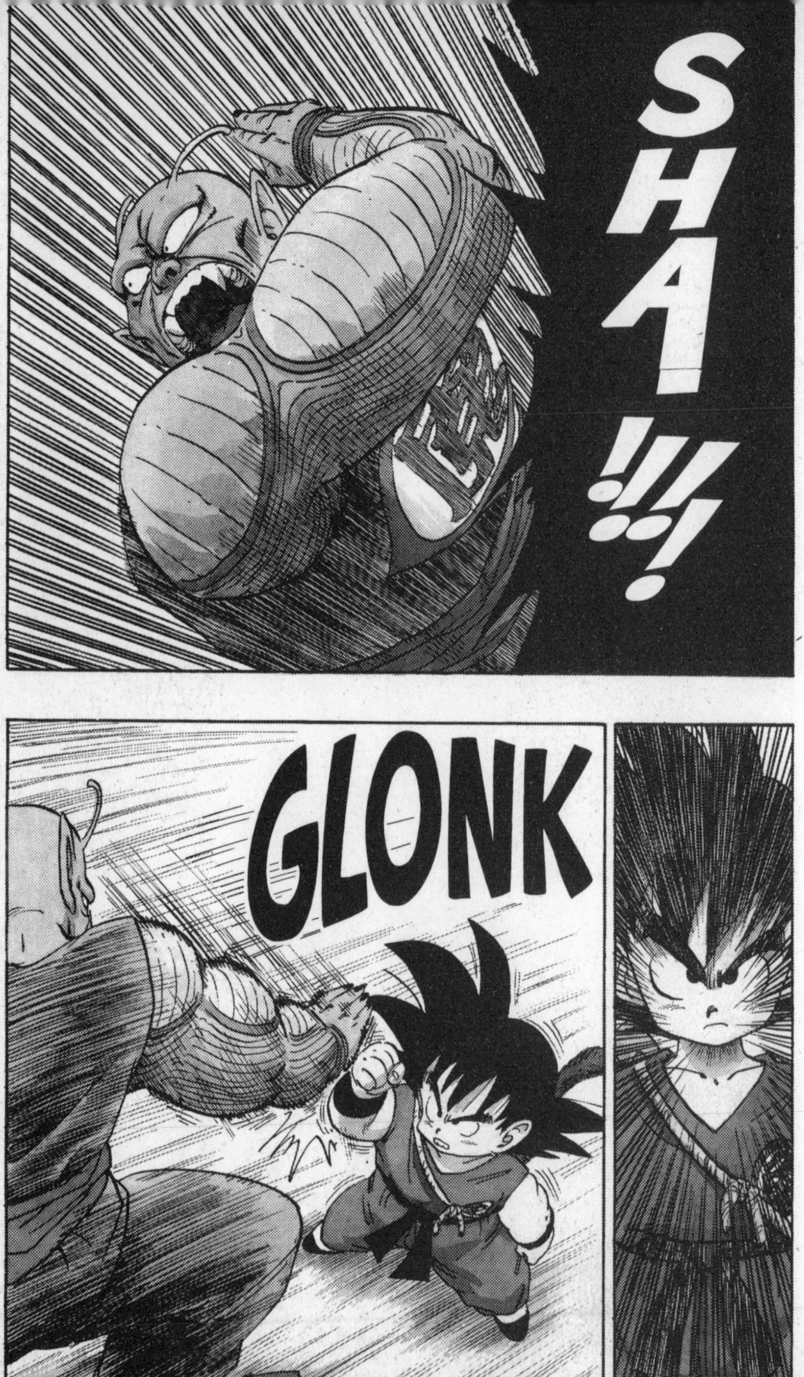
SHA!!!!
GLONK

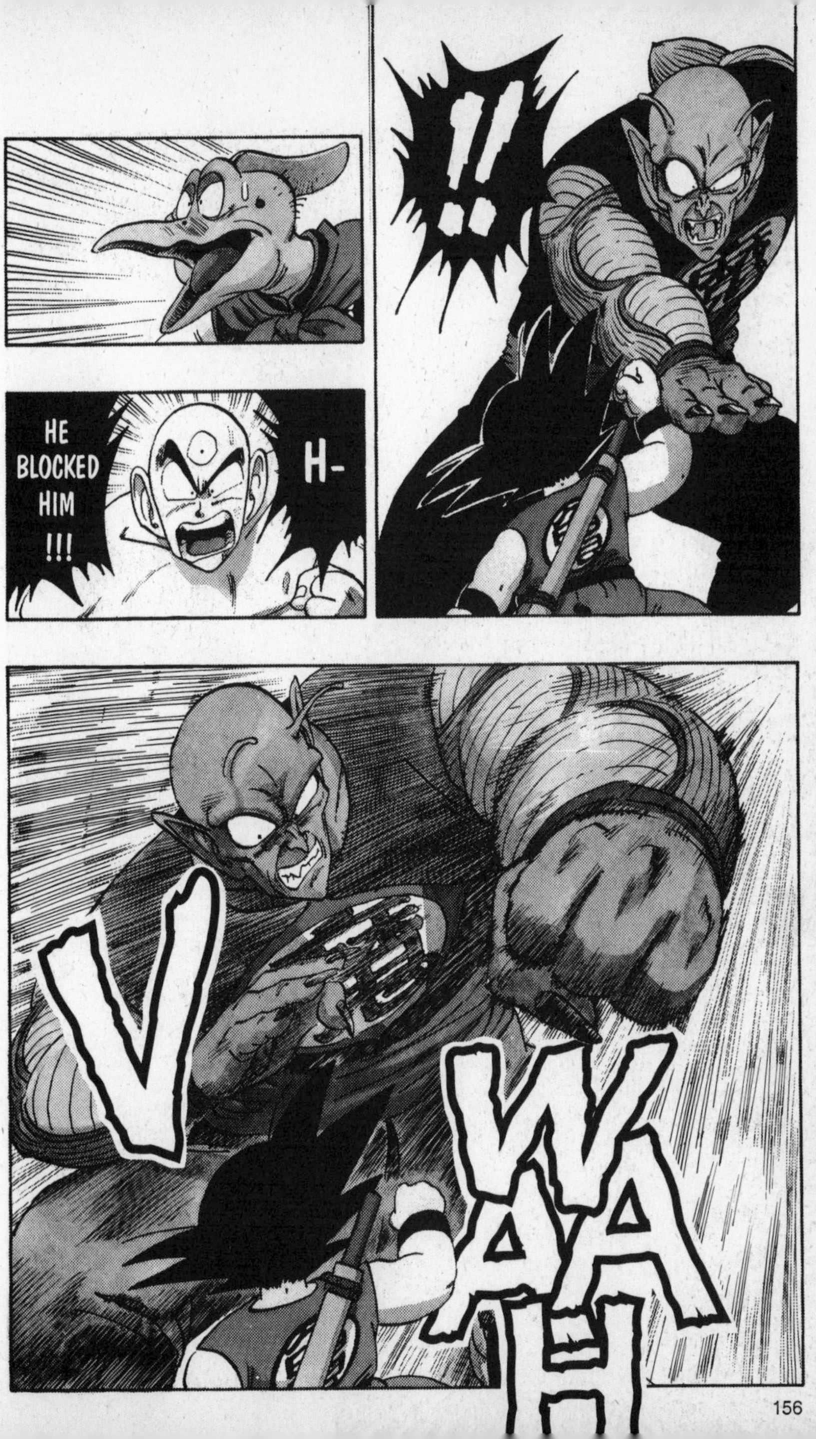
!!
H-
HE BLOCKED HIM !!!
V
WAAH

READ THIS WAY

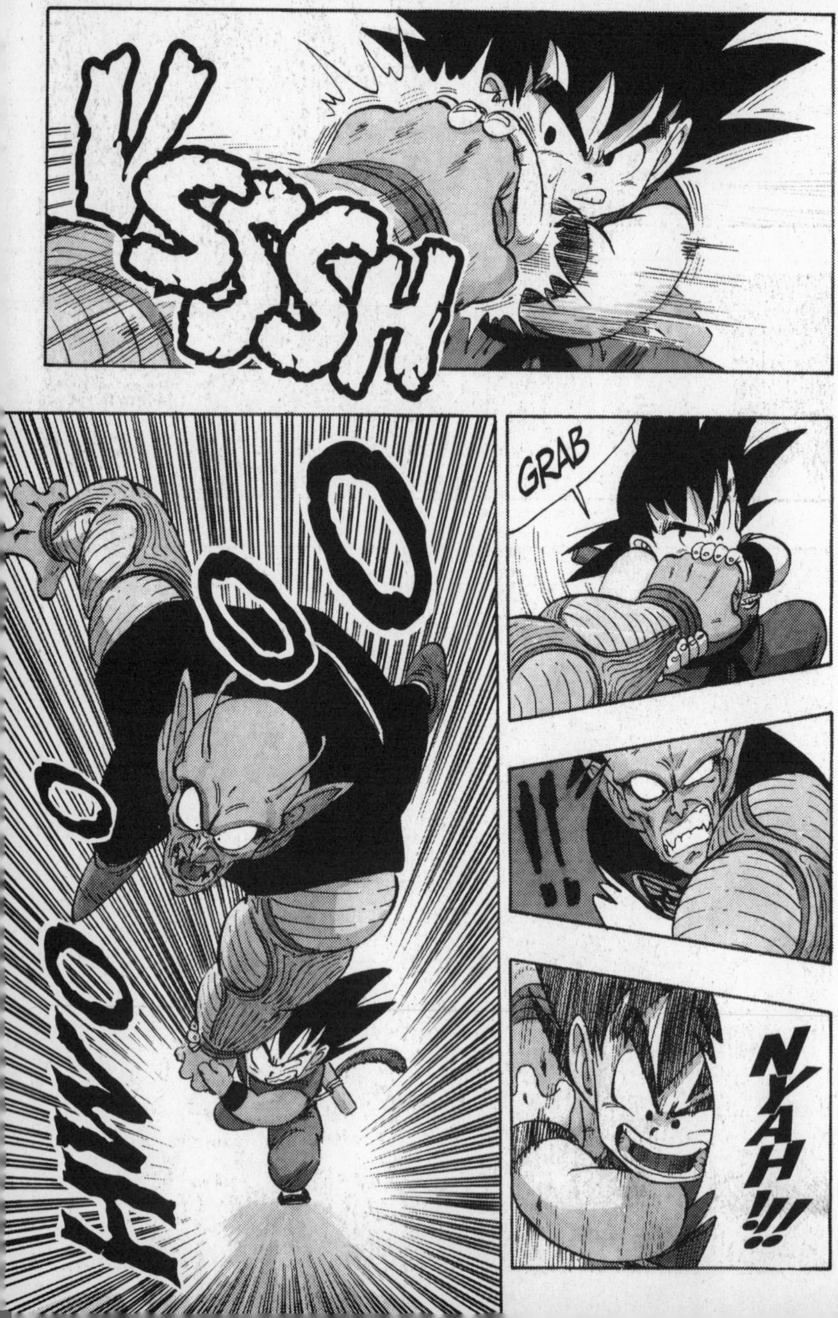
VSSH
GRAB
!!
NYAH!!!
WHOOOO

READ THIS WAY

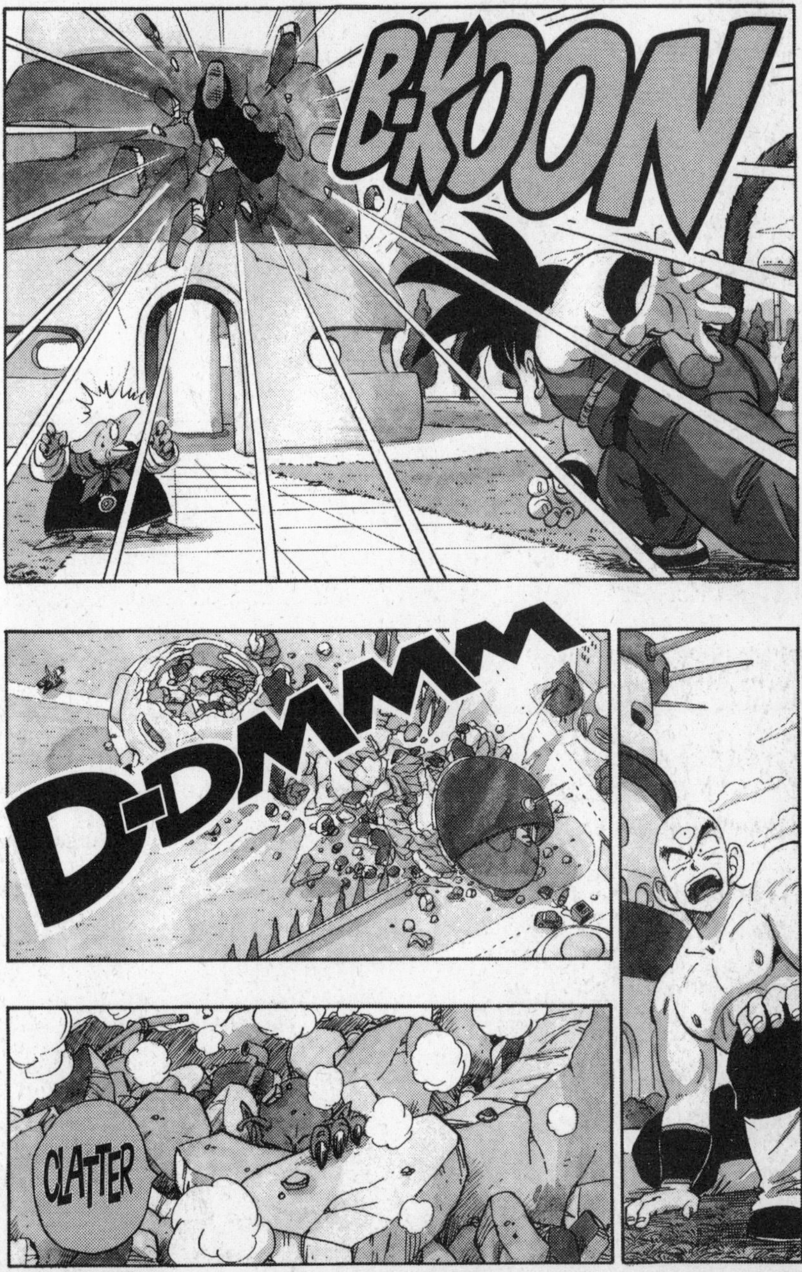
B-KOON
D-DMMMM
CLATTER

READ THIS WAY

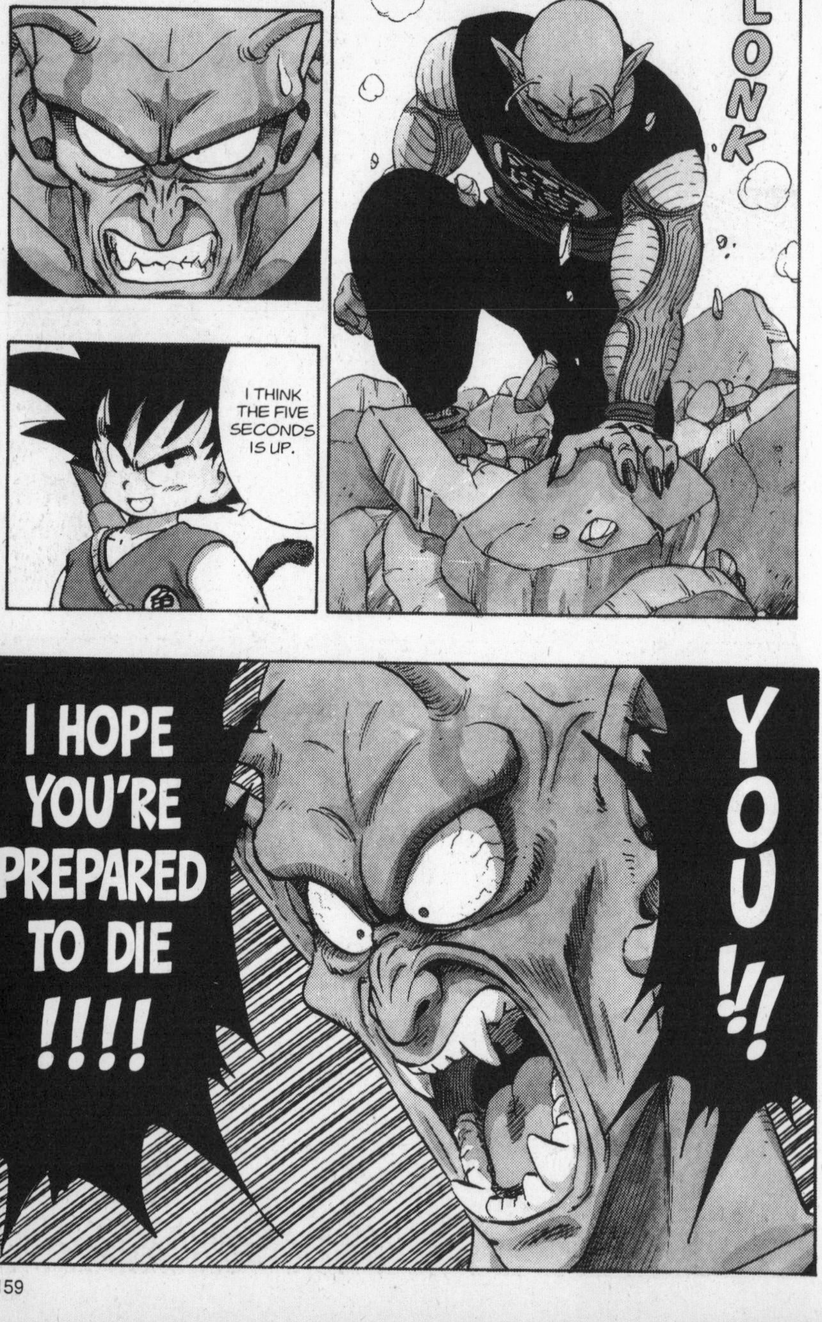
KLONK
I THINK THE FIVE SECONDS IS UP.
YOU!!!
I HOPE YOU'RE PREPARED TO DIE!!!!

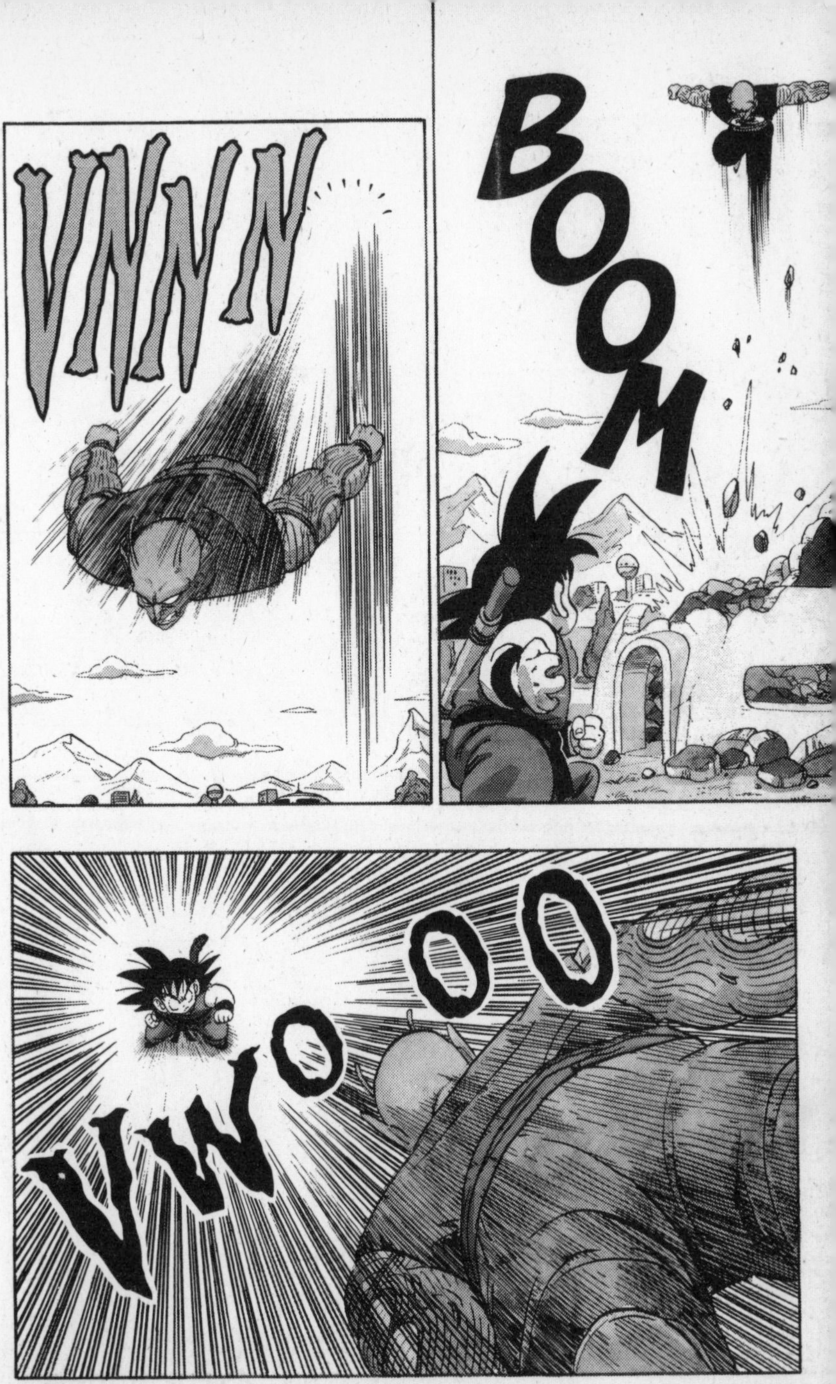
BOOM
VNNN
VWOOOOO

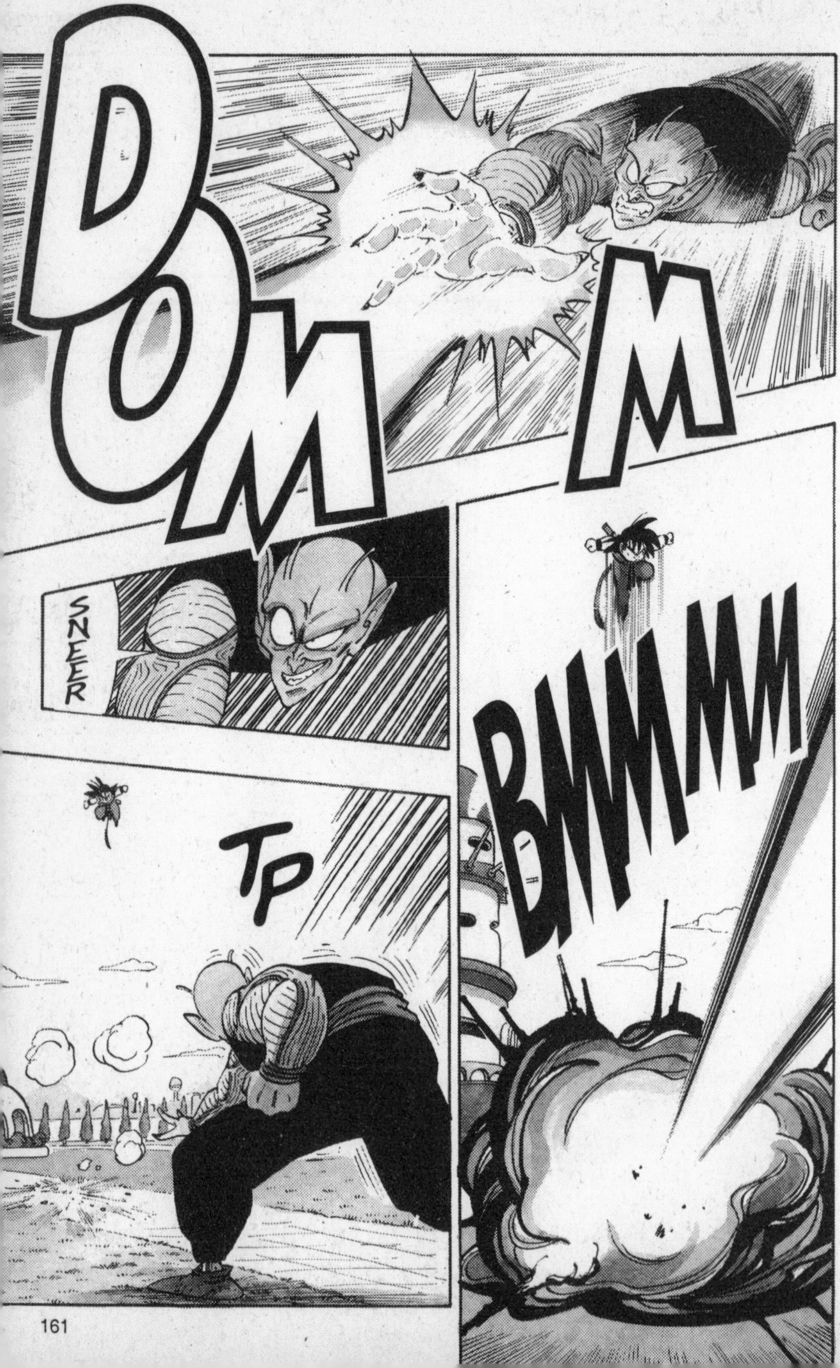
DOMMM
BAMMMMM
SNEER
TP

READ THIS WAY

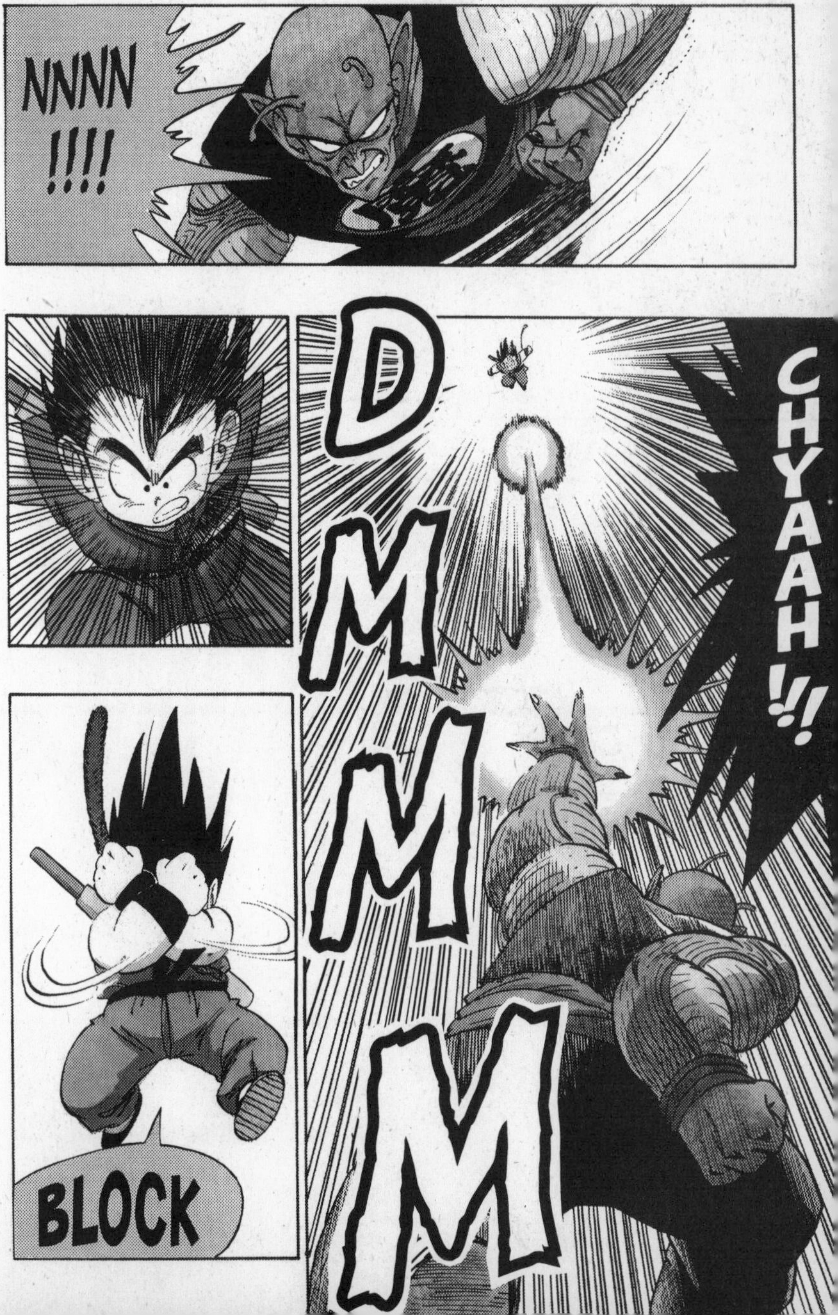
NNNN!!!!
CHYAAH!!!
DMMM
BLOCK

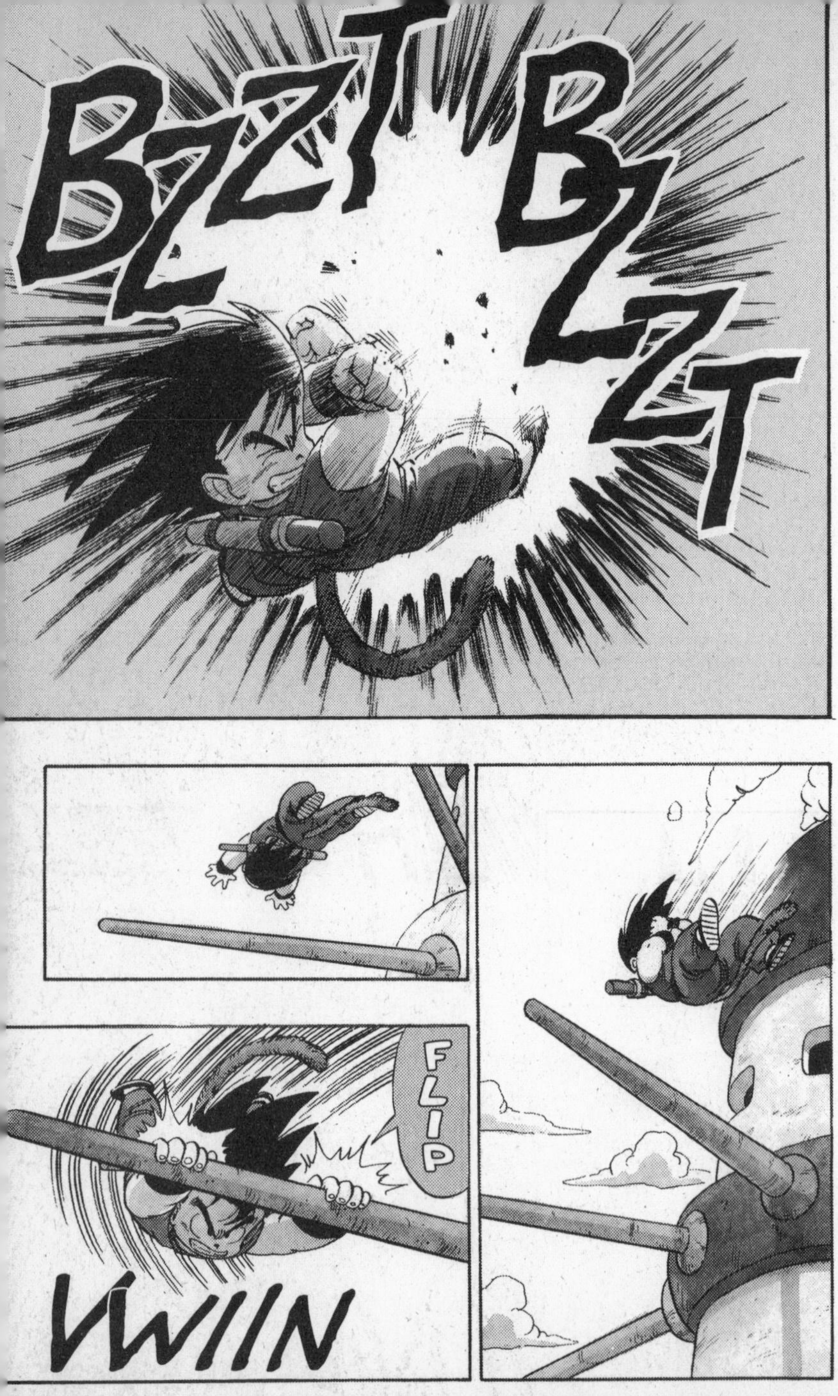
BZZT
BZZT
FLIP
VWIIN

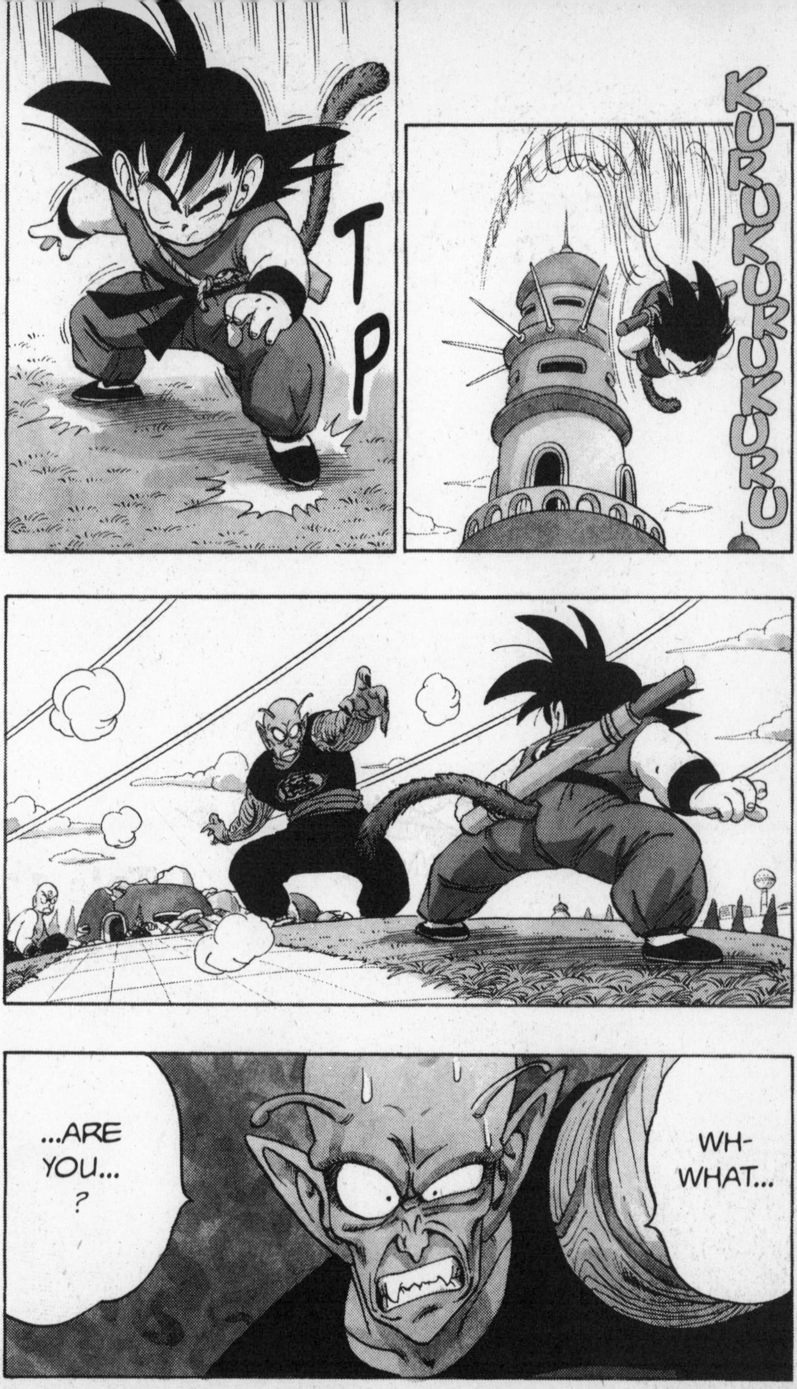
KURUKURUKURUKURU
TP
WH- WHAT...
...ARE YOU... ?

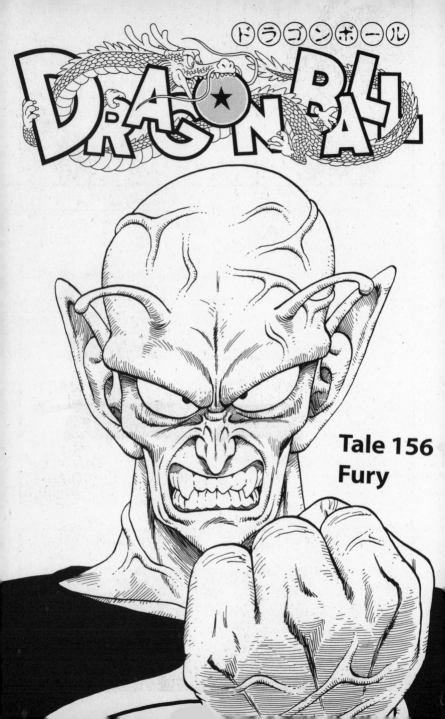

DRAGON BALL
ドラゴンボール

**Tale 156
Fury**

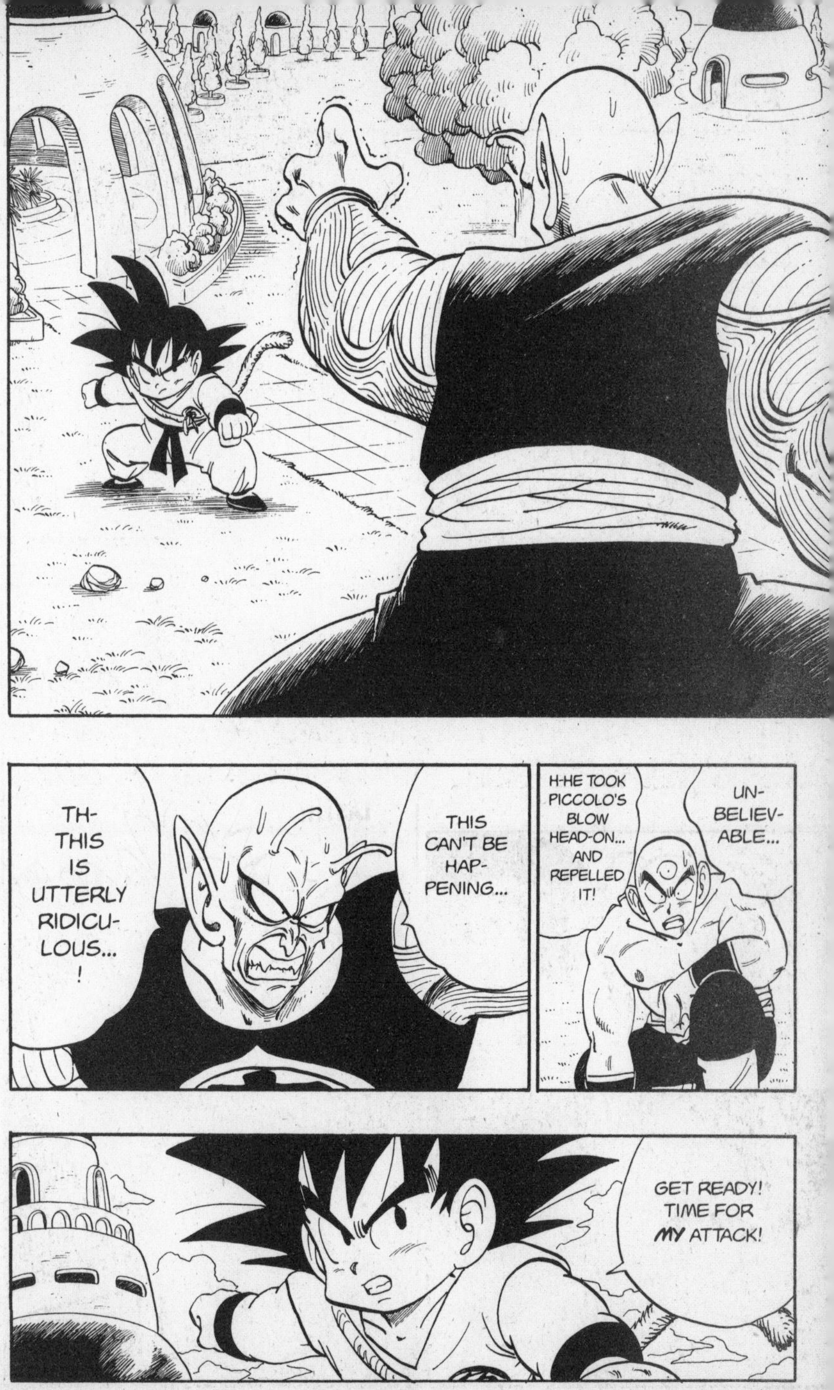
UN-BELIEV-ABLE...
H-HE TOOK PICCOLO'S BLOW HEAD-ON... AND REPELLED IT!
THIS CAN'T BE HAP-PENING...
TH-THIS IS UTTERLY RIDICU-LOUS...!
GET READY! TIME FOR *MY* ATTACK!

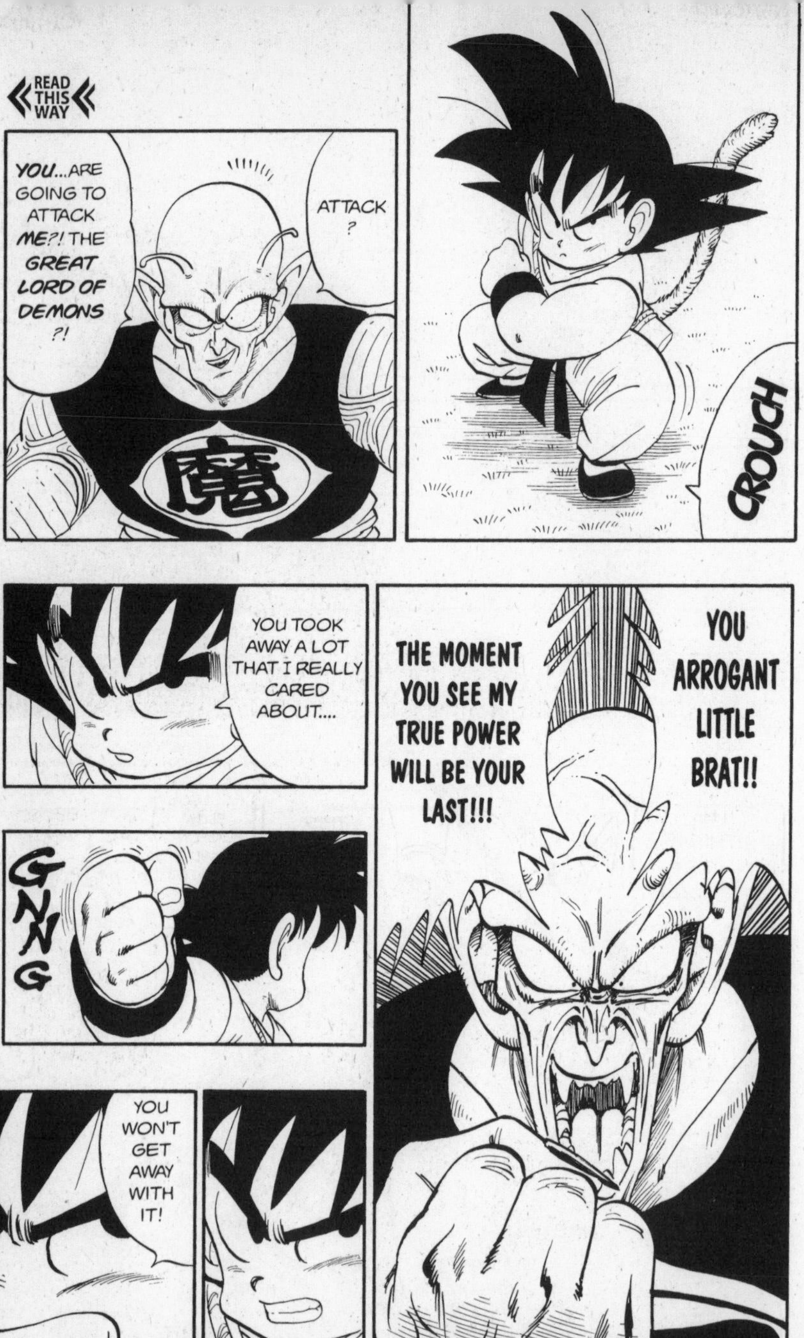
READ THIS WAY
CROUCH
ATTACK?
YOU...ARE GOING TO ATTACK ME?! THE GREAT LORD OF DEMONS?!
YOU ARROGANT LITTLE BRAT!!
THE MOMENT YOU SEE MY TRUE POWER WILL BE YOUR LAST!!!
YOU TOOK AWAY A LOT THAT I REALLY CARED ABOUT....
GNNG
YOU WON'T GET AWAY WITH IT!

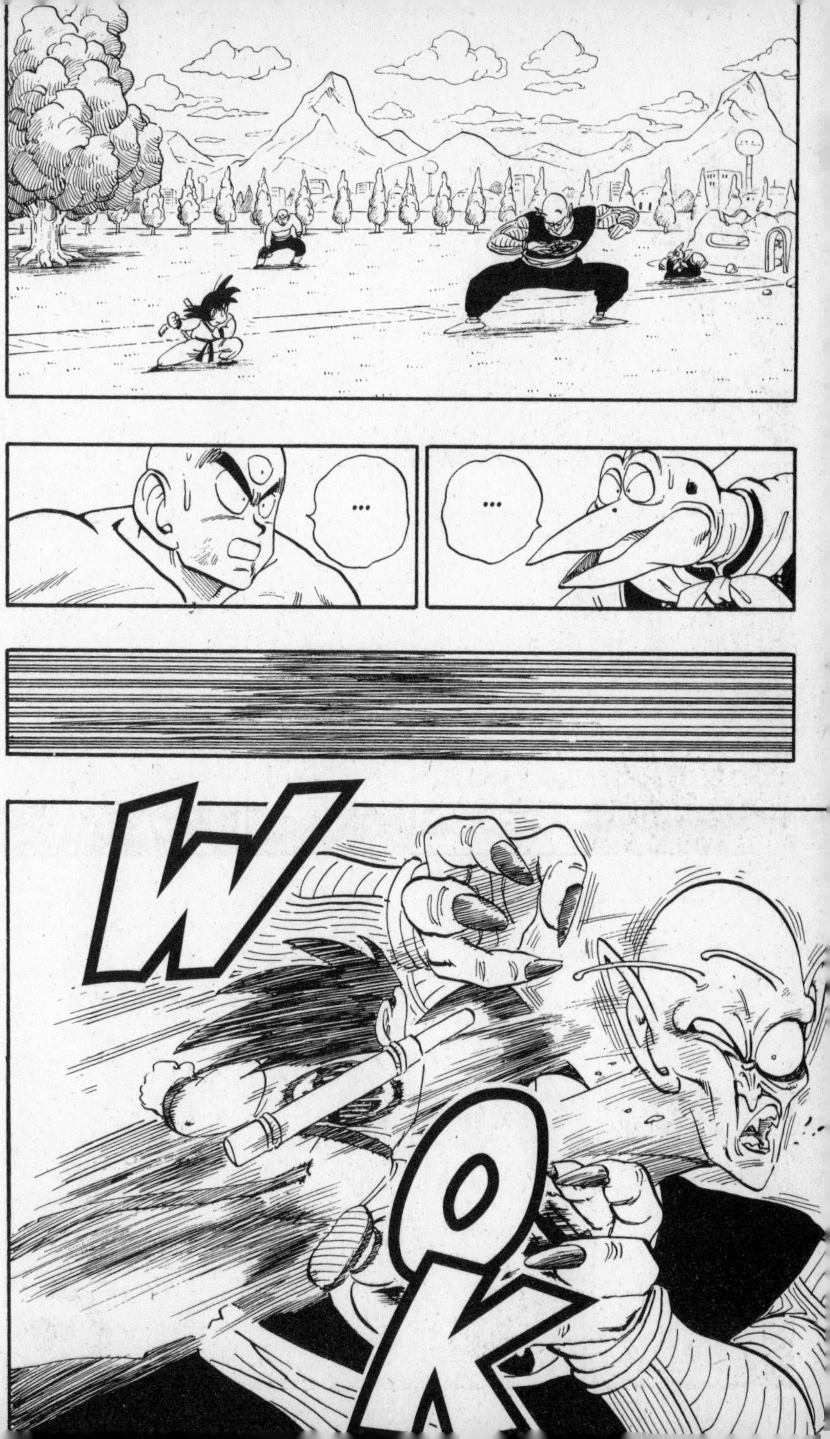
...
...
WOK

READ THIS WAY

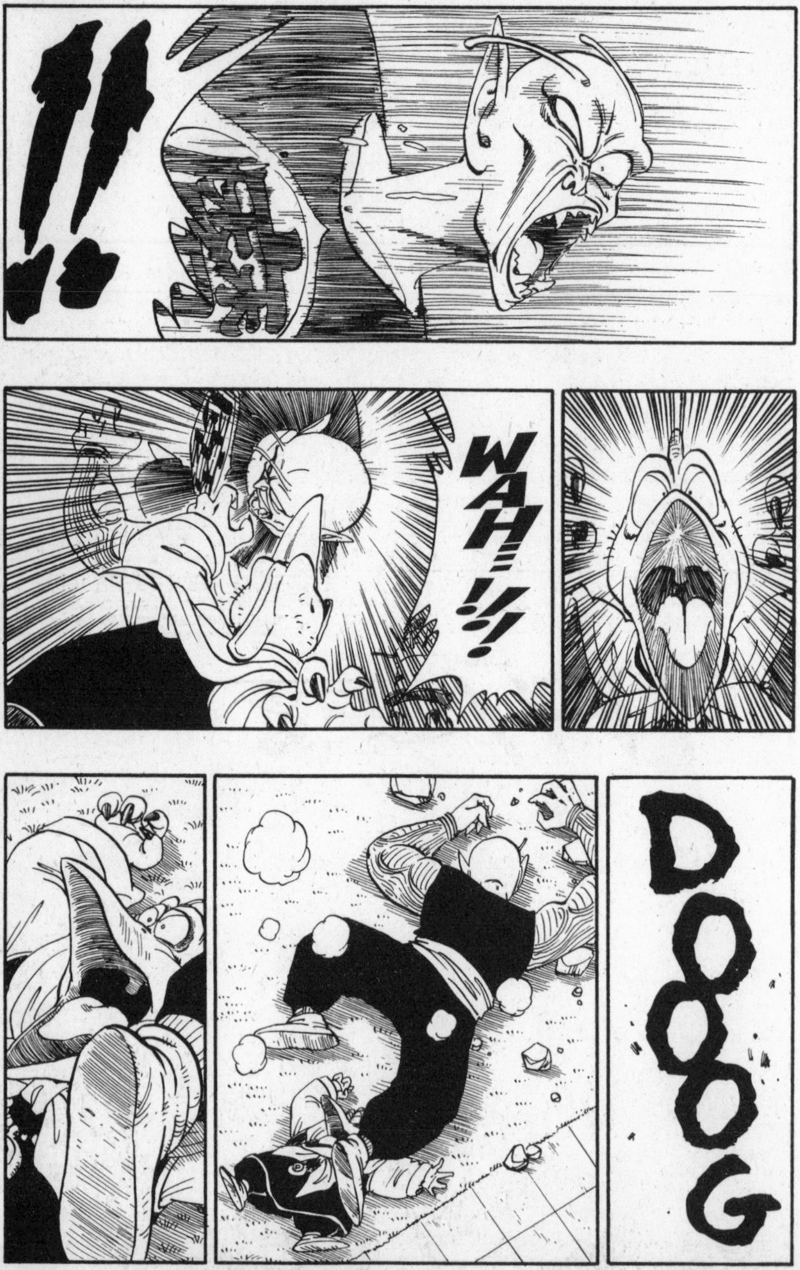
!!
WAH!!!
DOOOG

READ THIS WAY

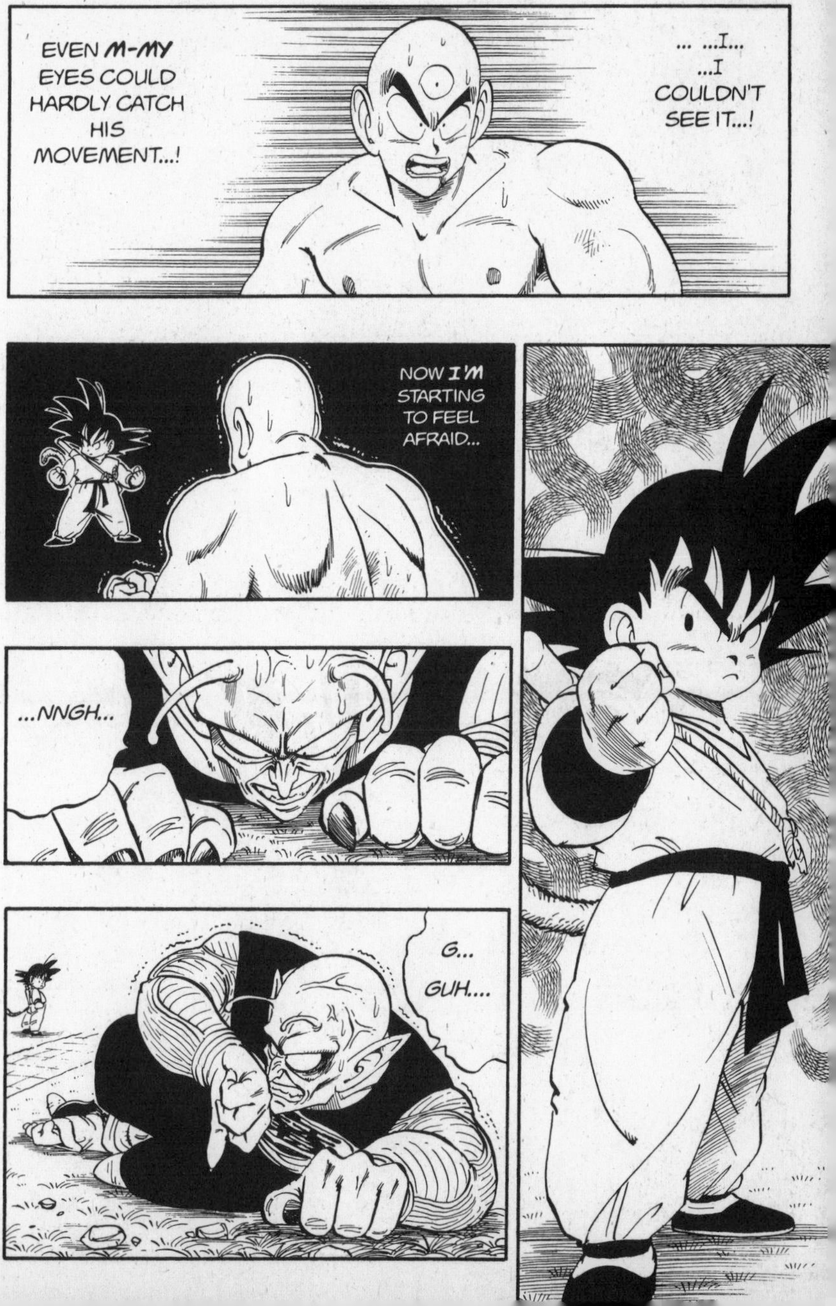
... ...I...
...I COULDN'T SEE IT...!
EVEN M-MY EYES COULD HARDLY CATCH HIS MOVEMENT...!
NOW I'M STARTING TO FEEL AFRAID...
...NNGH...
G... GUH....

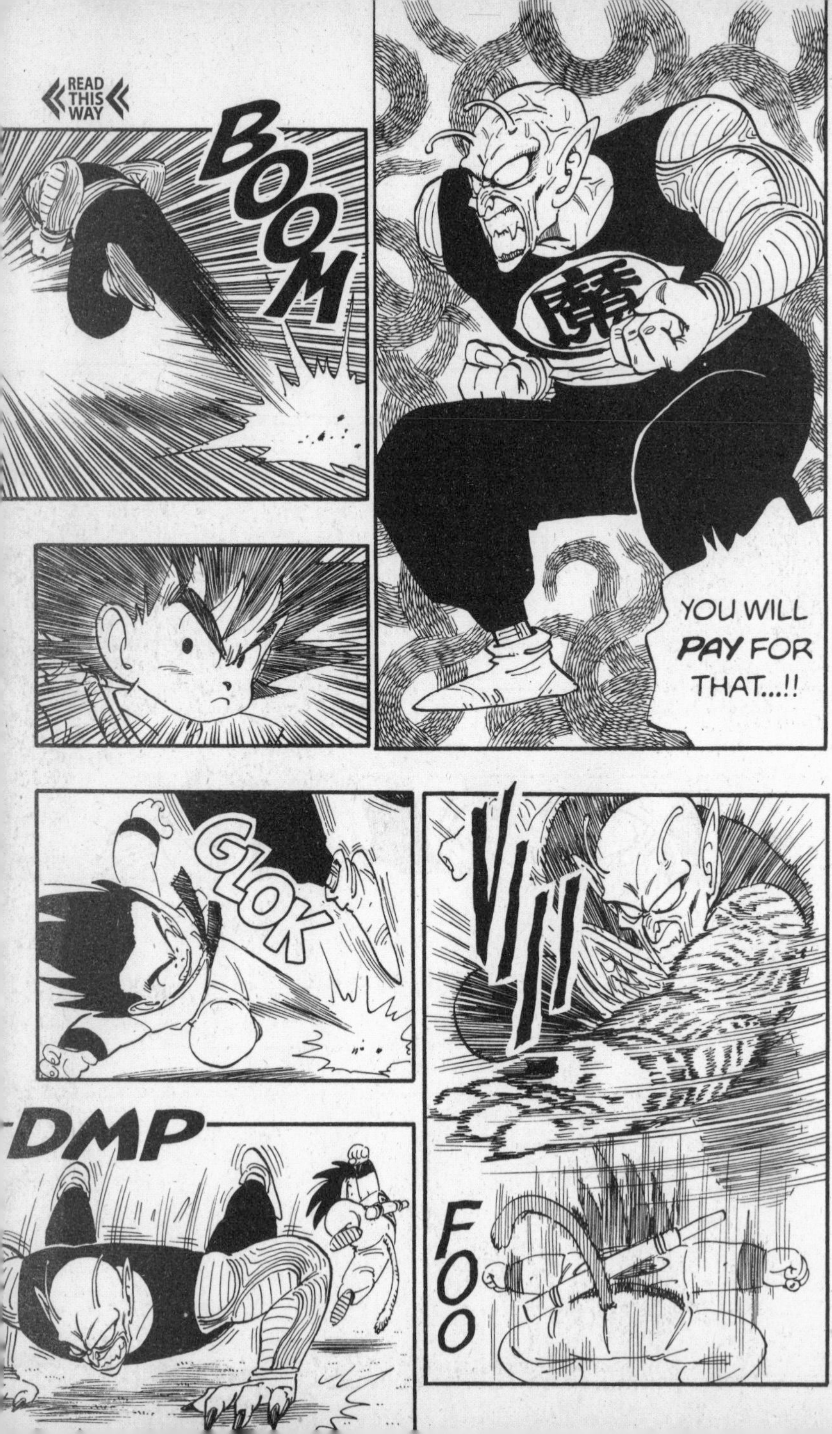

READ THIS WAY
YOU WILL PAY FOR THAT...!!
BOOM
GLOK
FOO
DMP

READ THIS WAY

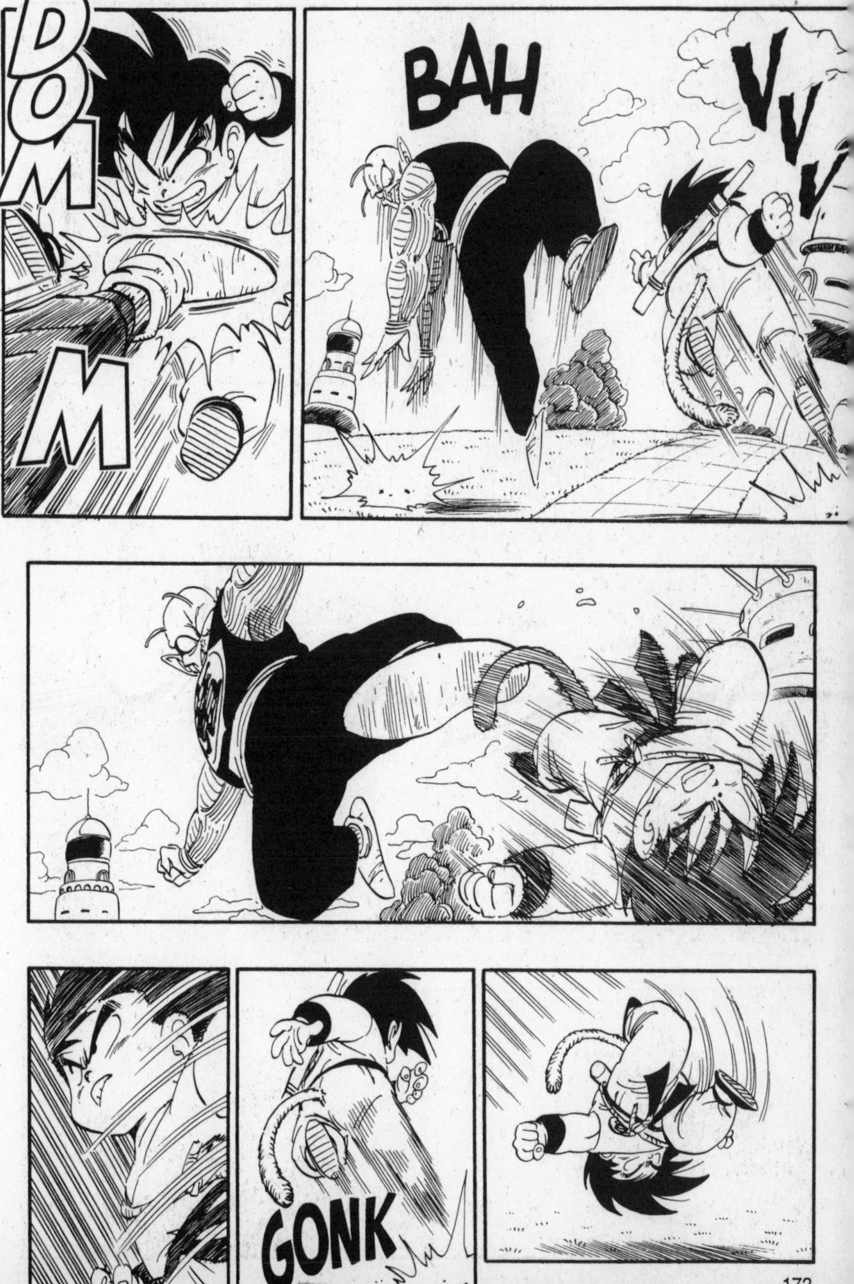
VVV
BAH
DOM
M
GONK

READ THIS WAY

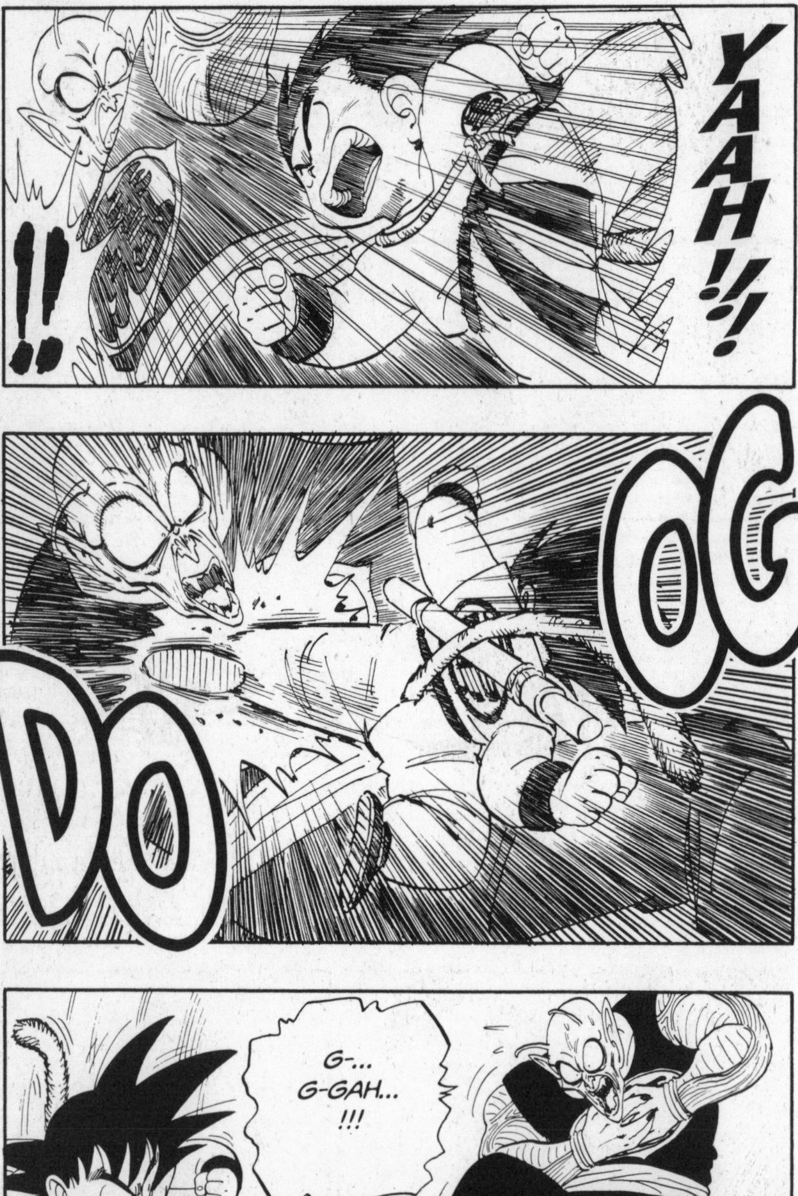

YAAH!!!
!!
DO
OG
G-...
G-GAH...
!!!

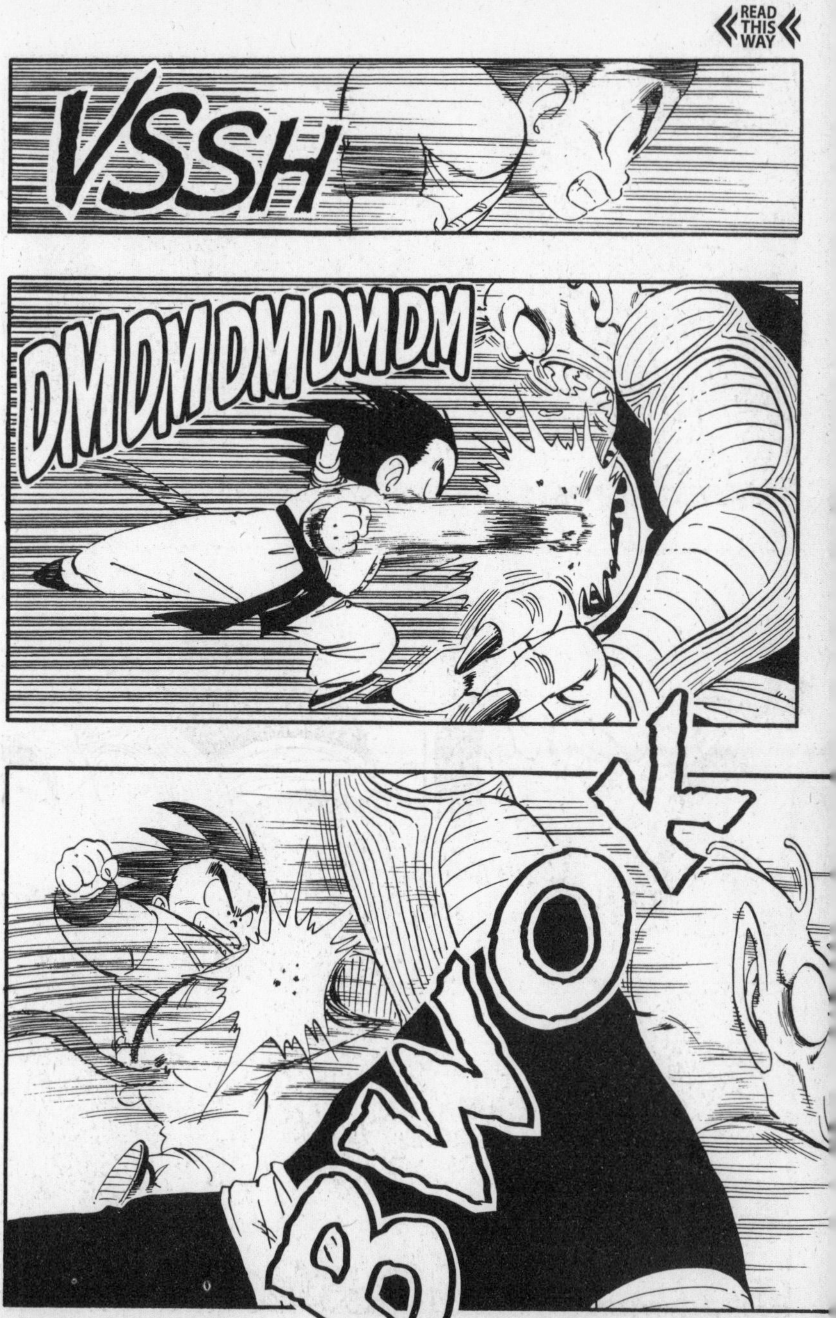
READ THIS WAY
VSSH
DM DM DM DM DM
BWOK

READ THIS WAY

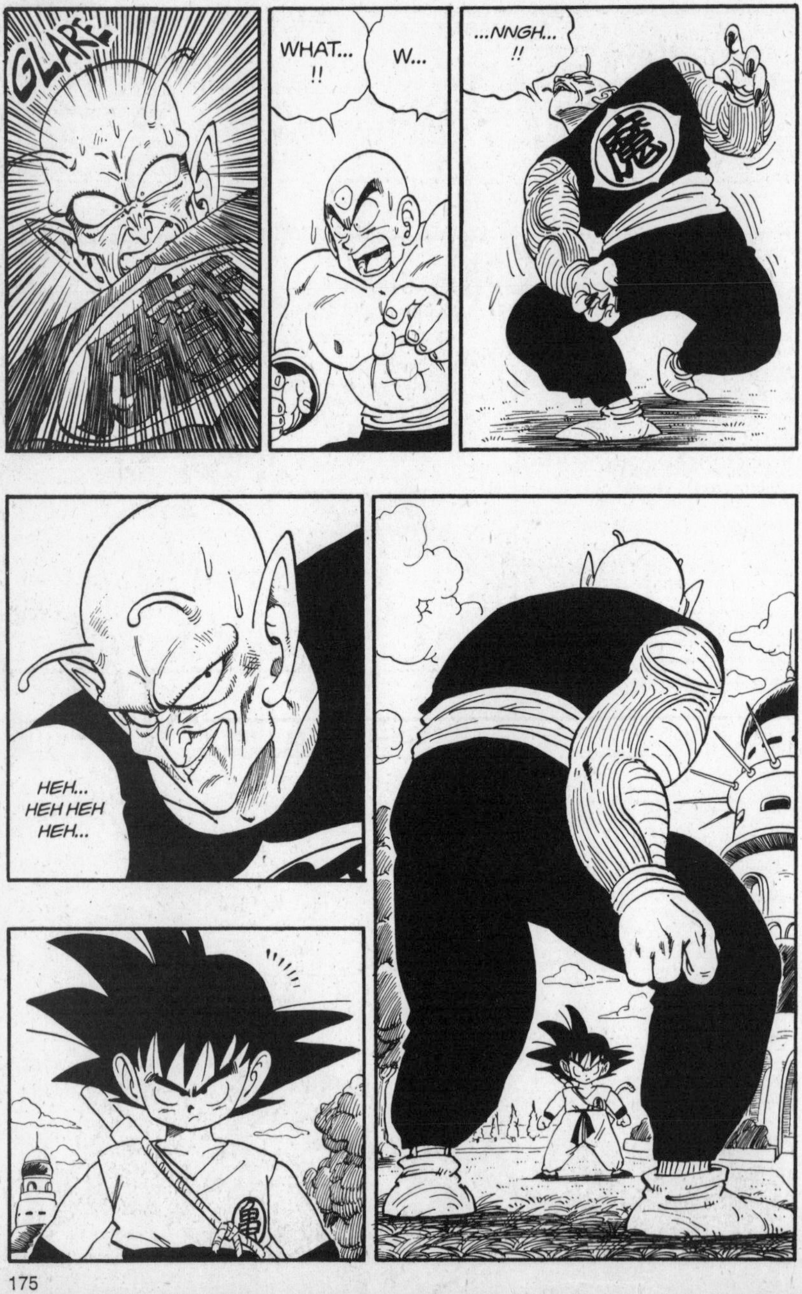
...NNGH... !!
W...
WHAT... !!
GLARE
HEH... HEH HEH HEH...

READ THIS WAY

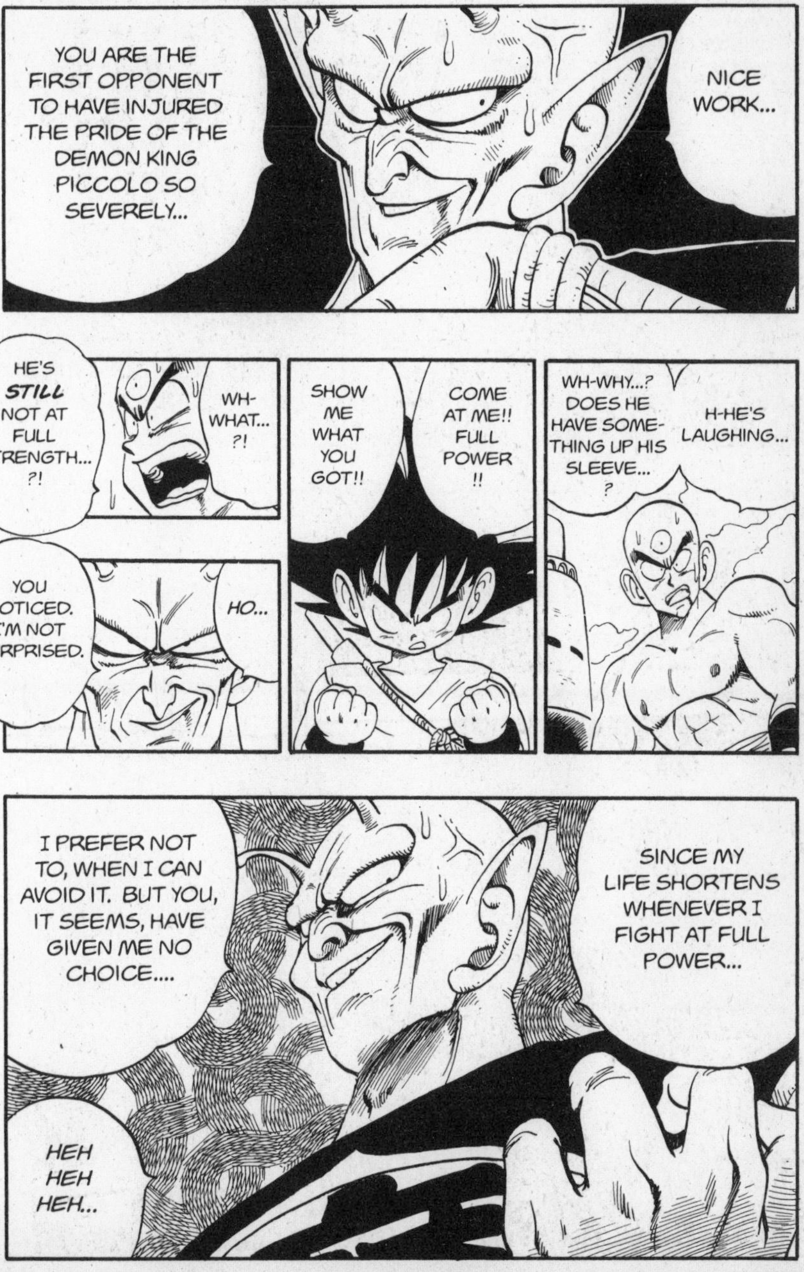
NICE WORK...
YOU ARE THE FIRST OPPONENT TO HAVE INJURED THE PRIDE OF THE DEMON KING PICCOLO SO SEVERELY...
H-HE'S LAUGHING...
WH-WHY...? DOES HE HAVE SOME-THING UP HIS SLEEVE...?
COME AT ME!! FULL POWER!!
SHOW ME WHAT YOU GOT!!
WH-WHAT...?!
HE'S **STILL** NOT AT FULL STRENGTH...?!
HO...
YOU NOTICED. I'M NOT SURPRISED.
SINCE MY LIFE SHORTENS WHENEVER I FIGHT AT FULL POWER...
I PREFER NOT TO, WHEN I CAN AVOID IT. BUT YOU, IT SEEMS, HAVE GIVEN ME NO CHOICE....
HEH HEH HEH...

READ THIS WAY

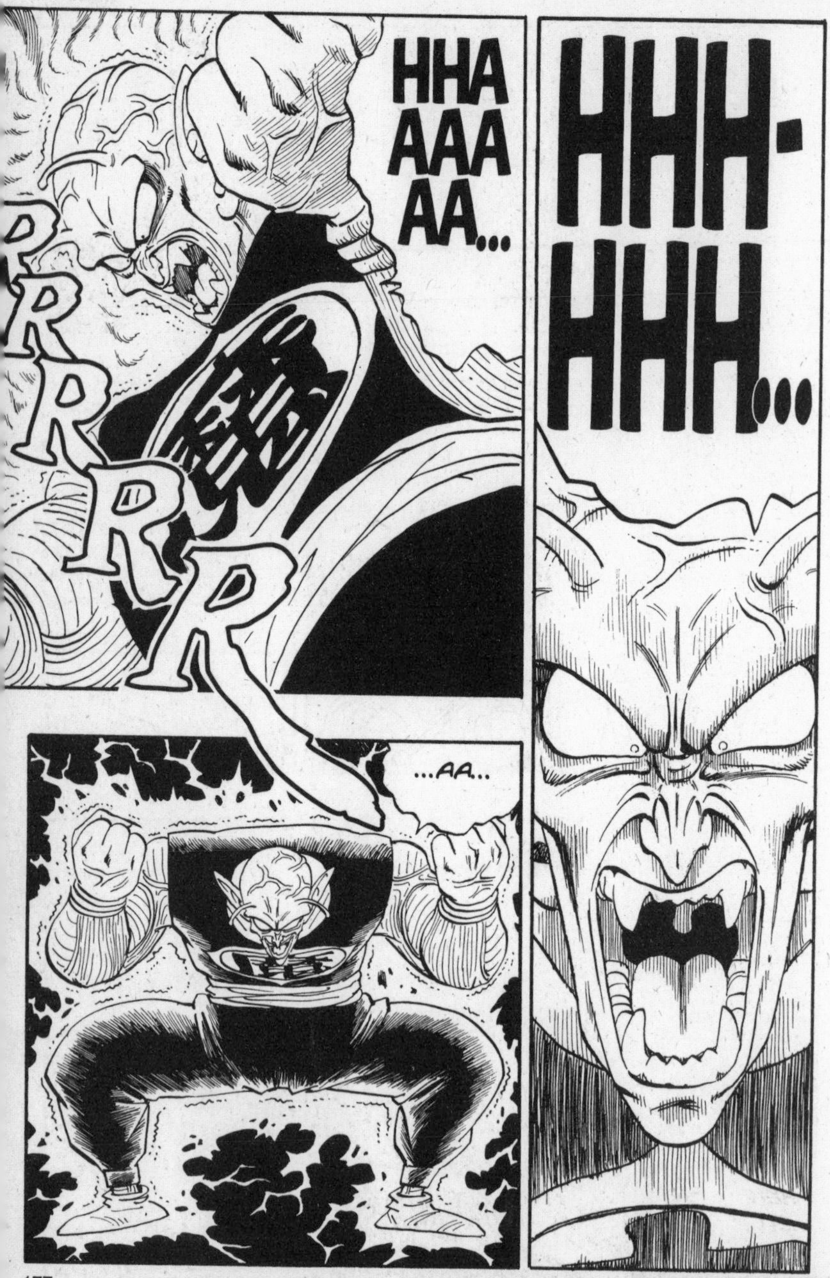
HHH-HHH-HHH...
HHA AAA AA...
RRRRR
...AA...

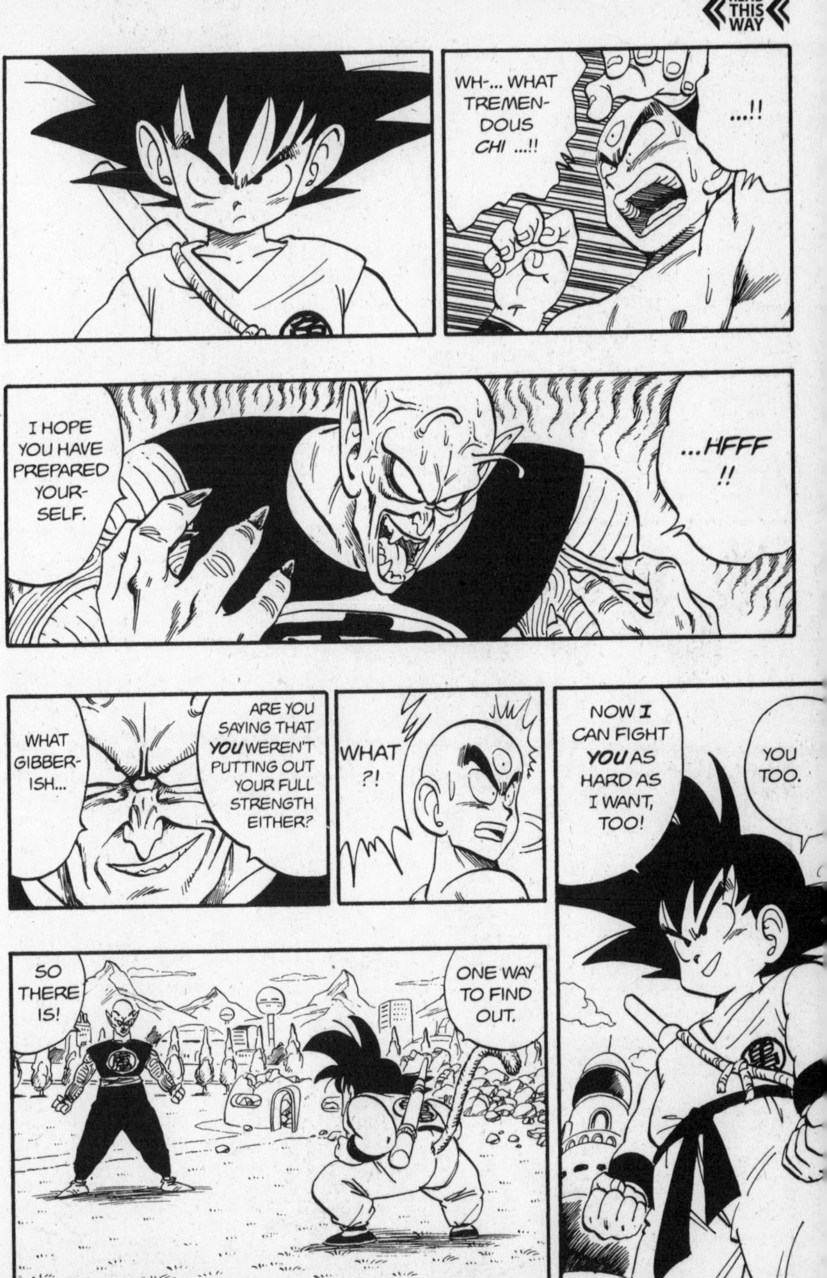
READ THIS WAY
WH-... WHAT TREMENDOUS CHI ...!!
...!!
...HFFF !!
I HOPE YOU HAVE PREPARED YOURSELF.
YOU TOO.
NOW I CAN FIGHT YOU AS HARD AS I WANT, TOO!
WHAT ?!
ARE YOU SAYING THAT YOU WEREN'T PUTTING OUT YOUR FULL STRENGTH EITHER?
WHAT GIBBERISH...
ONE WAY TO FIND OUT.
SO THERE IS!

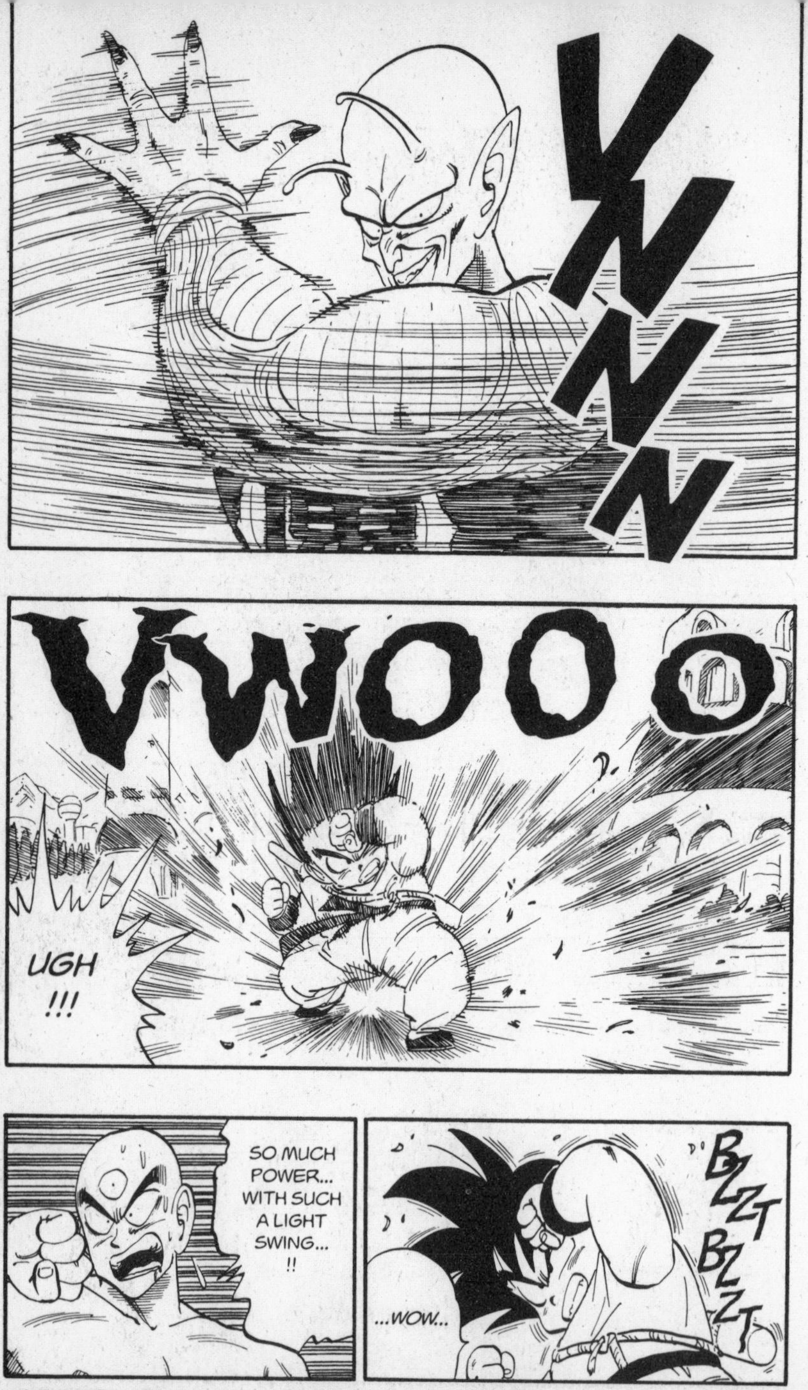
VNNN
VWOOO
UGH !!!
D BZZT BZZT
...WOW...
SO MUCH POWER... WITH SUCH A LIGHT SWING... !!

NEXT: Goku's...Counterattack?!

TITLE PAGE GALLERY

These title pages were used when Dragon Ball was originally published in 1988 in the Japanese Weekly Shonen Jump magazine.

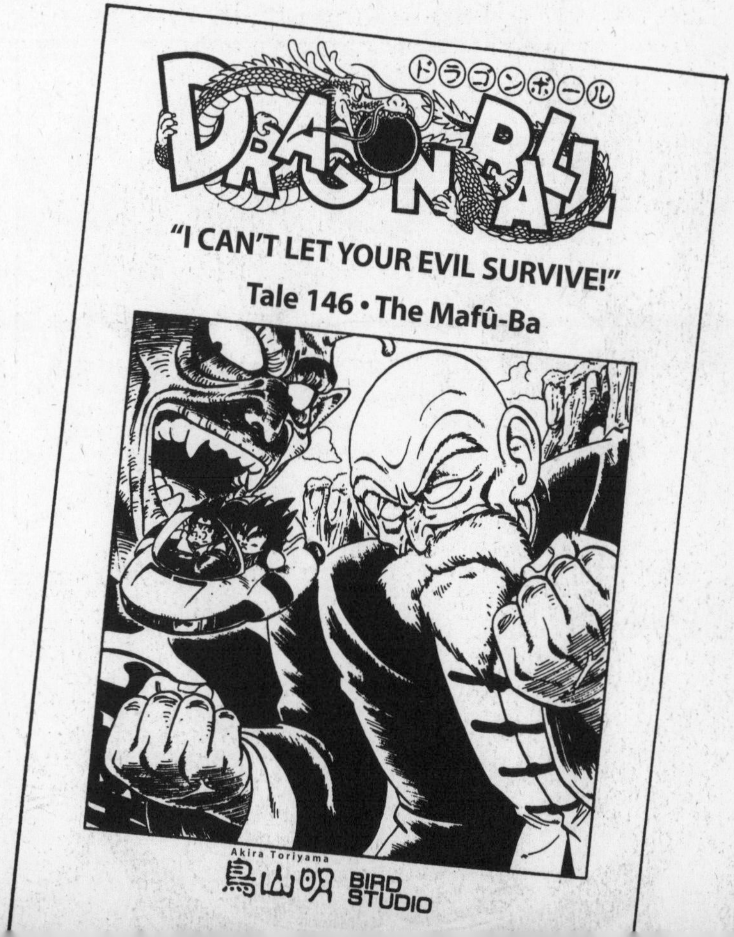

ドラゴンボール
DRAGON BALL
"I CAN'T LET YOUR EVIL SURVIVE!"
Tale 146 • The Mafû-Ba
Akira Toriyama
鳥山明
BIRD STUDIO

ドラゴンボール

DRAGON BALL

NO ONE CAN STOP ME NOW!!!

Tale 147 • The Demon King of Old…Restored!

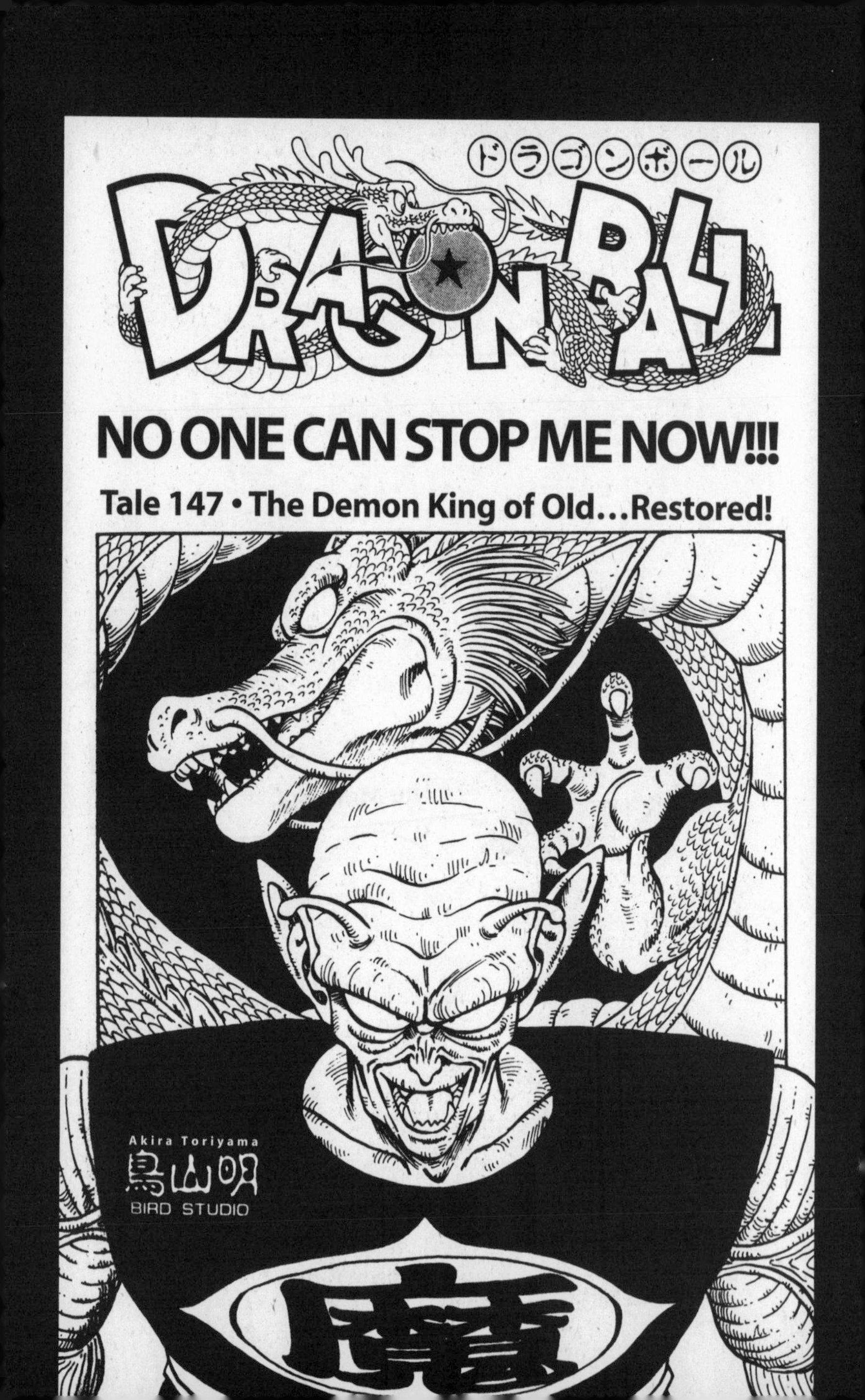
Akira Toriyama
鳥山明
BIRD STUDIO
魔

ドラゴンボール

DRAGON BALL

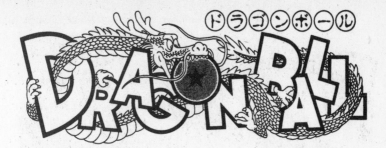

WHAT WAITS AT KARIN TOWER...?

Tale 148 • Go Ask Karin!

CAPSULE

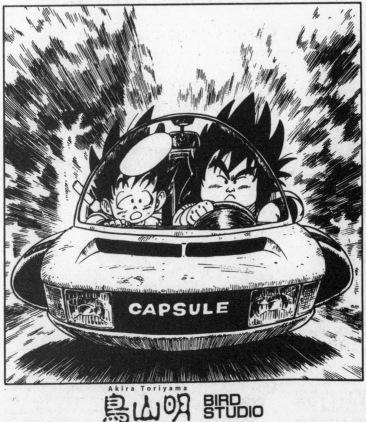

Akira Toriyama

鳥山明 BIRD STUDIO

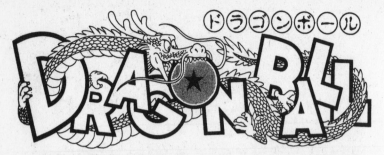

STEELED FOR DEATH, WHAT DOES THE DIVINE WATER TASTE OF???

Tale 151 • The Superest Super Water!!

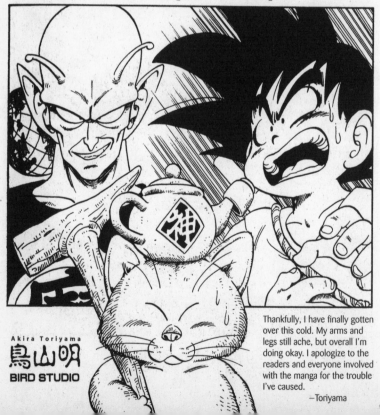

Akira Toriyama
鳥山明
BIRD STUDIO

Thankfully, I have finally gotten over this cold. My arms and legs still ache, but overall I'm doing okay. I apologize to the readers and everyone involved with the manga for the trouble I've caused.
—Toriyama

ドラゴンボール

DRAGON BALL

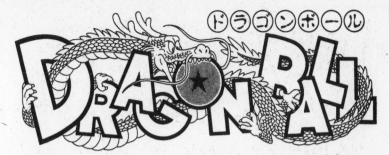

GOKU'S BACK...AND JUST IN TIME!

Tale 152 • Piccolo's World

BIRD STUDIO

Akira Toriyama

鳥山明

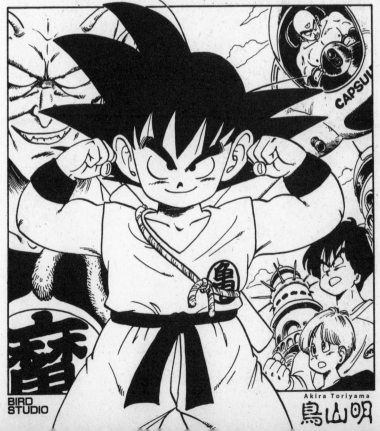

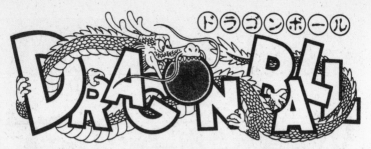

TO FIGHT THE MIGHTY PICCOLO!

Tale 153 • Tenshinhan's Resolve

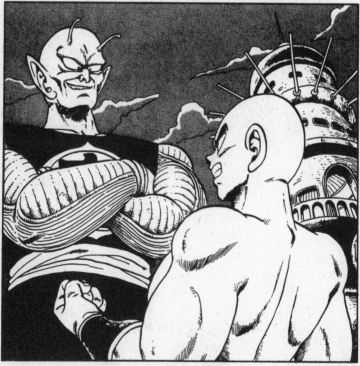

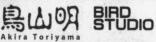

鳥山明 **BIRD STUDIO**
Akira Toriyama

IN THE NEXT VOLUME...

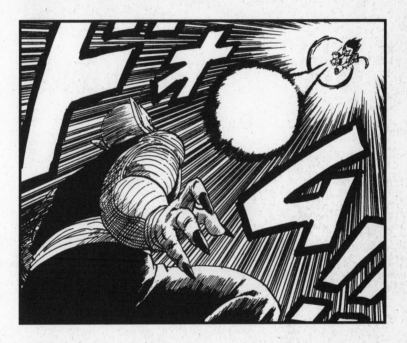

Goku is the world's only hope—but can even he defeat Piccolo, who can blast a city off the map by just flexing his biceps? As the battle turns even more brutal, Goku must gamble all his strength on the secret power of his monkey-tailed heritage! Then, in search of a way to stop Piccolo from ever taking over the world again, Goku's gaze turns skyward—to the heavenly realm of Kami-sama, creator of the Dragon Balls, deity of the Dragon Ball world. But Piccolo and Kami-sama share a shocking secret...all in the next volume of Dragon Ball!

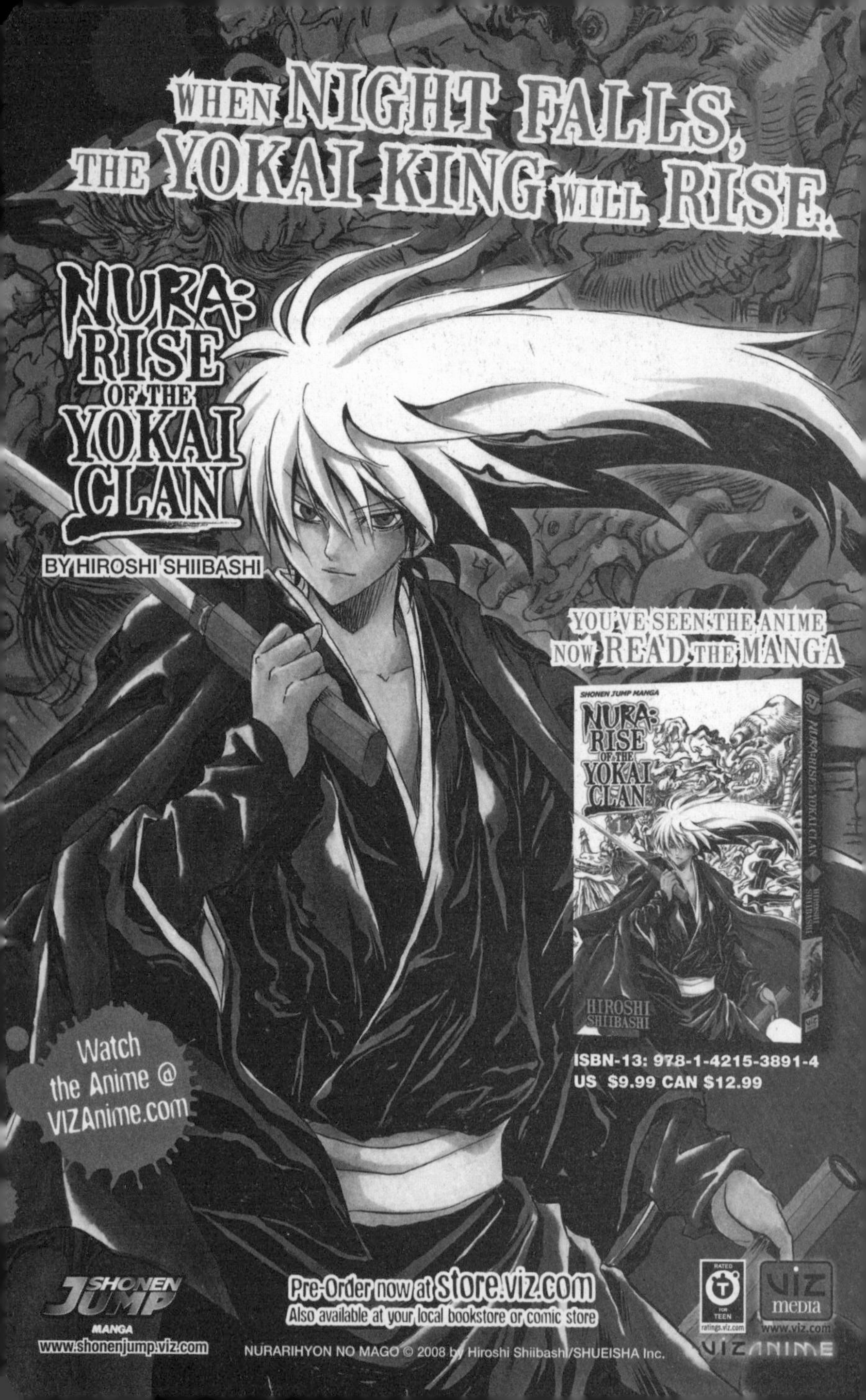

WHEN NIGHT FALLS, THE YOKAI KING WILL RISE.
NURA: RISE OF THE YOKAI CLAN
BY HIROSHI SHIIBASHI
YOU'VE SEEN THE ANIME NOW READ THE MANGA
SHONEN JUMP MANGA
NURA: RISE OF THE YOKAI CLAN
HIROSHI SHIIBASHI
ISBN-13: 978-1-4215-3891-4
US $9.99 CAN $12.99
Watch the Anime @ VIZAnime.com
SHONEN JUMP MANGA
www.shonenjump.viz.com
Pre-Order now at store.viz.com
Also available at your local bookstore or comic store
RATED T FOR TEEN ratings.viz.com
VIZ media www.viz.com
VIZ ANIME
NURARIHYON NO MAGO © 2008 by Hiroshi Shiibashi/SHUEISHA Inc.

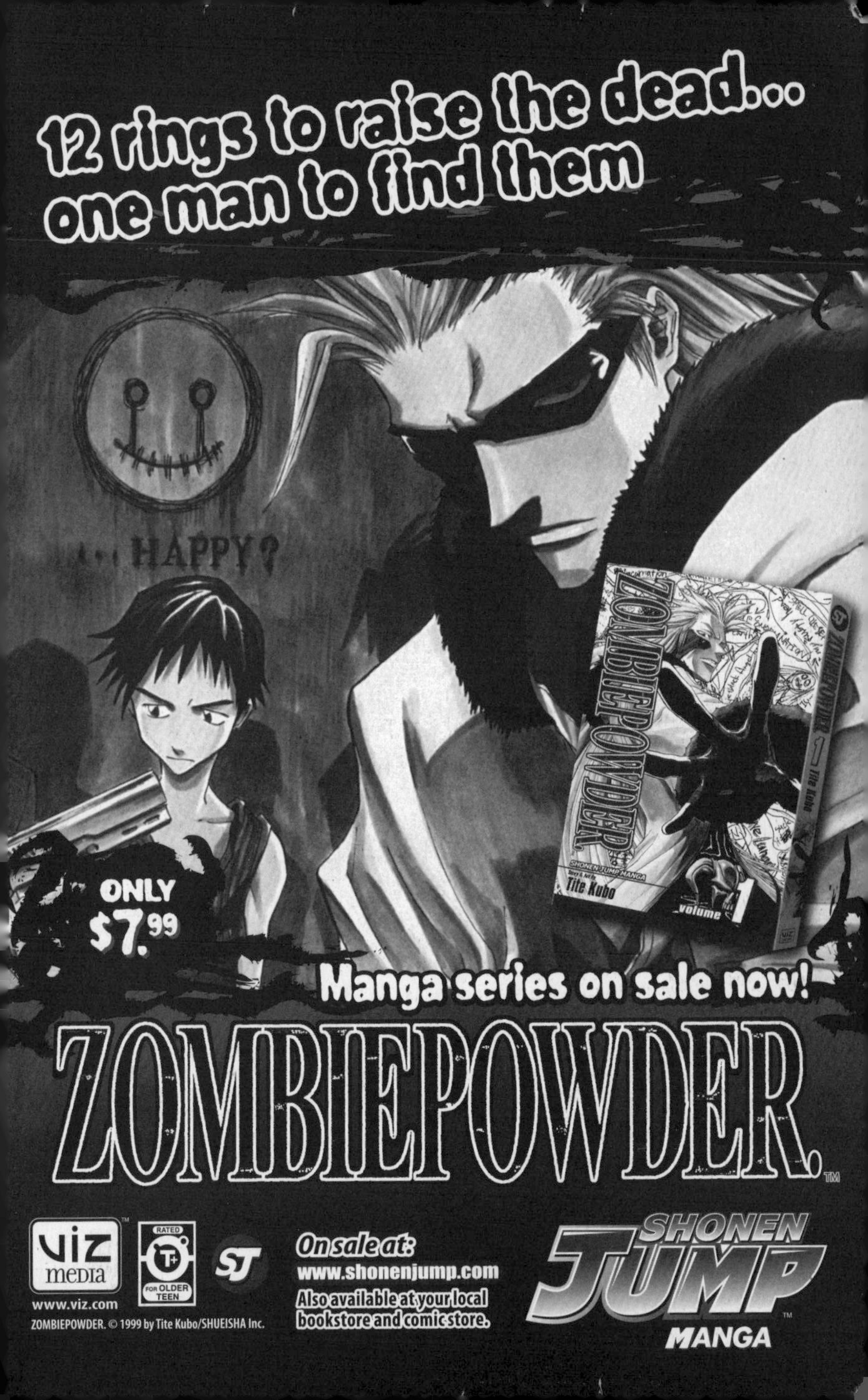

12 rings to raise the dead...
one man to find them
...HAPPY?
ZOMBIEPOWDER.
SHONEN JUMP MANGA
Story & Art by Tite Kubo
volume 1
ONLY $7.99
Manga series on sale now!
ZOMBIEPOWDER.™
viz media
www.viz.com
RATED T+ FOR OLDER TEEN
SJ
On sale at:
www.shonenjump.com
Also available at your local bookstore and comic store.
SHONEN JUMP™ MANGA
ZOMBIEPOWDER. © 1999 by Tite Kubo/SHUEISHA Inc.

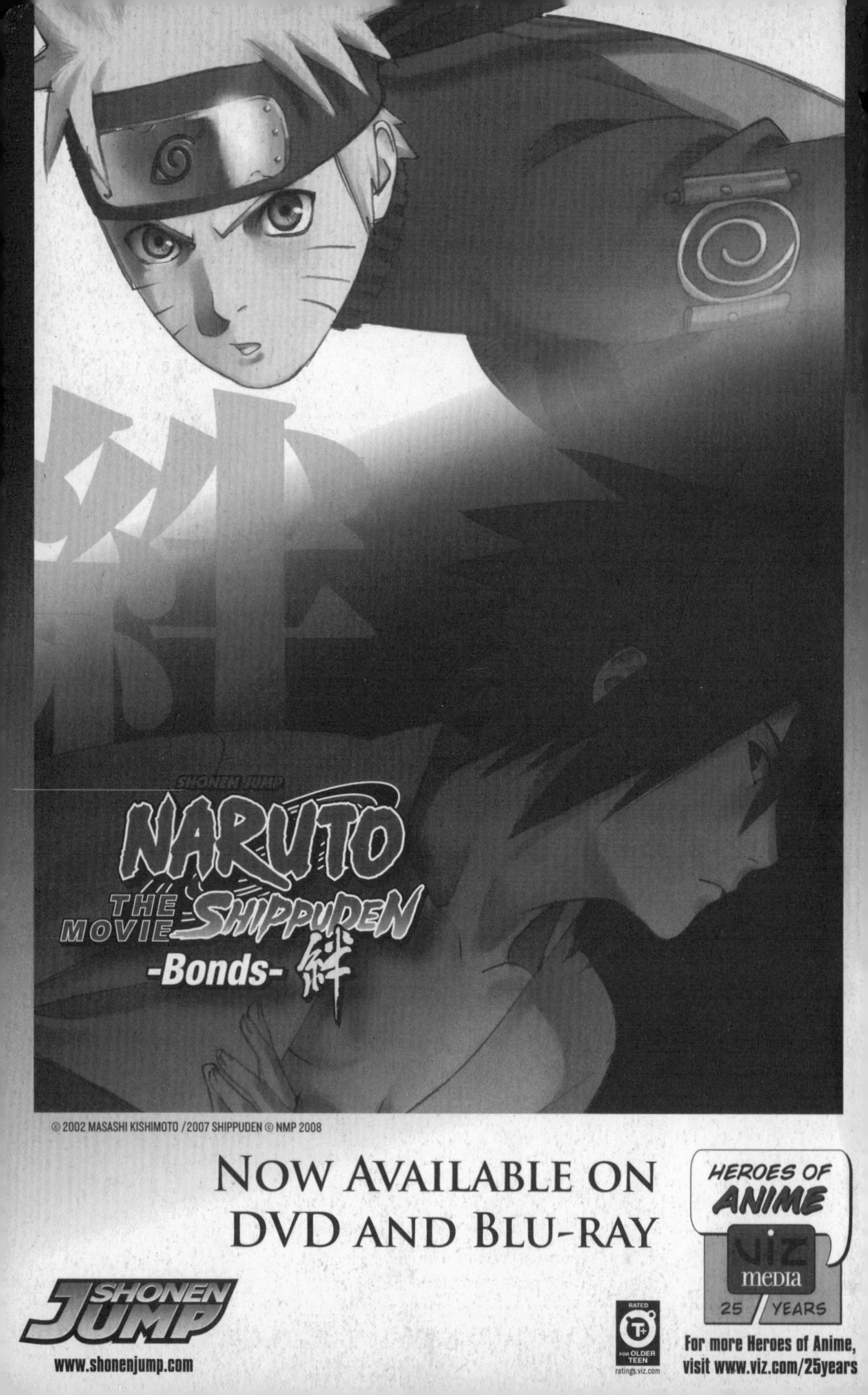
SHONEN JUMP
NARUTO
THE MOVIE
SHIPPUDEN
-Bonds- 絆
© 2002 MASASHI KISHIMOTO /2007 SHIPPUDEN © NMP 2008
NOW AVAILABLE ON
DVD AND BLU-RAY
SHONEN JUMP
www.shonenjump.com
RATED T+ FOR OLDER TEEN
ratings.viz.com
HEROES OF ANIME
VIZ media
25 YEARS
For more Heroes of Anime, visit www.viz.com/25years

The VIZ Manga App has some new friends...

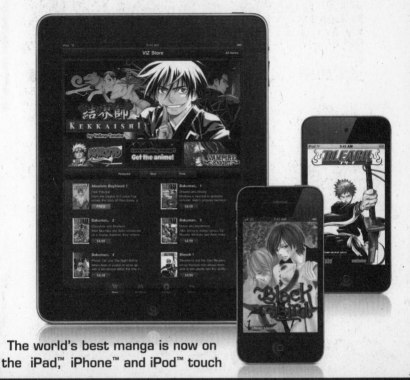

The world's best manga is now on the iPad,™ iPhone™ and iPod™ touch

---

To learn more, visit viz.com

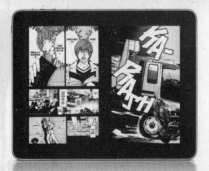

From legendary manga like *Death Note* to *Absolute Boyfriend*, the best manga in the world is now available on multiple devices through the official VIZ Manga app.

- Hundreds of volumes available
- Free App
- New content weekly
- Free chapter 1 previews

www.viz.com

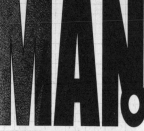
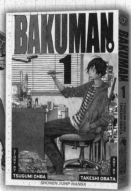

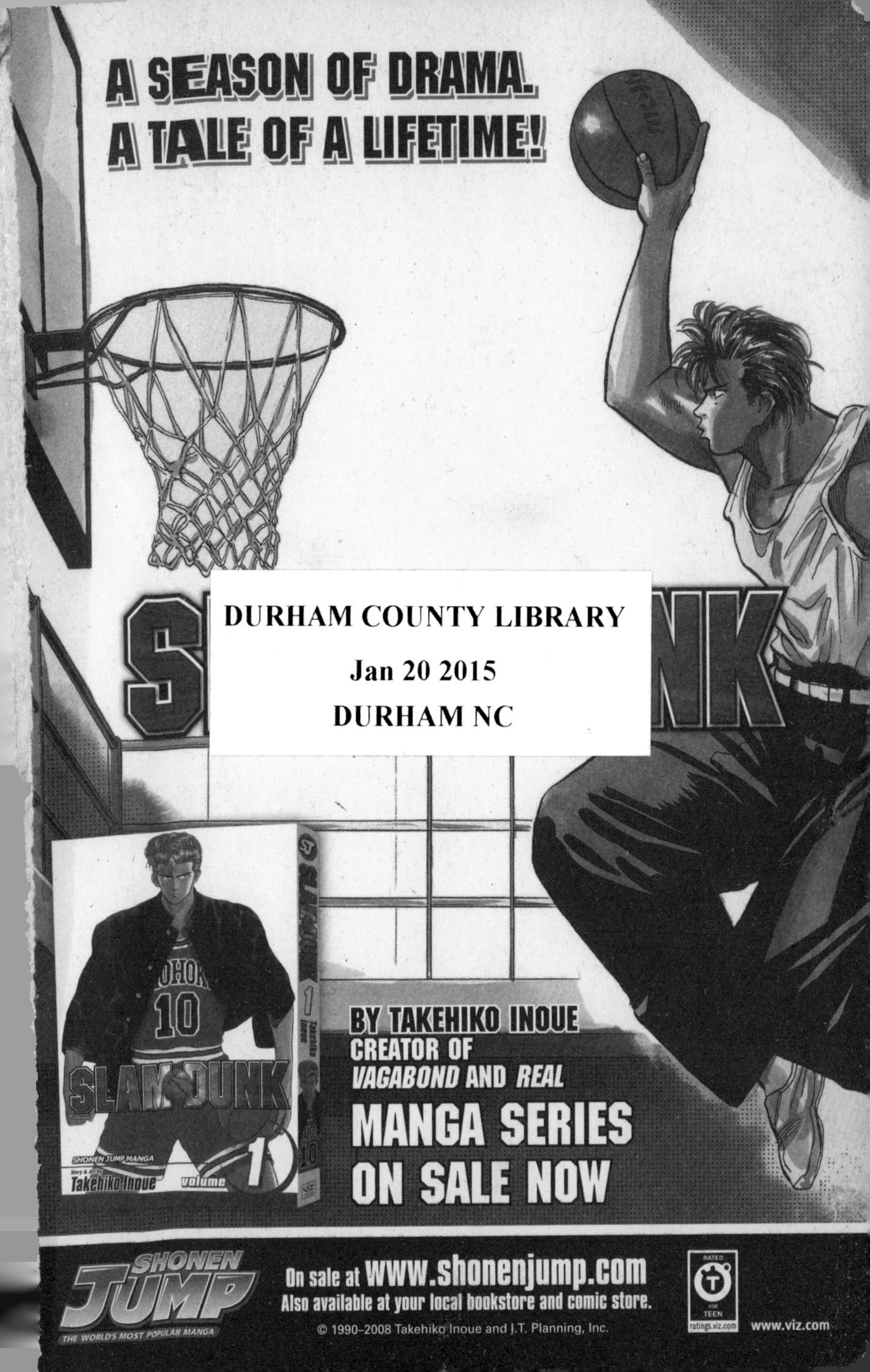

A SEASON OF DRAMA.
A TALE OF A LIFETIME!
BY TAKEHIKO INOUE
CREATOR OF
VAGABOND AND REAL
MANGA SERIES
ON SALE NOW
SLAM DUNK
SHONEN JUMP MANGA
Takehiko Inoue
volume 1
SHONEN JUMP
THE WORLD'S MOST POPULAR MANGA
On sale at www.shonenjump.com
Also available at your local bookstore and comic store.
© 1990–2008 Takehiko Inoue and I.T. Planning, Inc.
RATED T FOR TEEN
ratings.viz.com
www.viz.com

DRAGON BALL VOL. 13
SHONEN JUMP Manga Edition

STORY AND ART BY
AKIRA TORIYAMA

English Adaptation/Gerard Jones
Translation/Mari Morimoto
Touch-Up Art & Lettering/Wayne Truman
Cover & Graphic Design/Sean Lee
Senior Editor/Jason Thompson

In the original Japanese edition, DRAGON BALL and DRAGON BALL Z are
known collectively as the 42-volume series DRAGON BALL. The English
DRAGON BALL Z was originally volumes 17-42 of the Japanese DRAGON BALL.

Printed in Canada

Published by VIZ Media, LLC
P.O. Box 77010
San Francisco, CA 94107

10 9 8 7 6 5 4
First printing, August 2003
Fourth printing, December 2011

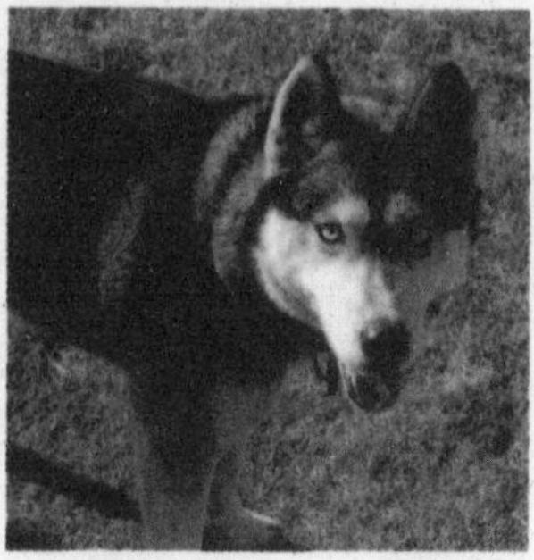

鳥山 明

This is our family dog, Matroshka. We took her name from the traditional Russian dolls. Her nickname is "Rosha," because it's a pain to constantly call her "Matroshka." I get cold easily, so I really envy her Siberian breed's ability to withstand cold. Even though she's female, she's super active and is constantly ramming my son and making him cry. No matter how busy I get, I always play with her once a day.

–Akira Toriyama, 1988

Widely known all over the world for his playful, innovative storytelling and humorous, distinctive art style, **Dragon Ball** creator Akira Toriyama is also known in his native Japan for the wildly popular **Dr. Slump**, his previous manga series about the adventures of a mad scientist and his android "daughter." His hit series **Dragon Ball** ran from 1984 to 1995 in Shueisha's **Weekly Shonen Jump** magazine. He is also known for his design work on video games such as **Dragon Warrior**, **Chrono Trigger** and **Tobal No. 1**. His recent manga works include **Cowa**, **Kajika**, **Sand Land**, **Neko Majin**, and a children's book, **Toccio the Angel**. He lives with his family in Japan.